Italian Violin Music of the Seventeenth Century

MUSIC: SCHOLARSHIP AND PERFORMANCE

Thomas Binkley, *General Editor*

WILLI APEL

*Italian Violin Music of the
Seventeenth Century*

EDITED BY THOMAS BINKLEY

INDIANA UNIVERSITY PRESS
BLOOMINGTON & INDIANAPOLIS

Translated and enlarged from *Die italienische Violinmusik im 17. Jahrhundert*,
© 1983 by Franz Steiner Verlag GmbH, Wiesbaden.

♾™ The paper used in this publication meets the minimum requirements of
American National Standard for Information Sciences—Permanence of Paper
for Printed Library Materials, ANSI Z39.48–1984.

Library of Congress Cataloging-in-Publication Data

Apel, Willi
  Italian violin music of the seventeenth century.
  (Music—scholarship and performance)
  Translation of: Die italienische Violinmusik im 17.
Jahrhundert.
  Bibliography: p.
  Includes index.
  1. Violin music—17th century—History and criticism.
2. Instrumental music—Italy-17th century—History and criticism. I. Binkley,
Thomas. II. Title. III. Series.
ML880.A6413   1990   787.2'0945'09032   88-45503
ISBN 0-253-30683-3 (alk. paper)
5 4 3 2 1 94 93 92 91 90

 *Contents*

The Composers and Their Published Music

Editor's Preface

The present book is an expanded translation of Professor Apel's book *Die italienische Violinmusik im 17. Jahrhundert* (published as volume XXI of the *Beihefte zum Archiv für Musikwissenschaft*, Wiesbaden, 1983), and itself a revision of nine articles that appeared in the *Archiv für Musikwissenschaft*, vols. XXX–XXXVIII (1973–1981). This translation is something of a harmony of the 1983 German publication and Professor Apel's own typescript translation into English. I have made a few corrections and many additions, and I have compiled a bibliography of original sources and selected modern editions as an aid to the violinist who does not have ready access to bibliographic tools and who wishes to secure this material for performance or study. The bibliography of original sources of the music discussed in this book are cited according to the standard *Répertoire international des sources musicales (RISM)* (a few discrepancies in orthography employed in the body of the book notwithstanding).

The brief biographical sketches preceding the discussion of each composer's work have been brought up to date in accordance with the *New Grove Dictionary of Music and Musicians* and other recent studies. I have combined the author's epilogue with other material at the beginning of the book to form an introduction that contains the rationale of the book, a short pre-history of violin music, and a discussion of the musical forms to be encountered in the text.

I have checked a great many of the original sources employed in the writing of this study, but it has not been possible for me to consult them all, nor have I attempted to repeat the research. In a few cases where I found what I consider to be interesting information I have added it silently. The reader is reminded that the original compositions still contain a wealth of information not captured in this or any other study, especially regarding notation and instrumentation.

Indeed, an investigation of the instrumentation in this repertory would make an interesting study. Not infrequently in the original publications there is disagreement between the *tavola* and the individual parts, with a piece ascribed to one instrument here, another there. For example, when a piece is indicated as suitable for *cornetto overo violino* and we find such idiomatic techniques as tremolo, the question arises whether the part is indeed suited to both instruments. Even when the instrumental attributions are consistent, it is not always clear what instrument is intended. *Violone* in the sixteenth century was often employed as a synonym for *viola da gamba*. The instruments bearing that name could, according to Ganassi, have as their lowest note the G at the bottom of the bass clef or the D below that. In the seventeenth century the term *violone* indicated a bass instrument, usually the smaller of the two, but often there is no distinction made between a viol, a violone (or contrabass), and a violoncello. Muffat referred to a *Contrabasso* of the Italians, which the Germans called *Violone*, while the smaller instrument was called *violoncino*. The term *Viola* was employed for the alto or tenor parts; it certainly meant an instrument of the violin family larger than the violin, but of no specific size, for existing examples reach a length of 48 cm (Stradivari) or 47 cm (Andrea Amati). The *Viola da braccio* is not an instrument distinct from the violin, but can be a violin or viola of any size, and may even refer to a violoncello, but not to a member of the viola da gamba family (one supposes). Incidentally, Buonamente in his *Settimo Libro* refers to *Basso di viola ò da Brazzo*; this tells us that *viola* means *da gamba* and indicates that *brazzo*, while designating the violin family, does not imply playing the instrument off the chest or shoulder, thus confirming the meaning of "violin family." The *Violetta* is taken to mean a violin in the repertory of this book, although I know of no good reason why it should not just as well refer to the rebec. The *Violino piccolo* is either a rebec (as called for in Monteverdi's *Orfeo*, where it is further identified as *alla franchese*), or a small violin tuned a fourth higher than usual, designed to capture the upper register not normally explored at that time on the normal violin. The *Lira* of Marenzio is surely a shortened form of *lira da braccio*; it should not be confused with the *Lirone*, which is a bass version of the early polyphonic *Lira da braccio*. The *Lirone* is a continuo instrument that produces a sound seldom heard today—a sustained string sound faintly reminiscent of a reed organ.

The wind instruments are more easily identified. The *Fagott* is the early bassoon, and probably so is the *Dolzaina* of Buonamente's *Libro Sesto*, where an alternate instrument, *Basso da Brazzo* (violone?), is indicated. The *Trombone* is encountered a good bit more often than modern performances would lead us to expect. The *Trombetta* is probably the *Tromba marina*, which is not a wind instrument at all. The *Tromba* of Cazzati is a natural trumpet, which he notes plays down a step if muted (*tromba serrata*). Like the violin, the *Tromba* plays the highest parts. The *Flauto*, also an instrument of the higher parts, is the recorder; while the *Piffero* is a shawm or early oboe, and *cornetto* is the generic term for that family, not always a treble instrument in this repertory.

Liuto, Chitarrone, and *Tiorbo* are interchangeable terms in the publications discussed in this volume, though the terms were also employed with distinct meanings in the seventeenth century.

If the original prints are inconclusive when it comes to designating instruments, they are equally unclear with regard to many musical details. Whether, and if so where, repeats are to be made; just how the notation of rhythm, meter, and tempo operates; and the use of this music in sacred as opposed to secular environments, as well as the bearing of that use on performance style are important issues that still require examination.

It is regrettable that Professor Apel was unable to study the entire corpus of Italian violin music preserved in prints and manuscripts throughout the world, but had to confine his work by and large to the significant printed sources. We are grateful nevertheless for what he was able to accomplish.

I have had much help in the preparation of this edition: Lewis Baratz worked up the initial RISM bibliography; Roger Freitas typed and checked endlessly, and caught me out on a myriad of details; and Lisa Cardwell prepared the music examples employing Theme© software.

THOMAS BINKLEY

Introduction

This is a book about violin music, not a book about violin playing. That is important in the light of a number of recent publications in the field of violin literature, for instance: G. Beckmann, *Das Violinspiel in Deutschland vor 1700* (Leipzig, 1918); A. Moser, *Geschichte des Violinspiels* (Berlin, 1923; 2d ed. by H. J. Nosselt, Tutzing, 1966); R. Aschmann, *Das deutsche polyphone Violinspiel* (Zurich, 1962); and D. Boyden, *The History of Violin Playing from Its Origins to 1761* (London, 1965). In all these books playing the violin is the subject of investigation, and the contents fully conform with their titles. The sources of violin music are studied almost exclusively from the viewpoint of playing—of technical requirements and achievements. *Tremolo, legato, portato, pizzicato, col legno, scordatura,* double stops, high positions: these and many other aspects of violin playing are traced to their origins and studied in their development.

In this context, an interesting and illuminating controversy developed between Boyden and Nosselt. In his *History of Violin Playing . . .* Boyden said that Moser's *Geschichte des Violinspiels* "is basically a history of violin music, not of violin playing" (p. 6, fn. 1). In the second edition of Moser's book, Nosselt refuted this statement, saying that if Boyden is suggesting that Andreas Moser presents a history merely of violin music, he is ignoring both the goals of the book and the carefully selected musical examples.[1] By and large, one must agree with Nosselt's statement that Moser's book is a history of violin playing, but the word "merely" (*lediglich*) throws a significant light on a situation that continues to exist: violin music is "merely" the unavoidable first step toward the really interesting and important subject, that is, violin playing.

What reason is there for the great interest in the technique of violin playing rather than in the music? This question arises in connection with early keyboard instruments as well: organ, clavichord, and harpsichord. These instruments, too, have undergone changes in playing and technique: consider the rapid runs that occur as early as ca. 1380 in some compositions of the Faenza codex; the "finger-breaking" passages to be found a hundred years later in the Buxheim Organ Book; the four-part pedal playing used about 1525 by Arnolt Schlick; the extremely difficult passages for the left hand that occur in some compositions of Thomas Preston and John Bull; and finally the steadily increasing virtuosity in the organ compositions of the north German masters of the seventeenth century. To be sure, in this field also there are important publications the titles of which refer to "-spiel," for instance A. G. Ritter's *Zur Geschichte des Or-*

gelspiels (Leipzig, 1884) and G. Frotscher's *Geschichte des Orgelspiels und der Orgelkomposition* (Berlin, 1935), but in both of them the contents do not really agree with the titles. Ritter's book is actually a history of early organ music, and in Frotscher's book the term *Orgelbau* (organ building) would be more appropriate than *Orgelspiel*. As far as I know, to the present day there is no book dealing specifically with the historical development of the playing of keyboard instruments.

Why is the situation with respect to the violin the opposite that for the keyboard? The main reason probably is that in the latter the playing technique is to a large extent preconditioned by the instrument—more specifically, by its keyboard mechanism; while the construction of the violin has no bearing on the way it is played. Briefly formulated, the difference is that a keyboard instrument has forty sound generators—keys, strings, pipes—for forty tones, while the violin has only four. Moreover, in spite (or because) of these limitations, the violin has turned out to be an extremely versatile instrument, the amazing capacities of which—suffice it to mention the use of higher and higher positions—were only gradually recognized and conquered. That may well explain why the technical advances in violin playing attract the attention of scholars while the music itself plays a secondary role. This state of affairs stands in need of correction. It is the purpose of the present book to offer a remedy, and to restore to violin music its rightful position of priority and primacy.

When, about twelve years ago, I first made plans for a book on early violin music, I had in mind a comprehensive publication similar in scope to my *Geschichte der Orgel- und Klaviermusik bis 1700* (Kassel, 1967; English translation by H. Tischler: *The History of Keyboard Music to 1700*, Bloomington, 1972). However, a preliminary study of the sources clearly showed that such plans were utopic, mainly because of the unexpectedly large number of the sources. While in the book on keyboard music I had to deal with about 250 sources for the period 1320–1700, there were more than 350 sources of violin music for the much shorter period 1580–1700. If only the keyboard sources for this shorter time are considered, there results a ratio of about 200 to 350: a clear indication of the fact that violin music was in much greater demand than keyboard music throughout the seventeenth century.[2]

Another difficulty in compiling the present study concerns the availability of modern editions that can be used for investigation. Here, once more, a comparison of keyboard and violin literature is interesting. In the former there are many of complete modern editions: for the fifteenth century, Paumann's *Fundamentum* and the Buxheim Organ Book; for the sixteenth the works of Hofhaimer, Schlick, Cavazzoni, Cabezon, Andrea Gabrieli, and Byrd; for the seventeenth those of Bull, Sweelinck, Scheidt, Scheidemann, Steigleder, Macque, Frescobaldi, Correa, Coelho, Froberger, Murschhauser, Fischer, Buxtehude, Böhm, Bruhns, Pachelbel, Kuhnau, Titelouze, Chambonnières, Louis Couperin, d'Anglebert, Nivers, Purcell, Cabanilles, and many others.[3] What is the situation in the field of violin music? To be sure, there are numerous editions of single compositions— e.g., an occasional piece by Cima, Castello, Bononcini, Legrenzi, and Torelli, but as far as I know, in all of seventeenth-century violin music there are only two masters whose complete works have been published, Corelli and Biber.[4] Everything else that is needed for a book on violin music requires study of the original sources.

This, in turn, leads to the third difficulty: studying the original scores of violin music takes much more time than keyboard music. Keyboard music is written in a simultaneous system of notation—a double staff, a tablature, or a score. Violin music, on the other hand, is usually written in part books, which first must be assembled into a score for the purpose of study. Perhaps that is why there are so many fewer editions of violin music than of keyboard music.

From this it must be clear why I had to adjust my original goal. The first step was limiting the study to Italian violin music, thus disregarding not only important contributions of English and French composers but also those of the German school, which boasts such masters as Johann Heinrich Schmelzer, Nikolaus Adam Strungk, Heinrich Ignaz Biber, and Johann Jakob Walther. And even in the area of Italian violin music, for which Claudio Sartori's *Bibliografia della musica strumentale italiana* was an essential help, it was necessary to limit my study further as the close of the seventeenth century approached. In the period before 1660 the sources can be managed with little difficulty, but after that date the number grows rapidly. In the 1660s there are about 25 prints, in the 70s 31, in the 80s 51, and in the 90s 68. Dozens of violinists, attempting to satisfy the clear desire for more violin music, brought out prints of an Opus 1, seldom however an Opus 2: Placuzzi, Guerrieri, Pasino, Penna, and Baldassini are examples of this group, the evaluation of which will have to wait for other scholars.

Finally let me identify what is meant by violin music. Basically, I have considered those works in which one voice, usually the highest, is specifically attributed to the violin—on the title page, in the part, or in the table of contents. Any attempt to extend the study would lead to a shoreless sea and to uncertainty: think of the many *canzone da sonar* between 1580 and 1620 whose parts are printed as canto, alto, tenore, and basso. Another area untouched are those pieces employing violin with voices, for example, arias or motets. In this book we consider only purely instrumental music.

Early Violin Music

The earliest published compositions for violin may be those found in a French publication from 1584, *Ballet comique de la Royne*, which contains the music for the marriage, celebrated with great pomp in 1581, of Monsieur le Duc de Joyeuse and Mademoiselle de Vaudremont, sister of the queen of France. The author and choreographer of the performance was Baltasar de Beaujoyeux, an Italian whose original name was Baldassaro da Belgioso and who was also known as Baltazzani. The music was written by Lambert de Beaulieu and Jacques Salmon.[5] Both acts of the ballet comique closed with an instrumental ballet consisting of a series of dances "exécutées de dix violons." The music is written in five parts, so there may have been two instruments to each part: violins for the two highest, viols for the lower ones and the bass. To be sure, this does not imply the first use of the violin in France, for, as David Boyden has shown, the violin was a favorite instrument at the French court from about mid-century, especially for dance music.[6]

About the same time in Munich, Italian string players were working under the direction of Orlando di Lasso. The *Dialoghi di Massimo Troiano . . .*, published in Venice in 1569, contains a description in both Spanish and Italian of the events connected with the marriage of Guglielmo VI, of Bavaria, and Renata of Lorraine. Seven *virtuosi* played both the violin and the viola da gamba (... *ma non solo della uiola di braccio ... ma ancora della uiola de gamba*; in Spanish, ... *non solo de la Vihuela de braço ... mas tambien de la Vihuela de pierna*). The music from the Munich establishment is preserved in the Hans Mielich codex (Munich ms. A) and contains only vocal compositions of the Willaert and Rore generation, not music composed especially for the violin.

The situation in France was different in this regard. The first of the two French ballets mentioned above are instrumental ballets. The first consists of four sections (the third in triple meter). In Weckerlin's transcription it comprises 92 measures. The closing *Grand Ballet* is much more extended, with fifteen or sixteen sections (three of them in triple meter), each of which represents a special dance step (*pas*). Fig. 1 shows the final section, which has interesting modulations.

FIGURE 1. BALLET COMIQUE (1582).

In 1589 a no less splendid festivity took place in Florence, at the marriage of Ferdinando de' Medici and Christiane de Lorraine. The music for this occasion was composed by Cavalieri, Malvezzi, Marenzio, and Caccini and was published in 1591 under the title *Intermedii et concerti, fatti per la comedia rappresentata in Firenze nelle nozze*. ... This publication contains, aside from vocal pieces with instrumental accompaniment, four purely instrumental *intermedii* that are designated *Sinfonia*.[7] *Secondo intermedio*, composed by Marenzio, carries the remark: "La sinfonia era composta di dua (sic) Arpe, due Lire, un Basso di Viola, due Leuti, un Violino, una Viola bastarda, ed un Chitarrone." The five part books are merely designated *Canto*, *Alto*, *Tenore*, *Settimo*, and *Basso*, so that the distribution of the instruments is not entirely clear. However, there is no doubt that the violin played the highest part, the *Canto*. Marenzio's *Sinfonia* consists of two sections: twelve measures in 4/4 time followed by eight measures in *proportio triple*. Fig. 2a shows the first section,[8] which consists of two phrases each of six measures; in the second section (Fig. 2b), these are transformed into four-measure phrases.

FIGURE 2. MARENZIO: SINFONIA (1591).

The next publication of interest to us comes from England in 1599. Anthony Holborne (ca. 1550–1600) published *Pavans, galliards, almains, and other short aires: both graue, and light, in fiue parts, for viols, violins, or other musicall winde instruments* (London: William Barley, 1599).[9] It contains 65 five-part compositions: 27 pairs Pavane—Galliarde (Nos. 1–54) followed by eleven single dances, among them two Almaynes (allemandes; Nos. 56 and 57). Most of these pieces, including the two allemandes, consist of three sections, as is customary for the pavane; the only exceptions are Nos. 60, 61, 64, and 65, which are in binary form. Many pieces carry poetic or possibly descriptive titles, for instance, the pavane *Patiencia* and the galliard *Hermoza* (Nos. 25 and 26) or the pair *Decevi* and *Myselfe* (Nos. 35 and 36). These compositions do not contain anything specifically violinistic, but in many of them the uninterrupted flow of their impressive melodies often extends over an entire section. Fig. 3 shows the upper part of the first section of the pavane *Patiencia*.

FIGURE 3. HOLBORNE: PATIENCIA (1599).

Forms of Italian Violin Music of the Seventeenth Century

A survey of the forms encountered in music is necessary because almost every form occurs with different designations, and every designation is used for a variety of forms. The results are confusing, and we shall try to clarify the situation with the following explanations.

It is important to realize that the word "form" is used here in the old (or old-fashioned) sense of the word, comparable to a vessel that can be filled with different fluids, or to a frame in which different pictures can be inserted: this in opposition to a view widely accepted today, that each composition generates its own form. Such a view is admissible and adequate for compositions of recent times—say, beginning with Mahler—but certainly not for those of the seventeenth century, a period whose entire art is characterized by a strong sense of traditional form.[10]

Binary Form: This is the simplest and most frequent type of violin music of the seventeenth century. First of all, it includes the innumerable dances that were written in this period: balli, balletti, allemandes, correntei, gigues, sarabandas, etc. However, this form also occurs with other designations, especially during the first half of the century. Rossi introduced the term *Sinfonia* (1607, 1608, 1613, 1622), which was adopted by Buonamente (1626), Marini (1629), Uccellini (1639, 1660, c.1665–1667), and Falconiero (1650). Another term for binary form is *Sonata*. It also was used first by Rossi, as a designation for binary form (1613, 1622); then by Merula as *Sonata per camera* (1651), followed by Legrenzi (1656) and G. M. Bononcini (1666) as *Sonata da camera*. Other designations for binary form are *Ritornello* (Marini, 1629), *Aria* (Buonamente, 1629), *Toccata* (Uccellini, 1660) and *Capriccio* (Falconiero, 1665; and G. B. Vitali, 1682, 1689).

Suite: This type consists of two or more dance movements, each in binary form, occasionally preceded by free movements (*Introduzione, Sinfonia, Preludio*). Before 1675 no general term for a suite existed in Italian violin music. If at all, suites are referred to by their initial movement. Thus, in the list of contents of Buonamente's *Libro VII* (1637), the last eight compositions are named *Sinfonia Prima–Sinfonia Ottava*, but actually they are suites, each of which consists of a sinfonia followed by a brando, a gagliarda and a corrente. Similarly, *Uccellini's suite Brando, Gaj, Amener, Gavotta* (1667) appears in the Contents as *Brando*. G. M. Bononcini, in 1675, was the first to designate suites as *Sonate da camera*. He was followed by Corelli (1685), C. A. Marini (1687), Colombi (1689), G. B. Vitali (1692), Bernardi (1692), T. Vitali (1695), and Caldara (1699). The term *Sonata* (without *da camera*) was used by G. B. Vitali (1684) and Corelli (1694, 1700). Torelli designated his suites as *Concerto da camera* (1696) or *Concerto per camera* (1690?). Finally, there exist the designations *Trattenimento* (G. B. Bononcini, 1685), *Divertimento* (T. Vitali, 1693; Buoni, 1693), and *Allettamento* (Buoni, 1693).

Suites occur very frequently in Italian violin music of the seventeenth century, but with no indication of tradition or development, because the suite is not a native type. It originated in France, and the Italian composers selected dances from the French repertory and combined them according to their own wishes and preferences. The only exceptions are the eleven *Brando* suites composed by Uccellini, G. M. Bononcini, Colombi, and G. B. Vitali between 1667 and 1685 according to the same scheme. However, their identity of form is not due to a musical tradition but to a court ceremonial.

Variations: About 80 Italian violin compositions belong to this type. It is striking that the designation *Partite*, which is always used for variations in the contemporary keyboard music, does not exist in the violin music. As with the other forms, a number of different designations were used. In the first three decades, variations were usually called *Sonata*, for instance, *Sonata sopra l'aria di Ruggiero* (Rossi, 1613), *Sonata E tanto tempo hormai* (Turini, 1621), *Sonata sopra la Novella* (Scarani, 1630), or *Sonata sopra l'aria della Scatola* (Buonamente, 1637). In the fourth decade the term *Sonata* disappeared, and variations were called *Aria*, particularly by Uccellini, for instance, *Aria sopra il Lantururù* (1642) or *Aria detta il Caporal Simon* (1645).

The great majority of variations from the first half of the seventeenth century are based on themes taken from the as yet unexplored repertory of popular song: *A voi dò vinto il cov, Bella che mi lieghi, Quest'e quel luoco, Cavallo zoppo, Quella bella Sirena, La mia Pedrina,* and others, in addition to those previously mentioned. Strangely enough, these themes, which apparently exist only in violin literature and have been ignored to the present day, completely disappear in the second half of the century. Along with them are a number of themes that frequently occur in other fields—keyboard music, lute music, some even in vocal music—and have been known for a long time. Most of them originated in the fifteenth century. The *Passamezzo (Pass'emezzo)* was used as a theme of variations for violin by Marini (1629), G. B. Vitali (1682), and T. A. Vitali (1695); the *Ruggiero* by Rossi (1613), Buonamente (1626) and Merula (1637) and Vitali (1603); the *Romanesca* by Rossi (1613, 1622), Marini (1620), and Buonamente (1626, 1637); the *Bergamasca* by Rossi (1622) and Uccellini (1642); the *Folia* by Falconiero (1650) and Corelli (1700). Even more frequently variations are based on short ostinati. *Ciacona* variations were written by Merula (1637), Uccellini (1642), Kempis (1644), Cazzati (1651, 1660), G. B. Vitali (1682), Corelli (1685), and Caldara (1699). The *Passacaglia* theme was used by Falconiero (1650), Marini (1655), Cazzati (1660), Pandolfi (1660), and G. B. Vitali (1682, 1698).

In addition to compositions whose titles show them to be variation sets, there are a number of pieces for which this indication is missing. To this "anonymous" group belong Cazzati's three *Capriccio* (1651, 1658, 1660) and three *Voltata* (1651), a *Balletto* by Marini (1655), a *Sonata* by Bertali (no date), a *Capricietto* by Pandolfi (1669), a *Sinfonia* by Stradella (no date), and two *Capriccio* by G. B. Vitali (1682).

Sonata: The term "sonata" is used here to designate a lengthy form consisting of several sections or movements that differ from each other by their tempo, their meter, their style, or other characteristics. The sonata is the most important and most interesting form of early Italian music; it was created and developed in this field and is the only form to which every composer in the present study has made a contribution.

In the first half of the seventeenth century, the sonata is occasionally referred to by the earlier term *Canzona*, for instance, by Viadana (1602), Sponga (1614), Picchi (1625), Frescobaldi (1628), and Cazzati (1642). Nearly all of Merula's numerous sonatas are designated *Canzona*. Often the term *Sinfonia* is used for sonata, by Sponga (1614), Mont'Albano (1629), Kempis (1644, 1649), G. M. Bononcini (1672), Colombi (1673),

Stradella (no date), Viviani (1678), Bassani (1683), Torelli (1687, 1692), and G. B. Bononcini (1685, 1686, 1687). The designation *Capriccio* was used by Cima (1610), F. and G. Sponga (1614, 1619), Cazzati (1669), Pandolfi (1669), G. B. Vitali (1669), and Viviani (1678).

The most frequently used designation is *Sonata*. The first to use it for a composition of this category was G. Gabrieli (1598, 1615), then Cima (1610), Rossi (1613), Turini (1621, 1624), Castello (1621, 1629), Fontana (about 1625), and later—to name only the most important composers—Buonamente, Cazzati, Neri, Legrenzi, G. M. Bononcini, G. B. Vitali, Corelli, Torelli, P. Degli Antonii, Ruggieri, Caldara, and Albinoni.

The meanings of the terms *Sonata da chiesa* and *Sonata da camera* are not properly understood even today. They occur for the first time in Merula's *Libro Terzo* of 1637, the title of which carries the remark *per chiesa e camera*. Obviously, *per chiesa* refers to the canzonas of the publication, perhaps also to the *Ruggiero* and the *Chiacona* (both variations), while the *Ballo* and the two *Balletto* are *per camera*. Neri's Opus 1 from 1644 also has the indication *in Chiesa & in Camera*, the former referring to the canzonas and sonatas, the latter to the correnti added at the end. A similar situation exists in Legrenzi's Opus 4, *Sonate da Chiesa, da Camera*, of 1656. The differentiation is particularly clear in G. M. Bononcini's *Trattenimenti* (Opus 9, 1675), where the *Tavola* lists five sonatas under the heading *Sonate da Chiesa* and some dances under *Sonate da Camera*. Usually, however, the two species are printed separately, for instance, sonatas in G. B. Vitali's *Sonate da Chiesa* (Opus 9, 1684) and in Ruggieri's *Suonate da Chiesa* (Opus 3, 1693), dances and suites in Cazzati's *Trattenimento per Camera* (Opus 22, 1660) or Corelli's *Sonate da Camera* (Opus 2, 1685).

In all the publications mentioned previously the terms *da chiesa* and *da camera* have the same meaning as in present-day usage: the former stands for sonatas, the latter for suites, or at least for single dances. But this is not always the case. In 1660 Pandolfi published two collections with the title *Sonate a Violino solo, per Chiesa e Camera*, which contains only sonatas in the proper sense of the word. The indication *per Chiesa e Camera* means that these sonatas could be performed in the church as well as in the "chamber" (in this case, the hall of the archducal palace at Innsbruck). Briefly stated, they are both church sonatas and chamber sonatas. The only difference may be that the former are accompanied on the organ, the latter on the harpsichord or spinet. Toward the end of the seventeenth century there appeared five publications containing sonatas written expressly and exclusively for "domestic use": Albergati's *Pletro armonioso composto di dieci Sonate da Camera* (1687), Ruggieri's *Bizzarie armoniche esposite in dieci Sonate da Camera* (1687), Veracini's *Sonate da Camera* (c.1694) and *Sonate da Camera* (1696), and Iacchini's *Sonate . . . per camera* (before 1695). Each of these prints consists of sonatas accompanied by instruments found in the home: for Albergati it is the cello and the harpsichord; for Ruggieri it is the theorbo, violone, or spinet; for Veracini the violone, harpsichord, or archlute; and for Iacchini the cello. The result of this investigation is that the term *sonata da camera* included not only suites but also sonatas, that is to say, chamber sonatas, not church sonatas intended to be accompanied by the organ.

During the course of the seventeenth century the structure of the sonata underwent a very interesting and significant development that has remained unnoticed to the present day. The earliest stage of the sonata is represented by numerous works that progress from beginning to end without interruption and are subdivided only by changes of meter, tempo, or thematic material. This structural principle is derived from the instrumental music of the sixteenth century. It is realized in many canzonas that are not considered here because they are not expressly written for violin. In the violin literature of the first half of the seventeenth century, and occasionally even later, there are many sonatas of this type, from Cima (1610) to Uccellini (Opus 5, 1649). Marini's *Sonata senza cadenza* (Opus 8, 1629) expressly refers to this type.

By writing a sonata with this title, Marini points to the second stage of the development, which could be designated *Sonata con cadenze*: a sonata divided by full cadences into several sections that differ in content and style. Most sonatas written between about 1620 and 1640 belong to this type, which could be called the cadence sonata. Merula, in his numerous canzonas created a special form of the sonata, consisting of three sections, with the middle section repeated. Legrenzi used this form in his Opus 2 (1652) and Opus 8 (1663).

About 1640 the third (and last) stage of the structural development began: the subdivision indicated by cadences was replaced by a distinct and unmistakable separation into individual movements. This type was created simultaneously by Cazzati in Bologna, in his *Canzoni a 3* (Opus 2, 1642), and by Neri in Venice, in *Sonate e Canzone* (Opus 1, 1644), in which the separation into movements is even clearer than in Cazzati's publication. From about 1640 to 1680 the number of movements varies from two to seven, with four being the most frequent. The type known today by the term "church sonata"—four movements in the tempo sequence slow, fast, slow, fast—occurs for the first time (more or less by chance) in Cazzati's Opus 8, of 1649, and then in G. B. Vitali's Opus 2, of 1667, and Opus 5, of 1669. In the 1680s this form predominated in Corelli (1681), Albergati (1683), and G. B. Bononcini (1687) and was used exclusively in Albinoni's Opus 1 (1694). Simultaneously another form of the sonata developed, in which the initial slow movement is omitted, resulting in a three-movement form fast, slow, fast. As early as 1668 Ziani had written several such sonatas in his Opus 7; and it appears quite frequently in G. B. Bononcini's Opus 5 (1687). In Albinoni's Opus 2 (1700), all six *Concerti* have the tempo sequence fast, slow, fast, which became obligatory for the concerto of the eighteenth and nineteenth centuries.

Concerto: This term is used here to designate a sonata that includes soloistic passages for the participating instruments. The actual development of the Baroque concerto took place in the first half of the eighteenth century, lying outside of our considerations. However, before 1700 there existed about 30 sonatas that paved the way for the later development. In many of these "concerto sonatas" the soloistic component is limited to sections in the middle of the composition, in which two instruments, one after the other (often overlapping) play a soloistic passage. Such a passage will be called a "double solo" in the following explanations.

The earliest concerto sonata is *Sonata per il Violoni* by Cima (1610), which has a double solo of twelve measures for violin and violone. *Canzone la Rizza* by Riccio (1620) begins with a violin solo of seventeen measures, and later there is a double solo of sixteen measures for violin and violone. Many sonatas by Castello contain extended solo passages. Sonata No. 7 of 1621 has a 34-measure double solo for violin and bassoon, and No. 8 has one of 29 measures for the same instruments. Sonata No. 9 by Fontana (about 1625) begins with a bassoon solo of 49 measures, and later has a violin solo of 24 measures. In Uccellini's *Libro Terzo* of 1642, Sonata No. 1 contains a double solo of twelve measures for violin and theorbo, No. 16 a triple solo of 24 measures for violin I, violin II, and theorbo. Both solo passages are unusual because they are not virtuosic, but are written in slow, sustained note values. Bertali's *Prothimia suavissima* (posthumous, 1672) contains a number of triple solos, all in virtuoso style; for instance, in No. 2 of *Duodena Prima* and in Nos. 7 and 10 of *Duodena Seconda*, all for violin I, violin II, and viola da gamba. *Sonata Prima* in Neri's Opus 2 (1651) consists of seven movements, the third of which is a solo for the two violins, the fifth a solo for the bass. Sonata No. 2 of Viviani's Opus 1 (1673) contains a twelve-measure solo for violin II and a double solo of 21 measures for violin I and viola.

Sonata No. 8 of Torelli's Opus 1 (1686) consists of six movements; the third is a duet for violin solo and violoncello solo, the fourth a solo for violin I (30 measures), and the fifth an even more extended solo (44 measures) for violin II. G. B. Bononcini's Opus 4 (also 1686) contains two concerto sonatas. The middle section of No. 5 begins with a 60-measure double solo for violin I and violin II, followed, after five measures *tutti*, by 54 measures of violoncello solo. No. 12 of this publication has an even more extended middle section of the same structure. In Ruggieri's Opus 1 (1689) five of the ten sonatas of the collection belong to this type. Nos. 5 and 7 contain extended and highly virtuosic double solos for violin and theorbo, while Nos. 5, 8, and 10 have single solos for the same instruments. Buoni's Opus 2 (1693) contains two concerto sonatas, Nos. 5 and 12, both with the same structure for the soloistic components: an 80-measure double solo for violin I and violin II, seven measures *tutti*, and a 32-measure solo for bassetto.

In all the concerto sonatas that have been mentioned, two or three instruments participate as soloists, as in a double or triple concerto. Not until Torelli's Opus 6 of 1698, is a composition to be found, Concerto No. 6, in which only one instrument, violin I, appears as soloist.

The concerto grosso also has its beginning in the seventeenth century. An exceptionally early example is *Sinfonia prima* by Francesco Sponga (Usper), of 1619. Not until 1651 does this type reappear, in Neri's Opus 2, which probably contained six concerti grossi, but only Nos. 10 and 12 have been preserved. In the second half of the seventeenth century five compositions of this type were written: three concerti grossi by Stradella (about 1670), Corelli's *Sinfonia* of 1689 (WoO, No. 1), and Torelli's Concerto Opus 5, No. 12, of 1698. Within the field of our study, these are the last representatives of a development that, in the eighteenth century, led to the famous concerti grossi by Corelli, Bach, and Handel.

NOTES

1. "Wenn freilich Boyden meint, Andreas Moser biete hier lediglich eine Geschichte der Violinmusik, so entspricht dies weder der Zielsetzung . . . noch etwa den von ihm souverän gewählten Notenbeispielen. . ." (p. 10).

2. Another interesting case of opposites is found in the nature of the source material: in the keyboard sources manuscripts play a much greater role than in violin music, e.g.,

the Turin, Lynar, and Lüneburg manuscripts, the Spanish manuscripts, etc., while violin literature is contained primarily in prints, a further evidence of popularity.

3. For example, the more than thirty publications in *CEKM*.

4. In this regard see also the listing of trio sonatas in E. Schenk, *Die italienische Triosonate* (=*Das Musikwerk*, vol. VII) (Bologna, 1954).

5. Modern edition by J. B. Weckerlin, in *Chefs-d'oeuvres de l'opéra classique français* (Paris, 1880–1902). See Jacquot 1963, p. 171.

6. BoydenH, pp. 54ff.

7. D. P. Walker, ed., *Les fêtes du mariage de Ferdinand de Medici et de Christine de Lorraine*, Florence, 1582 (Paris, 1963); further, H. M. Brown, *Sixteenth-century Instrumentation: The Music of the Florentine Intermedii*, MSD XXX, 1973.

8. Complete in *Orgel und Klavier in der Musik des 16. Jahrhunderts* (Leipzig, 1910), p. 312.

9. Modern edition: London Pro Musica Edition (London, 1980).

10. In my *Harvard Dictionary of Music* (Cambridge, 1944; 2d ed., 1969) I tried, under the rubric "form" to unravel this confusion by distinguishing between "form in music" and "form(s) of music." [This distinction is blurred in Don Randel, *The New Harvard Dictionary of Music* (Cambridge, 1986)—ed.]

The Composers and Their
Published Music

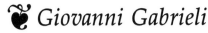 Giovanni Gabrieli

Giovanni Gabrieli, a nephew of Andrea Gabrieli, was born in 1557 in Venice. From about 1575 to 1579 he was active at the court chapel of Munich, under Orlando di Lasso. In 1584 he became second organist and in 1586 first organist at San Marco in Venice, succeeding his uncle. He died in 1612 in Venice.

Gabrieli's *Sacrae Symphoniae* of 1597, a collection of motets for six to eighteen voices, includes several instrumental compositions. Two are remarkable because for the first time in printed music a part is specifically designated *Violino*. One of these compositions is the famous *Sonata pian'e forte*, the other a fifteen-voice *Canzona per sonar Quarto toni*.[1] The sonata is written for eight voices divided into two choirs, the first for cornetto and three trombones, the second for violin and three trombones. The title carries the remark *alla quarta bassa*, which could be incorrectly interpreted as an indication to play the composition a fourth *lower* than it is written. The correct interpretation, however, is that it is notated at the lower fourth and therefore is to be played at the *higher* fourth. The same transposition is employed by Salomone Rossi in *Il primo libro delle Sinfonie* (1607), where it is indicated unequivocally by the remark "Va sonata alla Quarta alta." That this is also the correct interpretation for Gabrieli's *Sonata pian'e forte* is borne out by the fact that the *violino* part, as notated, descends to *d*, a fourth below the lowest tone of the violin.[2]

The cornetto and violin, instruments that in many compositions of the seventeenth century are used as alternatives ("per il Cornetto over Violino"),[3] appear in Gabrieli's *Sonata pian'e forte* as partners of equal rank. They either alternate with each other or combine their forces, each supported by three trombones, to produce a magnificent sonority and a splendid example of Renaissance-Baroque instrumentation.

In 1615, three years after Gabrieli's death, *Canzone e sonate del Signor Giovanni Gabrieli* was published. It contains seventeen canzonas of five to twelve parts; one sonata each of fourteen, fifteen, and 22 parts; and finally *Sonatta Con Tre Violini*.[4] In contrast to *Sonata pian'e forte*, this work is not dependent on sonority but on the transparency of its counterpoint as well as the constant change of the motifs and their treatment. Fig. 4 shows three motifs, each presented in a different manner: the first in imitation, the second as a complementary motif, the third in parallel motion.

NOTES

1. Modern edition in *Istituzioni e monumenti dell'arte musicale italiana*, vol. II, Nos. VI and XVI. Also printed in HAM, No. 173, and WasielewskiS, No. IV.

2. Transposition is a very complicated proposition in music of the sixteenth and seventeenth centuries. Clef configuration, chiavetta, various traditions concerning the performance of vocal music with instruments, and, of course, the Kammerton/Chorton practice, all have left their marks on musical practice, the discussion of which goes beyond the limits of this book.

3. See, in this regard, CulM.

4. Modern edition of this print by M. Sanvoisin; *Sonatta* is printed in WasielewskiS, No. VII.

FIGURE 4. GABRIELI: SONATTA CON TRE VIOLINI (1615).

SOURCES

Sacrae Symphoniae . . . senis 7, 8, 10, 12, 14, 15, & 16, tam vocibus, quam instrumentis, editio nova. Venice: Angelo Gardano, 1597.   RISM G86.

Austria: Vienna Österreichische Nationalbibliothek Musiksammlung (S,A,T,B, parts 5–12).

Great Britain: London, British Library.

Italy: Brescia, Archivio del Duomo (lacks parts 10–12); Ferrara, Biblioteca comunale Ariostea; Piacenza, Archivio del Duomo.

Spain: Montserrat, Monasterio de Montserrat.

West Germany Augsburg, Staats- und Stadtbücherei (lacks S); Regensburg, Bischöfliche Zentralbibliothek.

Yugoslavia: Ljubljana, Narodna in univerzitetna knjiznica (A, 5).

Editions:

Istituzioni e monumenti dell'arte musicale italiana, vols. 1–2. Milan: Edizioni Ricordi, 1939.

Opera Omnia, vol. 1, parts 1–3. Venice: Fondazione Giorgio Cini; Mainz: Universal Edition, 1969.

Canzoni et sonate del Signor Giovanni Gabrieli a 3. 5. 6. 7. 8. 10. 12. 14. 15. & 22. voci, per sonar con ogni sorte de istrumenti con il basso per l'organo. Venice: Stampa del Gardano, appresso Bartolomeo Magni, 1615.   RISM G88.

Czechoslovakia: Prague, Státní knihovna CSR (Organ).

Italy: Bologna, Civico Museo (T incomplete); Rome, Biblioteca Musicale Governativa del Conservatorio di Santa Cecilia (A,T,B, part 5).

West Germany: Augsburg, Staats- und Stadtbücherei (lacks B); Kassel, Murhard'sche Bibliothek der Stadt Kassel und Landesbibliothek.

Edition:

Michel Sanvoisin, ed., *Le Pupitre* 27. Paris: Heugel et Cie., 1971.

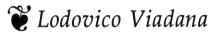 Lodovico Viadana

*The real name of this composer was probably Grossi, but he called himself Viadana
after the little city near Modena where he was born about 1560. From 1593 to 1597
he was chapelmaster at the cathedral of Mantua, from 1602 at the monastery San
Luca in Cremona, from 1608 at the cathedral of Concordia, and from 1610 to 1612
at the cathedral of Fano. Later he entered the monastery of San Andrea in Gualtieri
(near Viadana), where he died in 1627.*

Lodovico Viadana was chiefly a composer of vocal music. Especially well known is his
Opus 12 from 1602: *Cento Concerti Ecclesiastici a Una, a Due, a Tre, & a Quattro voci.
Con il Basso Continuo per Sonar nell'Organo.* It is a collection of sacred vocal music except
for its closing composition, *Canzon francese* for violin, two cornetti, trombone, and bass.
The bass is not independent but duplicates the lowest segment of the upper parts. Thus
it is not a separately composed *basso continuo* but a *basso seguente* (the original designation
is *In Risposta*). The length of the canzona is 110 breves, and, as is frequently the case,
there are several sections, each based on a different theme. These themes are not treated
in the customary four-voice imitation but occur only in the two upper parts (violin and
cornetto I). They alternate at the same pitch level, so that they answer each other in the
manner of an echo. Viadana vas familiar with this technique from earlier echo pieces
and especially from the double-chorus compositions of the Venetian school. In the present
composition, of course, the performers are not a large group of singers but only two
instrumental soloists. Moreover, Viadana's canzona contains numerous extended rests so
that the four-voice setting is actually reduced to two parts, and only at the middle and
again at the end do all the instruments play together. The general character of this canzona
may be illustrated by its initial theme, seen in Fig. 5 (the *basso seguente* is omitted).

FIGURE 5. VIADANA: CANZON FRANCESE (OPUS 12, 1602).

Let us compare this "melody" with that of Antony Holborn's pavane *Patiencia* from
1599 (Fig. 3). In the English pavane the violin part is highly expressive, while liveliness
and activity are the dominating principle in the Italian canzona. *Canzon francese* has an
interesting structure and instrumentation, with a frequent exchange of violin and cornetto
I in the upper parts and of cornetto II and trombone in the lower ones. In the closing
section of the canzona the initial motif of the first (and last) theme is treated in stretto

(Fig. 6). Also noteworthy is the repeated change from *e* to *eb* (see the asterisks). Viadana's canzona is characteristic of Italian violin music with its lively melodic contour and its varying of structure.

FIGURE 6. VIADANA: CANZON FRANCESE (OPUS 12, 1602).

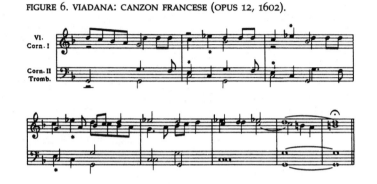

In 1610 Viadana published his Opus 18, a collection of instrumental compositions entitled *Sinfonie musicali a otto voci*. It contains eighteen sinfonias with the indication *per concertare con ogni sorte di strumenti*, that is, without specific reference to the violin.

SOURCES

Cento concerti ecclesiastici, a una, a due, a tre, & a quattro voci, con il basso continuo per sonar nell'organo, nova inventione commoda per ogni sorte da cantori, & per gli organisti....
Opus 12. Venice: Giacomo Vincenti, 1602.   RISM V1360.
Edition:
Claudio Gallo, ed., *Monumenti musicali mantovani*, vol. 1. Mantua: Istituto Carlo D'Arco per la storia de Mantova; and New York: Bärenreiter, 1964 (excerpts).
Reprints:
Venice: Giacomo Vincenti, 1603.   RISM V1361.
    Italy: Fabriano, Biblioteca comunale (Organ).
Venice: Giacomo Vencenti, 1604 (3d printing).   RISM V1362.
    Italy: Fabriano, Biblioteca comunale (A,T,B).
Venice: Giacomo Vincenti, 1605 (4th printing).   RISM V1363.
    East Germany: Dresden, Sächsiche Landesbibliothek, Musikabteilung (S, A incomplete).
    Italy: Bologna, Civico Museo.
    West Germany: Augsburg, Staats- und Stadtbibliothek (S,A,T,B,b.c.).
Venice: Giacomo Vincenti, 1607 (5th printing).   RISM V1364.
    Great Britain: London, British Library (S).
Venice: Giacomo Vincenti, 1608 (6th printing).   RISM V1365.
    West Germany: Regensburg, Bischöfliche Zentralbibliothek (S).
Venice: Giacomo Vincenti, 1610 (7th printing).   RISM V1366.
    Italy: Siena, Biblioteca dell'Accademia Musicale Chigiana (A,T, B incomplete).
Venice: Giacomo Vincenti, 1612 (8th printing).   RISM V1367.
    East Germany: Saalfeld, Heimatmuseum, Bibliothek (T,B, b.c.).
    Italy: Rome, Biblioteca Musicale governativa del Conservatorio di Santa Cecilia (A).
    West Germany: Regensburg, Bischöfliche Zentralbibliothek (S,A,T,B, b.c.).

Sinfonie musicali a otto voci ... commode per concertare con ogni sorte de stromenti, con il suo basso generale per l'organo, novamente composte, & date in luce. Opus 18. Venice: Giacomo Vincenti, 1610.   RISM V1407.

    Great Britain: Oxford, Bodleian Library (I: S,A,T,B; II: S,A,T,B, organ).

    Italy: Bologna, Civico Museo.

    West Germany: Munich, Bayerische Staatsbibliothek, Musiksammlung (S I).

Salomone Rossi

Salomone Rossi was probably born on August 19, 1570 in Mantua, where for many years (1587 to 1628 ?) he was a composer and viol player at the court of the Gonzagas. He came from an old Jewish family and in all his publications called himself "Ebreo." Particularly well known today is his Hashirim asher lish'lomo *(The songs of Solomon) (1622–23), in which the texts are printed in Hebrew. He also published the earliest ensemble vocal music with a continuo part (reflecting a practice of performance that went back at least two generations),* Il secondo libro de madrigali ... *(1602). His sister was a virtuoso singer (known as "Madama Europea"), but she and Salomone seem not to have been related to other musicians by the name of Rossi at the Mantuan court. Rossi probably perished during the destruction of the ghetto and the severe plague following the sack of Mantua in 1630.*[1]

Between 1607 and 1662 Salomone Rossi published four books with instrumental music, the first three written for viols, the fourth for violin. However, their content as well as their style are so closely related that all of them have to be included in this study.

    The first publication, from 1607, *Il primo libro delle sinfonie et gagliarde a tre, quatro, & a cinque voci.... Per sonar due Viole, overo doi Cornetti, & un Chittarrone, o altro istrumento da capo,* contains 27 compositions in the following order (the consecutive numbering has been added):

Tre voci:	Sinfonia prima–quinta decima	Nos. 1–15
Quattro voci:	2 Sinfonia	Nos. 16, 17
	2 Gagliarda	Nos. 18, 19
	1 Sonata	No. 20
Cinque voci:	2 Sinfonia	Nos. 21, 22
	1 Gagliarda	No. 23
	1 Sinfonia	No. 24
	2 Gagliarda	Nos. 25, 26
	1 Passeggio d'un balletto	No. 27

It should be noted that Rossi's music is still rooted in the early tradition insofar as his compositions—unlike Viadana's—were published with neither a *basso continuo* nor a *basso seguente* part. Thus a designation such as *tre voci* correctly indicates the number of performing instruments. However, in the general practice of the seventeenth century the continuo part is not counted, so that for a *sonata a tre* (trio sonata) four or more instruments are required: frequently two violins; viol or violone (or later violoncello); and organ, harpsichord, harp, theorbo, or some similar instrument or a combination of continuo instruments.

The twenty *sinfonie* of Rossi's *Il primo libro*, contain a new type of violin music, which was further developed by several other composers: short and very attractive pieces that (in a very positive way) one might think of as the bagatelles of the seventeenth century. Rossi's sinfonias usually consist of two sections, each repeated. Some of them, however, such as Nos. 11 and 13 (each but seventeen bars long) are continuous; while others, such as No. 22, *Sinfonia grave a 5*, have three sections, with the structure ‖:9:‖:7:‖:11:‖. Often there is an opening passage of short imitation between the two upper parts. This is the case in the three-voice Sinfonia No. 5, in which the initial motif recurs in the second section in triple meter, not notated in imitation but in homophonic style. Fig. 7 shows the beginnings of both sections.

FIGURE 7. ROSSI: SINFONIE QUINTA A 3. (1607).

The *Sonata a 4.* (No. 20) is the most extended composition of the collection (54 measures). It is not a sonata in the usual sense of the word but a fugue with the theme

Frequently the theme

is used as a counterpoint so that this sonata is reminiscent of the later freely treated double fugue.

Rossi's *Il secondo libro delle Sinfonie è Gagliarde à Tre voci per sonar due Viole, & un Chitarrone con alcune delle dette a Quattro, & a Cinque, & alcune Canzoni per sonar à Quattro nel fine* (1608) contains 35 pieces (the numbering of Nos. 1–32 is original; Nos. 33–35 are unnumbered in the original):

21 Sinfonia à 3	Nos. 1–21
2 Sinfonia à 4 & à 3 si placet	Nos. 22, 23
1 Gagliarda à 4 & à 3 si placet	No. 24
2 Sinfonia à 4 & à 3 si placet	Nos. 24, 25

5 Sinfonia à 5 & à 3 si placet   Nos. 27–31
1 Gagliarda à 5 &   3 si placet   No. 32
3 Canzona per sonar à 4   Nos. 33–35

All sinfonias are in binary form except for Nos. 5, 11, 18, 23, and 29 which are continuous (the ternary form is not represented in this collection). Sinfonia No. 16 shows by its bold chromaticism, especially by the use of diminished thirds in the bass (mm. 2, 4, and 9), that Rossi was familiar with the revolutionary practices of his time. The three canzonas at the end of the collection are in binary form, as are most of the sinfonias, but these are more extended. Moreover, they begin with four-voice imitation, rather than the two-voice imitation of the sinfonias.

FIGURE 8. ROSSI: SINFONIA NO. 16 (1608).

Rossi's third book, *Il terzo libro de varie Sonate, Sinfonie, Gagliarde, Brandi, e Corrente per sonar due Viole da braccio, & un Chitarrone, o altro stromento simile*, probably appeared in 1613, but only a third printing from 1623 is preserved.[2] It contains:

6 Sonata   Nos. 1–6
9 Sinfonia   Nos. 7–15
8 Gagliarda   Nos. 16–23
3 Brando   Nos. 24–26
7 Corrente   Nos. 27–33

The six sonatas are quite unlike the common sonata derived from the canzona. Nos. 1, 2, and 6 are each about 50 measures in binary form. No. 1, *Sonata prima detta La Moderna*, begins with a very effective passage, one of the most impressive manifestations of the *stile moderno*. Later on, another "modern" passage occurs: two parallel seventh chords. Fig. 9 shows the beginning of this sonata.

FIGURE 9. ROSSI: SONATA PRIMA DETTA LA MODERNA (1613).

The other sonatas, all skillfully written little pieces, are variations: No. 3, *sopra l'aria della Romanesca* (eight variations); No. 4, *sopra l'aria di Ruggiero* (eight variations); No. 5, *sopra l'aria Porto celato il mio nobil pensiero* (nine variations). At the end of each piece there is the remark "Se replica l'ultima parte ma piu presto" (repeat the final section faster). No. 6, *Sonata in dialogo detta la Viena*, is indeed a dialogue between the two strings. At first they speak to each other with extended and highly expressive solo passages (twelve to fifteen measures), later with shorter and more precise fragments (one to three measures), giving the impression that the dialogue becomes increasingly excited. This is truly a remarkable and unique composition.

The six sonatas are followed by nine sinfonias of which *Sinfonia ottava* (No. 14) is especially noteworthy. It is an early example of the seventeenth-century style of organ music called *durezze e ligature*, which is characterized by the frequent use of dissonances (*durezze*) and suspensions (*ligature*). A number of dance pieces follow: *Gagliarda prima* does not have the customary binary form of seventeenth-century dances but consists of three sections (ten, eight, and sixteen measures)—a structure derived from the six-teenth-century pavane. *Brando secondo* (*brando* is Italian for *branle*) and *Corrente settima* carry the remark "Aria di Gio. Battista Rabini. Fabricate le parti del Autore," indicating that their melodies are by Rubini (an otherwise unknown composer), but the three-part settings are by Rossi.

In 1622 there appeared Rossi's *Il quarto libro di varie Sonate, Sinfonie, Gagliarde, Brandi, et Corrente per sonar due Violini et un Chitarrone o altro Stromento simile. . .* which is for violins. Its contents are:

12 Sonata	Nos. 1–12
6 Sinfonia	Nos. 13–18
1 Gagliarda	No. 19
4 Gagliarda, La sua Corrente	Nos. 20–23
1 Gagliarda	No. 24
2 Gagliarda, La sua Corrente	Nos. 25, 26

2 Brando   Nos. 27, 28

1 Sonata a Quattro Violini e doi Chitarroni   No. 29

As this list indicates, the contents of Book IV are similar to those of Book III. Sonatas Nos. 1–4 each consist of two sections—each to be repeated—with the second section about twice as long as the first and more varied. Sonatas No. 5–12 are all variations (as are three of the *Libro terzo*) based on popular songs: *Aria francese, Aria di Tordiglione, Aria di un Balletto, Aria E tanto tempo hormai, Aria del Tenor di Napoli, Aria della Romanesca, La Scatola,* and *La Bergamasca*.[3] *E tanto tempo hormai* (No. 8) consists of four variations on a theme that was also used by Turini (1622), Buonamente (1626), and Uccellini (1642). It is but 21 measures long and consists of three equal phrases. *Sonata sopra l'Aria del Tenor di Napoli* (No. 9) has only three variations but is twice as long. The main outline of the bass (tenor) is shown in Fig. 10a.[4]

FIGURE 10. ROSSI: a. TENOR DI NAPOLI (1622). b. LA SCATOLA (1622).

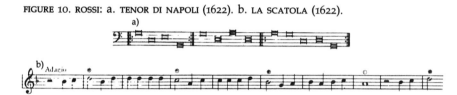

Sonata undecima detta La Scatola is based on a theme that was also used by Buonamente (1631) and Uccellini (1645), the latter quoting the beginning of the text: "Tu m'hai rotto la scatola da gli aghi ch'a voi tu me le paghi se la ragion vorra." The melody is a paraphrase of the passamezzo, either the *passamezzo antico* in minor (Rossi and Buonamente) or the *passamezzo nuovo* in major (Uccellini). Fig. 10b shows the beginning of Rossi's composition. The first variation is *adagio*, the next seven are *presto*, and the final two are again *adagio*, once more with the remark "Si replica l'ultima parte ma piu presto."

Except for the short and continuous No. 16, all the sinfonias have the same binary structure as the first four sonatas and are somewhat shorter. As in *Terzo libro*, there is one sinfonia (No. 17) in *Quarto libro* in *durezze e ligature* style. It is certainly not by chance that this composition is written in E minor, a tonality felt to express solemnity and mysticism. This key was used for many *durezze* compositions for organ, including the three *Toccate per l'elevazione* in Frescobaldi's *Fiori musicali* (1635).

FIGURE 11. ROSSI: SINFONIA QUINTA (1622).

As for the dances, in contrast to those in *Terzo libro*, these gagliardas and correnti are usually presented in pairs, e.g., *Gagliarda Ottava detta la Soriana—La sua Corrente.*

Rossi's *Libro quarto* closes with *Sonata a quattro Violini e due Chitarroni*, possibly the earliest composition specifically written for four violins. It consists of two sections, the second probably repeated, yielding the form A B B. The instruments are arranged in two choirs, each consisting of two violins and one chitarrone. In the first section the two choirs alternate in rather extended phrases for 40 measures, then close with eight measures in which they answer each other in the manner of an echo (*Forte, Piano*). In the second section all the instruments play together, apart from the short passage where the two choirs alternate. Parallel fifths, which are by no means rare in Rossi's compositions, occur in two places.

From the standpoint of musical history, the 55 sinfonias are the most significant items in the four books. With them Rossi created a type of composition that was cultivated further by other composers. Moreover, these short pieces reveal him as a master of miniature art. They represent a microcosmos that may well be placed side by side with that of Bartók.

NOTES

1. See Joel Newman and Fritz Rikko, *A Thematic Index to the Works of Salomon Rossi* (Hackensack, NJ, 1972).

2. RISM lists this work as Opus 12, with a date of 1638.

3. Note that in violin literature (Turini, Rossi, Marini, Buonamente, Uccellini, and others) there are variation pieces under the title *Sonata*, while in the contemporary keyboard music (Macque, Trabaci, Mayone, Frescobaldi, and others) these always are entitled *Partite*, which indicates that they contain several *parte* (sections, variations). The modern meaning of *Partita* (suite) appears for the first time with Johann Krieger in 1697 (cf. ApelG, p. 649) and with J. S. Bach.

4. The *Intavolature de cimbalo* of Antonio Valenti of 1576 contains variations on a "tenore grande alla Neapolitana," vaguely similar to Rossi's. Cf. ApelG, p. 270.

SOURCES

Il primo libro delle sinfonie et gagliarde a tre, quatro, & a cinque voci . . . per sonar due viole, overo doi cornetti, & un chittarrone o altro istromento da corpo. Venice: Ricciardo Amadino, 1607.   RISM R2763.

Italy: Bologna, Civico Museo (S I).

West Germany: Augsburg, Staats- und Stadtbücherei (S I and II, A, b.c.).

Editions:

Studio per Edizione Scelte, Florence, 1980 (facsimile).

Fritz Rikko and Joel Newman, eds., 3 vols. New York: Mercury Music Corp., n.d.

Il secondo libro delle sinfonie e gagliarde e tre voci, per sonar due viole, et un chittarrone, con alcune delle dette a quattro & a cinque, & alcune canzoni per sonar a quattro nel fine. Venice: Ricciardo Amadino, 1608.   RISM R2764.

Austria: Vienna, Österreichische Nationalbibliothek Musiksammlung (S I and II, B).

West Germany: Augsburg, Bischöfliche Zentralbibliothek.

Edition:

Fritz Rikko and Joel Newman, eds. Florence: Studio per Edizione Scelte, 1980 (facsimile).

Il terzo libro de varie sonate, sinfonie, gagliarde, brandi e corrente. Venice: Alessandro Vincenti, 1623 (probably published first in 1613, see text).   RISM R2767.
   Poland: Wroclaw, Biblioteka Uniwersytecka (S I and II, B).
Reprint:
Il terzo libro de varie sonate, sinfonie, gagliarde, brande e corrente per sonar due viole da braccio, & un chittarrone, o altro simile stromento . . . terza impressione. . . . Opus 12. Venice: Alessandro Vincenti, 1638.   RISM R2768.
   Great Britain: Oxford, Bodleian Library (S I and II, B).
Edition:
Il Seicento Musicale Italiano, vol. 2. Rome: Pro Musica Studium, 1980.

Il quarto libro de varie sonate, sinfonie, gagliarde, brandi, e corrente per sonar due violini et un chittarrone o altro stromento. Venice: Alessandro Vincenti, 1622.   RISM R2765.
   Italy, Bologna, Civico Museo (S II, b.c.).
Reprint:
Venice: Alessandro Vincenti, 1642 (*nuovamente ristampate*).   RISM R2766.
   West Germany: Kassel, Murhard'sche Bibliothek der Stadt Kassel und Landesbibliothek (S I and II, B).

Andrea and Giovanni Paolo Cima

The brothers Andrea and Giovanni Paolo Cima (there was also a Giovanni Battista Cima, who may have been related to them) were active in the musical life of Milan. Andrea, who was born about 1560, was organist at Santa Maria della Rosa about 1617. His music was included in anthologies such as B. G. Bonometti's Parnassus Musicus Fernandeus *of 1615 (RISM 1615[13]), and that may be the basis of Riemann's contention that Andrea was later chapelmaster at the cathedral in Bergamo. Giovanni was organist and chapelmaster at Santa Celso in Milan beginning in 1610, but he had been active as a composer long before that, having published his first collection in 1599.*

In 1610 Gio. Paolo Cima published *Concerti ecclesiastici . . . Messa e doi Magnificat & Falsi Bordoni a 4. & sei Sonate per Istrumenti a due, tre, quattro . . . con la partitura per l'Organo.* The six sonatas are designated as follows:

Capriccio d'Andrea Cima	No. 1
Sonata per Cornetto, over Violino	No. 2
Sonata per il Violino	No. 3
Sonata à 3.	No. 4
Sonata A 4.	No. 5
Capriccio d'Andrea Cima. A 4.	No. 6[1]

The publication consists of five part books: *Canto, Alto, Tenore, Basso,* and *Partitura,* the last of which needs explanation. For Sonatas Nos. 1, 2, and 3 (all *a 2.*) the *partitura* (score) consists of two systems; for No. 4 (*a 3.*) of three; and for Nos. 5 and 6 (both *a 4.*) only of the bass, which in the *Basso* part book is named *Basso Principale* and in the *Partitura, Basso continuo.*.

For Nos. 1–4 the *partitura* is a tablature, representing what today is called a "score." It occasionally differs from the individual parts—in some places where the parts have a rest, the score has notes. Thus, in the Capriccio by Andrea Cima (No. 1), in mm. 76–84 first the *Canto*, then the *Basso* each have a four-measure rest, whereas there are notes in the score at these places. Another example is a passage from G. P. Cima's Sonata No. 2 (Fig. 12).

FIGURE 12. G. P. CIMA: SONATA PER CORNETTO, OVER VIOLIN (1610).

Here the violone has a three-measure rest, while the organ plays a counterpoint to the violin's ascending chromatic scale. Also, in m. 5 of Fig. 12, the violone and the organ begin with an imitation of the violin, while no counterpoint is notated anywhere else. Probably this was improvised by the organist by playing the bass part of the preceding measures, as is indicated in Fig. 12 in small notes.

This publication is the first in which the designations *a due*, *a tre*, etc., are used in the way that became customary during the seventeenth and early eighteenth centuries, that is, to indicate the number of instrumental parts without taking into account the *basso continuo*. Hence, *a due* means a composition for which there are three part books, *a tre* one with four part books, etc.

In the two contributions by Andrea Cima (Nos. 1 and 6), 108 and 87 measures respectively, about ten themes or motifs are treated imitatively without interruption; for this type of composition H. Riemann introduced the term *Flick-Kanzona* (patchwork canzona). The fact that both compositions are named *capriccio* indicates a conservative practice, for it was in the 1560s that instrumental pieces were so named (e.g., Vincenzo Ruffo, *Capricci in musica, a 3, a commodo di virtuosi*, Milan, 1564). The term *sonata* came into common use in Italy about 1600, after Gabrieli's *Sonata pian'e forte* of 1597. Stylistically, also, these capriccios are conservative, for their note values never go beyond eighth notes. Nevertheless, these compositions show both technical skill and lively imagination.

The four contributions by Gio. Paolo Cima, all termed "sonata," differ from those of his elder brother first in the frequent occurrence of sixteenth-note passages. In many details they join the mainstream of Italian Baroque style, perhaps most strikingly in *Sonata per Cornetto, over Violino* (No. 2). Near the end of this piece a chromatic scale is used as a motif, first five times within the interval of a fourth

then spread over an octave (see Fig. 12), and finally expanded, as if by force, to encompass an eleventh as a solo passage in the bass (from *E* to *a'*). The new style manifests itself more subtly in *Sonata per il Violino* (No. 3), for instance in its initial theme (Fig. 13), which expands over a seventh in a highly expressive design.

FIGURE 13. G. P. CIMA: SONATA PER IL VIOLINO (1610).

The theme recurs twice, so that a rondo-like form results. Near the middle of the sonata the violin has a highly virtuosic solo passage, which is then repeated by the violone two octaves lower. This is the first appearance of an important concerto principle, one that recurs in many later compositions.

    Sonata a tre, Violino, Cornetto, & Violone (No. 4) is the earliest example of the setting generally known as "trio sonata." For *Sonata. A 4.* (No. 5), no instruments are specified. Perhaps it could be regarded as a sort of string quartet with *basso principale* for the organ. This sonata contains three sections in which short, precise motifs are treated in multiple imitation: the first (Fig. 14a) five times; the second (Fig. 14b) thirteen times; the third (Fig. 14c), an echo motif, six times.

FIGURE 14. G. P. CIMA: SONATA A 4. (1610).

    G. P. Cima's four sonatas are important both historically—many of the ideas found in them were further developed by later composers—and artistically. *Sonata per il Violino* (No. 3) is especially noteworthy and is considered by some the first great masterwork of the violin literature of the seventeenth century.

NOTE

    1. Modern edition of No. 3 in BeckmannVS, No. 2; Nos. 2–4 in K. Grebe, *G. P. Cima: Drei Sonaten* (1957); No. 4 in SchenkT, No. 1. In the Grebe edition important details of the original voice leading are not recognizable.

SOURCES

Concerti ecclesiastici a una, due, tre, quattro voci, con doi a cinque, et uno a otto, messa, e doi Magnificat, & falsi bordoni a 4., & sei sonate, per istrumenti a due, tre, e quatro di Giovanni Paolo Cima, organista della gloriosa Madonna ... con la partitura per l'organo.

Milan: Simon Tini & Filippo Lomazzo, 1610 (contains works by both Cimas). RISM C2229/1610⁴.

    Italy: Bologna, Civico Museo (S, A, T, B, score); Verona: Biblioteca capitolare.

❧ *Francesco and Gabriel Sponga (Usper)*

Francesco Sponga was born in Poreč (Parenzo), in Istria. He called himself "Usper" after his patron, Lodovico Usper, to whom he dedicated his first publication, Ricercate . . . di Francesco Sponga (1595), in which he designated himself as a pupil of Andrea Gabrieli. He was active as an organist in Venice, from 1598 at the Scuola Grande di San Giovanni Evangelista and from 1614 at the Church of San Salvatore. He died in 1641. Gabriel Sponga, about whose life nothing is known, was his nephew.

In 1614 there appeared *Messa e Salmi . . . & insieme Sinfonie . . . di Francesco Usper*, a collection of sacred vocal music to which are added at the end *Sinfonia a 6.*, *Sinfonia a 6. di Gabr. Sp.* [Gabriel Sponga], and *Sinfonia a doi Violini di Gabr. Sp.* Here the term "sinfonia" is used not for short pieces in binary form (as it is by Rossi) but for extended compositions of 95, 134, and 86 measures respectively. The most interesting composition is the second Sinfonia (for two violins and four unspecified instruments), with its constant change of ideas in various structures, frequently divided between two choirs. *Sinfonia a doi Violini* is a rather insignificant composition, with its initial eight measures repeated at the end.

    In 1619, another publication by Francesco Usper appeared, entitled *Composisioni armoniche . . . Opera Terza*. There are no extant copies of this collection of motets and ten instrumental compositions, but the instrumental pieces are preserved in a transcription by A. Einstein:[1] two sinfonias, three sonatas (two of them by Gabriel Sponga), three canzonas, and two capriccios. *Sinfonia prima*, is an early predecessor of the concerto grosso.[2] This eight-voice composition of more than 130 measures includes two long sections for a *concertino* of three instruments: the first (24 measures) for two violins and b.c., the second (62 measures) for flute, viol (or chitarrone), and b.c. *Sonata a tre* (two violins, bassoon, and b.c.) by Gabriel Sponga is not very attractive (there is, for instance, a section in which a one-measure motif is repeated fourteen times), but it is noteworthy for a tremolo passage (Fig. 15a), numerous echoes (*piano*, *forte*), and a passage marked *ligate* (Fig. 15b). The remaining eight instrumental pieces of this publication are not specifically designated for violin.

FIGURE 15. GABRIEL SPONGA: SONATA (1619).

NOTES

1. EinsteinC, vol. III.
2. A. Einstein, "Ein Concerto grosso von 1619" in *Kretzschmar Festschrift* (Leipzig, 1918), p.26.

SOURCES

Messa e salmi da concertarsi nel'organo et anco con diversi stromenti, a cinque voci, et insieme sinfonie, et motetti a una, due, tre, quattro, cinque, et sei voci. Venice: Giacomo Vincenti, 1614.   RISM U116.
     Italy: Bologna, Civico Museo (S, A, T, B, 5, 6).

(Canto) Compositioni Armonische nella quali si contengono motetti, sinfonie, sonate, canzoni, & capricce, a 1. 2. 3. 4. 5. 6. 7. & 8 voci con basso continuo et in fine in Battaglia a 8 . . . Opus 3. Venice: Stampa del Gardano, appresso Bartolomeo Magni, 1619.   [No RISM number, reported lost in the Second World War (SartoriB); originally preserved in Berlin.]
     Italy: Bologna, Civico Museo.

 Marc'Antonio Negri

Marc'Antonio Negri was a singer and vice maestro di capella at St. Mark's in Venice, where for several years he was an assistant to Monteverdi. In 1616 he was appointed abbot of the monastery at Veglia. He published two books of Affetti amorosi: *the first (1608) is a collection of three-part vocal music, the second (1611) is a collection of music for one, two, and five voices with continuo, to which he added three instrumental sonatas. Sonata prima and seconda, for doi violini, are short pieces of twelve and fourteen measures respectively, the latter being a short-interval canon. Sonata terza is a fanfare for wind instruments.*

SOURCES

Affetti amorosi libro secondo. Venice: Ricciardo Amadino, 1611.   RISM N363.
     Belgium: Brussels, Bibliotheque Albert Ier.
     Italy: Genoa, Biblioteca universitaria.

Giulio Belli

Giulio Belli (born c. 1560, died after 1621) was a pupil of Tomaso Cimello in Naples. Later he entered a Franciscan monastery. He became maestro di capella at the Catedrale d'Imola in 1590, then at Santa Maria in Carpi, and subsequently at the church of the Cà Grande in Bologna. He moved about rather a lot, working in Ravenna, Reggio, Forli, and returning to Imola. In his Concerti ecclesiastici of 1613, *he calls himself* Maestro di Capella della Catedrale d'Imola. *This collection of canzonas closes with a* Canzone Doi Cornetti *over* Violini & Trombone *in trio setting (two violins, bass, and b.c.). It consists of three sections: 57 measures in duple meter, six in triple, and eighteen in duple). The third section begins like the first (with the two violins exchanged), then continues differently.*

SOURCES

Concerti ecclesiastici a due et a tre voci. Venice: Bartolomeo Magni, 1613.   RISM B1771.
    Austria: Vienna, Österreichische Nationalbibliothek Musiksammlung (S I and II, B, b.c.).
    Italy: Bologna, Civico Museo; Bologna, Archivio di San Petronio.
    Poland: Wroclaw, Biblioteka Uniwersytecka (lacks b.c.).
Reprint:
Frankfurt: Nikolaus Stein, 1621.   RISM B1772.
    East Germany: Dresden, Sächsische Landesbibliothek, Musikabteilung (B, b.c.).
    France: Paris, Bibliothèque du Conservatoire national de musique (S I and II, organ incomplete; lacks B).
    Poland: Warsaw, Biblioteka Uniwersytecka (S II).

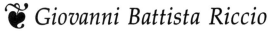

Giovanni Battista Riccio

Giovanni Battista Riccio (fl. 1609–1621) was an organist at the confraternity of San Giovanni Evangelista, where his contract described him as a violinist. In 1620 he published Il terzo libro delle Divine Lodi musicali, *a collection of motets in which eleven instrumental pieces are inserted at various places. Six pieces are for one or two violins, e.g.,* La Finetta *for violin, trombone, and b.c.;* La Grilletta *for two violins in Ecco and b.c.; and* La Rubina *for two violins, trombone, and b.c. The canzona* La Rizza *(for two violins and b.c.) begins with an eighteen-measure section for violin I solo, while in the subsequent section an eight-measure melody is performed first by violin II solo, then by violin I solo. Thus the principle of the concerto is more fully realized here than in Gio. Paolo Cima's* Sonata per il Violino *(1610).*

SOURCES

Il terzo libro delle devine lodi musicali . . . accommodate per concertare nell'organo, con le quattro antifone alla Gloriosa Vergine, e molti motteti, a 1. 2. 3. & 4. voci, et alcune canzoni da sonare a una 2. 3. et 4. stromenti. Venice: Stampa del Gardano, appresso Bartolomeo Magni, 1620.   RISM R1285.
    West Germany: Frankfurt, Stadt- und Universitätsbibliothek (S,A,T,B, score).
Edition:
Florence: Studio per Edizione Scelte, 1979 (facsimile).

 Innocentio Vivarino

Innocentio Vivarino (c.1575–1626) seems to haved lived all his life in Adria (Veneto), where was an organist and a singing teacher. He must have been an important figure in the musical life of the city, for he was a member of the Compagnia del Ss Sacramento. In 1620 he published Il primo libro de Motetti . . . con otto Sonate per il Violino ò altro simile stromento. *The eight sonatas[1] all belong to the same type, namely, that of the solo sonata (violin and b.c.). Their structure also is very uniform, since they all consist of three short sections, with the meter sequence* C, 3, C; *e.g., No. 2 has the structure* C *(mm. 1–23), 3 (mm. 24–36),* C *(mm. 37–58). Their content is as insignificant as that of Riccio's pieces.*

NOTE

1. Modern edition of No. 2 in RiemannH, p. 115 (only the initial section); No. 7 in A. Schering, "Zur Geschichte der Solosonate . . .," in *Riemann-Festschrift* (Leipzig, 1909), p. 319.

SOURCES

Il primo libro de motetti . . . da cantarsi a una voce, con otto sonate per il violino o altro simile stromento. Venice: Stampa del Gardano, appresso Bartolomeo Magni, 1620. RISM V2252.
　　West Germany: Frankfurt, Stadt- und Universitätsbibliothek.
Edition:
Luigi Pieressa, ed., *Eight Sonatas.* Padua: G. Zanibon, 1976.

Giulio Mussi

Giulio Mussi of Lodi in Lombardi (dates unknown) was Maestro di Capella dell'Illustre Comunità di Perdenon. Il primo libro delle Canzoni . . . opera quinta *(1620) contains sixteen canzonas. Instruments are specified only for the next-to-last piece, L'Amaltea, which is written for* doi Violini ò Cornetti in Ecco *and b.c. In the first section (mm. 1–71) and the final one (mm. 93–108), the first violin is used as a solo instrument, the second violin for short echoes. By way of contrast, the middle section (mm. 72–92), marked* Ecco insieme, *is a duet with echoes. Fig. 16a shows the* Ecco solo, *Fig. 16b the* Ecco insieme.

SOURCES

Il primo libro delle canzoni da sonare a due voci . . . con il basso per l'organo, et nel fine una toccata in ecco a doi soprani, Opus 5. Venice: Alessandro Vincenti, 1620.　　RISM M8225.
　　Italy: Bologna, Civico Museo.
　　West Germany: Munich, Bayerische Staatsbibliothek, Musiksammlung (S, B, b.c.).

Reprint:
Venice: Alessandro Vincenti, 1625 (*novamente ristampate, & corrette*)   RISM M8226.
   Poland: Wroclaw, Biblioteka Uniwersytecka (B, b.c.; lacks S).

FIGURE 16. MUSSI: L'AMALTEA (1620).

Adriano Tomaso Banchieri

Adriano Tomaso Banchieri (1568–1634) was born in Bologna, studied with Gioseffo Guami, and entered the Benedictine order, where he acquired the name Adriano. As an organist, he worked in Siena, Lucca, and Imola and at various Dominican houses. He was one of the founders of the Accademia dei Floridi in Bologna, an academy visited by Monteverdi, where he sported the name "Il Dissonante." His Primo libro delle Messe e Motetti *ends with* Sonata, due Violini e Trombone sopra l'aria del Gran Duca, *in which a popular song is heard again and again (Fig. 17). As with many works by Banchieri, this composition is full of charm and spirit and may well please today's listeners as it pleased those in the past.*

SOURCES

Primo libro delle messe e motetti concertato con basso e due tenori nell'organo. Opus 42.
Venice: Alessandro Vincenti, 1620.   RISM B811.
   Italy: Bologna, Civico Museo.

FIGURE 17. BANCHIERI: SONATA SOPRA L'ARIA DEL GRAN DUCA (1620).

🎵 *Giovanni Martino Cesare*

About the turn of the seventeenth century, Giovanni Martino Cesare, c.1590(?)–1667, and his brother Giovanni Francesco were active at the court in Vienna. Later Cesare was a trombonist in Udine, then a cornetist in Günzburg (near Augsburg), from where he went to Munich to teach cornetto in the service of Duke Maximilian. From 1615 on he was a cornettist there. His Musicali melodie per voci et instrumenti, published in Munich in 1621, is lost, but its contents are known through notes made by A. Einstein: fourteen motets and fourteen canzonas arranged according to the number of voice parts (A 1., A 2., etc.[1]). Six of the canzonas are for Cornetto ò Violino, *among them* La Gioia, *the beginning of which is worth noting for its jumping motion (Jumps of joy? Fig. 18).[2]*

NOTES

1. See SartoriB, p.1621b.
2. The instrumental pieces of Cesare, Belli, Riccio, and Vivarino are transcribed in EinsteinC, vol. III.

FIGURE 18. CESARE: LA GIOIA (1621).

SOURCES

Musicali melodie, per voci et instrumenti, a una, due, tre, quattro, cinque, e sei. Munich: Nikolaus Heinrich, 1621.   RISM C1752.
  West Germany: Frankfurt, Stadt- und Universitätsbibliothek (part 2); Regensburg, Bischöfliche Zentralbibliothek (parts 1, 2, 3, score for organ).

 Dario Castello

> *Nothing is known about the life of this important composer except what the titles of his publications indicate. In his first book, of 1621, Dario Castello calls himself* Capo di Compagnia de musici d'Instrumenti da fiato *(leader of the wind instrument players); in his second book, of 1629 (the dedication to Emperor Ferdinand II is dated 1627),* Capo di Compagnia d'Istrumenti, *both times at San Marco in Venice. He must have been quite popular in his time for both books were reprinted in the 1650s.*

Dario Castello's first publication carries the title *Sonate concertate in stil moderno, per sonar nel organo, overo spineta con diversi istrumenti, a 2. & 3. voci, con basso continuo, libro primo.* His second is called *Sonate concertate in stil moderno, per sonar nel Organo overo Clavicembalo ... libro secondo.*[1] The compositions in these two collections are written for numerous instruments—winds and strings—which are nearly always specified. Furthermore they are the first publications known to us that contain only sonatas: compositions that are not merely named so but are sonatas in the proper sense of the word, as we shall see.

  Book I contains twelve sonatas, book II, seventeen. As may be expected of a composer who was head of the Istrumenti da fiato, twenty of these sonatas are written for wind instruments, such as soprano (probably recorder), cornetto, fagotto (or viola), and trombone (or violeta). The nine remaining sonatas require participation of the violin, as follows:

Book I,	Nos. 7, 8	à 2: Sopran (Violino), Fagott, b.c.
	Nos. 9–11	à 3: Violino (2), Fagott, b.c.
	No. 12	à 3: Violino (2), Trombone (Violeta), b.c.
Book II,	Nos. 15, 16	à 4: Violino (2), Violeta, Viola, b.c.
	No. 17	à 4: Violino (2), Cornetto (2), b.c.

Castello's sonatas are designated *concertate in stil moderno*, very likely because the participating instruments occasionally have virtuoso solo passages, either short phrases or fairly extended sections, most of which carry the designation *solo*. The latter are of particular interest since—along with similar ones in G. P. Cima's sonatas—they are early realizations of the principle of the concerto. Among the nine violin sonatas listed above, six have highly virtuosic solo sections of fifteen to twenty measures, usually near the middle of the composition. In Book I, in Sonatas Nos. 7 and 8, the concerto section begins with a violin solo followed immediately by a solo for bassoon; in Nos. 9 and 11 it consists of a violin duet with subsequent bassoon solo; in No. 12 the concerto is confined to a quiet violin duet of 28 measures; and in Book II, No. 17, the concerto of violin I and cornetto I is enhanced by echoes from violin II and cornetto II.

In Castello's publications the part books are fully provided with bar lines, practically always in the manner they are drawn today, that is, at the distance of a whole note (*semibrevis*). In this respect Castello was far ahead of his time, for except for a 1630 publication by his successor Scarani, such bar lines do not recur until after 1650.

A particularly important innovation of Castello's is the consistent use of tempo indications: *adasio, alegra* (also *alegro*), and *presto*. This is their first appearance in violin literature, and for many years they remain unique. It is not until the 1630s that printed music included tempo indications. For instance, Frescobaldi's *Primo libro delle canzoni*, as published in 1628 by Robletti, has no such indications; but the 1634 reprint by Vincento, (entitled *Canzoni da sonare*) provides them. Obviously, during the first three decades of the seventeenth century the concept of the "notated" tempo was still firmly rooted in the minds of composers and musicians. Only gradually did they realize that it was possible to modify the tempo within certain limits by prescriptions such as *adagio* or *allegro*.[2] Castello wrote tempo indications in all his sonatas, sometimes as many as ten. See, for example, the following schematic representation of Sonata No. 8 of Book I. (The second line shows the number of measures in a particular meter [D = duple time; Tr = triple time]; and vertical lines indicate full cadences at the ends of sections.)

Castello: Sonata, Book I, No. 8

Section	1	2a	b	3	4a	b
Meter	22 D	4 D	11 D	29 Tr	2 D	16 D
Tempo	allegro	adasio	allegro		adasio	presto
Instrumentation	violin and bassoon				violin solo	

	c	d	5a	b	c	
	2 D	19 D	28 Tr	3 D	6 D	
	adasio	presto		adasio	presto	
	bassoon solo		violin and bassoon			

The only sections with no tempo indication are the two in triple time, both of which have the time signature 3/2. To judge from the context, section 3 should be played slowly, section 5a quickly. (The variability of the time signature 3/2 is clearly shown by Sonata No. 9 of Book I, which also has two such sections, one marked *allegro*, the other *adasio*.) In the sonata represented here the four *adasio* passages are only short introductions to fast passages, resulting in an effect of surprise, as, for instance, at the beginning of section 4 (Fig. 19).

FIGURE 19. CASTELLO: OTTAVA SONATA (1621).

In other sonatas there are short *adasios* at the ends of *allegro* passages as well as fairly extended independent *adasio* sections.

Above we mentioned that Castello's compositions are sonatas in the modern sense of the word. This means that they are lengthy compositions (100 to more than 200 measures) with several (mostly five or six) sections of contrasting character separated by full cadences, frequently also by fermatas. They are unlike the "sonatas" that actually belong to the category of the fugue (Rossi's *Sonata* from 1607), the variation (Turini's *Sonata E tanto tempo* from 1621), the suite (G. M. Bononcini's *Sonate da camera* of 1667), or yet other types (for instance, binary form). Thus, Castello's sonatas stand at the very beginning of the development of the modern sonata, a development to which Cazzati, Legrenzi, Corelli, and many other composers have contributed.

Castello's sonatas are characterized by a great variety of ideas and treatment. Occasionally sections of a sonata are related to each other by thematic variation, but the prevailing impression is that of change, of contrast. Even within the same section the picture changes frequently, sometimes in a logical development, sometimes by means of surprising effects. Among the latter, the sudden transitions from an expressive *adagio* to a lively *allegro* are especially noteworthy, as, for instance, in Sonata No. 9 of Book I, for two violins and bassoon (which is tacit at this place), shown in Fig. 20.

FIGURE 20. CASTELLO: NONA SONATA (1621).

Several sonatas close with an extended pedal point, above which the violins or other instruments play impressive cadential passages. Fig. 21 shows (in abbreviated writing) the closing measures of Sonata No. 11 of Book I.

FIGURE 21. CASTELLO: UNDECIMA SONATA (1621).

Also remarkable are the many details that are typical of the fanciful—even fantastic—style of the early Baroque period, for instance, the frequent use of *alla zoppa* rhythms or the rhapsodic-virtuoso writing in the solo passages. The first excerpt in Fig. 22 shows the beginning of the violin solo from the last sonata of *Libro secondo*, which, by the way, is much more virtuosic than the subsequent solo for the cornetto, thereby demonstrating that Castello was as familiar with the violin as with wind instruments.[3]

FIGURE 22. CASTELLO: SONATA DECIMA SETTIMA (1629).

Sonata No. 17 of Book II is written for two violins and two cornetti; violin I and cornetto I play the upper voices of a two-violin and b.c. setting, while violin II and cornetto II (they are named *Risposta di Violino* and *Risposta di Cornetto*) are occasionally used for echoes. This design makes for a fascinating interplay of the four instruments. For this sonata the *basso continuo* part book does not have a single-voice thorough bass but rather a score notated on two systems. We have already encountered this method in the sonatas by G. P. Cima, and we shall find it again in the works of Fontana, Marini, and other later composers. How can this practice be explained? Does it mean that "the violinist was allowed freedom of nuance in tempo and that the accompanist would (thus) be able to follow,"[4] as has been said with reference to Marini? Or was the upper part of the score actually played by the organist, who in a way supported the violinist? Modern players, of course, will sharply reject such an interpretation, but certain facts indicate beyond doubt that the violin indeed was doubled by a suitable register of the organ. Castello's *Sonata Decima Settima* (Book II, No. 17) offers particularly convincing evidence for this interpretation. The upper voice of its score does not always agree with either of the two soprano instruments (violin I and cornetto I); rather it doubles one then the other. Sometimes the change occurs so quickly that the upper part of the score actually becomes an independent melody, which, I have no doubt, was played on the organ. Fig. 22b shows one of these passages (mm.12–16).

It could be argued that the organist could not possibly play the often fast violin or cornetto passages at the same time as the chords demanded by the thorough bass. However, in this sonata, the lengthy organ bass has no figures. The same is true of the two sonatas *a sopran solo* (Nos. 1 and 2 of Book II), which are also printed in score. All the other sonatas have the common thorough bass with figures, as was customary at that time. Thus, Castello's use of figured bass offers yet another example of what we shall call "doubling practice," referring to the fact that in certain compositions the soprano part (usually the violin) was doubled on the organ.

All in all, Castello turns out to be a very imaginative composer. Violin music (as well as music for wind instruments) is indebted to him for many important innovations. That he was admired by his contemporaries is attested to by the fact that his *Libro primo* was reprinted twice in 1658, once in Venice (Francesco Magni) and once in Antwerp (Phalèse). Fortunately, his importance is being recognized again today; see the list of modern editions in note 1.

NOTES

1. Modern editions of Book II, Nos. 1 and 2 are in DM, No. 37; of Book I, Nos. 3, 5, 8, and 12 and Book II, Nos. 7, 11, 12, 15, 16, and 17 in *Recent Researches in the Music of the Baroque Era*, vols. 23 and 24 (Madison: A-R Editions, 1977).

2. Apel employs the term "tempo" in the sense of "tempo markings." It is clear that in the seventeenth century these markings also had affective meanings.

3. With regard to such writing, Moser writes: "Triads in 32d notes across all strings are frequent, and many chains of trills in Presto would cut a good figure even with Tartini" (MoserG, p. 17). The trills are found only in Sonata No. 2 of Book II for "soprano solo," probably the recorder. I have found no chains of trills.

4. IselinM, p. 32.

SOURCES

Sonate concertate in stil moderno, per sonar nel organo, overo spineta con diversi istrumenti, a 2. & 3. voci, con basso continuo, libro primo. Venice: Stampa del Gardano, appresso Bartolomeo Magni, 1629 (originally published in 1621; no extant copy).   RISM C1459.
    Poland: Wroclaw, Biblioteka Uniwersytecka. (S I and II, B; lacks score).
Reprints:
Venice: Francesco Magni, 1658.
    Great Britain: Oxford, Bodleian Library.
Antwerp: Les héritiers de Pierre Phalèse, 1658.
    Great Britain: Durham, Cathedral Library.
Editions:
Florence: Studio per Edizione Scelte, 1979 (facsimile).
Eleanor Selfridge-Field, ed., *Recent Researches in the Music of the Baroque Era*, vols. 23, 24. Madison: A-R Editions, vol. 23, 1977 (selections).

Sonate concertate in stil moderno per sonar nel organo overo clavicembalo con diversi istru-menti, a 1. 2. 3. & 4. voci, libro secondo. Venice: Stampa del Gardano, appresso Bartolomeo Magni, 1629.   RISM C1462.
    Poland: Wroclaw (Parts 1, 2 incomplete, 3, 4; lacks b.c.).
Reprints:
Venice: Bartolomeo Magni, 1644.   RISM C1463.
    Great Britain: Oxford, Bodleian Library.
    Italy: Florence, Biblioteca Nazionale Centrale (lacks part 3).
Antwerp: Les héritiers de Pierre Phalèse, 1656.   RISM C1464.
    Great Britain: British Library (lacks parts 1, 2, 3).
Editions:
Florence: Studio per Edizione Scelte, 1981 (facsimile).
Madison: A-R Editions, vols. 23, 24, 1977.

 *Francesco Turini*

> *Turini, the son of Gregorio Turini, a native of Brescia, was born in 1589 in Prague. In 1601, at the age of twelve, he became organist at the court of the Emperor Rudolf II. After the emperor's death, in 1615, Turini went to Italy. He was active as an organist at the cathedral of Brescia from about 1620 until his death in 1641.*

In 1621 Francesco Turini published *Madrigali . . . con alcune Sonate a due, et a tre. Libro primo,* a collection of madrigals to which are appended four compositions for violin: *Sonata a 2., Sinfonia a 3., E tanto tempo hormai,* and *Il Corisino.* The last two pieces are each named *Sonata a Tre.* Although this publication is not completely preserved, there exists a complete reprint from 1624, in which two more instrumental pieces are added: *Sonata a 3.* and *Gagliarda a 3.* The first of these six compositions is scored for violin, bass, and b.c.; all the others have the trio scoring two violins, bass, and b.c.

All these compositions are important, and they certainly deserve the attention they have received through modern editions.[1] The very beginning of the first composition, *Sonata a 2.,* diverges unmistakably from the stereotype of the canzona: a few long sus-tained notes form a melody that with some justification is inscribed "cantabile" in the modern edition. A very similar melody is found in Rossi's *Sonata prima detta la Moderna* from 1613 (see Fig. 9), but it is written for the viola.

Sonata E tanto tempo hormai consists of five variations on a song that was also used for variations by Rossi (1622), Buonamente (1626), and Uccellini (1642). Turini's variations are not all the same length, having 27, 22, 24, 22, and 24 measures respectively. Riemann tried to resolve the problem of the unequal length of these early pieces by rewriting the bass parts of the variations so that they would all be 23 measures in length.[2] However, in the variations of Rossi, Buonamente, and Uccellini the theme unmistakably has a length of 21 measures and consists of three phrases, A B B, each of seven measures. In Turini's composition the first two variations are in duple meter (**C**), the third and the fourth in triple meter (3), and the fifth also in triple meter but with blackened notes (the *color* of mensural notation). Variation 2 has a passage with echo effects (*forte, piano*).

Sonata Il Corisino is characterized by a predominating theme:

against which various other themes appear as a counterpoint. This very interesting and fascinating composition consists of three sections in which the meter varies in the same manner as in the variations of *E tanto tempo hormai*: the first section is in duple meter, the second in triple, and the third in triple meter with blackened notes. In both compositions the notation indicates not only meter but also tempo (or at least the proportion), as it normally does in the mensural notation of the fifteenth and sixteenth centuries. If we use as a basis the duration of the *semibrevis*, the present-day whole note, which Michael Praetorius indicates in his *Syntagma Musicum* II (1619), pp. 87–88, the following metronome tempi result:

c	○ = M.M. 21; ♩ = 42; ♪ = 84
3	○ = M.M. 21; ♩ = 63; ♪ = 126
3 *colr*	♩. = 63; ♪ = 189

Turini's most important work is *Sonata a 3.* of 1624. This extended composition of about 150 measures consists of four sections separated by full cadences.

Sonata a 3. (1624)

Section	1	2	3a	b	c	d	4a	b.	c	‖
Meter	27 D	39 D	17 D	15 D	13 D	10 D	8 D	19 Tr	10 D	

Section 1 is a *Grave* that begins with sustained chords, but it soon becomes more lively by means of sixteenth-note passages. Section 2 is a fugue with a chromatic theme in half notes,

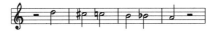

and a lively counter theme. Section 3 consists of four divisions of contrasting character. It begins with a dialogue of the two violins in quick motion, during which the bass has a rest (a); then follows a division *a 3.*, in which each instrument plays a lengthy sequential passage (b); in the next division violin II plays a three-measure passage in eighth notes that is extended to four measures by violin I and finally to six measures by the bass (c); and in the fourth division violin I and II alternate, first in short groups of sixteenth notes, then of 32ds, and close with a double trill in sixteenths (d). The fourth section (d) is itself divided in three parts: the first contains sustained chords; the second is in triple meter with the three instruments playing a free canon; and a coda in *alla breve* meter that leads to a truly daredevil act by the two violins. Fig. 23 shows the beginning and the close of this sonata.

FIGURE 23. TURINI: SONATA A 3. (1624).

The third section of this sonata and the fourth section of Castello's sonata (discussed on p. 36) are early examples of a type of passage that remained important until the end of the seventeenth century. A section—later a movement—is divided into numerous sub-sections that differ from each other in meter, tempo, scoring, or compositional technique (e.g., chordal or fugal style), or other characteristics. We shall refer to such passages as "contrast sections" or "contrast movements." They were cultivated mainly in the Venetian school, while the Bolognese school is characterized by a tendency toward unification.

NOTES

1. Modern edition in G. Leonhardt, *Francesco Turini: 6 Sonaten* (Vienna, 1956); "E tanto tempo" also in SchenkT, No.2.
2. RiemannH, pp. 107–111.

SOURCES

*Madrigali a una, due, tre voci, con alcune sonate a due et a tre, libro primo.*Venice: Bartolomeo Magni, 1621.　　RISM T1388.
　　Italy: Ferrara, Biblioteca comunale Ariostea (T I and II, B; lacks b.c.).
Reprint:
Venice: Stampa del Gardano, appresso Bartolomeo Magni, 1624.　　RISM T1389.
　　Belgium: Brussels, Conservatoire Royal de Musique, Bibliothèque (T I and II, B, b.c.).

France: Paris, Bibliothèque nationale.
Great Britain: Oxford, Christ Church Library.
Italy: Bologna, Civico Museo.
Poland: Wroclaw, Biblioteka Uniwersytecka.
Edition:
Vienna: Universal Editions, 1957, 2 vols.

. . . novamente ristampati, & dall'istesso auttore ricorretti di molti errori che sono occorsi nella prima stampa, & aggiuntovi dal medemo alcuni madrigali & sonate. Venice: Alessandro Vincenti, 1624.   RISM T1390.
Austria: Vienna, Österreichische Nationalbibliothek, Musiksammlung (T I and II, B, b.c.).
Italy: Verona, Biblioteca capitolare.
West Germany: Kassel, Murhard'sche Bibliothek der Stadt Kassel und Landesbibliothek (lacks Tenor I).

 Giovanni Battista Fontana

Giovanni Battista Fontana, a very important master of early violin music, was a native of Brescia. He was active in Rome, Venice, and Padua, where he died of the plague in 1630 (1631?). His compositions are preserved in a single publication that appeared in 1641. The dedication praises Fontana as "one of the most singular virtuosos the age has seen."

Fontana's *Sonate a 1. 2. 3. per il Violino, o Cornetto, Fagotto, Chitarrone, Violoncino o simile altro Istromento* contains eighteen sonatas. Nos. 1–6 are for violin solo and b.c.; Nos. 7, 8, and 11 for two violins and b.c.; Nos. 9, 10, and 12 for bassoon, violin, and b.c.; Nos. 13, 14, 15, 17, and 18 for bassoon, two violins, and b.c.; and No. 16 for three violins and b.c.[1] The publication consists of four part books: *Canto I, Canto II, Basso,* and *Partitura.* In the Partitura the six solo sonatas are printed in score on two systems (as are the solo sonatas of Cima and Castello); for the rest only the *basso continuo* is printed.

In various respects, Fontana's work is close to that of Castello. Both composers wrote only true sonatas, that is, extended compositions (Fontana's longest, No. 9, has 213 measures) subdivided into a number of clearly separated sections. Fontana's subdivisions are somewhat less clear than Castello's since there are no tempo indications. However, other details, especially cadences and change of meter and scoring, provide sufficient clues for analysis.

Sonata seconda. Violino solo

Section	1a	b	c	2	
Meter	91 D	39 Tr	3 D	48 D	

Sonata settima. A doi Violini

Section	1	2a	b	c	3a	b
Meter	17 D	7 D	5 D	10 D	9 Tr	37 D
Instrumentation	violin I	violin I	violin II	violins I and II	violins I and II	

4a	b	5a	b
25 D	10 D	9 Tr	12 D
violin I	violins I and II	violins I and II	

Sonata decima. Fagotto e Violino

Section	1a	b	c	d	e	2
Meter	20 D	7 D	3 D	3 D	4 D	11 D
Instrumentation	violin, bassoon	violin	bassoon	violin	bassoon	violin, bassoon

3a	b	c	4a	b	c	d
8 D	16 D	20 D	8 Tr	8 Tr	15 Tr	30 D
violin, bassoon	bassoon	violin	violin	bassoon	violin, bassoon	

Sonata 17. Fagotto con due Violini

Section	1	2	3	4	5
Meter	10 D	22 Tr	39 D	11 D	10 Tr
Instrumentation	violins I and II	bassoon	tutti	violin II, bassoon	violin I

6	7	8a	b
15 Tr	18 D	11 Tr	11 D
tutti	violin I, bassoon	tutti	

The diagrams of four of Fontana's sonatas show that their structures are far from uniform. Some have only a few sections (No. 3, with no inner cadences, therefore consists of only one "movement"), while others have as many as four, five, and even nine sections. It might be possible to combine some of the shorter sections into a single one of greater length, but that would leave much to the subjective judgment of the present-day observer.[2]

Although Fontana's sonatas are not designated *concertate in stil moderno*, they are concerto sonatas almost to the same degree as Castello's. In the case of Sonatas Nos. 1–6, for *violino solo*, no *concertato* is possible except when the violin has an occasional rest, during which the organ surfaces as the solo instrument (for instance, in mm. 51–59 of *Sonata seconda*). In Sonatas Nos. 7–18, however, all *a* 2. or *a* 3., the participating instruments are treated in concerto style, having solo passages of various lengths. Thus, the

Sonata settima (as indicated in the diagram) has a short solo passage for violins I and II in section 2 as well as a long one of 25 measures in section 4, while *Sonata nona* begins with a 48-measure solo for bassoon followed by a 23-measure solo for violin.

A peculiarity of the formal structure of Fontana's sonatas is that short sections or subdivisions recur later. Thus, in *Sonata settima* (see the diagram) section 3a is identical with section 5a (with the two violins exchanged), and in *Sonata 17* section 1 recurs as 8b, but with the addition of the bassoon. In *Sonata quarta decima* two entire sections recur (in reverse order), according to the scheme A B C D C B E.

Fontana's style is similiar to Castello's but certainly more modern, in the sense that it tends toward unusual, surprising, and fantastic passages, in which the mentality of the early Baroque manifests itself with exceptional clarity. The techniques of imitation, sequence, and repetition, which Castello quite frequently employs, play only a subordinate role in Fontana's work, which is dominated by frequent changes of ideas, by unexpected passages, and especially by the sudden eruption of highly virtuoso passages during quiet motion. Fig. 24 shows an example from *Sonata seconda* in which three half notes are followed immediately by septuplets, then sextuplets.

FIGURE 24. FONTANA: SONATA SECONDA (C. 1625).

Alongside such extravagant passages, however, there are many examples showing that Fontana "better understood how to develop and extend melodic threads than did his predecessor."[3] A particularly impressive example is to be found in *Sonata nona*, in which a long solo for the bassoon (mm. 1–48) is followed by a somewhat shorter solo for the violin (mm. 49–72), the beginning of which is shown in Fig. 25. Although this sonata (as well as a few others) is rather quiet throughout, it always remains interesting and captivating. Sudden eruptions of virtuoso passages, like the one in Fig. 24, occur only in duple-meter sections, while the sections in triple meter progress evenly, with logically developed motifs.

FIGURE 25. FONTANA: SONATA NONA (C. 1625).

Fontana is probably the most important composer of early Baroque violin music, having mastered both the virtuoso and the cantabile style of the violin (and of the bassoon). He is at home with the techniques of sudden and surprising change as well as consequential development. He is not lacking in inner contradiction, for precisely through that device he creates works that hold the listener in suspense.[4] It is gratifying that his work is available to a large extent in modern editions. Fontana certainly deserves such an honor, and it is to be hoped that his compositions, now easily accessible, will find the attention that should be paid to them.

NOTES

1. Modern edition in IselinM, example 13; and HAM, No. 198. Nos. 1–6 and 9–12, edited by F. Cerha, in DM, facsimiles 13–15 and 409–411. Nos. 4 and 8 in WasielewskiS, Nos. XII–XIII. No. 10 in SieglingS. No. 14, edited by Schenk, in DM, facsimile 442.

2. The significance of cadences in Fontana's sonatas was recognized in TorchiM, p. 46. How one could suggest that these sonatas are in three movements (Foreword to GieglingS) is incomprehensible to me.

3. RiemannH, p. 113.

4. TorchiM, p. 46, recognizes these contradictions, but is too critical of them, describing them as "dry and odd-mannered." The article *Fontana*, in MGG, wanders far from the mark, comparing Fontana's sonatas to the "perfected style" of around 1700 and calling them "remarkably helpless, lacking in ideas, and illogical in the joining of sections."

SOURCES

Sonata a 1. 2. 3. per il Violino, o cornetto, fagotto, chitarone, violoncino, o simile altro istromento. Venice: Bartolomeo Magni, 1641.   RISM F1475.

Great Britain: Oxford, Bodleian Library (S I and II, B, score).

Italy: Bologna, Civico Museo; Florence, Biblioteca Nazionale Centrale.

Poland: Wroclaw, Biblioteka Uniwersytecka.

Editions:

Florence: Studio per Edizione Scelte, 1978 (facsimile).

Friedrich Cerha, ed. Vienna: Verlag-Dolbinger (Diletto Musicale, vols. 13–15), 1962.

Giovanni Picchi

In F. Caroso's Nobiltà di dame *of 1600, Giovanni Picchi is depicted as one of three instrumentalists on the title page and mentioned among the "Professori da ballare." In 1615 he was organist of the Casa Grande at Venice, a position he still held in 1625. In 1623 he was appointed organist at the Scuolo di San Rocco in Venice, and the following year he applied for the position as second organist of San Marco, but without success.*

Picci's first publication known to us, *Intavolatura di Balli d'Arpichordo*, of 1621, is a remarkable collection of idealized dances for harpsichord, among them a *passamezzo antico*, consisting of six variations in which the well-known theme is presented in a fascinating manner.[1] Four years later, there appeared his *Canzoni da sonar con ogni sorte d'Istromenti a Due, Tre, Quattro, Sei, & Otto Voci* in nine part books—*Prima Parte* to *Ottava Parte* and *Basso Continuo*. It contains nineteen canzonas in five groups: *A due voci* (Nos. 1–6), *A tre voci* (Nos. 7–9), *A quattro voci* (Nos. 10–13), *A sei voci* (Nos. 14–16), and *A otto voci* (Nos. 17–19). In each of the groups *A due*, *A tre*, and *A sei* the last composition (i.e., Nos. 6, 9, and 16) is called *Sonata*. Some of the canzonas carry precise and interesting indications of the instruments to be used, for instance: *Doi Violini, ò Cornetti* (Nos. 1, 4, and 5); *Trombone, & Violini* (Nos. 3 and 6); *Doi Violini, & Flauto* (No. 9); *Doi Tromboni, & doi Violini* (No. 12); *Quattro Tromboni, & doi Violini* (No. 15); and *Doi Violini, doi Flauti, Trombone, & Fagotto* (No. 16). Three of the four-part canzonas (Nos. 10, 11, and 13) are for wind instruments, without participation of the violin. The three six-part compositions are written for double choir. In Nos. 14 and 15 one choir consists of three trombones, the other of two violins and one trombone; in Sonata No. 16, a choir of two flutes and one trombone contrasts with another of two violins and one bassoon. In such diverse and interesting instrumentations Picchi, like Castello, shows himself to be a Venetian. The three eight-part canzonas, Nos. 17–19, are merely designated *A doi chori*, with no instruments specified.

In contrast to those of Castello, Picchi's canzonas lack tempo indications and are subdivided only by the change of meter. Ten canzonas (including Nos. 2, 4, 12, and 19) consist of three sections D, Tr, D; four (Nos. 1, 9, 10, and 13) of five in the order D, Tr, D, Tr, D; and three (Nos. 5, 7, and 16) are entirely in duple meter. Canzona No. 8 also is basically in duple meter, but it is interrupted at three places by a refrain of six measures. In no. 17 the two meters change very frequently.

Stylistically, Picchi's canzonas remain within the limits of what was customary at the time. Some sections are fugatos or fugues based on a single theme; in others a number of motifs are briefly imitated; and still others reveal homophonic, sequential, alternating, or even soloistic components. Why three of the compositions are called *sonata*, is difficult to understand, since they do not differ from the others in structure or in style.

Anyone expecting to find in Picchi's canzonas the sort of interesting traits exhibited in the passamezzo for harpsichord may be disappointed. The fascinating and always interesting passages of Castello or Fontana are lacking, for the musical action proceeds in a regular and some might say pedantic manner. Nevertheless, there are many particulars that merit attention. Canzona No. 8 for two violins and trombone is especially attractive.

Canzoni No. 8.

1a	b		2a	b		3a	b		4	‖
45 D	6 Tr		8 D	6 Tr		9 D	6 Tr		35 D	‖

The three sections in triple meter (1b, 2b, and 3b) have the same form—three measures in full chords followed by their echo—and constitute an effective refrain. This canzona is noteworthy not only for this pleasant effect but also because of the composition of sections 1a and 4. The former is a fugato whose theme begins with a motif that moves through the steps of a fourth in a characteristic rhythm. Toward the end of this section this motif reappears, played by all three instruments in stretto. In section 4 it is used once more in descending motion, in a remarkable manifestation of the cyclic principle. Fig. 26a shows the beginning of the canzona, Figs. 26b the first, and 26c the second stretto.

NOTE

1. Modern edition by O. Chilesotti in *Biblioteca di rari musicali*, vol. II (Milan, n. d.); the passamezzo is abbreviated in HAM, No. 154b.

FIGURE 26. PICCHI: CANZONA OTTAVA (1625).

SOURCES

Canzoni da sonar con ogni sorte d'istromenti a due, tre, quattro, sei et otto voci, con il suo basso continuo. Venice: Alessandro Vincenti, 1625.   RISM P2042.
    Italy: Bologna, Civico Museo.
    Poland: Wroclaw, Bibilioteka Uniwersytecka.
Edition:
Florence: Studio per Edizione Scelte, 1979.

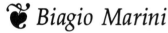 *Biagio Marini*

> *Biagio Marini was born about 1597 in Brescia. In 1615 he was appointed violinist at San Marco in Venice (working under Monteverdi). From 1620 to 1623 he worked as organist and chapelmaster in Brescia, and from 1622 in Parma. From 1623 until about 1645 he served at the Wittelsbach court in Neuburg on the Danube. He spent time in Brussels and Düsseldorf; and he returned to Italy at various times (1634, 1649, and 1652), working in Brescia, Padua, Ferrara, Milan, and Venice. He died in Venice in 1666.[1]*

In 1617 Marini published his Opus 1: *Affetti musicali ... accomadate da potersi suonar con Violini Cornetti et con ogni sorte de Strumenti Musicali.* In a way, it is the earliest collection in which all the compositions are for violin and in which the violin is named first.[2] The publication contains an irregularly arranged collection of 27 pieces of various kinds: three balletti, eleven sinfonias, three sonatas, three canzonas, two arias, two brandi, one gagliarda, and one capriccio. Fourteen of these pieces are in trio scoring (two violins, bass, and b.c.); five are violin duets (with b.c.); seven are for violin, bass, and b.c.; *La Orlandina* has an optional bass (*Basso se piace*); and *La Gardana* is for violin solo and b.c. Altogether, nineteen compositions have survived for two violins and bass, and eight for one violin and bass. The bass is always to be played on the organ, with or without an accompanying instrument (such as viola da gamba or bassoon). Thus, Marini is the second composer (Cima was the first) to write for solo violin.

    In the formal structure of his compositions, Marini shows a strong tendency toward a subdivision into short sections that close with a full cadence. Usually these sections are of irregular length, indicating that they do not conform to the principle of symmetrical construction. In the following structural analyses of five pieces only those sections are shown that are clearly marked by full cadences. The numbers refer to measures of a whole note (*semibrevis*).

Vendramino Balletto	¢	6	6	|	Tr	8	8	|	¢	3	3	3	3	5	6
Martinenga Symfonia	¢	9	13	15	24								
Gardana Symfonia	¢	6	15	15	9	3							
Bordiera Aria	¢	4	4	5	5	4	4						
Aguzzona Sonata	¢	13	20	14	35	14	7						

The last piece is noteworthy for its length and greater continuity.

Like other composers of the time (Cima, Castello, and Fontana), Marini adopts the practice of adding the violin solo parts in the *basso continuo* part book (*basso principale*), resulting in a two-system score whose upper system is the violin part. However, he does not do this in all cases. For instance, there is a score for *La Gardana Symfonia*, but only a *basso continuo* for *Il Monteverdi Balletto*. Does this mean that in the former piece Marini intended that the violin be doubled by the organ, while in the latter it was a solo violin in the real sense of the word?

Finally, a few details of style should be noted. Near the end of *Il Vendramino Balletto* the two violins play a motif in Lombard rhythm (*alla zoppa*), first alternating, then simultaneously, with a most remarkable effect. Violin I plays the minor third bb'–g', while violin II plays the minor third d'–b♮' (see Fig. 27a). The result is a false chromatic relation similar to the one in Viadana's canzona (see Fig. 6) but considerably more effective. Probably there will be those who will try to eliminate this nuisance by means of editorial accidentals. Well, they cannot be helped.[3]

Fig. 27b (the end of *La Albana Symfonia*) shows passagework in both violins with an f, which is not changed into the leading tone, f♯, until the cadence. Also interesting is the close of *La Bemba Canzone in Ecco*, with its fading of the final echo (Fig. 27c). Lastly, note the tremolo in *La Foscarina Sonata con il tremolo* (Fig. 27d). It precedes by seven years the famous tremolo in Monteverdi's *Combattimento* (1624).

In 1618 Marini published his Opus 2: *Madrigali e Symfonie*, a collection of thirteen madrigals[4] and twelve instrumental pieces: two canzonas, three synfonias, three *Balletto e Symfonia*, two gagliardas, and two correnti. Unfortunately, this publication is incompletely preserved (the *Bassus*, which according to Sartori, was in the State Library of Berlin, is probably lost).[5]

Compared with Opus 1, the most important advances in Opus 2 are the greater length of the compositions and, particularly, the nearly uninterrupted continuity of the voice parts. Three of the compositions are marked *Violino* (in the part book *Canto I*): *La Rizza*, No. 1, a canzone of about 130 measures, one section of which is marked *Tardo*; *La Bombarda*, No. 5, a somewhat shorter canzona; and *La Rocha*, No. 11, a gagliarda for *Basso e Violino*, in which all the sharps up to e♯ are used. It is especially unfortunate that the *Bassus* of this composition is not preserved. Fig. 28 shows the beginning of the violin part of this gagliarda; it consists of only two sections, not (as was customary in the sixteenth century) of three.

FIGURE 27. MARINI: AFFETTI MUSICALI (OPUS 1, 1617).

FIGURE 28. MARINI: LA ROCHA GAGLIARDA (OPUS 2, 1618).

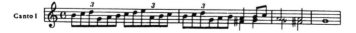

La Malipiera Sinfonia, No. 7, one of the compositions not designated for violin, contains a noteworthy passage with triplets and double-stops (Fig. 29).

FIGURE 29. MARINI: LA MALIPIERA SINFONIA (OPUS 2, 1618).

Marini's Opus 3, *Arie Madrigali et Correnti,* appeared in 1620. This publication, of which only the score is preserved, ends with six instrumental pieces, the last of which is for violin: *Romanesca Per Violino Solo e Basso se Piace.*[6] It consists of seven variations (*parte*) of the Romanesca bass; the fifth and sixth are named *Gagliarda*, the last, *Corrente*. Variations 1–4 have the mensuration sign **C** (*tempus imperfectum*) and, consequently, bar lines that separate notes having the value of four (occasionally two) half notes. Actually, however, the Romanesca bass (or the Romanesca melody) is in triple meter and requires bar lines at the distance of three half notes. Fig. 30a shows under the original bar lines; Fig. 30b the correct ones.

FIGURE 30. MARINI: ROMANESCA (OPUS 3, 1620).

Here, as in Rossi's Romanesca (1613) and Frescobaldi's Romanesca (in *Toccate d'intavolatura*, 1615), a seemingly mistaken time signature is employed for the first four variations, while the Gagliarda variations, Nos. 5 and 6, and the Corrente variation, No. 7, seem to have the correct time signature, 3. The reason is that the sign **C** here still has the meaning, derived from older mensural practice, of *tactus*, that is, of a measuring of time (tempo). Variations 1–4 are to be played in "normal" tempo (about • = M. M. 21, 𝅗𝅥 = 42, ♩ = 84), while in the gagliardas the whole note is divided into three half notes, so that a faster tempo results: • = 21, 𝅗𝅥 = 53, ♩ = 126).[7] In the third variation, *in altro modo*, the bass notes are twice as long as in variations 1, 2, and 4, and therefore it is written in what today would be termed 3/1 meter, which corresponds to *adagio*. The closing Corrente, like the Gagliardas, has the time signature three, but is notated in shorter note values (quarter notes instead of half notes) and is therefore twice as fast as the Gagliardas. Thus, although Marini's Romanesca has no tempo indications, by its notation, it is divided into various tempi:

Moderate	Slow	Moderate	Fast	Very fast
Var. 1,2	Var. 3	Var. 4	Var. 5,6	Var. 7

The beginnings of these sections are shown in Fig. 31.

FIGURE 31. MARINI: ROMANESCA (OPUS 3, 1620).

We now come to a publication that has attracted much attention in the literature on violin playing, that is, Marini's Opus 8: *Sonate Symphonie Canzoni, Pass'emezzi, Balletti, Correnti, Gagliarde e Retornelli.*[8] It appeared in 1629 in Venice, but the dedication shows that the manuscript was completed in 1626 in Neuburg on the Danube, where Marini served at the Palatine court of Wittelsbach. Containing 69 compositions, it is one of the most extensive collections of violin literature of the seventeenth century. The following is a summary of its contents (the *Tavola* reproduced in Sartori, vol. II, p. 1626 m is not complete; I have added consecutive numbering):

I. A 2.
    Nos. 1–12   Sonata prima–duodecima
    No. 13   Sonata senza cadenza, decima terza
    No. 14   Capriccio per decima quarta

II. A 3.
    Nos. 15–19   Sinfonia prima–quinta
    No. 20   Sonata sopra la Monica
    Nos. 21–43   Balletti, Corrente, Gagliarde
    Nos. 44–51   Ritornello primo–octavo
    No. 52   Sonata a 3. in Ecco

III. A 4.
    Nos. 53–58   Canzona prima–sesta

IV. A 6.
    Nos. 59–62   Canzone septima–decima

V. Per il Violino Solo
    Nos. 63–66   Sonata prima–quarta
    No. 67   Capriccio
    No. 68   Pass'e mezzo
    No. 69   Sonata per l'organo & violino ò cornetto.

Nine pieces (Nos. 6, 8, 9, 17, 18, 54, 55, 58, and 59) are written for wind instruments (recorder, cornetto, bassoon, trombone). The violin participates in the remaining 60 compositions, the most important of which are the seventeen compositions called *Sonata*, to which the two *Capriccio* (Nos. 14 and 67) may be added. According to their scoring, they fall into four groups:

Two violins and b.c.: 8 sonatas (Nos. 1–5, 7, 13, and 20) and capriccio (No. 14)
Violin, bass, and b.c.: 4 sonatas (Nos. 10, 11, 12, and 69)
Three violins and b.c.: sonatas (No. 52)
Violin and b.c.: 4 sonatas (Nos. 63–66) and capriccio (No. 67)

In Sonatas Nos. 10 and 12 the bass is marked *ad libitum*, so that they can also be performed in the scoring violin and b.c. Indeed, in these sonatas the bass (bassoon) is practically identical with the b.c., in contrast to No. 11, in which the bassoon has several solo passages, so that it is an essential part of the musical structure. As for the upper parts, there is a choice between violin and cornetto in seven sonatas (Nos. 2–5, 13, 63, and 69), while the remaining twelve compositions are exclusively for the violin. In Nos. 14 and 64–67 this exclusiveness is conditioned by the fact that these pieces have passages with double-stops, which, of course, are not possible on the cornetto. In some other sonatas the occurrence of long, uninterrupted passage-work—without rests for breathing—may have prohibited the use of the cornetto.

The four solo sonatas (Nos. 63–66) are represented in the *basso continuo* part book by a score notated on two systems, as is the case in some of Castello's sonatas, where the violin is doubled on the organ. Marini also contributes evidence for the doubling practice in the passage reproduced in Fig. 32, from the first solo sonata (No. 63).

FIGURE 32. MARINI: SONATA PRIMA, PER IL CORNETTO Ò VIOLINO SOLO SEMPLICE (OPUS 8, 1629).

Shall we assume that the organist suddenly stopped playing at the two places where the violin sets in after a 32d rest? It is hardly thinkable. A strong argument against this thesis is the fact that in these solo sonatas there are lengthy passages in double-stops which—although printed in the score—were probably played by the violinist alone. We may therefore conclude that doubling was an *ad libitum* practice: the organist played along with the violinist, not necessarily all the time, but only where it appeared suitable according to a previous agreement. To put it briefly: the organ was to support not to overpower the violin.

Another interesting contribution to performance practice is provided by *Sonata in Ecco con tre violini* (No. 52), mainly because of the remark that the first of the three violinists should be visible on the podium, but not the two others, who play double echoes here and there (according to the *basso continuo* part book, *Il Primo Violino deve essere visto, e gli altri due no*). Thus, the acoustical impression is enhanced by the theatrical effect of an echo "behind the scene."

For the last composition of Opus 8, *Sonata per l'Organo e Violino o Cornetto*,[9] Marini also wrote a score for the organ. Its upper voice, however, is by no means identical to the violin part (as it is in the solo sonatas), but is a new and independent part for which Marini provides interesting instructions for registration: "The organist must play the *basso* and the *secondo soprano* [the violin part is the *primo soprano*] with one octave flute register and pedal, or one can play the *secondo soprano* on a violin or trombone at the octave."

For a structural analysis of the sonatas the cadences are the decisive indication, as they are in the sonatas of Castello and Fontana. Marini confirms the correctness of this method by designating No. 13 as *Sonata senza Cadenza*. This sonata flows from beginning to end with no interruption, as do *Sonata in Ecco* (No. 52) and *Sonata per l'Organo e*

Violino ò Cornetto (No. 69). The other sonatas are divided into three to six sections that end with full cadences. Schematic representations of two such sonatas follow:

Sonata decima. Violino e Basso (No. 10)

1	2	3a	b	c	‖
15 D	16 D	30 D	10 Tr	16 D	

Sonata quarta. Per il Violino per sonar con due corde (No. 66)

1	2	3	4a	b	5	6a	b	‖
30 D	20 D	32 D	12 Tr	21 D	11 D	21 Tr	12 D	

Section 2 is *con due corde*; later there are the indications *tardo, presto, affetti* (i.e. affective improvisation?), *f*, and *p*; section 6 is to be repeated.

Note that the sections marked off by cadences are not at all uniform, but are nearly always further subdivided by the use of different motifs or various techniques of composition.

Sonata sopra A voi do vinto il cor (No. 7) has a completely different structure. As its title suggests, this "sonata" actually consists of four variations of a popular song that, like *E tanto tempo ormai* (see pp. 23, 36, 39, and 41 n.1) has the structure A B B. The length of the phrases is not the same in each variation: A most often has eight measures and B nine measures, so that the song has a total length of 26 measures. *Sonata sopra la Monica* (No. 20), also based on a popular song, is treated in a more complicated manner. I have not succeeded in finding a wholly satisfactory analysis. However, an easily recognizable four-measure refrain occurs at the beginning, the end, and three more times at irregular distances (Fig. 33).

FIGURE 33. MARINI: SONATA SOPRA LA MONICA (OPUS 8, 1629).

The second half of this refrain is somewhat similar to the closing phrase of the well-known song *La Girometta*.[10] On the other hand, there is no relation between Marini's *Sonata sopra la Monica* and *Partite sopra la Monica* by Frescobaldi (in *Toccate d'Intavolatura*, 1614).

The content of Marini's sonatas represents an important advance in the field of violin technique: Marini was the first to use double-stops and *scordatura* on the violin (on the viola da gamba and on the lute both techniques had been used during the sixteenth century). It has been assumed that Marini learned double-stop playing from German violinists he met during his stay at Neuburg, from 1623 to 1645,[11] however, Marini's Opus 2, printed in 1618 in Venice, contains a short passage in double-stops (see Fig. 29). At any rate, in his Opus 8, eight years later, he goes far beyond this first attempt. Double-stop passages of four to twenty measures are found in Nos. 14, 52, 64, 65, and

66. In *Capriccio, che due violini sonano quattro parti* (No. 14), two violins play double-stops simultaneously, producing a four-voice passage. And in *Capriccio per sonare il violino con tre corde a modo da lira* (No. 67), there are several places with three-voice chords, even a four-voice one at the end (Fig. 34; in the next-to-last measure, note the delayed leading tone).

FIGURE 34. MARINI: CAPRICCIO PER SONAR IL VIOLINO CON TRE CORDE (OPUS 8, 1629).

Sonata seconda d'inventione per il Violino (No. 64) is famous as the first (and, for several decades, the last) attempt to use *scordatura* on the violin: the highest string is tuned down from *e″* to *c″*, so that passages in parallel thirds can be fingered as passages in parallel fifths.[12]

More important than these experiments are Marini's endeavors to write in a specifically violinistic style. Thus, in *Sonata terza variata* (No. 65) there is a place where the violin enters on *e″*. In *Sonata prima a doi violini* (No. 1), violin I has a skip of two octaves, from *c‴* and *c′*, while violin II simultaneously skips from *a″* to *a*. There are many other examples of wide leaps, but they do not provide conclusive evidence for advances in violin technique since they occur in sonatas for *violino ò cornetto*. To this category belongs the example given by Iselin[13] as well as the passage in Fig. 35, in which the sign ～ means "repeat the same motif on another degree of the scale."

FIGURE 35. MARINI: SONATA QUARTA A DOI VIOLINI Ò CORNETTI (OPUS 8, 1629).

While these examples cannot be regarded as evidence of Marini's advanced violin playing, they are, unfortunately, typical of his style in another sense, since they reveal his predilection for sequential modulating repeats: the initial, one-measure motif of Fig. 35 is played four times, followed by six repeats of its first half. Constructions of this kind occur again and again. The climax of this mannerism is reached in *Sonata terza variata* for violin solo (No. 65), in which, judging from its title, Marini especially strives for changes of ideas. Indeed, in the 146 measures of this sonata, about twenty different themes or motifs can be distinguished but the principle of *variatio* is ruined by the principle of *repetitio*. This sonata begins with eight measures in quiet motion followed in m. 9 by a half-measure motif in very fast note values (32ds and sixteenths), which appears eight times on various degrees of the scale. Then, the entire section (mm. 1–15) is transposed to the lower fifth, so that altogether the motif is heard no fewer than sixteen times. Mm. 39–50, in 3/2 meter, consists of six repeats of a two-measure phrase; in mm. 90–93 an irrelevant motif in sixteenth notes appears seven times in descending sequence, and so on. Certainly, good ideas are not lacking in Marini's sonatas; for example, *Sonata prima a doi violini* (No. 1) begins with the beautiful melody reproduced in Fig. 36.

FIGURE 36. MARINI: SONATA PRIMA A DOI VIOLINI (OPUS 8, 1629).

Unfortunately, the overall impression is marred by eight repetitions—three of its full length, two of the first two measures, and three more of the entire melody. This technique of repetition sets Marini apart from Fontana, who is always mindful of change, novelty, and even surprise. A few compositions from Marini's Opus 8 have sufficient artistic significance to merit special attention today. Perhaps the most attractive is *Sonata sopra A voi dò vinto il cor* (No. 7), a set of variations on an extended and interesting theme. In each of the four variations it is interpreted in a lively and diverting manner. Among the solo sonatas, *Sonata quarta per il Violino solo* (No. 66) includes several good passages, for instance, the twenty-measure section in double-stops and, later, a short series of trills to be played first *Tardo*, then *Presto*, then *Tardo* again. However, here too there are repeats of irrelevant motifs.

The remainder of Marini's Opus 8 merits a few remarks. The *Sinfonie*, Nos. 15–19 (No. 17 is for wind instruments), all have the form ‖:A:‖:B:‖, which is different from the multisectional *sinfonie* of Marini's Opus 1, but the same as Rossi's *sonatas* from 1622. Here, also, there are often excessive repeats. For instance, in *Sinfonia quinta* (No. 19), the first section is quite impressive, but the second suffers from a passage in which a one-measure motif is repeated ten times, sometimes by the first violin, sometimes the second.

The large collection of dances (Nos. 21–43) begins with eight pairs of *Balletto—Corrente* (the first balletto lacks the corrente), then four single correnti and four gagliardas. All these dances are in binary form, as are the sinfonias. The eight ritornellos (Nos. 44–51) are designated in the *Tavola* as *Ritornello primo, [secondo, etc.] del Tuono*, but have no recognizable relation to the eight church modes. Perhaps they were used as refrains in connection with strophic songs (for instance, arias). Except for the one-section *Ritornello terzo* they are all in binary form with an extension ranging from ‖:14:‖:12:‖ (*Ritornello quarto*) down to ‖:4:‖:3:‖ (*Ritornello ottavo*). As for the ten canzonas (Nos. 53–62), six (*prima, quarta, quinta, ottava, nona, decima*) require participation of the violin. For instance, *Canzona prima* is written for four violins (or cornetti) and *Canzona ottava* is in double-choir style with the interesting scoring of two violins against four trombones. The canzonas include quite a few passages of splendid sonority, although they, too, are not free from annoying repeats. This is especially true of *Canzone quarta*, a composition of 84 measures in which the motif

is played no fewer than 22 times. Iselin calls *Canzona quinta* a "Prachtstück," in which 24 measures are filled with the alternation "of an unbelievably primitive little motif."[14]

The *Pass'e mezzo* (No. 68) consists of ten *parte* (variations), the seventh of which is noteworthy for the remark *larga di Batutta* (sic) and for its chromaticism. Side by side with normal progressions such as

there are many unusual ones such as

Riemann reproduces the entire variation, though not without changing this construction (and similar ones) into the "normal" progression[15]

All in all, Marini's Opus 8 plays an important role in the development of violin technique, although from the musical point of view it makes rather conflicting impressions. Many good ideas and interesting constructions are to be found side by side with trivialities that tend to diminish the total picture.

We do not encounter publications by Marini containing violin music again until the 1640s: *Corona melodica*, Opus 15, 1644, a collection of motets to which four *Sonate per 2 Violini* are added; and *Concerto terzo*, Opus 16, 1649, a collection of madrigals that closes with two balletti. The sonatas of *Corona melodica* would be of great interest, coming as they do between those of Opus 8 (1629) and those of Opus 22 (1655) but unfortunately only the continuo of this publication is preserved. The complete *Concerto terzo* is preserved, and with it the two balletti (for two violins, alto viola, tenor viola, and b.c.), both of which are suites. The first consists of *Entrada grave, Balletto prima parte, Seconda parte Galliarda, Terza parte Corrente, Ritirata, Quarta parte Corrente seconda, Ritirata, Quinta parte Brando,* and *Ritirata finale.* The three ritirati are identical except for somewhat more lively figuration in the third. The second *Balletto* has the same form, except that the *Quinta parte Brando* is replaced by a *Quinta parte Allemand,* and the three ritirati are identical. The simple, homophonic style and the regular structure of almost all the dances (8 + 8, 12 + 12, 16 + 16) show that these balletti were written for some court festivity, as does the dedication to Leopoldo Guglielmo, archduke of Austria. As for the musical content, only one detail is significant: in the first suite the first section of the *Balletto* closes with the dissonant cadence generally known as the "Corelli clash":

It is interesting to note a certain similarity in the misattribution of the Corelli clash and the so-called Landini cadence: the latter is found as early as Machaut, the former long before Corelli in Steffano Landi's *Il Sant'Alessio* from 1634.[16]

It is regretable that of Marini's instrumental compositions from his middle period, that is, between Opus 8 of 1629 and Opus 22 of 1655, nothing more than two relatively harmless court ballets remain.

More than 25 years lie between Opus 8 and his last opus for violin, Opus 22, which appeared in 1655 in Venice under the title *Diversi generi di Sonate, da Chiesa, e da Camera, a Due, Trè, e a Quattro*.[17] The publication contained:

Balletto primo–quarto	Nos. 1–4
Zarabanda prima–quarta	Nos. 5–8
Corrente prima–quarta	Nos. 9–12
Sinfonia primo–sesto tuono	Nos. 13–18
Sonate per due violini	No. 19
Sonata violino e basso	No. 20
Sonata prima a 3. sopra Fuggi	No. 21
Sonata seconda a 3.	No. 22
Sonata terza per tre violini	No. 23
Sonata a 4. Due violini, viola e basso	No. 24
Passacaglie a 3. et a 4.	No. 25

The following remark is added on the title page: *Con l'Alfabeto alle più proprie per la Chitarra alla Spagnola a beneplacito*. Indeed, the *basso continuo* for Nos. 1 and 3–12, that is, all the dancelike pieces except the *Balletto secondo*, are provided with letters A, B, C, etc., indicating chords to be played on the guitar, probably according to the system of Pietro Milloni, which was the most popular at the time.[18]

The publication consists of four part books: violin I, violin II, *Viola e Basso*, and b.c. In the third part book only one part is notated; that probably means that both instruments played the same part, with the viola an octave higher than the bass. The only exception is *Sonata A 4. Due violini, viola, e Basso* (No. 24), for which this part book contains two different voice parts, one for *Viola ò Trombone*, the other for *Basso*. This sonata, therefore, is the only composition for four instruments plus continuo.

Balletto primo consists of four variations (*Prima–Quarta Parte*) of a dancelike theme in double meter and a fifth (*Quinta Parte*), in triple meter, marked *Corrente, Presto*. All the variations have the same continuo, which is modified for the fifth variation because of its triple meter. The theme has the structure ‖:4:‖:8:‖, showing a tendency toward symmetrical phrasing (*Vierhebigkeit*), which manifests itself in many other dances of Marini's Opus 22.

Balletto secondo is much more important. It consists of *Entrata grave, Balletto allegro, Gagliarda, Corrente*, and *Retirata*.[19] It is a suite, but it lacks a basic characteristic of this type, namely, unity of tonality: the *Entrata* is clearly in the key of E major (with modulation to B major), the *Balletto* is in G major, the *Gagliarda* and the *Corrente* are in A minor, and the *Retirata* begins in F major and closes in D major. The three dances have a symmetrical two-part form, the *Balletto* and the *Gagliarda* with ten measures in each part, the *Corrente* with twelve. Artistic climaxes of the composition are found in the initial and closing movements, both of which are written in chordal style throughout. The rhythmic formula in mm. 10–12 reminds one of a courteous or even courtly bow: ♩ 𝄾 ♪♪ 𝄾 ♪♪ 𝄾 ♩. In the *Retirata* this gesture is even more decisive, since its ten measures consist exclusively of this rhythmic formula; its strange modulations remind one of Gesualdo and seem to bestow on these farewell bows a grotesque, satiric character (Fig. 37).

FIGURE 37. MARINI: RETIRATA (OPUS 22, 1655).

Balletto terzo and *quarto* each consist of a single movement in binary form, the former with the structure ‖:6:‖:6:‖, the latter with ‖:2:‖:8:‖. In the second part of *Balletto quarto*, which is named *Allemano*, a short motif that sounds like a gentle bird's cry is played seven times in succession by violin I.

The sarabandas are in strictly symmetrical binary form with four-measure phrases in each part, except for *Sarabanda seconda*, which has fourteen measures in each part. The correnti also show a marked tendency toward regular phrasing. In all the sinfonias except the last (No. 18), Marini employs the traditional short binary form, which continues without interruption. Similar to the sinfonias in Merula's Libro IV (1651), Marini's sinfonias carry designations referring to the church modes, *Primo—Sesto Tuono*. Possibly they were employed as versettes in psalmody, although some of them have a rather worldly, almost dancelike character.

The most important compositions of Marini's Opus 22 are the six sonatas (Nos. 19–24). Nos. 20, 22, and 23, each consist of three movements separated not only by double bars (occasionally also by starting on a new line) but by the designation *Prima Parte, Seconda Parte, Terza Parte.*[20] The other three sonatas are subdivided only by cadences, Nos. 19 and 24 into three sections, No. 21 into two.

Sonata per due violini (No. 19)

1a	b	2	3a	b	
28 D	26 D	23 Tr	8 D	5 D	‖
dolcemente	allegro		dolcemente	allegro	

Sonata violino e basso (No. 20)

Prima parte	Seconda parte	Terza parte		
1	2	3a	b	‖
33 D	39 D	14 Tr	15 D	
	allegro		fast	

Each sonata is individually shaped and has its own remarkable and impressive traits. *Sonata per due violini* (No. 19) begins with an extraordinarily beautiful section, named *Dolcemente*, in which a sustained eight-measure theme is played four times in succession at the distance of seven measures (the initial and final notes coincide), each time transposed to the fifth (or lower fourth), on C, G, D, and A, as is outlined in Fig. 38.

FIGURE 38. MARINI: SONATA PER DUE VIOLINI (OPUS 22, 1655).

No less impressive is the theme of the *Prima Parte* of *Sonata Violino e Basso* (No. 20). It bears an unmistakable resemblance to the theme of a sonata written in 1610 by Giovanni Paolo Cima (compare Fig. 39 with Fig. 13). Note the replacement of the broken seventh chord by a triadic motion, the enlargement of the subsequent skip from a sixth to a sixth plus an octave, and the continuation in the manner of an *andamento*: Marini's theme clearly represents a noteworthy advance (which is not the same as progress).

FIGURE 39. MARINI: SONATA VIOLINO E BASSO (OPUS 22, 1655).

Sonata No. 21, named *sopra Fuggi dolente core*, is essentially a lively three-voice fugue whose theme reminds one of the French song *Ah vous dirai-je maman*, known today through Mozart's variations.

The fourth sonata, inscribed *Sonata seconda A 3.* (No. 22; for two violins, bass, and b.c.), begins with a beautiful *Grave* in sustained chords, followed by a section in 3/2 meter that "was one of the most remarkable that Marini wrote."[21] A highly irregular structure in the bass and numerous syncopations in the two upper parts generate a feeling of restlessness, a nervous tension that is possibly unique in seventeenth-century violin music.

In the fifth sonata, *Sonata terza per 3 violini* (No. 23), written for three violins and b.c., the continuo is unusually high. It is notated in the C clef, and its lowest note is *d*, so that all the instruments—three violins and organ—combine to produce an exceptionally bright sonority.

The last sonata, *Sonata A 4. Due violini, viola, e Basso* (No. 24; actually a string quartet with continuo), begins with a very beautiful duet for the bass and the first violin in slow tempo. It is followed first by a *tutti, allegro* and then by a section in triple meter with a most interesting progression. It consists almost entirely of a single basic element of music, the descending fifth, which is repeated time and again, always in the same rhythm, (♪ ♩♩), but in a highly peculiar and unexpected distribution: first three times separately; not at all in the next three measures; then incessantly in the next twelve measures in one or another voice part, on one or another degree of the scale, sometimes in parallel thirds: it sounds like a never-ending ringing of bells (Fig. 40).[22]

The closing composition, *Passacaglio* (No. 25), consists of *Introduzione* (five measures), *Prima parte* (26 measures), *Seconda parte* (sixteen measures), *Terza parte* (26 measures), and *Finale* (six measures). The actual *Passacaglio* (*primo–terza parte*) is remarkable because it does not have the usual form of an ostinato, but is a rondeau, which was customary

FIGURE 40. MARINI: SONATA A 4. DUE VIOLINI, VIOLA E BASSO (OPUS 22, 1655).

in France. In addition it does not—as with Buxtehude and Bach—increase in virtuosic polish, but remains stately from beginning to end:

Passacaglio (No. 25)

R R A R R :‖: B R R :‖: C R R :‖
Prima parte   Seconda parte   Terza parte
(R is a four-measure refrain.)

In the history of music, Marini is known mainly by his Opus 8, *Sonate Symphonie Canzoni* . . . of 1629, in which he proves to be an outstanding violin virtuoso. But it is especially in his Opus 22, *Diversi generi*, of 1655, that he wrote compositions of truly high musical rank, and these are the works that secure him a place of honor in the development of Italian violin music. The six sonatas especially are great works of art and deserve much more recognition than they have received.

NOTES

1. IselinM is a detailed study of Marini's life and instrumental music. See also T. D. Dunn, "The Sonatas of Biaggio Marini: Structure and Style," *MR* XXXVI (1975):161.
2. Complete transcription of Opus 1 in EinsteinC, vol. X. Modern edition of individual pieces in IselinM; ScheringB, No. 192; and (partially garbled) ReimannH, pp. 96 and 99.
3. A chromatic effect in Schering's edition of *La Gardana* (ScheringB, No. 192) is inauthentic. The sharp before the C in the fourth from the last bar, according to the practice that extended from the sixteenth century to Bach, applies as well to the next C, in the third from the last bar.
4. Among them the first published musical love letter.
5. In IselinM, Opus 2 appears in the list of works but is not discussed in the text.
6. Modern edition of all pieces in TorchiA; three also in WasielewskiS, Nos. IX (two correnti) and X (*La Romanesca*).
7. The metronome indications are in accordance with the *rechten mässigen Takt* of M. Praetorius (*Syntagma Musicum* III, p. 87).
8. Complete transcription in EinsteinC, vol. X.
9. Modern edition by A. Schering in *Riemann-Festschrift* (Leipzig, 1910), p. 320.
10. See, for example, ApelG, p. 471, Fig. 503. A similar motif occurs in an aria in Uccellini's Opus 4 (1645) with the text *Caporal Simon*.
11. IselinM, p. 28.
12. Examples in MoserG, p. 95; BeckmannV, appendix 5; and BoydenH, p. 131. The piece is frequently cited according to the *Tavola* as "Sonata per il Violino, d'inventione," whereas the title in the music reads more clearly, "Sonata d'inventione per il Violino."

This, then, is an "invention sonata" and not a sonata for an "invention violin," as correctly noted in IselinM, p. 32, note 5.

13. IselinM, p. 29.

14. Ibid., pp. 26–27.

15. RiemannH, p. 105, m.1.

16. See H. Goldschmidt, *Studien zur Geschichte der italienischen Oper im 17. Jahrhundert*, vol. 1 (Leipzig, 1901), p. 212.

17. Modern edition of Nos. 1–4, 19, 20, 21, 23, 24, and 25 in TorchiA, pp. 19ff. (accidentals not always dependable); Nos. 19 and 20 in WasielewskiS, Nos. XXI and XXII; No. 22 in IselinM, supplementary fascicle 12.

18. See Johannes Wolf, *Handbuch der Notationskunde* (Leipzig, 1909), vol. II, p. 173. For a further, more detailed study of the early guitar, see James Tyler, *The Early Guitar: A History and Handbook*, Early Music Series 4 (Oxford, 1980).

19. In all parts except the b.c. it is written "Pretirata," which is probably a mistake.

20. TorchiM, p. 53, calls Marini the "creatore della sonata à più parti signalamente divisi." But Cazzati was the one (in 1642) who clearly divided the sonata into movements.

21. IselinM, p. 42.

22. How one can call this movement, with its nearly fanatical emphasis on the descending fifth, "correntencharakter" is beyond me (IselinM, p. 42).

SOURCES

Affetti musicali ... nella quale si contiene, symfonie, canzon, sonate, balletti, arie, brandi, gagliarde & corenti, a 1. 2. 3., acomodate da potersi suonar con violini, corneti, et con ogni sorte de strumenti musicali. Venice: Stampa del Gardano, appresso Bartolomeo Magni, 1617.   RISM M657.

Poland: Wroclaw, Biblioteka Uniwersytecka (S I and II, B, basso principale).
Edition:
Florence: Studio per Edizione Scelte, 1978.

Madrigali et symfonie a una, 2. 3. 4. 5. ... Opus 2. Venice: Stampa del Gardano, appresso Bartolomeo Magni, 1618.   RISM M658.

Great Britain: British Library (S II).
Italy: Bologna, Civico Museo (S I).

Arie, madrigali et corenti a 1. 2. 3. ... Opus 3. Venice: Stampa del Gardano, appresso Bartolome Magni, 1620.   RISM M659.

Italy: Bologna, Civico Museo.
Edition:
Antique Musicae Italica Monumenta Birxiensia 8. Milan: Antique Musicae Studiosi, 1970.

Sonate, symphonie, canzoni, pass'emezzi, baletti, corenti, gagliarde, & retornelli, a 1. 2. 3. 4. 5. & 6. voci, per ogni sorte d'istrumenti.... Opus 8. Venice: Stampa del Gardano, appresso Bartolomeo Magni, 1629.   RISM M663.

Poland: Wroclaw, Biblioteka Uniwersytecka (S I incomplete, S II, T, B incomplete, 5, 6).

Corona melodica et diversis sacrae musicae floribus concinnata, duabus, tribus, quatuor, quinque, sex & pluribus vocibus ac instrumentis disticta. Opus 15. Antwerp: Les héritiers de Pierre Phalèse, 1644.   RISM M666.

Belgium: Bibliotèque Royale Albert Iᵉʳ (b.c.).

Concerto terzo delle musiche da camera ... a 3, 4, 5, 6 e più voci. ... Opus 16. Milan: Camagno, 1649.   RISM M667.

Italy: Florence, Biblioteca Nazionale Centrale (S,A,T,B, V I and II, b.c.).

Per ogni sorte d'istromento musicale, diversi generi di sonate, da chiesa, e da camera, a due, tre, & a quattro, con l'alfabeto alle più proprie per la chitarra alla spagnola ... libro terzo. Opus 22. Venice: Francisco Magni, 1655.   RISM M671.

Great Britain: Oxford, Bodleian Library (V I and II, Viola, b.c.).
Italy: Bologna, Civico Museo.
Poland: Wroclaw, Biblioteka Uniwersytecka (lacks V I).
Edition:
Florence: Studio per Edizione Scelte, 1979 (facsimile).

🎵 *Tarquinio Merula*

Tarquinio Merula was born in Cremona. In 1622 he was chapelmaster at Santa Maria Maggiore in Bergamo, in 1623 court organist in Warsaw, in 1628 organist at Sant'Agata and chapelmaster at the cathedral of Cremona, from circa 1633 to 1642 again in his former position in Bergamo, and in 1652 once more at the cathedral of Cremona. He died there a few years later.

In 1615 Merula's *Il primo libro delle Canzoni a quattro* appeared, containing twelve canzonas, two allemandes, and one corrente. It requires only brief mention since it is designated *per sonare con ogni sorte de strumenti musicali*. The part book for the *Basso generale* contains the following interesting remark: "Benche per maggior facilità di tutti li Signori Organisti vi sia posto il basso continuo alle presenti Canzoni, laudo nomdimeno il partirle" (Although for the greater convenience of all the organists there is given here only the *basso continuo* for the present canzonas, I nonetheless recommend making a score).

In 1624, when Merula published his Opus 6, *Il primo libro de Motetti e Sonate e Sonate concertati*, he called himself *Organista del Re di Polonia*. Aside from motets the publication contains two sonatas for violin or cornetto, bass and b.c. (the *Basso* part book is lost). Like so many canzonas of the time, these sonatas owe their interest not so much to the significance of their ideas as to their frequent change. They also contain some unusual rhythmic constructions. In mm. 11 and 13 of the first sonata, both the violin and the continuo have the rhythm ♩♪♪♪♪♩.[1] The second sonata contains sequential settings of a motif comprising five beats in 4/4 meter or four beats in 3/2 meter. Fig. 41 shows the beginning of the latter sequence.

FIGURE 41. MERULA: SONATA SECONDA (OPUS 6, 1624).

The first sonata begins with a phrase of three measures, which is immediately repeated at the upper fourth. Every musician knows this method of beginning a composition from Bach's *Italian Concerto* (where, as in most cases, the initial phrase is transposed to the upper fifth). It was used by many other violin composers of the seventeenth century, e.g., Cazzati, Stradella, Bononcini, and Corelli. We shall name it "incipit repeat."

In 1628 there appeared Merula's *Libro secondo de Concerti Spirituali con alcune Sonate*, a collection of motets with two instrumental pieces. In the text they are named *Canzone Prima* and *Canzone Seconda*, and they are scored for two violins, bass, and b.c. They differ from the sonatas of Opus 6 in their formal structure, which is characterized by two internal repeat signs: A:‖:B:‖:C. Merula had already used this format for the majority of the canzonas of his *Primo libro delle Canzoni,* and it recurs time and again in his later publications. The exact meaning of these repeat signs is not entirely clear. They indicate at least repetition of the second section (A B B C), and probably also of the first (A A B B C). In both sonatas the middle section consists of two parts, one of them in triple meter; and in each piece the third section is a shortened variant of the first, which is also characteristic of Merula's formal practices.

Two publications from the late 1630s—like *Primo libro delle Canzoni* of 1615—contain exclusively instrumental compositions: *Il secondo libro delle canzoni da suonare a tre, duoi, Violini e Basso . . . opera nona*, 1639, and *Canzoni overo sonate concertate per chiesa e camera a due et a tre. . . . Libro terzo, opera duodecima,,* 1637. Obviously *Libro secondo*, Opus 9, had appeared some time before 1637, the year in which the *Libro terzo*, Opus 12, had its first printing, which has not been preserved.

Libro secondo contains twelve canzonas, all in the trio scoring two violins, bass, and b.c.[2] Again, each work consists of three sections, separated by internal repeat signs. In addition to their structural uniformity, these canzonas also display similarities of content. The first section (A) is in duple meter (except that of No. 12, which is in triple meter) and is always written in fugal style. The second section (B) nearly always consists of two parts, one in duple meter (D), the other in triple (Tr). The exceptions are No. 6, with three parts—D Tr D; No. 9, with three parts—Tr D Tr; No. 10, with only one part, in Tr; and No. 12, with only one part, in D. Of course, the various parts differ not only in their meter but also—more importantly—in their style. Nearly half of the sections are three-voice fugatos; about five may be regarded as violin duets, for instance B1 (first part of section B) of Canzona No. 1; two are homophonic with the indication *Tremolo*[3] (B2 of Nos. 8 and 12); and in three instances there is a homophonic tremolo with a subsequent *presto* fugue (B2 of Nos. 3 and 5, B1 of No. 9). Fig. 42 shows the transition from the tremolo to the *presto* of Canzona No. 5. There is a special significance in the contrast of the soft vibrations of the slow tremolo and the rapid repercussions of the *presto*: both are repetitions of a note, but they are entirely different in character and effect.

The last section (C) of these canzonas is either a shortened version of the first (e.g., in Nos. 1 and 12) or a coda of three or four measures (e.g., in Nos. 5 and 9). In the latter case, the three-sectional structure is reduced to one of two sections plus coda.

The sections or parts written in fugal style are based on short, lively themes, many of them beginning with a repercussion of the initial note. The first theme of *Canzon nona*

FIGURE 42. MERULA: CANZON QUINTA DETTA LA CORFINA (OPUS 9, 1639).

Canzon terza detta la Benaglia

Meter	A		B1	2	3		C	
	18 D	: || :	31 Tr	8 D	24 D	: || :	14 D	
Style	fugue,		fugue,	homo-	fugue,		shortened	
	theme a		theme a'	phonic	theme b		version of A	

(Theme a' is a variant in triple meter of theme a.)

Canzon nona detta la Cancelliera

Meter	A1	2		B1	2		Coda	
	31 D	17 D	: || :	20 D	13 D	: || :	3 D	
Style	fugue,	fugue,		homo-	fugue,			
	theme a	theme b		phonic	theme c			

is an exception; it represents a type that in the eighteenth century was called *andamento* (continuity, development; see Fig. 43a). No less interesting is the second theme of this canzona (part A2 in the diagram); its energetic design reminds one of Vivaldi (Fig. 43b). The initial theme of the *Canzon undecima detta la Fontana* begins with no fewer than twelve repetitions of the first note. Here the compositional technique of repercussion is pushed to the very limit of what is permissible.

FIGURE 43. MERULA: CANZON NONA DETTA LA CANCELLIERA (OPUS 9, 1638).

In 1637 Merula's Opus 12 appeared: *Libro terzo. Canzoni over sonate concertate per chiesa e camera a due et a tre.*[4] As far as is known today, this is the first appearance of the terms *da chiesa* and *da camera*, which play such an important role in the later development of Italian violin music. Merula's category per chiesa probably includes the canzonas contained in his publication, while *per camera* refers to the other compositions—variations and dances. To be sure, the canzonas have a rather worldly character, especially the first, *La Gallina*. Based on a theme imitating the sound of hens, it is similar to, though not quite as realistic as, the motif for "La Gallina" in Farina's *Capriccio stravagante* (see Fig. 50).

Merula's *Libro terzo* contains seventeen canzonas *a due* and seven compositions *a tre*: *Ruggiero, Chiacona*, three entitled *Ballo*, and two entitled *Canzon*. The group *a due* contains twelve canzonas for two violins and b.c. followed by five canzonas for violin, violone, and b.c. The first three compositions *a tre*: *Ruggiero, Ballo detto Eccardo*, and *Chiacona*, are designated *a doi violini et a 3. col Basso*, which means that they can be performed by either two violins and b.c. or two violins, bass, and b.c. Indeed, in the *Ballo* and in the *Chiacona* the violone part parallels the b.c. In the *Ruggiero*, however, the violone part is independent, and in variations 3 and 6 it is used as a solo instrument, playing the characteristic figurations of these two variations. Thus the complete instrumentation is two violins, bass, and b.c.

In the nineteen canzonas of the *Libro terzo*, in place of the older *basso seguente*, which Merula had used in *Libro secondo*, he employs an organ bass; from the very beginning it supports the fuguing upper voices with chords, as was a common practice. In the canzonas *Ruggiera* and *L'Ara*, he goes one step further by beginning the fugal theme with the organ, then giving it to the strings. Fig. 44 shows this practice.

FIGURE 44. MERULA: CANZON LA RUGGIERA (OPUS 12, 1637).

The first 25 measures of *La Pedrina* are printed in the continuo part book in the form of a three-voice score, with the upper voice parts identical with violins I and II. This is another example of the doubling practice we have encountered in compositions by Cima, Castello, Fontana, and Marini.

The structure of the canzonas is the same as in *Libro secondo*, that is, with two internal repeat signs dividing the composition into three sections or, occasionally, into two and a coda. However, the second section, which in the earlier collection nearly always consisted of two parts, is in most cases continuous, while the third is a shortened version of the first.

As in *Libro secondo*, some canzonas of *Libro terzo* begin with fugal sections whose themes are of the type known as *andamento*.[5] Two of these are reproduced in Fig. 45. The two collections are similar in some ways but differ in many others. They differ conspicuously in the treatment of first sections. In the canzonas of *Libro secondo* they are always written in fugal style, while in *Libro terzo* an antiphonal style is frequently used: this also is a kind of imitation, but of entirely different character and effect. In some

FIGURE 45. MERULA: a. LA TRESCHIA; b. LA MERULA (OPUS 12, 1637).

canzonas (e.g., Nos. 5, 7, and 11) the answer (*comes*) is on the same degree of the scale as the subject (*dux*), in contradiction to the basic principles of a fugue.

In the canzona *La Pedrina* (No. 3) the first section is neither fugal nor imitative, but consists of an eight-measure theme and seven variations. Actually, the theme and all the variations are reduced to seven measures each because the final measure coincides with the initial measure of the subsequent variation:

The same theme had been used by Turini in his *Sonata Il Corisino* of 1621 (see p. 40). It is one of the many popular songs preserved in the violin music of the early seventeenth century.

The canzonas *La Maruta* and *La Dada* each have a section notated in measures of three half notes (*minimae*) and marked *prestissimo*. Why, in a fast tempo, are long notes, rather than quarter notes or even eighth notes used? The answer is that the principles of mensural notation still prevailed, according to which the *semibrevis* is the shortest note that can be divided into three parts (*prolatio maior: semibrevis* = 3 *minimae*). The shorter values could only be subdivided into two parts. Measures with three quarter notes occur in Uccellini's *Libro terzo* of 1642—whether for the first time is uncertain. Incidentally, these two canzonas are the only ones that have tempo indications. This is surprising, since among the twelve canzonas of *Libro secondo*, six have tempo indications.

The remaining compositions of *Libro terzo* need only brief mention. The *Ruggiero* consists of six variations of the well-known theme, which here has the form A B B, with each phrase comprising six measures (not the usual eight). The *Chiacona* consists of 32 lively and attractive variations on a *basso ostinato* in 3/2:

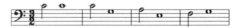

and a coda in which the *ostinato* is stated once in duple meter.[6] Canzona *La Treccha* contains a section consisting of twelve variations on the same *ostinato*. *Ballo detto Eccardo* is divided into three sections of twelve, fifteen, and five measures respectively, all in triple meter, followed by a variation of these three sections. The third section is especially interesting because of the disjunct motion of its upper part (Fig. 46). *Ballo detto Gennaro* consists of four sections of eleven, eight, twelve, and nine measures respectively; *Ballo detto Pollicio* also of four sections, but of more regular length, that is, eight, eight, ten, and sixteen measures, all in 3/2 meter and in the style of a gagliarda.

FIGURE 46. MERULA: BALLO DETTO ECCARDO (OPUS 12, 1637).

Merula's last publication of violin music, *Il quarto libro delle canzoni da suonar a Doi, et a Tre*, Opus 17, appeared in 1651. Three different scorings are represented, all with b.c.:

Canzona a doi Violini	Nos. 1–9
Canzona a 2, Violino e Basso	Nos. 10–17
Canzona a 3, doi Violini e Violone	Nos. 18–25
Sonata a 3, doi Violini e Violone	Nos. 26–28
Sinfonie di tutti gli tuoni a 3, doi Violini e Violone	Nos. 29–36

Canzonas Nos. 1–23 have the structure A:‖:B:‖:C, that is, two rather extended sections and a third that is either a much shortened version of the first or a coda of two to four measures. An exception is Canzona No. 9, *La Calzoletta*, its third section being a nearly complete repetition of the first (but with 24 instead of 34 measures). At least in this case, there can be little doubt that the two internal repeat signs refer only to the second section (A B B C) and not to the first (A A B B C), since that repeat would cause the first section to be played three times—a rather unlikely situation.[7]

In the fugal sections of his late canzonas Merula prefers to use a tonic answer in the first exposition, as he frequently does in his earlier canzonas. Thus, in the first canzona of Opus 17, *L'Ariberta*, the expositions of both the initial section and the triple-meter section are answered at the unison. The same procedure is used for the initial themes of Canzonas Nos. 3, 7, and 9, while in Nos. 11, 12, 13, and others, the answer is in the bass at the lower octave. In some canzonas Merula uses an interesting procedure, starting the answer at the tonic but turning it to the dominant (or lower dominant) after one or two measures. At the beginning of Canzona No. 6, *La Illica* (Fig. 47), as in some canzonas of Merula's *Libro terzo*, the initial statement is followed not by a counterpoint to the answer but by a rest. Several other composers of the time—Cazzati, Bertali, Uccellini, and Bononcini—occasionally used this procedure for the expositions of their fugatos or fugues. The advantage of this method, and obviously the reason for using it, is that the second violin is as clearly audible as the first, without being concealed by counterpoint.

The two last Canzonas, Nos. 24 and 25, are decidedly different. They have neither internal repeat signs nor internal cadences, but are continuous from beginning to end. Moreover, in addition to the customary dedicatory designations (*La Valcharenga, La Brena*) they carry references to popular songs: *Sopra a (sic) Donna Mortale* and *Sopra Nò nò,*

FIGURE 47. MERULA: CANZONE SESTA, LA ILLICA (OPUS 17, 1651).

the latter with the remark *per camera.*[8] At first, one is inclined to assume that these compositions, like so many canzonas or sonatas, are sets of variations, but this assumption turns out to be incorrect. Actually, both pieces are free "fantasias" based on their respective themes. The theme *Donna Mortale* is particularly engaging (Fig. 48), and the canzona derived from it is one of Merula's most attractive compositions.

FIGURE 48. MERULA: CANZONE SOPRA DONNA MORTALE (OPUS 17, 1651).

Sonata prima, seconda, and *terza* of *Libro quarto* are each designated *per camera.* As early as 1624, as an appendix to a collection of motets, Merula had published two pieces designated *Sonata* that conform in every respect to the contemporaneously prevailing conception of sonata form. The sonatas of 1651, however, show entirely different and unexpected traits: first, they are all in triple time throughout (the *prima* and *terza* in 3/2, the *seconda* in 3/4); second, the *prima* and *seconda* consist of three independent sections, each of which is to be repeated, while the *terza* consists of two such sections; and third, all three sonatas are written in a homophonic style throughout, occasionally enriched by figuration but without even a hint of genuine polyphony or of imitative counterpoint. All these features combine to bestow on these compositions the stamp not of a sonata but of dance music. This is doubtless why they are marked *per camera,* but why *sonata?* The beginnings of *Sonata prima* and *seconda* are reproduced in Fig. 49 (the violone part is omitted because it is identical with the *basso continuo*).

FIGURE 49. MERULA: a. SONATA PRIMA; b. SONATA SECONDA (OPUS 17, 1651).

Merula's *Libro quarto* closes with *Sinfonie di tutti gli tuoni,* a collection of eight short pieces of fourteen to twenty measures each and called *Primo tuono, Secondo tuono,* etc., up to *Ottavo tuono.* One wonders for what purpose such short uninterrupted movements were written. In Buonamente's *Libro VII* of 1637, the purpose of the eight sinfonias is clear: they serve as introductions to suites. Merula's sinfonias, which are much shorter than Buonamente's and not written in binary form, probably had a quite different function. Most likely, they are a collection of versicles that were used during the service as introductions to the psalmody. This assumption is reinforced by the fact that each sinfonia is ascribed to one of the church modes. Normally, such versets were written for the organ. Here they are written for a string trio with organ accompaniment.

With few exceptions, Merula's instrumental compositions are canzonas. For this type he used (probably invented) a fixed form from which he deviated only four times: in the two canzonas of Opus 6, which he wrote in 1624, during his stay in Poland; and in the last two canzonas of Opus 17, of 1651. One is inclined to regard such persistence as a compositionally inferior trait, particularly in comparison with the entirely free forms of Merula's contemporary Buonamente. However, it should be borne in mind that there is a difference only in degree, not in essence, when Bach wrote all his suites according to the scheme Allemande, Courante, Sarabande, Gigue, or when he (as did many others) wrote each dance movement in binary form. Moreover, in all these cases the phenomenon of oft-repeated formal schemes exists only for the surveying historian, not for the one who performs or listens to an individual composition.

NOTES

1. I have dealt with this pattern in "Drei plus Drei plus Zwei = Vier plus Vier," *Acta musicologica* XXXII (1960):29.

2. Transcription in EinsteinC, vol. IX; new edition of Nos. 9 and 6 in WasielewskiS, Nos. XV and XVI; No. 6 in HAM, No. 210.

3. During the sixteenth and succeeding centuries the term *tremolo* took on several meanings having in common the idea of a rapid alternation involving a main note: various sorts of trills, repetition of a single note, and vibrato (eighteenth century). Monteverdi aimed at a clearly articulated tremolo (Book VIII, 1638) with sixteen to the bar, while Marini's "tremolo with the bow" and "tremolo with the instrument" are not clearly defined. There is little in sixteenth- and seventeenth-century sources to imply the modern tremolo effect, which is a color of sound.

4. Facsimile in *Biblioteca musica Bononiensis*, Sect. IV, No. 150 (n.d.). Modern edition in RiemannB, No. 90; *La Gallina* and *La Ruggiera* in RiemannO, vol. III, pp. 108 and 112; *La Strada* in ScheringB, No. 184. The beginning of the canzona *L'Ara* is in RiemannH, p. 145, mistakenly presented as a composition by Marini.

5. Fugue subjects of great length, sometimes of more than one phrase.

6. Variations 1–11 are in RiemannH, pp. 121–123, in reduced values and with the misleading comment "six times more" (instead of 21 times).

7. The article *Merula* in MGG states: "They [the canzonas] usually consist of a series of clearly defined parts, the first and last of which are sometimes repeated in their entirety." In the present case, that would mean part A would be played four times.

8. Does the remark *per camera* mean that the composition is not suitable for the *chiesa*? Why would it not be suitable? Because the text is objectionable? It would be of great interest to learn whether the texts of the many songs mentioned in these studies

(*E tante tempo, A voi dò vinto, Questa bella Sirena, etc.*) are preserved in literary sources, and perhaps also published in philological studies.

SOURCES

Il primo libro delle canzoni a quattro voci per sonare con ogni sorte de stromenti musicali, aggiontovi due alemane, & una corrente. Venice: Stampa del Gardano, aere Bartolomeo Magni, 1615.   RISM M2352.
> Great Britain: British Library (basso generale).
> Italy: Bologna, Civico Museo (S,A,B, basso generale); Rome, Biblioteca Apostolica Vaticana-Chigiana (S,A,T).

Edition:
Adam Sutkowski, ed., *Opere Complete di Tarquinio Merula*, vol. 1A. Brooklyn: Institute of Medieval Music, 1974.

Il primo libro de motetti, e sonate concertati a due, tre, quatro, e cinque voci, co'l basso per l'organo. . . . Opus 6. Venice: Alessandro Vincenti, 1624.
> Italy: Bologna, Civico Museo (S,A,T, organ; lacks B).

Canzoni overo sonate concertate per chiesa e camera a due et a tre . . . libro terza. Opus 12. Venice: Alessandro Vincenti, 1637.   RISM M2353.
> Italy: Bologna, Archivio dell'Accademia filarmonica (V I and II, Violone, b.c.).
> Poland: Wroclaw, Biblioteka Uniwersytecka (V I, b.c. incomplete).

Edition:
Biblioteca Musica Boneniensis, Section IV, No. 150. Bologna: Fiorni Editore Bologna, 1969 (facsimile).

Il secondo libro delle canzoni da suonare a tre, duoi violini, & basso . . . con il basso generale. Opus 9. Venice: Alessandro Vincenti, 1639.   RISM M2354.
> Italy: Bologna, Civico Museo (S I and II, B, b.c.).

Later edition, 1655. RISM M2355.
> Great Britain: Durham Cathedral (complete).
> Poland: Wroclaw, Biblioteka Uniwersytecka.
> West Germany: Kassel, Murhard'sche Bibliothek der Stadt Kassel und Landesbibliothek (S I, b.c.).

Edition:
Adam Sutkowski, ed., *Opera Complete di Tarquinio Merula*, vol. 2A. Brooklyn: Institute of Medieval Music, 1974.

Libro secondo de concerti spirituali con alcune sonate a due, tre, quattro, et cinque voci. Venice: Alessandro Vincenti, 1628.   RISM M2339.
> Great Britain: London, British Library (basso principale).
> Italy: Bologna, Civico Museo.

Il quatro libro delle canzoni a suonare a doi & a tre . . . . Opus 17. Venice: Alessandro Vincenti, 1651.   RISM M2356.
> Great Britain: Durham, Cathedral Library (V I and II, Violone, b.c.).
> Italy: Bologna, Civico Museo (V I and II).
> Poland: Wroclaw, Biblioteka Uniwersytecka.

Edition:
Adam Sutkowski, ed., *Opere Complete di Tarquinio Merula*, vols. 3A and 4A. Brooklyn:
Institute of Medieval Music, 1974.

✌ *Carlo Farina*

*Farina was born about 1600 in Mantua. From 1625 to 1629 he was concertmaster
at the court in Dresden, probably under Heinrich Schütz. In 1637 he was in Danzig
and later seems to have returned to Italy, where it is supposed he died of the plague
in 1649.*

In 1626 Farina published *Libro delle Pavane, Gagliarde, Brandi . . . a 2. 3. 4. voce* [sic], *con
il basso per sonare*. It was followed in 1627 by Book II, with a German title, *Ander Theil
neuer Paduanen, Gagliarden, Couranten, französischen Arien . . . a 2. 3. 4. voci*; and Book
III, *Il terzo libro delle pavane, gagliarde, brandi, mascherata . . . a 3. 4. voci*. Two publications
appeared the following year: *Il quarto libro delle pavane, gagliarde, balletti, volte, . . . a
2. 3. & 4. voci*; and *Fünffter Theil neuer Pavanen, Brandi, Mascheraden, Balletten, Sonaten
mit 2. 3 und 4 Stimmen*. All these works were published in Dresden. Since all five books
are very similar in content and appeared within three years, it is best to consider them
as a unit. Taken together they offer 24 pavanes, 32 gagliardas, eighteen correnti, three
brandi, nine voltas, four arias, three mascheratas, two passamezzos, thirteen balletti,
ten sonatas, six sinfonias, two canzonas, and one capriccio.

Each volume was published in four part books: *Canto, Alto, Tenor,* and *Basso*.[1] Books
I, IV, and V contain compositions *a 2, a 3,* and *a 4*; Book III *a 3* and *a 4*; and Book II all
a 4. According to older usage, all of them include the *Basso*. According to the usual
practice of the thorough-bass period (for instance, in Cima's publication of 1610), the
four-voice pieces (all the pavanes and other dances) are *a 3* (two violins, tenor, and b.c.);
the three-voice ones (sinfonias and six sonatas) are *a 2* (two violins and b.c.); and the
two-voice ones (four sonatas, two canzonas) are *a 1* (violin and b.c.). For some unknown
reason the *Basso* has figures only for the pavanes and the sonatas.

It is generally assumed that all these compositions are for the violin. While we do
not wish to dispute this assumption, we must point out that instruments are specified
only for the last six pieces of Book III (the sinfonias), which in the *Canto* and *Alto* carry
the remark "per sonare con doi Violini over Cornetti." Is it permissible to conclude then
that some of the remaining compositions are written for other instruments? In the books
with Italian titles (Books I, III, and IV) Farina calls himself *Sonatore di Violino*, while in
the two with German titles, he calls himself *Violist* and states that the compositions
therein are "to be played enthusiastically upon the viols."

In the literature on violin music only one of the more than 120 pieces in Farina's five
books has received attention, *Capriccio stravagante a 4*, in Book II. In this enormous
composition of 375 measures (without counting the repeats indicated for several sections),
Farina uses all sorts of tricks (among them three-voice chords played "con il legno") to

imitate various instruments—*Lira, Pifferino, Trombetta, Flautino,* and *Tamburo*—and animals—*La Gallina, Il Gallo, Il Gatto,* and *Il Cane.* Wasielewski, who described the capriccio at some length,[2] declared it to be a piece of only modest significance.[3] This assessment was sharply criticized by Beckmann, who raised the capriccio to the rank of a "cheerful string serenade."[4] To my mind, *Capriccio stravagante* is best forgotten. This is not to deny that it contains some interesting details. The motif Farina uses in order to characterize *La Gallina* and *Il Gallo* (Fig. 50a) is a remarkable invention; and indeed it was adopted by Merula in his *Canzone La Gallina* (1637), by Uccellini in his *Aria maritata insieme la Gallina e il Cucco* (1642), and by the keyboard composer Alesandro Poglietti in his *Capriccio über das Henner und Hannengeschrey* (about 1680). The *Cane* is characterized by a short passage with strongly dissonant chords (Fig. 50b) that strikingly imitate the barking of a dog.

FIGURE 50. FARINA: CAPRICCIO STRAVAGANTE (1627).

Of Farina's ten sonatas, five are in Book I, three in Book IV, and two in Book V. Some are noteworthy for their great length, for instance, *Sonata detta la Moretta* (Book I, No. 23), with 348 measures; or *Sonata detta la Capriola* (Book I, No. 22), with 295.[5] Like most sonatas of the 1620s, they consist of a number of sections that close with full cadences. However—more frequently than in the sonatas by Castello, Fontana, and Buonamente— there are cadences after short passages that can hardly be regarded as separate sections. As for details of style, let us first consider the six sonatas written for two violins and b.c.: Book I, Nos. 21, 22, and 23; Book II, Nos. 20 and 21; Book V, No. 15. The imitative treatment of a motif, a technique used by Buonamente with admirable superiority, is completely unknown to Farina. In his tendency to repeat short motifs he resembles Marini, even exceeds him. Thus, in the *Sonata detta La Capriola* (Book I, No. 22), the motif shown in Fig. 51a is repeated eleven times, that in Fig. 51b, sixteen times. Very frequently Farina makes use of the technique exemplified by Fig. 51c, shifting a motif from one upper part to the other in immediate succession, a technique he may have invented. It differs from the method known as "complementary motif" insofar as the two parts combine into a single one. By the way, this motif is repeated fifteen times.

FIGURE 51. FARINA: a, b. LA CAPRIOLA; c. LA MORETTA (1626).

Extended passages in parallel thirds are also very common. All these procedures may seem pedantic, even fatiguing. The "adagio" sections—that is, those notated in longer note values—are more impressive, although they are indicative of routine rather than inspiration.

On the whole, the four sonatas for solo violin and b.c. (Book I, Nos. 24 and 25; Book IV, No. 22; and Book V, No. 16) are shorter than those for two violins and also less repetitious. In *Sonata detta la Franzosina* (Book I, No. 24) and *Sonata detta la Desperata* (Book V, No. 16) Farina writes double-stops in an interesting notation, a sort of tablature in which only the higher note appears. A number written beneath it indicates the distance to the lower one. A footnote reads: "il numero serve per la distantia della nota che va sonata sotto" (the number indicates the distance from the note to be sounded below).

A more successful repertory than the capriccio and the sonatas are Farina's dance pieces. Each book opens with a number of pavanes, and those of Book I are especially noteworthy. Their quiet motion (never exceeding eighth notes) agrees with the character of this dance, and their extended melodies continue without interruption over some 20 to 30 measures. They are reminiscent of the English pavanes of about 1600. In the pavanes of the other books Farina often goes beyond these limits by using short motifs, sixteenth-note passages, and other devices to enrich the picture. Some may feel they disturb it. Occasionally they contain interesting details, for instance in Book IV, No. 3, the sequence

is repeated ten times as a *basso ostinato* and several times as a *soprano ostinato* (Fig. 52).

FIGURE 52. FARINA: PAVANA (BOOK IV, NO. 3, 1628).

While all the pavanes are tripartite, thirteen of the 32 gagliardas are in the more contemporary form ‖ : A : ‖ : B : ‖ . The structure of the gagliardas is more modern than that of the pavanes, for they frequently are divided into phrases of four bars (that close with a dotted whole note), complementing the requirements of the dance if not always the musical expression. However, there are some phrases of seven, eleven, and thirteen bars.

In Book II, Gagliarda No. 13 is noteworthy for its chromaticism; and in Book III, Nos. 8 and 11 are interesting for their tonality, A major, which is an unusual key for 1628. The brandi and the mascheratas are likely to have been played at court festivities since they all consist of twenty short sections, each of which obviously represents a dance step. From a musical point of view, these pieces are interesting. The various sections are of irregular length: the brandi of Book V begin with three sections of ten measures and close with sections of thirteen or fourteen measures. The mascherata from the same book begins with sections of four, five, and eight measures and closes with a section of sixteen measures in triple meter called *La sua Gagliarda*. Section 14 of this mascherata has a complicated rhythm—five measures in 6/4 (Fig. 53).

FIGURE 53. FARINA: MASCHERATA (BOOK V, 1628).

In compositions by Farina and other composers of the period there are examples of the simultaneous occurrence of a scale degree with its chromatically altered octave, for instance, *b* against *bb*.[6]

NOTES

1. The mention of *Cinque fasc.* in SartoriB probably results from the fact that the Landesbibliothek Kassel owns, in addition to the complete set of prints, a manuscript copy of the *Basso*, on the title of which Farina is promoted from *sonatore* to *senatore*.

2. J.W. von Wasielewski, *Die Violine und ihre Meister*, 3d ed. (Leipzig, 1893), p. 59.

3. "Musikstück von untergeordneter Bedeutung," ibid., p. 61.

4. "Lustige Streichserenade," BeckmannV, p. 15; see also the article *Farina* in MGG.

5. The numbers are taken from the original editions.

6. See Willi Apel, *Accidentien und Tonalität in den Musikdenkmälern des 15. und 16. Jahrhunderts* (Berlin, 1936), pp. 35–37; and the remarks in the Preface to the second edition, in *Collection d'études musicologiques*, vol. XXIV (Baden-Baden, 1972).

SOURCES

Libro delle pavane, gagliarde, brandi, mascharata, aria franzesa, volte balletti, sonate canzone, a 2. 3. 4. voce, con il basso per sonare. Dresden: Wolfgang Seiffert (Gimel Bergen), 1626.   RISM F97.

    West Germany: Kassel, Murhard'sche Bibliothek der Stadt Kassel und Landesbibliothek (4 parts).

Ander Theil neuer Paduanen, Gagliarden, Couranten, Französischen Arien, benebst einem kurzweiligen Quodlibet von allerhand seltzamen Inventionen, dergleichen vorhin im Druck nie gesehen worden, sampt etlichen Teutschen Täntzen, alles auff Violen anmutig zugebrauchen, mit vier Stimmen. Dresden: Autor (Gimel Bergen), 1627.   RISM F98.

    East Germany: Dresden, Sächsische Landesbibliothek, Musikabteilung (cantus only).

    West Germany: Kassel, Murhard'sche Bibliothek der Stadt Kassel und Landesbibliothek (4 parts).

Edition:

Padua: G. Zanibon, 1955.

Il terzo libro delle pavane, gagliarde, brand: mascherata, arie franzese, volte, corrente, sinfonie, a 3. 4. voci, con il basso per sonare. Dresden: Autor (Gimel Bergen), 1627.   RISM F99.

    West Germany: Kassel, Murhard'sche Bibliothek der Stadt Kassel und Landesbibliothek (4 parts).

Il quarto libro delle pavane, gagliarde, balletti, volte, passamezi, sonate, canzon: a 2. 3. & 4. voci, con il basso per sonare. Dresden: Johann Gonkeritz, 1628.   RISM F100.

West Germany: Kassel, Murhard'sche Bibliothek der Stadt Kassel und Landesbibliothek (4 parts).

Fünffter Theil neuer Pavanen, Gagliarden, Brand: Mascharaden, Balletten, Sonaten, mit 2. 3. und 4. Stimmen auff Violen anmutig zugebrauchen. Dresden: Gimel Bergen, 1628.   RISM F101.

West Germany: Kassel Murhard'sche Bibliothek der Stadt Kassel und Landesbibliothek (4 parts).

Giovanni Battista Buonamente

Until 1622, Giovanni Buonamente lived in Mantua, where he certainly was acquainted with Salomone Rossi (was he perhaps his pupil?). Then he went to Vienna, where he served as chapelmaster to the empress. In 1627 he was in Prague when Emperor Ferdinand II was crowned King of Bohemia. In 1630 he went to Assisi, where he died in 1637.

Four publications by Buonamente with violin music appeared in 1626, 1629, 1636, and 1637. They are called *Libro quarto* to *Libro settimo* and were obviously preceded by *Libro primo* to *Libro terzo*, which are lost.[1]

Buonamente's book from 1626, *Il quarto libro de varie Sonate, Sinfonie, Gagliarde, Corrente, e Brandi per sonar con due Violini, & un Basso di Viola*, consists of three part books for string instruments, that is, without a *basso continuo*. The supposition that a fourth part book for organ existed and is lost is invalidated by the fact that *Libro quinto* and *settimo* have the same string trio scoring (two violins and bass). Very likely Buonamente followed the example of Rossi, whose *Il primo libro* (1607) also lacks a continuo.

The contents of Buonamente's *Libro quarto* are as follows:

Sonata Prima–Decima	Nos. 1–10
Sinfonia Prima–Deima	Nos. 11–20
Gagliarda Prima–Undecima	Nos. 21–31
Corrente Prima–Terza Decima	Nos. 32–44
Brando Primo–Quarto	Nos. 45–48
Le tanto tempo hormai	No. 49
Ballo del Gran Duca	No. 50

Sonatas Nos. 1–4 are sonatas in the proper sense of the word, that is, continuous compositions in which various motifs are treated in various styles: alternating, duet, homophonic, imitative, or fugal. Nos. 5–10, like Sonatas Nos. 5–12 in Rossi's *Libro quarto* of 1622, are variations based on popular songs: *Poi che me rimena* (six variations on a 24-measure theme), *Ruggiero* (seven variations on a 24-measure theme), *Bella che mi lieghi* (six variations on a 24-measure theme), *Romanesca* (eight variations on an eight-measure theme in 3/2), *Questo è quel luoco* (seven variations on a sixteen-measure theme), and *Cavaletto zoppo* (fourteen variations on an eight-measure theme). Two more variation sets are found at the end of the collection: *E tanto tempo* (eight variations on a 21-measure theme; this theme was also used by Turini) and *Ballo del Gran Duca* (four variations on a 28-measure theme). This *Ballo* is of special interest because it is not a popular song but a court dance. From its lightly figured bass one can derive a "tenor" consisting of seven sections (dance steps?) that are similar to each other but cadence on different scale degrees (Fig. 54a).

FIGURE 54a. BUONAMENTE: BALLO DEL GRAN DUCA (1626).

In the literature on violin playing Buonamente is almost totally disregarded because his compositions have no technical details worthy of note. They are, however, important from a musical point of view, especially Sonatas Nos. 1–4. They are sonatas in the true sense of the word and indicate with exceptional clarity methods of composition that are characteristic of all later violin sonatas. Therefore we shall try to give a short description of each one.

Sonata prima consists of three sections, each of which closes with a full cadence. In the first section (mm. 1–33) three motifs are treated in imitation. Their speed increases: the first consists of half and quarter notes, the second of quarter and eighth notes, the third of eighth and sixteenth notes. The second section (mm. 34–50) is homophonic in half and whole notes (hence, notated *adagio*) and in *durezze* style with modulation from C major to E major and then to G major. The third section (mm. 51–76) is again in fugal style, first with a new motif that appears nine times in stretto. Then it returns to the first section, with motifs 2 and 3 reappearing in reverse order. At the end of the sonata motif 2 reappears in augmentation (Fig. 54b).

FIGURE 54b. BUONAMENTE: SONATA PRIMA (1626).

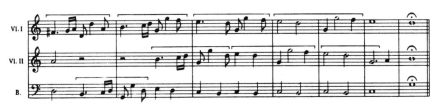

Sonata seconda is continuous, without cadences, and imitative throughout, using six motifs, the second of which also appears in inversion. In the last part (mm. 36–60) Buonamente returns first to motif 1, then to motif 2, but, as always, with a change of treatment.

Sonata terza is also continuous. In mm. 1–47 six motifs are treated in imitation. Then follows a part in triple time (mm. 48–84), which begins with the two violins in parallel thirds, continues with alteration, and closes with a seventh motif, whose imitations appear in shifted positions (Fig. 55). The final part (mm. 85–97) is in even meter, with the seventh motif in augmentation and in stretto.

FIGURE 55. BUONAMENTE: SONATA TERZA (1626).

Sonata quarta, like *prima*, consists of three sections. The first (mm. 1–46) begins with a sort of double theme (Fig. 56) whose first, somewhat antiquated, half is heard only twice; the second half, which is modernistic and violinistic, is thoroughly imitated and recurs repeatedly during the further course of the sonata. Several other motifs follow, and finally there is a part in 6/4 meter (mm. 28–46). The second section (mm. 47–99) is in duple meter, beginning with a homophonic *adagio* and continuing with lively imitations of various motifs, among which motifs 1a and 1b (Fig. 56) also reappear briefly. The third section begins in triple meter (mm. 100–113) and closes with a part in duple meter (mm. 114–123) in which motif 1b again predominates.

FIGURE 56. BUONAMENTE: SONATA QUARTA (1626).

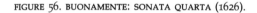

Buonamente's sonatas are characterized by regular development and consistency but are always interesting and full of inner liveliness. There are no sudden eruptions of virtuosity, as in the works of Castello and Fontana, nor are there pedantic repetitions, as in those of Marini and Farina. Buonamente was the first violin composer to make use of such devices of school counterpoint as inversion, augmentation, and stretto. In his later publications he also wrote canons.

The variations in *Libro quarto*, whose themes and structures have already been indicated, suffer from the stereotype repeat of the same formulation ("formula variation"). They are based on themes that—as may be expected in popular songs—are often banal, causing Buonamente to make at least the final variation of each cycle more interesting and variable. Thus, in the final variation of *Sonata quinta sopra Poi che mi rimena* he writes short scale passages in 32d notes that are cut off abruptly, reminding one of Fontana. The fifth variation of *Sonata nona sopra Questo è quel luogo* is especially interesting because the four-measure phrases of the theme are expanded into five-measure phrases.

The sinfonias have the binary form that Rossi had established for this type. For the gagliardas, which both Rossi and Marini wrote in binary form, Buonamente employs the ternary form that was traditional in the sixteenth century, when the gagliarda was the after-dance of the pavane, which always consisted of three sections. Frequently the sections comprise ten or twelve measures, for instance, in *Gagliarda prima* (No. 21): ‖ : 10 : ‖ : 10 : ‖ : 12 : ‖. The correnti and the brandi have binary form. The last brando (No. 48) has an introduction called *Avanti il quarto brando*. The ninth sinfonia (No. 19), the eighth gagliarda (No. 28), and the twelfth corrente (No. 43) are all in D major, a tonality that was unusual at the time. One might perhaps combine them into a suite. In the tenth sinfonia (No. 20) there are four measures of *presto*, then three measures of *adagio*; these are two of the very few tempo indications in *Libro quarto*. The content of the sinfonias and the dance pieces are always interesting and stimulating. These compositions as well as the sonatas deserve new editions.

Three years after his *Libro quarto*, in 1629, there appeared Buonamente's *Il quinto libro de varie sonate, sinfonie, gagliarde, corrente, & ariette per sonar con due Violini & un basso di viola*. It is dedicated not by the author to a person of rank but by the printer to the author, probably because of his fame and his position at the Viennese imperial court; "Al molto illustro Signor . . . Cavalier Gio. Battista Buonamente, Musico di Sua Maestà Cesarea . . . Devotissimo Servitore di Cuore Alessandro Vincenti." Although the title begins with *Il quinto libro de varie Sonate*, this publication contains no sonatas, only sinfonias, gagliardas, correnti, and arias. It begins with two suites (*Sinfonia, Gagliarde, La sua Corrente*), which may well be regarded as the first examples of the *sonata da camera*. There follow *Sinfonia terza–undecima, Corrente prima–nona*, and *Aria prima–decima quinta*. All the pieces are scored for string trio (two violins and bass), but a remark at the end of the *Tavola* states that the arias can also be played "con un Violino solo e'l Basso." For all the pieces, including the two gagliardas, Buonamente uses binary form. Arias appear here for the first time in violin music.[2] These pieces are short, very lively, and charming, and they fit the violin as if made to order, as the beginning of *Aria prima* shows (Fig. 57).

FIGURE 57. BUONAMENTE: ARIA PRIMA (1629).

In several arias there are typically violinistic wide skips, such as

$\quad$ or $\quad$ (in eighth notes).

Buonamente's *Libro sesto* (1636) deviates from his three other known books in several respects. *Libro quarto, quinto*, and *settimo* each contain a mixed repertory of sonatas, variations, sinfonias, dances, and ariettas, but *Libro sesto* is limited to sonatas and canzonas. On the other hand, it has a greater variety of scoring. All the compositions in the other books are for two violins and bass (without b.c.), while the works in *Libro sesto* range from *a 2* to *a 6*, all with a figured thorough bass. There is also an interesting—

though wholly accidental—difference from the bibliographical point of view. Only one copy of each publication exists today: *Libro sesto* in the State Library (*Landesbibliothek*) of Kassel, the other three at the University Library of Wroclaw. This is probably why Torchi completely ignores Buonamente (none of his publications exist in Italy), and why Riemann ignores the three books in Poland and considers only *Libro sesto*.[3]

The publication of 1636, in which Buonamente calls himself *Maestro di Capella nel Sacro Convento di San Francesco d'Assisi*, has the title *Sonate, et Canzoni a due, tre, quattro, cinque et a sei voci . . . Libro sesto*. The contents (all with b.c.) are:

Sonatas à 2;	Nos. 1–4 due Violini
	No. 5 Cornetto e Violino
Canzonas à 2:	No. 6 Canon Violino, e Dolzaina ò Basso da Brazzo
Sonatas à 3:	No. 9 doi Violini, & Basso da Brazzo ò Faggotto
	Nos. 10, 11 3 Violini
Sonatas à 4:	No. 12 4 Violini
	No. 14 2 Violini & doi Bassi
Canzonas à 4:	No. 13 [unspecified]
	No. 15 4 Viole da Brazzo
	Nos. 16–18 [unspecified]
Canzon à 5:	No. 19 (Violino), Cornetto, 3 Tromboni
Sonatas à 5:	No. 20 (Violino), Cornetto, 3 Tromboni
Sonatas à 6:	No. 21 (Violino), Cornetto, 3 Tromboni
	No. 22 sei doi Violini, ò Cornetti and quattro Tromboni, ò Viole da Brazzo
Canzon à 6:	No. 23 quattro Tromboni, e doi Violini

For these compositions Buonamente employs various instruments of the Venetian school: cornetto, trombone, bassoon, and theorbo. Of special interest from the violinistic point of view are No. 10 and 11, for three violins, and No. 12, for four. On the other hand, the term *violino solo* is missing, not only here but in Buonamente's entire output.

The *tavola* at the end of each part book lists the instrumentation for most of the compositions. Additionally there are indications in the music regarding instrumentation. For example, the *Basso* part book lists No. 17 as *Canzona a 4: Basso da Brazzo da Gamba,* while in the *tavola* it is given simply as *Canzon à 4*. In No. 21 the *L'Auto atiorbato* is designated in the *Quinto* part in the music but not in the *tavola* The dolzaina is probably the dulzian (the early bassoon) not the sixteenth-century dulzaina, a capsule reed instrument sounding (according to Zacconi) like a mute crumhorn.

The question arises why some of the compositions are called sonata and others canzona. Nettl assumed that the difference was in the *Aufführungsvorschrift*, the fact that instruments are specified for the sonatas but not for the canzonas.[4] This assumption is not plausible or conclusive. William Newman thinks that the sonatas differ from the canzonas in their "greater freedom and variety in the scoring and ideas,"[5] but this opinion cannot be maintained either; and his statement that the sonatas contain "numerous passages in 32d notes" is incorrect. Thus, the question remains unanswered, and it will be best not to recognize any differentiation between the sonatas and the canzonas of *Libro sesto*.

Some of these compositions are considerably longer than what was normal at the time, especially *Canzon seconda a 2* (No. 8; Nos. 6–8 are erroneously called *Canzon, Canzon prima, Canzon seconda*), with 206 measures, and *Sonata seconda a 3* (No. 10), with 182 measures. On the other hand, *Sonata prima a 2* (No. 1) is unusually short, with only 68 measures. What is Buonamente's attitude regarding cadences that divide the composition into several sections? While the composers of the 1620s—Castello, Turini, and Fontana—tend to divide their sonatas into a fairly large number of short sections, Buonamente clearly prefers no interruption. Eleven compositions of *Libro sesto* have no cadences, ten have one cadence, and only two have two cadences: *Canzon seconda a 2* (206 measures) and *Sonata terza a 3* (158 measures).

As mentioned, the sonatas of Marini and Farina include passages with as many as 30 repetitions of a theme or a motif—certainly not a very happy sign of the era. This was not a passing phenomenon, as one might hope, but actually the beginning of a development that continued and even increased in quite a few violin compositions of the third and fourth decades of the seventeenth century, especially in works for two violins. This manner of writing (it might be called "repeat technique") is a specific stylistic trait of the early period. It is certainly of slight artistic value, but it is historically important.

This technique manifests itself with special clarity at the very beginning of Buonamente's *Libro sesto*. In *Sonata prima a 2* (No. 1), in a passage of eighteen measures, the same motif is repeated 28 times, first seven times in its full form (Fig. 58a), then reduced to its first half. *Sonata seconda a 2* shows a more extensive use of the same device, with 26 repeats of a one-measure motif (Fig. 58b), followed by four repeats of its second half. Fortunately, these are extreme cases, and in the other compositions the number of repeats is tolerable.

FIGURE 58. BUONAMENTE: a. SONATA PRIMA; b. SONATA SECONDA (1636).

We shall limit ourselves to a detailed description of two sonatas from *Libro sesto*.

Sonata quarta a due (No. 4) consists of two sections of 72 and 80 measures respectively, separated by a full cadence. Each section is subdivided into several parts of individual stamp that follow each other without interruption. In the first part of the first section (mm. 1–40) a quiet theme, consisting of half and quarter notes, is imitated by the two violins. It appears four times in its full length of eight measures, then several times slightly modified and shortened, but in such a way that the initial motif

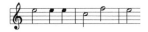

is always preserved and clearly audible. A second part of twenty measures follows without interruption. It is governed by a one-measure motif in eighth notes, contrasting strongly with the first part. The third part is again of a sharply contrasting character, that is, homophonic and with the remark *affetti* (tremolo?). In the first part of the second section, 45 measures with the tempo signature 3, two themes are treated in imitation. It is interesting to note that this part in triple meter is provided with bar lines in each part book, while elsewhere there are no bar lines at all. This practice, which is also found in other compositions of the period, may indicate that triple meter was felt to be more "accentuating" than even meter. The second part comprises 22 measures in **C**, which is unusual. The theme, which consists mostly of half notes, is heard four times in imitation. Then this quiet is interrupted by a motif in sixteenth notes that recurs five times at intervals of one-and-a-half measures. This change from quiet to fast, from darkness to light, is typical of early Baroque style. Fig. 59 shows the beginning of this passage. The last twelve measures of the sonata are a shortened variant of the beginning. Performing a composition like this would be a rewarding experience for two violinists who are not interested in virtuosity but in music of high artistic value.

FIGURE 59. BUONAMENTE: SONATA QUARTA (1636).

Sonata a 4. Violini (No. 12) is one of the few compositions for four violins.[6] In spite of its considerable length (175 measures) it has only one cadence, at m. 149, before a closing section in triple meter. Within this frame an extremely fascinating picture unfolds. It attracts the listener not by its variety of colors (the four instruments have the same tone color) but by the variety of the design—the multitude of ideas and the diversity of their treatment. The themes or motifs appear in close succession and are too numerous to be discussed here. Some are fairly extended, others short and precise; some are in sustained motion, others pass rapidly. No less diversified are the methods Buonamente uses to present these ideas: normal four-voice imitation, paired imitation, double fugue with theme and counter theme, inverted imitation, stretto, division into two choirs, repeat of motifs, and parallel motion, among others. Echo-like restatement—an obvious device in a composition for four violins—occurs only once (mm. 27–28) and without any in- dication such as *ecco* or *forte-piano*. It is therefore being used only as a compositional method, not as an acoustical effect. Indeed it seems that this effect, which was popular in the first two decades of the seventeenth century, was getting old-fashioned about 1630, at least in violin music. On the organ, which with its numerous registers is almost preordained for the echo, it continued to be used throughout the seventeenth century. Fig. 60 reproduces a short passage from Buonamente's truly fascinating sonata for four violins. These ten measures include in close succession three strettos on three different scale degrees, a four-voice imitation, and the echo-like repetition mentioned above.

FIGURE 60. BUONAMENTE: SONATA A 4. VIOLININI (1636), MM. 21–30.

Canzona No. 6, which is inscribed *Canon Violino e dolzaina ò Basso da brazzo*, is a canon of 116 measures beginning with the dolzaina and answered by the violin after five measures at the octave plus a fifth. From beginning to end it has exceedingly lively and energetic material.

One year after Buonamente's *Libro sesto*, in 1637, there appeared his *Il settimo Libro di Sonate, Sinfonie, Gagliarde, Corrente, et Brandi a tre, due Violini et Basso di Viola, ò da Brazzo*. The additional remark *Nuovamente composte dal Cavalier Gio. Battista Buonamente e raccolte, e date in luce da Alessandro Vincenti* . . . suggests that this book—like *Libro quinto*—originated, not with Buonamente, but with the printer, Vincenti, whose dedication (to Gio. Francesco Cavazzi) praises Buonamente as one of the "più splendido Maestro di questi tempi." At any rate, the notice *Nuovamente composte* should not be taken literally. We know that at least one composition, *Sonata sesta* . . . *sopra L'aria della Scatola*, was written in 1627, ten years before the publication of *Libro settimo*.[7]

Libro settimo contains the following compositions:

Canon. Sonata prima detta la Monteverdi	No. 1
Sonata prima–nona	Nos. 2–10
Sinfonia prima–ottava	Nos. 11–18

The scoring is the same as in *Libro quarto* and *quinto*, that is, two violins and bass, without continuo.

The canon that opens the collection, like many other compositions of the time, is dedicated to Monteverdi. Very likely it is an early work, and to me it seems less interesting than the one in *Libro sesto*. The theme is repeated at the distance of four measures and in unison and progresses rather monotonously in fairly large note values that are twice interrupted by passages in sixteenth notes.

Among the nine sonatas that follow, two are variation sets: *Sonata quinta sopra l'aria della Romanesca* (with nine variations) and *Sonata sesta sopra l'aria della Scatola* (with thirteen). The *Romanesca* theme had been used by Buonamente in his *Libro quarto*, and the *Scatola* theme appears as early as 1622 in Rossi's *Il quarto libro* (see Fig. 10b). Rossi's variations are simpler and more appealing than those by Buonamente, in which the formula technique (mentioned in connection with the variations of *Libro quarto*) plays too large a role.[8]

The remaining seven sonatas are sonatas in the proper sense of the word. *Sonata prima detta la Rovetta* (No. 2) flows for 250 measures in 3/2 meter without a cadence. In spite of this monotony, it contains some interesting details, for instance, a passage of 23 measures, in which a pregnant motif appears in numerous variants, starting on different beats of the measure (hence, with shifted accents), with the interval of the descending fifth replaced by the octave, the sixth, and the ascending fifth, and with inversion of the initial notes or of the entire motif. Fig. 61 shows the beginning of this passage.

FIGURE 61. BUONAMENTE: SONATA PRIMA (1637).

Sonata seconda detta la Videmana (No. 3) has an interesting structure. Its initial theme begins with two successive thirds

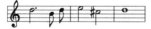

a motif that is heard at least 60 times, sometimes slightly varied. However, unlike the design in Sonatas Nos. 1 and 2 of *Libro sesto*, these repetitions appear, not within a limited section, but spread out over the 170 measures of the sonata. Therefore, this is not an extreme instance of repeat technique but a most remarkable realization of the principle of unification.

Sonata ottava detta la Cavazza (No. 9) is best interpreted as an extended and very lively triple fugue. It is interrupted by a slow section marked *Grave*, which is not related to the themes of the fugue. The sonata can be schematically represented as follows (there is only one cadence, before the *Grave*):

Section	1a	b	c	2a	b
Measures	1–18	19–81	82–89	90–117	118–144
Theme	a	a,b,c,	b	Grave	a,b,c

Each theme is of an individual design and therefore clearly recognizable: the first (a) by a repercussion in eighth notes, the second (b) because of its unusual rhythm (2 + 3 + 3),[9] and the third (c) by its continuous sixteenth-note motion. All three themes appear in diverse combinations and in inversion. Fig. 62 shows a passage from section 1b (mm. 20–24) that gives an idea of Buonamente's inventiveness and admirable compositional technique.

FIGURE 62. BUONAMENTE: SONATA OTTAVA (1637).

The sonatas of *Libro settimo* are followed by eight sinfonias. At the beginning of *Sinfonia prima* Buonamente explains what these pieces are meant to be: "Ogni sinfonia ha il suo Brando, Gagliarda, e Corrente." As introductions to suites, they are similar to those at the beginning of *Libro quinto*, of 1629, but they include an additional dance, the brando. Thus, Buonamente's decisive role in the development of the Italian suite, the *sonata da camera*, becomes apparent. It is possible that sinfonias were combined with dance pieces even earlier, but Buonamente took the decisive step from possibility to reality, from variable combinations to a definite form.

All the sinfonias have the traditional binary form ‖ : A : ‖ : B : ‖ , with an average of 30 measures for each section. With only one exception they include a passage in 3/2, either at the end of A or at the beginning of B. Regarding these triple-meter passages Buonamente says: "Quando si entra nella Ciasqualtera non si altera il tempo di prima, ma si seguita l'istessa misura" (When you begin the sesquialtera, do not change the original beat but continue in the same measure). Of course, *tempo* does not have the present meaning of "speed" but means the *tempus* of mensural notation, that is, the value of the *brevis*, which, according to Buonamente's remark, remains unchanged. The only difference is that in C it is divided into two *semibreves (tempus imperfectum)*, in 3/2 into three *(tempus perfectum)*. Thus, a triple-meter measure has the same duration as a duple-meter measure, and this is what Buonamente means by *l'istessa misura*. His explanations therefore confirm the proportional interpretation of triple meter that we have repeatedly stressed; but, at the same time, they probably indicate that this traditional interpretation was no longer self-evident. As for the dances, the gagliardas are in C 3/2, the correnti in C 3. Therefore, the latter semibreves are twice as fast as the former.

From the musical point of view, the brandi deserve special attention. Two particularly impressive examples of musical and violinistic inventiveness occur at the beginning and end of the brando from *Sinfonia seconda* (Fig. 63a) and at the beginning of the brando from *Sinfonia sesta* (Fig. 63b).

FIGURE 63. BUONAMENTE: a. BRANDO FROM SINFONIA SECONDA;
b. BRANDO FROM SINFONIA SESTA (1637).

How is one to evaluate the work of Buonamente? The article *Buonamente* in MGG assesses only his violinistic achievements (high positions, wide skips, etc.), and the *Enciclopedia della Musica* (Milan, 1963), which appeared ten years later, repeats the same statement in Italian translation. I think that such an evaluation is insufficient and misleading. Although Buonamente is not without interest from the point of view of violin playing (as appears from Figs. 57, 60, and 62), his main significance is as a composer. He wrote many pieces, especially sonatas, of great interest and high artistic value. While Castello, Fontana, and Scarani actually had no successors, Buonamente stands at the beginning of the development that leads to Merula, Cazzati, Legrenzi, and finally to Corelli and his contemporaries. He was the first violin composer to make use of the devices of school counterpoint. Furthermore, he must be regarded as the founder of the Italian suite, the *sonata da camera*.

NOTES

1. See Paul Nettl, "Giovanni Battista Buonamente," *ZfMW* IX (1927): 531. For Books IV, V, and VII, I worked from the transcriptions in EinsteinC, vol. I.
2. In keyboard music, we encounter arias as early as 1588, with Marco Facoli (modern edition in CEKM, vol 2, 1963).
3. RiemannH, pp. 117ff.
4. Nettl, p. 533.
5. NewmanS, p. 114.
6. Others are by Rossi, 1622; Marini, 1629; Uccellini, 1660; Legrenzi, 1666 and 1673; and Vivaldi (*Concerto* No. 10, from *L'Esstro armonico*, 1712, which Bach transcribed for keyboard, four hands).
7. According to a letter of Buonamente, dated September 19, 1627 (Nettl, p. 542).
8. The article *Buonamente* in MGG (by Paul Nettl), mentions variations on *Cias'rupola*, which I have been unable to find. Is this an error? In a letter of March 24, 1627 published by Nettl (*ZfMW* IX [1927]:542) Buonamente mentions *ciastrupola* but clearly in the meaning of a proportional sign (sesquidupla? sequitertia?).
9. See W. ApelD, p. 29. As I was able to discover later, this rhythm occurs frequently in Spanish organ music of the seventeenth century (ApelG, pp. 501, 522, 529, 534, and 756). One is reminded of the political situation of the time, when parts of northern Italy were under Spanish rule.

SOURCES

Il quarto libro de varie sonate, sinfonie, gagliarde, corrente, e brandi per sonar con due violini & un basso di viola. Venice: Alessandro Vincenti, 1626.   RISM B4941.
    Poland: Wroclaw, Biblioteka Uniwersytecka.

Edition:
Florence: Studio per Edizione Scelte, 1982.

Il quinto libro de varie sonate, sinfonie, gagliarde, corrente, & ariette per sonar con due violini & un basso di viola . . . Venice: Alessandro Vincenti, 1629.   RISM B4942.
Poland: Wroclaw, Biblioteka Uniwersytecka (Canto II incomplete; lacks B).

Sonate, et canzoni a due, tre, quattro, cinque et a sei voci . . . *libro sesto* . . . *con il suo basso continuo.* Venice: Alessandro Vincenti, 1636.   RISM B4943.
Great Britain: Oxford, Bodleian Library.
West Germany: Kassel, Murhard'sche Bibliothek der Stadt Kassel und Landesbibliothek. (V I and II, T, B, 5, b.c.).
Poland: Wroclaw, Biblioteka Uniwersytecka (lacks V II).

Il settimo libro di sonate, sinfonie, gagliarde, corrente, et brandi a tre, due violini et basso di viola, o da brazzo . . . Venice: Alessandro Vincenti, 1637.   RISM B4944.
Poland: Wroclaw, Biblioteka Uniwersytecka (Canto I; lacks Canto II, B).

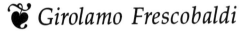 Girolamo Frescobaldi

Girolamo Frescobaldi was born in 1583 in Ferrara, where he grew up in an exciting musical environment. The most illustrious performers and composers of the day, including Luzzaschi, Gesualdo, and several southern Italian keyboard artists, were active in the city. In 1604 Frescobaldi went to Rome, where he established a brilliant career, enjoying a pension from the influential Antonio Barbarini. He died in Rome in 1643. While he is remembered especially for his keyboard music, it is important to note that he also composed for the voice, lute, and violin.

In 1628, Robletti published *Il primo libro delle Canzoni* . . . *accomodate, per sonare ogni sorte de stromenti. Da Girolamo Frescobaldi* . . ., a collection of 25 canzonas, of which Nos. 1–3 are for *violino solo over cornetto* and No. 4 is for *violino solo.*[1] It is interesting to compare these compositions with the six organ canzonas that had appeared one year earlier, in Frescobaldi's *Secondo libro delle toccate.* As may be expected, they are simpler and less pretentious. While the organ canzonas are written in a fully developed keyboard scoring with an intricate interplay and fusion of the voice parts, the violin canzonas are duets of violin and bass, to which only the simple chords of the thorough bass give a fuller sonority. On the other hand, there are some similarities. The principle of variation (variation canzona), which Frescobaldi uses in his organ canzonas with a high degree of sophistication,[2] is also found in the violin canzonas, although more rarely. Fig. 64 shows three passages from *Canzona seconda,*[3] which are characterized by a motif of three descending notes and its inversion.

In the organ canzonas Nos. 1–4, each section closes with a passage in toccata style whose complexity provides a most effective contrast to the fugal style of the preceding sections. The violin canzonas also have such passages, but, again in a much simpler style (see Fig. 65).

FIGURE 64. FRESCOBALDI: CANZON SECONDA (1628).

FIGURE 65. FRESCOBALDI: CANZON SECONDA (1628).

Il primo libro delle canzoni was also published in Rome, in the same year (1628), by Masotti,[4] but in score and with slightly different contents. Added at the end is *Toccata per Spinetta, e Violino*, which is the most interesting composition for violin written by Frescobaldi.[5] It resembles *Sonata per l'Organo e Violino ò Cornetto* from Marini's Opus 8 in that in both compositions the keyboard instrument has an independent part for the right hand, which competes with the violin part. Marini has the organist's left hand playing the supporting bass. ("Dovendo l'organista sonar il basso . . ."), while Frescobaldi writes a *Basso* for this part and has the spinet player's left hand playing figurations similar to those in the right hand.[6] These are joined by the violin, so that in the main section of the toccata—that is, after twelve measures *Violino solo* and twelve measures *Spinettina sola*—three voice parts rival each other, mostly alternating with short figurations.

NOTES

1. Modern edition in DM, vol. 87 (F. Cerha), as Nos. III, I, V, and IV, along with one canzona (not specified for the violin) taken from a print published by Masotti, in Rome, in the same year.

2. ApelG, p. 462, Fig. 492.

3. Ibid., No. I.

4. See SartoriB, 1628j and 1628i; this reminds one of Chopin, whose works were also published simultaneously by several different publishers.

5. Modern edition in DM, vol. 46 (F. Cerha); and CEKM 30, III, p. 65 (W.R. Schindle).

6. The opening of the toccata is marked "comincia violino solo," and the score is written in two staves, one with treble clef for the violin and one with bass clef. After twelve measures the score changes to three staves, one with the soprano clef and two with the bass clef. The indication "violino tace" appears above the soprano staff, and "spinettina solo" is written below it. Later the remark "segue Spinettina è Violino" appears at a place where there are four staves, one with treble clef for the violin, a soprano and bass clef pair for the spinet, and an independent bass clef. This scoring implies the presence of a third player in addition to the principals. The same system is encountered in *Toccata per Spinetta sola over Liuto* (one two-staff system for the solo instrument and one bass-clef line) and in *Canzona Ultima, detta la Vittoria*.

SOURCES

Il primo libro delle canzoni a una, due, tre, e quattro voci, accomodate per sonare ogni sorte de stromenti. Rome: Giovanni Battista Robletti, 1628.   RISM F1868.
> Italy: Bologna, Civico Museo (S I and II, B I and II; lacks b.c.).
> Poland: Wroclaw, Bibliotecka Uniwersytecka (lacks S II).
> United States: Washington (D.C.), Library of Congress, Music Division (lacks S II).
> West Germany: Lüneburg, Ratsbücherei und Stadtarchiv der Stadt Lüneberg, Musikabteilung (S I and II, B I and II; lacks b.c.).

Reprint:

In partitura, il primo libro delle canzoni a una, due, tre e quattro voci, per sonare con ogni sorte di stromenti, con dui toccate in fine. Rome: Paolo Masotti, 1628.   RISM F1869.
> Italy: Bologna, Civico Museo.
> Great Britain: London, British Library.
> West Germany: Lüneburg, Ratsbücherei und Stadtarchiv der Stadt Lüneburg, Musikabteilung; Wolfenbüttel, Herzog-August-Bibliothek, Musikabteilung.

Canzoni da sonare a una, due, tre, et quattro con il basso continuo ... libro primo [new edition of 1628, with supplement]. Venice: Alessandro Vincenti, 1634.   RISM F1870.
> Italy: Bologna, Civico Museo; Pistoia, Archivio capitolare della Cattedrale (S incomplete).
> Great Britain: London, Royal College of Music (S I and II, B I and II, b.c.).
> Poland: Wroclaw, Biblioteka Uniwersytecka (lacks S I and II).
> West Germany: Kassel, Murhard'sche Bibliothek der Stadt Kassel und Landesbibliothek (S I, b.c.).

Edition:

Florence: Studio per Edizione Scelte, 1981. (Contains works of both 1628 and 1634 editions.)

🎵 *Ottavio Maria Grandi*

> *Of Grandi's life nothing is known beyond what appears with the title of his Opus 2 from 1628. A pupil of Alfonso Pagani of Bologna, he was organist at the Basilica della Ghiara in 1625 and from 1626 to at least 1630 at the cathedral Chiesa Della Miracolosissima Madonna dei Servi in Reggio Emilia, where he was also Professor di Violino. His lost Opus 1 was dedicated to Alfonso d'Este, and his (incomplete) opus (see below) was dedicated to Franceso d'Este—indications that he had some connection to Ferrara.*

Grandi's Opus 2 *Sonate per ogni sorte de stromenti a 1. 2. 3. 4. & 6. con il Basso per l'organo,* contains twenty sonatas, four of which require the use of the violin. Nos. 1 and 2 are for violin solo and b.c., No. 19 is for four trombones and one violin, and No. 20 is for three trombones and three violins.[1]

Unfortunately, Opus 2 is not completely preserved. The first violin (*Soprano I. parte*), which is indispensable for the solo sonatas, is missing. However, sections of *Sonata prima,* which have been preserved by G. Beckmann,[2] clearly reveal Grandi's importance for the development of violin playing. Beckmann says about this sonata, which includes a section of 32 measures in double-stops, "It is likely that Grandi was the first to attempt writing a two-voiced contrapuntal movement for the violin."[3] Indeed, in Grandi's double-stop section the two parts occasionally move in a truly contrapuntal independence of the rhythm, while in Marini's Opus 8 (1629) they always sound simultaneously. Fig. 66 shows the beginning of Grandi's double-stop section.

FIGURE 66. GRANDI: SONATA PRIMA (OPUS 2, 1628).

NOTES

1. The last eleven pieces are also found in the manuscript Wroclaw, Biblioteka Uniwersitecka 111, compiled by Adam Jarzebski.
2. See BeckmannV, Anhang, No. 4.
3. Ibid., p. 19.

SOURCES

Sonate per ogni sorte di stromenti a I. 2. 3. 4. & 6. con il basso per l'organo ... Opus 2. Venice: Stampa del Gardano, appresso Bartolomeo Magni, 1628.   RISM G3479.
    Great Britain: British Library (S, second part).
    Italy: Bologna, Civico Museo (Organ, lacks title page).
    Poland: Wroclaw, Biblioteka Uniwersytecka (B, third part).

🎵 *Bartolomeo Mont'Albano*

Bartolomeo Mont'Albano was born in Bologna, perhaps about 1590. He entered the Franciscan order in 1619. In 1629 he became chapelmaster in Palermo, where he published his only known volumes of music. About 1642 he returned to Bologna, in 1647 he directed music for the General Chapter of his order in Rome, and in 1650 he went to Venice, where he died shortly thereafter.

In 1629 Mont'Albano published a book in Palermo with the title *Sinfonie ad uno e doi Violini, a doi, e Trombone, con il partimento per l'Organo, con alcune a quattro Viole.* It contains thirteen sinfonias: four for violin solo and b.c.; two for two violins and b.c.; two for two violins, trombone, and b.c.; and five for four viols.[1] In spite of the designation *Sinfonia*, all these compositions are actually sonatas.

Mont'Albano has been called "self-willed and occasionally ingenious."[2] This characterization is particularly true of the four solo sonatas, whose violin parts contain virtuoso passages reminscent of Castello or Fontana. Along with them are numerous repeats of short motifs, like those that occur frequently in the works of Marini.

Mont'Albano's sinfonias for violin solo average 60 measures in length and are filled with frequently changing ideas. Nos. 1, 2, and 4 are written without cadential interruptions and without tempo indications. In striking contrast, *Sinfonia terza Sghemma* consists of four sections marked by cadences. These are subdivided into nine parts in which *Tardo* and *Presto* alternate, the *Tardo* parts in the singing style of the violin, the *Presto* parts consisting of repeats of short motifs:

Sinfonia terza Sghemma

Section	1	2a	b	3a	b	4a	b	c	d	
Meter	11 D	10 D	6 D	6 D	8 D	10 D	5 D	10 D	5 D	‖
Tempo	(Tardo)	Presto	Tardo	Presto	Tardo	Presto	Tardo	Presto	Tardo	‖

The piece begins with a four-measure phrase ending with a rest, after which the phrase is repeated at the upper fifth. This method of beginning a composition (incipit repeat) has been mentioned in connection with Merula's *Sonata prima* from 1624 (Opus 6). Of course, neither Merula nor Mont'Albano invented this principle. Its development probably began in the sixteenth century, and it extends as late as the Classic (Beethoven's "Waldstein" Sonata) and Romantic (Wagner's *Tristan*) periods.

Mont'Albano's publication has several noteworthy details. For instance, in *Sinfonia prima Arezzo*, a motif of three eighth notes is imitated at the interval of the upper second (Fig. 67). This passage vacillates between *f* and *f♯*, an effect that was frequently used at the time. Sinfonias Nos. 1 and 5 close not with a trill but with the ornamentation that Caccini calls *trillo* in the Preface to his *Le nuove musiche* of 1602 (Fig. 68).[3]

FIGURE 67. MONT'ALBANO: SINFONIA PRIMA AREZZO (1629).

FIGURE 68. MONT'ALBANO: SINFONIA TERZA SGHEMMA (1629).

Mont'Albano's compositions for two violins (with or without trombones) differ strikingly from those for solo violin. While the latter are a sort of fireworks display presented to an astonished audience in Palermo, the sinfonias for two violins are the works of a composer who has had a thorough training in counterpoint and fugue (probably in Bologna). All four have the structure D Tr D—Nos. 5, 6, and 7 continuously, with no cadence; No. 8 with each section closing with a cadence. All these sections or parts are written according to the rules of the fugue; and in Sinfonias Nos. 6 and 8, the third section is based on the same theme as the first. All the sinfonias for two violins move in usual note values, except for *Sinfonia settima Castelletti* (published by Wasielewski), which has a passage in 32d notes toward the end.

The sinfonias for four violas, Nos. 9–13, have the same general character as Sinfonias Nos. 5–8.

NOTES

1. Modern edition of No. 4 in GeiglingS, No. 2; of No. 7 in WasielewskiS, No. XIV.
2. TorchiM, p. 43.
3. One notices that Mont'Albano, who usually employs accidentals in the modern way, that is to say, retaining their validity for a whole measure, here places a sharp sign before each *g* in the ornament, but not for the *f*. This is in accordance with a practice that can be followed back to Kotter's organ tablature of 1513. See ApelA, p. 30.

SOURCES

Sinfonie ad uno, e doi violini, a doi, e trombone, con il partimento per l'organo, con alcune a quattro viole. Palermo: Giovanni Battista Maringo, 1629.   RISM M3304.
    Italy: Bologna, Civico Museo (4 parts).

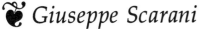 *Giuseppe Scarani*

> *Giuseppe Scarani was a Carmelite monk in Manuta, where he was the organist in 1628. In 1629 he was a singer at St. Mark's Basilica in Venice. In 1641 he was again in Mantua, this time as court organist.*

Scarani had composed two volumes of two-part madrigals by 1628, and in 1630 a publication appeared in Venice with the title *Sonate concertate a due, e tre voci di Giuseppe Scarani Organista, Musico della Serenissima Republica. . . . Dedicate alla Sacra Maestà di Ferdinando Terzo. . . . Libro Primo, Opera prima.* He published his Opus 2, *Concerti ecclesiatici,* in 1641 and also composed some motets.[1]

Although nowhere in the 1630 publication is the violin expressly mentioned (the *Tavola* as well as the titles use the indications *A due Canti; A due, Canto e Basso;* etc.), these sonatas are unmistakably violinistic in concept and style and are clearly related to the documented violin music of the Venetian school.

Scarani calls his compositions *Sonate concertate*, the same designation that Castello used for his publications of 1621 and 1627. Scarani very likely adopted the designation from him, as the two musicians were active in Venice—Castello as head of the wind instrument players of San Marco, Scarani as singer at St. Marks Basilica and possibly also organist. Both of them were permitted to dedicate their books to members of the imperial family: Castello his *Libro secondo* to Emperor Ferdinand II, Scarani his *Libro primo* to the emperor's son, "Sacra Maestà di Ferdinando Terzo."[2]

In some musical aspects also, Scarani proves himself to be Castello's successor. Both his publication and Castello's contain only sonatas, called *concertate*. Castello's additional remark, *in stil moderno*, is missing in Scarani's music, probably because his sonatas have no soloistic sections, an element that plays an important role in Castello's sonatas. A logical conclusion would be that these solo sections, which we are inclined to correlate to the term concerto, are indicated, not by *concertato*, but by *stil moderno*. This style was "modern" for only about fifteen years, from 1615 to 1630 (perhaps the concerto grossi of Francesco Sponga [Usper] of 1619 belong in this category). Both Venetian composers provide all the voice parts of their sonatas with barlines at a regular distance, thus dividing them into measures of equal length. This procedure was not used by any other violin composer of the early Baroque period. Scarani may be more conservative in this matter since he places the barlines at the distance of a *brevis*, while Castello anticipates the present-day usage of separating notes to the value of a *semibrevis* (whole note). Finally, Scarani follows Castello's example of providing his compositions with numerous and often surprising tempo indications.

Scarani's eighteen sonatas fall into three groups of six, each with a different scoring: Nos. 1–6 *a due Canti* (two violins and b.c.), Nos. 7–12 *a due Canto e Basso* (violin, bass, and b.c.), and Nos. 13–18 *a tre due Canti e Basso* (two violins, bass, and b.c.). No. 2, *sopra Il Gazella* (sic), and No. 18, *sopra La Novella*, are variations. The remaining compositions are sonatas in the proper sense of the word. Their structure is determined by their inner cadences: Nos. 1, 7, and 9 have none; Nos. 3, 5, 6, 8, and 10–17 each have one; and No. 4 has two. (Cadences considered here are only those that close with a whole note in all voices. Nos. 5 and 12 have cadences that close with half notes, but with fermatas, thus effectively changing them into whole notes.)

By far the most frequent structure consists of two sections. In comparison with the sonatas of the 1620s (by Castello, Fontana, Marini, and Mont'Albano), this form may be regarded as something of a backward step since we are inclined to regard the section structure of the early sonata as the predecessor of the late Baroque sonata (of Corelli and Bach). Actually the structural development of the sonata did not move in a straight line but along a crooked path.

Another interesting aspect of Scarani's sonatas is the ample use of tempo indications. Scarani sometimes applies them even more frequently than did Castello, particularly in Sonata No. 3, which has eleven tempo marks:

Sonata terza

Section	1a	b	c	d	2a	b
Meter	11 D	6 D	5 D	16 D	18 Tr	15 D
Tempo	largo	allegro	adasio	allegro	allegro	adasio; affetto

	c	d		e	f	g	
	2 D	6 D		14 D	4 D	5 D	
	allegro	adasio; affetto		allegro	adasio	presto	

The sonata consists of two sections each subdivided by change of tempo or meter into numerous parts of contrasting character. In such contrasting parts—which later become contrasting movements—there is a tendency toward disunity, which is a distinguishing mark of the sonatas of the Venetian school, from Castello and Scarani to Neri and Legrenzi, and finally to Ruggieri. Particularly interesting is the segment 2b–2d of Scarani's *Sonata terza*, an extended *adasio* that is quite unexpectedly interrupted by two measures of *allegro*. Fig. 69 shows an excerpt from this segment, in which the various indications are placed exactly as in the original voice parts.

FIGURE 69. SCARANI: SONATA TERZA (1630).

The indication *allegro* appears later in *Canto II* than in *Canto I* and in the *basso continuo*; it was a common practice in the seventeenth century to indicate changes of tempo not at a rest but at the first note after the rest. In mm. 57 and 74 the b.c. has the indication *adasio*, while the upper parts are marked *affetto*, a combination that is also found in other sonatas. Here we do not wish to enter into a discussion of the many problems presented by the term *affetto*. We assume that in the present case it has the meaning of "expression," so that we are dealing with an *adagio con affetto* in the modern sense of the words. Very likely *affetto* also indicates a special bowing technique, either the exciting *tremolo* (as in

Monteverdi's *Combattimento*) or the sensitive *portato*, which is produced by a slight up-and-down movement of the right hand.

In order to provide additional material for the study of this problem (which is one of performance rather than music history), Fig. 70 shows a passage from Sonata No. 15. Each of the three main instruments plays a sustained theme marked *affetto*, while a motif in short note values serves as a counterpoint.

FIGURE 70. SCARANI: SONATA NO. 15 (1630).

The *affetto* theme consists of diminished intervals (fifth, fourth, and seventh). Scarani's predilection for sudden changes of tempo can be seen in this sonata. The *adasio* shown in Fig. 70 continues for another fifteen measures. It is followed unexpectedly by two measures of *presto*, which, in turn and no less abruptly, are followed by another *adasio*, with which the sonata ends (Fig. 71). Measure 88 is notated with *f*—not *f♯*—and m. 90 with *b♭*—not *b♮*.

FIGURE 71. SCARANI: SONATA NO. 15 (1630).

More important from the musical point of view than these bizarre effects is the idea, realized in several sonatas, of presenting the same motif in a fast tempo and then in a slow one, as occurs toward the end of Sonata No. 6 (Fig. 72).

FIGURE 72. SCARANI: SONATA SESTA (1630).

This sonata is called *sopra Re, mi, fa, sol, la* and, as far as I know, is the only composition based on this pentachord. The theme is first presented in whole notes in *adasio* and reappears, in numerous variants of rhythm and meter, in a stimulating exchange with other motifs. It never becomes tedious yet retains its character of a head motif for the entire composition. In a very similar manner Scarani treats the hexachord in Sonata No. 9 (the usual designation *sopra ut, re, mi, fa, sol, la* is missing here). In a way, this compositon is also nearly unique. While the hexachord has often been used as a theme in vocal and organ music (by Morales, Palestrina, Byrd, Bull, Sweelinck, Frescobaldi, and Froberger), as far as I know, there are only two hexachord compositions for violin: Scarani's Sonata No. 9 and the first *allegro* from Corelli's Sonata No. 1, Opus 1 (1681).

Scarani's preferred style of composing is the free fugato based on one or on two themes, occasionally on extended themes of the type called in the eighteenth century *andamento* (continuation, development), as in his Sonata No. 14 (Fig. 73).

FIGURE 73. SCARANI: SONATA NO. 14 (1630).

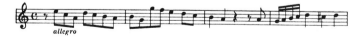

Not all of Scarani's themes are as interesting as this one, but they are always treated in a stimulating and lively manner. Within the course of a compositon, themes or motifs reappear with a shift of rhythm, that is, with a changed accentuation, a technique that was also used by Buonamente (see Fig. 55) and Mont'Albano (see Fig. 67). Compared with the fugato, other styles of composition—such as complementary technique, sequential continuation, or parallel motion—are relatively rare. Thus, Scarani plays an important role in the history of the fugue.

Finally, let us consider the two variation sonatas. The *basso continuo* part book of *Sonata seconda* carries the remark *Sopra Il Gazella*. The conjecture that this sonata is a set of variations is confirmed by the fact that the bass consists of three statements (not separated from each other) of a theme comprising 33 whole notes (the first statement has only 31) and having the form A B B: the same form as in the songs *E tanto tempo* and *A voi do vinto*. The *Gazella* theme is notated in C but obviously has to be read in 3/2, as does the *Romanesca* theme (see Fig. 30). Thus interpreted, the theme has 22 measures, eight for A and seven for B. Fig. 74 shows the beginning of the first statement (first variation) and the transition from the first to the second.

FIGURE 74. SCARANI: SONATA SECONDA SOPRA IL GAZZELLA (1630).

The bass serves as the foundation for two upper parts that continue without interruption and in a manifold exchange of motifs, thus radically differing from the formula technique, which has produced many mediocre, but also some very famous, variations (for instance, Bach's Goldberg Variations). In addition to the change of motifs there is a most interesting variability of tempo. The first variation is *adasio*, except for the repeat of B, which is marked *presto*; the second variation begins with three measures *presto*, then passes over to *adasio*, and closes with three measures *presto*; the third variation is to be played *adasio* throughout.

Scarani's other variations, *Sonata 18. Sopra la Novella*, shows entirely different traits. While the structure of the *Gazella* variations is completely obscured by various means (in this respect it resembles variations of the twentieth century), the structure of the *Novella* composition is entirely clear: it consists of eight variations marked *Prima Parte*, *Seconda Parte*, ... *Ottava Parte*.[3] The theme is clearly recognizable in the upper part of the last variation, at the conclusion of the composition. This procedure is just as valid as the normal practice of placing the theme at the beginning. It has a length of 21 measures, the same as *E tanto tempo*, but is in 3/2 meter and does not have the form A B B. The remark "Va portata tutta larghissima" at the beginning of the work points out another striking contrast to the changes of tempo in the *Gazella* variations. In each variation of the *Novella* theme, short, but by no means trivial, motifs are treated very skillfully, and the invariability of the slow tempo makes the musical substance all the more impressive.

All in all, Scarani's *Sonate concertate*, Opus 1, can claim an important place in the history of violin music not only because of some interesting details but also because of its artistic value. The scarcity of clarifying cadences, the frequent changes of tempo, the unusual shifts of accentuation, and other similar techniques bestow on Scarani's sonatas (except the last) a character comparable to the *chiar'oscuro* of painting. Nor would the word "insecurity"—so often used today—be out of place. We mention this expressly in order to suggest that these compositions, published in 1630, might well be closer to present-day feelings than are many "secure" compositions of a later period.

NOTES

1. According to Eleanor Selfridge-Field in *Grove*, vol. 16, p. 549.
2. He reigned as Emperor Ferdinand III from 1637 to 1657. He was not only a serious music lover, as his father had been, but also a well-known composer. See Josef-Horst Lederer, "Ferdinand III," in *Grove*, vol. 6, p. 470.
3. Cf. note 3, p. 24. Scarani employed the term *Partita* for a single variation, not for the whole work, which he called *Sonata*.

SOURCES

Sonate concertate a due, e tre voci di Giuseppe Scarani organista, musico della serenissima Republica.... Dedicate alla Sacra Maestà di Ferdinando terzo ... libro primo. Opus 1. Venice: Bartolomeo Magni, 1630.   RISM S1167.
   Poland: Wroclaw, Biblioteka Uniwersytecka (S I and II, B, b.c.).

🎜 *Guglielmo Lipparino*

Guglielmo Lipparino (Lipparini), who flourished at the beginning of the seventeenth century, was an Augustinian monk at San Giacomo in Bologna, and a pupil of Tiburtio Massaino. From 1609 to 1633 he was musical director at the cathedral in Como. By 1635 he had returned to Bologna.

Lipparino published numerous collections of vocal music (canzonettas, motets, masses), among them *Sacri Concerti a una, due, tre et quattro Voci ... con alcune Sonate a due e tre Voci*, Opus 13, 1635. This publication contains more than twenty motets and eight sonatas—five for violin, violone, and b.c.; and three for two violins, violone, and b.c.[1] The continuo is not figured.

The structure of Lipparino's sonatas is unusually simple. Nos. 2, 5, 6, and 8 are pieces of 70 to 100 measures in duple meter throughout and without cadences. The four remaining sonatas have a middle section in triple meter. No. 4 has no interruptions, while Nos. 1, 3, and 7 have a cadence at the close of the first section. Since these sections close with a half note, not with a whole note, one might speak of only mild interruption. At any rate, the structural simplicity of these Bolognese sonatas is in striking contrast to the multisectional form of the Venetian sonatas.

Stylistically, also, Lipparino's sonatas are simple and conservative. The voice parts are written in the note values commonly used before 1600—half notes, quarter notes, eighth notes, and only occasional short runs in sixteenth notes. A conservative attitude is also evident in the use of an A-minor cadential formula with postponed leading tone:

Sonata No. 3 begins with ten measures for violin I solo and has an eight-measure passage for violin II solo in the triple-meter section. However, these solo passages (as well as some shorter ones in other sonatas) are not at all virtuosic, but remain within the limits of moderation that are characteristic of Lipparino's entire output.

In *Sonata La Paleota*, No. 2, Lipparino twice quotes the *Ruggiero* melody in the violin part, but in an interesting shortened version (in Fig. 75 the normal rhythm is shown in small notes). The same idea of quoting a popular song within a sonata recurs in *Sonata La Malvezza*, No. 7, in which the well-known *Bergamasca* melody appears three times (in violins I and II and in the violone), also in a shortened version, reduced from four to three measures.

FIGURE 75. LIPPARINO: SONATA LA PALEOTA (1635).

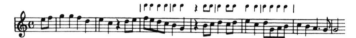

Lipparino's sonatas are unpretentious but by no means uninteresting. They are neither modern nor brilliant but are nevertheless valuable and stimulating.

NOTE

1. The *Tavola* indicates the scoring only with the words *Doi canti e basso* or *Basso e Canto*, while in the part books the designation is *violino C* in the *Canto Primo* and *Tenore* part books, *Violone* in the *Basso* part book.

SOURCES

Sacri concerti a una, due, tre, et quattro voci, con le litanie delle Beata Vergine Maria che si cantano nella Santa Casa di Loreto, et alcune sonate a due e tre voci . . . con il suo basso continuo. Opus 13. Venice: Alessandro Vincenti, 1635.   RISM L2578.
    Italy: Bologna, Civico Museo (SI, T third part, B, b.c.).

Marco Uccellini

Marco Uccellini was the first Italian violin composer whose entire life fell within the seventeenth century. He was born about 1603, possibly in Modena. From about 1640 to 1665 he directed instrumental music at the Este court in Modena (but none of the music for the entertainments he produced there has survived). In 1647 he was chapelmaster at the cathedral there, and later chapelmaster at the Farnese court in Parma. He is thought of as the founder of the Modena school of violin music. He died in Forlimpopoli in 1680.

Uccellini's first book with violin music is not preserved. In 1639 he published his *Libro secondo: Sonate Sinfonie et Correnti a 2. a 3. et a 4. per sonar con diversi Istromenti*. His activity as a violin composer extends to an Opus 9 from 1667 and includes about 100 sonatas, 75 sinfonias, 75 correnti, 25 arias, and twenty miscellaneous compositions. In this large output the designation *canzona* (to which Merula adhered throughout his oeuvre) hardly ever occurs.[1] Even in Uccellini's last publication there are 25 sinfonias with the same binary form as in Salomone Rossi's *Il primo libro* from 1607, although with greatly enlarged contents.

Uccellini's *Libro secondo* contains twelve sonatas, six sinfonias, and twelve correnti. Sonatas Nos. 1 and 2 are *a due*, for violin, bass, and b.c.; Nos. 3–8 are also *a due*, for two violins and b.c.; Nos. 9 and 10 are *a tre*, for two violins, bass, and b.c.; and Nos. 11 and 12 are *a quattro*, the former for two violins, two basses, and b.c., the latter for three violins, bass, and b.c. For four sonatas the bass instrument is specified: *Trombone* (No. 1), *Tiorba* (No. 2), *Basso da Viola* (No. 10), and *Trombone ò Fagotto* (No. 12). The parts for *Tiorba* and *Basso di Viola* carry almost the same thorough-bass figures as the *basso continuo*, an indication that full chords—similar to those played on the organ or harpsichord—were occasionally played on these string instruments. All the sinfonias and the first six correnti are written for two violins and b.c. The last six correnti are for violin and b.c., a scoring indicated in the *Tavola* and with each correnti by the remark *a Violino solo*; it is missing in the title, where it should appear as *a 1*.

The great majority of Uccellini's sonatas are in three sections. Their form is not indicated by two inner repeat signs (as in Merula's canzonas) but by the middle sections being written in triple meter. Nine sonatas have this structure, with Nos. 1, 5, 6, 8, 10, and 12 having no cadences (D Tr D); and three having a cadence either before the triple-meter section (Nos. 2 and 3: D | Tr D) or after it (No. 4: D Tr | D). Nos. 7 and 11 have enlarged forms, though without a cadence. The only sonata entirely outside this framework is No. 9; *Sonata nona in canone*. It is a canon of 85 measures between violin I and the bass, with the bass starting at a distance of five measures and at the lower octave, while in violin II the various motifs of the canonic melody are more freely imitated. It is one of the most impressive compositions in *Libro secondo*.

In the sonatas in three sections the initial one usually consists of several (occasionally as many as six) fugatos based on different themes or motifs. Some appear only two or three times, and others are more fully imitated in fairly extended subdivisions; but occasionally we find the all too frequent repeats of an irrelevant motif that (as has been mentioned before) are an unwelcome component of early seventeenth-century violin music. The triple-meter section in some sonatas is written as a canon, in others as a fugato with one or two themes. The final section varies considerably in length (from ten to 58 measures) and accordingly in the number of motifs. In addition to canon and fugato there are passages in parallel thirds, in complementary motifs, or in chordal (homophonic) style, the last especially in the sonatas *a quattro*.

The more extended fugatos (or fugues) contain passages with free, nonthematic material that can be regarded as episodes. They are an early manifestation of a principle that plays an important role in the fully developed fugue. In *Sonata seconda*, near the end of the first section, the theme has a syncopated rhythm (2 + 3 + 3). It starts on various beats of the measure (similar to Buonamente's procedure in Fig. 55), but it is also dovetailed with itself so that its last note coincides with the first note of the next presentation. Suddenly, this lively and intricate play is stopped by a rest, after which the even and quiet motion presents another sharp contrast. This segment is shown in Fig. 76 (the *basso continuo* is identical with the theorbo, except for the notes in small print).

FIGURE 76. UCCELLINI: SONATA SECONDA (OPUS 2, 1639).

In Sonatas Nos. 6 and 12, Uccellini writes the initial fugato according to the principles of the double fugue: introducing two themes at the outset, the second of which (b) forms the counterpoint to the first (a) but also constitutes its continuation and completion (a + b). Fig. 77 shows the beginning of *Sonata duodecima*, which is also interesting for its sonority: the upper structure is performed by three violins, the lower by wind instruments—trombone or bassoon together with the universal wind instrument, the organ.

Sonata undecima, unlike all the other sonatas, does not begin with a fugato but with an introduction of thirteen measures in five-part chordal style. This passage is repeated at the end of the sonata, as is indicated by the remark *Da Capo*. Fig. 78 shows the beginning of this prelude and postlude, which is also noteworthy for its modern treatment of tonality.

Although none of the sonatas of *Libro secondo* are completely satisfactory as total works of art, they contain numerous details of great interest that reveal Uccellini to be a gifted composer.

The sonatas are followed by six sinfonias, written in the miniature form previously encountered in Salomone Rossi's *Il primo libro* of 1607 and *Il quarto libro* of 1627; in Marini's Opus 8 of 1626; and in Buonamente's *Settimo Libro* of 1627, where they serve as introductions to suites. Uccellini's sinfonias consist of the usual two sections, each

FIGURE 77. UCCELLINI: SONATA DUODECIMA (OPUS 2, 1639).

FIGURE 78. UCCELLINI: SONATA UNDECIMA (OPUS 2, 1639).

repeated. An exception is *Sinfonia sesta a 2 Violini in canon*. The (unique) copy in the University Library of Wroclaw has a slip with the following remark in German (probably written about 1700): "N.B. The other voice of this sixth sinfonia must be begun from the end and fiddled backwards all the way to the beginning. The sign at the beginning, ꝏ, is the final of the other voice." Indeed, this is a retrograde canon of about 90 measures.[2]

Uccellini's *Libro secondo* closes with twelve correnti, the last six of which belong to the relatively few compositions of the early seventeenth century that are written for Violino solo (violin and b.c.).

In 1642, there appeared Uccellini's [*Il Terzo Libro delle*] *Sonate, Arie, et Correnti a 2. e 3. per sonar con diversi Instromenti. . . .*[3] Its contents are:

Sonatas à 2:	Nos. 1, 3	Violino, Tiorba
	No. 2	Violino, Trombone
	Nos. 4–11	Violino (2)
Sonatas à 3:	No. 12	Violino (3)
	Nos. 13–19	Violino (2), Basso
Arias à 3:	Nos. 20–28	Violino (2), Basso (Violone in part book)
Correnti:	Nos. 29–41	[unspecified]
	No. 31	(alternate performance as violin solo)
	No. 42	Violin solo (second violin in part book)

(The scoring of Sonata No. 14 is given in the *Tavola* as two violins and bass, but in the part book for *violino secondo* it is listed as "a tre violini." For Sonatas 1–3, the bass parts are in the part book marked *Canto primo*, and the violin parts are in *Canto secondo*. For the sonatas for two violins and bass, *Canto primo* contains the bass and *violino secondo*, and *Canto secondo* contains the *violino primo* part.)

Nine of these compositions require the participation of a bass instrument. For Nos. 1 and 3, the theorbo is specified, while for Nos. 2, 13, and 15–19 a bowed bass such as violone or viola da gamba may have been intended. As in *Libro secondo*, the bass parts of these nine sonatas have nearly the same thorough-bass figures as the *basso continuo*, an indication that chords were occasionally played on them. It should come as no surprise that bass instruments such as the violone or viola da gamba were played chordally in the first half of the seventeenth century: as early as 1542—exactly 100 years before Uccellini's *Libro terzo*—Ganassi made liberal use of double-stops for the viola da gamba in his *Regola Rubertina*.

Two of the sonatas are canons. *Sonata settima, La Fortunata, Canon a due Violini* is a normal canon in which violin I imitates violin II at the unison after four measures. Much more problematic is *Sonata duodecima, La Tartaruga*, which in *Canto II* is said to be *A tre Violini, Sopra Iste Confessor, in Canone*. The following is the solution for this rather intricate riddle canon: the *Violino primo* part (which is printed in *Canto II*) contains mainly passages in short notes (quarters, eighths, and sixteenths). But here and there, whole notes (*semibreves*), mostly in groups of three or more, if read in immediate succession, form the melody of the hymn *Iste Confessor*. It is played by violin III as a *cantus planus* (that is, an uninterrupted succession of whole notes), while violin II plays a free counterpoint in short note values. If all the figurations in fast notes are disregarded, there results a two-voice canon whose main voice (violin III) is the hymn melody played without interruption in whole notes, while the imitating voice (violin I) has the same melody but interspersed with rests.[4] Here is the beginning of the canon:

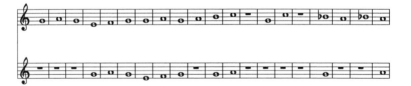

A cryptic hint at this solution is provided by the title *La Tartaruga*, the tortoise, which moves slowly, as do the notes of the hymn melody. Such canons with rests were known in the fifteenth century, for example, on the tune *L'homme armé*. This piece by Uccellini represents a Modenese tradition of canonic art that reached its apex in G.B. Vitali's *Artificii musicali* of 1689.

These two canonic sonatas are each played in one continuous movement. But among the remaining seventeen sonatas, which are sonatas in the proper sense of the word, there are eight that are continuous without a cadence, six with only one inner cadence, and three with two cadences. Another aspect of the formal structure is the change of sections in duple and triple meter. As in *Libro secondo*. Uccellini's basic form is tripartite with a middle part in triple meter. However, enlarged structures with two parts in triple meter are much more frequent in *Libro terzo* than in *Libro secondo*. Four sonatas of this type have no inner cadence, according to the scheme D Tr D Tr D (Nos. 10, 14, 16, and 18); three have one cadence: D Tr | D Tr D (Nos. 1, 5, and 13); and one has two cadences: D Tr | D | Tr D (No. 11). Several sonatas (for instance, Nos. 1, 2, and 5) are cyclic insofar as the last section begins with the initial theme but continues with different constructions.

Sonata La Poggia, No. 1, for violin, theorbo, and b.c., has (as was stated previously) the structure D Tr | D Tr D. The following schematic presentation shows the essential details of its contents:[5]

Sonata prima La Poggia

Section	1a	b	c	2a			b	c
Meter	13 D	20 D	23 Tr	5 D	5 D	4 D	26 Tr	10 D
Tempo	slow	allegro	fast	slow			allegro	
Instrumen-	violin,			violin	theorbo	violin	violin, theorbo	
tation	theorbo			solo	solo			

The first section begins with a slow introduction in whole and half notes, the only case of this kind in Uccellini's *Libro secondo*. An allegro in fugue style (1b) follows immediately. The final part of the first section (1c), in triple meter, begins with a phrase of seven measures that is transposed twice to other scale degrees. This technique is very unusual in Italy but is reminiscent of a method common in Spanish organ music of the seventeenth century. Called "modulating passages,"[6] they appear in Spain shortly after 1600, in the works of Aguilera de Heresia (d. 1627), and there is no doubt that they originated in that country. Uccellini's modulating passages are much less extended than those of Aguilera, nor do they adhere to the principle of modulating to the fifth (or fourth), which is always observed by the Spanish organ masters. Fig. 79 shows Uccellini's modulating passage (without the *basso continuo*, which is practically identical with the theorbo).

FIGURE 79. UCCELLINI: SONATA PRIMA LA POGGIA (OPUS 3, 1642).

The second part of this sonata begins with a short section (2a) in which both instruments play soloistic passages. Once more, the principle of the concerto is realized, as it was 22 years earlier in the works of Castello. However, Uccellini's solo passages are not at all virtuosic (as Castello's were) but are written in sustained note values, thus emphasizing the expressive style of the violin. Solo passages of a similar character occur in Sonatas Nos. 4, 16, and 19. Fig. 80 shows the soloistic section of *Sonata La Vendramina*, No. 16, in which the two violins and the theorbo appear one after the other with short solo passages that are expressly referred to in the *basso continuo* (Fig. 80; the b.c. for the theorbo solo passage is omitted since it is identical with the theorbo voice part). One might assume that such slow solo passages were played with improvised ornamentations, somewhat similar to the adagios of Corelli's Sonata, Opus 5 (1700), though perhaps less elaborate.

FIGURE 80. UCCELLINI: SONATA SESTADECIMA LA VENDRAMINA (OPUS 3, 1642).

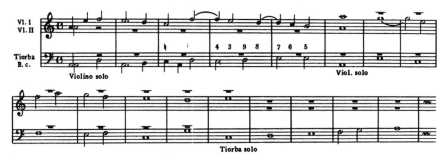

Another interesting sonata of Uccellini's *Libro terzo* is No. 15, *La sorella mi fa fallare.* Its title might lead one to suppose that it is a set of variations on a popular song. Actually the title can be divided into solmization syllables as follows: *La so(l) re la mi fa fa la re.* Like the famous *Lascia fare mi* (= *la sol fa re mi*), it yields a theme that dominates the entire sonata. Fig. 81a shows the transcription of the words into a melody, and Fig. 81b shows the theme as it appears at the beginning of the sonata. In spite of its artificial derivation, this theme is of great musical value and more interesting than most of the themes invented by Uccellini. And this sonata, in which the theme appears time and again in one or another voice part, in one or another rhythmic transformation, is the most interesting and valuable in Uccellini's *Libro terzo*.

FIGURE 81. UCCELLINI: SONATA QUINTADECIMA LA SORELLA MI FA FALLARE (OPUS 3, 1642).

The last sonata, *Sonata decima nona la Febre*, is clearly in the key of C minor. Although the signature is limited to *bb*, the chromatic alterations *eb* and *ab* occur so frequently within the course of the composition that it would be entirely possible, and even preferable, to transcribe it with a key signature of C minor. In Uccellini's later publications his predilection for the flat keys is even more apparent, but in general the violin composers of the seventeenth century tend to enlarge the system of keys "upwards," that is, toward the sharp keys.

The first eight arias in *Libro terzo* are variations based on popular songs, among them *Ciacona*, *Bergamasca*, *E tanto tempo hormai* (which Turini had used in 1621), and *Quest'e quel loco* (which we have encountered in Buonamente's *Libro quarto* of 1626). The sixth set of variations is almost literally taken over from Buonamente, resembling a set in which "the four-measure phrases of the theme are expanded into five-measure phrases" (see p. 77). The theme *Il Lantururù*, of *Aria settima*, is new. It consists of two sections, of four and eight measures respectively, and has eight variations, the last one in *presto*. The variations of *E tanto tempo* are particularly attractive. They are not composed according to the tiring principle of formula variation but contain various motifs and figurations.

Aria nona is not a set of variations but a piece of program music. It is called *L'emenphrodita* (Hymen-Aphrodite), with the remark "Maritati insieme la Gallina e il Cucco fanno un bel concerto." Here the hen is married, not to the cock (as in Farina's *Capriccio stravagante*), but to the cuckoo; and together they make *un bel concerto*, she with the same crackle as Farina's *La Gallina* (Fig. 50), he with the well-known cry of the cuckoo.

The correnti at the end of *Libro terzo* are, as usual, binary and symmetrical, with two sections each of eight, twelve, fourteen, sixteen, or eighteen measures. Some, however, are not symmetrical, for instance, *Corrente quarta*, with the scheme ‖:14:‖:18:‖.

In 1645 there appeared Uccellini's *Sonate Correnti et Arie da Farsi con diversi Stromenti si da Camera come da Chiesa à uno à due, et à tre . . . opera quarta*, which we will abbreviate as *Libro IV*.[7] The title contains the same reference to *da Camera* and *da Chiesa* as does Merula's *Libro terzo* of 1637. Of all of Uccellini's publications, this is the most comprehensive. It contains, first of all, 30 sonatas: (Nos. 1–6) for violin and b.c. (*a uno*, as the title says); Nos. 7–14 for violin, bass, and b.c. (*a due*); Nos. 15–22 for two violins and b.c. (also *a due*); and Nos. 23–30 for two violins, bass, and b.c. (*a tre*). There follow twenty correnti and fifteen arias, all for two violins and b.c., but with violin II *ad libitum* for all the correnti and for the first ten arias.

This publication is especially interesting because of its large number of sonatas. They are uniform in having only one middle section. The enlarged forms, which are quite frequent, particularly in *Libro terzo*, are not represented here. The structure indicated (or, at least, suggested) by the cadences shows a decided preference for no interruption. Sixteen sonatas consist of one "movement" (to anticipate a term from the later development of the sonata), eleven have two movements, and three have three. The following are examples of each type:

Sonata prima a Violino solo detta la Vittoria trionfante (violin and b.c.)

Section	1a	b	c	d	‖
Meter	61 D	12 D	72 Tr	74 D	
Tempo		adagio		fast	‖

Sonata decima quarta a Violino e Basso (violin, bass, and b.c.)

Section	1	2a	b	c	‖
Meter	40 D	47 Tr	18 D	34 D	
Tempo	allegro	allegro	grave	allegro	‖

Sonata quarta a Violino solo detta la Hortensia virtuosa (violin and b.c.)

Section	1a	b	2	3a	b	
Meter	10 D	15 D	50 Tr	6 D	12 D	‖
Tempo	adagio	allegro		adagio	allegro	

Several sonatas are cyclic in the same manner as was described for those in *Libro terzo*. Thematic unity is even stronger in those sonatas in which the theme of the triple-meter section is derived from the initial theme. Fig. 82a shows the theme of *Sonata prima detta la Vittoria trionfante*, which refers to some triumphant victory of the time (section 1b of the above schematic representation is independent of the theme). Sonatas Nos. 8, 9, 11, 12, and 13 are also monothematic.

FIGURE 82a. UCCELLINI: SONATA PRIMA (OPUS 4, 1645).

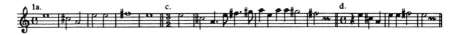

The following are some particularly noteworthy details. In Sonata No. 2, for violin and b.c., the last sixteen measures of the triple-meter section present another example of the "Spanish" modulating passages, since a four-measure phrase is transposed to four other scale degrees (B♭ major, E♭ major, C minor, B♭ major). Sonata No. 21, for two violins and b.c., contains a short solo passage in slow note values, similar to that shown in Fig. 80. Sonatas Nos. 3, 16, and 26 all begin with fairly extended *adagio* or *grave* sections (that of No. 26 is 33 measures long) that might be associated with the first movement of the later *sonata da chiesa*—although Uccellini's introductory *adagios* do not conclude with cadences, but pass over without interruption to the subsequent *allegro*.

The sonatas of *Libro IV* are especially noteworthy from the point of view of tonality, even more so than those in *Libro terzo*. The key of C minor, which in the earlier publication was represented by one sonata, occurs here in four (Nos. 4, 5, 9, and 17), and No. 20 is in the parallel major of E♭. Flats beyond E♭, such as A♭, D♭, and even G♭ appear repeatedly. Fig. 82b shows the last measures of Sonata No. 20, in E♭ major. The effect of a minor chord shortly before the final major chord is used in several sonatas by Uccellini, obviously in order to increase the brilliance of the ending in a major key. The range of the sharp notes is also extended, especially in Sonata No. 22, which is in the key of B minor and which contains a short *grave* section with D♯, A♯, and E♯.[8]

FIGURE 82b. UCCELLINI: SONATA VIGESIMA (OPUS 4, 1645).

The correnti in *Libro IV* are for *violino solo* with violin II *ad libitum*. The following remark appears at the end of the *Tavola*: "Avertasi che tutte le Correnti di presenti libri vanno sonate presto." In other words, all the correnti in this book are to be played *presto*. They are in binary form and symmetrical, either exactly (for instance, ‖:14:‖:14:‖, ‖:16:‖:16:‖) or approximately (for instance, ‖:12:‖:14:‖), as is usual for dance pieces of the period. Later (for instance, in those of Bach), the second section is considerably longer than the first. Uccellini's correnti have attractive melodies, as have hundreds of others written during the seventeenth century.

Libro IV closes with fifteen compositions called *Aria* that fall into two groups. Nos. 1–10 are short pieces in approximately binary form (for instance, ‖:6:‖:7:‖, ‖:9:‖:10:‖), and all are in duple meter.[9] *Aria nona* has leaps of a fifth (so fitting for the violin), played simultaneously by the two violins at the distance of a third, resulting in a succession of II$_7$ chords (Fig. 83).

FIGURE 83. UCCELLINI: ARIA NONA (OPUS 4, 1645).

The last five arias are all variation sets: No. 11, on *Caporal Simon* (seven variations on a ten-measure theme); No. 12, on *Il Bigaran* (five variations on a thirteen-measure theme); No. 13, on *Questa Bella Sirena* (ten variations on an eight-measure theme); No. 14, on *La mia pedrina* (nine variations on a twenty-measure theme); and No. 15, on *La Scatola da gli agghi* (five variations on a sixteen-measure theme). As is true of many variations of the period, they are mainly interesting because of the themes, not the variations, which conform to the stereotype. Together with those used by Rossi, Marini, Buonamente, and others, these themes represent an unexpectedly rich mine of early Italian popular song. Except for the *Scatola*, which had been used in 1622 by Rossi (see Fig. 10b), all the popular songs selected by Uccellini have new texts, although some of the melodies may well be of older origin. The *Scatola* melody is a paraphrase of the sixteenth-century *passamezzo nuovo*, and the melody for *Caporal Simon* closes with the refrain:

which occurs in Marini's *Sonata sopra la Monica* of 1629 (see Fig. 33) as well as in the well-known song *La Girolmetta*.

In 1649, there appeared Uccellini's *Sonate over Canzoni da farsi a Violino solo e Basso Continuo, Opera quinta . . .*, here abbreviated as *Libro V*. This publication consists of two part books, *Canto* and *Partitura*, and contains twelve sonatas for violin and b.c., one for two violins and b.c. (No. 13, a canon *alla rovescia*), and No. 14, called *Tromba sordina per sonare con un Violino* in the *Tavola* and on the part but *Trombetta . . .* in the *partitura* part book.[10] In the *Partitura* all the pieces are printed in a two-system score whose upper part is identical with the violin part printed in the *Canto*. This is another example of a practice that raises the question whether the violin part was duplicated by the right hand of the organ part (see the discussion in connection with compositions by Castello and Marini, pp. 37–38, 52). The practice was *ad libitum*: the organist could duplicate various passages in the violin part, at his own discretion or in agreement with the violinist. It has been argued that it was impossible for the organist to play the fast figurations of the violin part at the same time as the chords indicated by the thorough-bass figures of the *basso continuo*. In Castello's case this objection is irrelevant because his scores have no thorough-bass figures. Uccellini's scores do have such figures, but surprisingly few of them, as can be seen by comparing the sonatas of his *Libro V* with the solo sonatas (Nos. 1–6) of *Libro IV*, which have a normal *basso continuo*, not a *Partitura*. For example, the first sonata of *Libro IV* has about 120 bass notes with figures, the first sonata of *Libro V* only sixteen, although they are about the same length (210 versus 216 measures). Thus, in the former sonata the organist had to play chords all the time, in the latter only occasionally, so that it was entirely possible to play extended passages in unison with the violin. In order to remove the last scruples about this "doubling practice," we should like to mention the "Pianoforte sonatas with Violin accompaniment" that were written from about 1740 to 1780 by Mondonville, Schobert, Edelmann, and others, in which the violin (or flute) frequently plays in unison with the pianoforte.[11]

Compared with the sonatas in *Libro IV*, those in *Libro V* shows a departure from the continuous type of structure in favor of a three- or four-part form. Half of the compositions consist of either three sections (Nos. 2, 4, 5, and 7) or four (Nos. 1, 8, and 11). See the following diagrams for Sonatas Nos. 1 and 4:

Sonata prima

Section	1	2	3	4	
Meter	11 D	60 D	87 Tr	42 D	
Tempo	slow			fast	

Sonata quarta

Section	1a	b	c	2a	b	3	
Meter	9 D	15 D	41 Tr	12 D	62 Tr	28 D	
Tempo	adagio	allegro		largo		fast	

The first section of *Sonata prima* is a slow introduction in homophonic style that corresponds to the first movement of a normal *sonata da chiesa*, all the more since it closes with a full cadence. The second section is a fugato whose theme played first on the organ, consists of whole, half, and quarter notes:

It differs strikingly from the themes commonly used in violin music of the time and reminds one of an organ ricercar. Themes of this type are found in several other sonatas, for example, in No. 6:

or in No. 7:

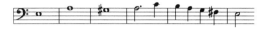

Such themes, however, are not treated strictly (as they would be in a ricercar) but serve as the point of departure for fast figurations on the violin.

The "Spanish" modulating passages mentioned in connection with Uccellini's *Libro IV* (see Fig. 79) are even more frequent and more extended in *Libro V*. In the first section of *Sonata seconda*, a three-measure phrase appears on four scale degrees, first on *d*, then transposed to *g*, *e*, and *a*. In the triple-meter section of *Sonata quarta* the modulating technique is used three times for a phrase of four measures, then several times for a shortened variant of this phrase. This method, which combines modulation with abbreviation, was used very frequently by Spanish organ masters active about the middle of the seventeenth century, for example, by Jose Ximenez (Jimenez)[12] (organist in Saragossa, 1654; died 1672). Uccellini's *Sonata ottava* also contains an interesting modulating passage.

In the sonatas of *Libro III*, Uccellini tended toward cyclic treatment; in *Libro IV* he made use of monothematic techniques. In *Libro V* the initial themes frequently recur in the further course of the sonata, either transformed into triple meter or in halved note values. In some sonatas Uccellini goes a step further, using these transformations for extended passages or even entire sections. For instance, near the middle of section 4 of *Sonata prima* (see diagram above) there is a seven-measure passage that is the exact diminution of the fourteen measures of section 2. And in *Sonata terza*, the initial section of 45 measures in duple meter is followed by an even longer one in triple meter; the first 45 measures are identical with those of the initial section, but transformed from 4/4 to 3/2. Thus, two sections of a sonata exhibit the same relationship as that between sixteenth-century dances and their after-dances. The violin style of these sonatas shows an increase in virtuosity over the solo sonatas of *Libro IV* (Nos. 1–6). Nearly every sonata contains extended passages with 32d notes; such passages are rarely found in the sonatas of Castello and Fontana. The singing style of the violin is also properly taken into account, especially in the slow introductions and in the beginnings of the fugatos, where the sustained notes of the violin compete with those of the organ. The range of the violin has been enlarged,[13] and there is frequent use of legato signs, either short curves or brackets (‿‿).

Sonata ottava[14] is particularly attractive, with its boldly rhapsodic introduction, the unexpected change from *d* to *db* and from *a* to *ab*, and the abrupt *alla zoppa* rhythms (Fig. 84). At the end of the triple-meter section, in an extended modulating passage, a four-measure phrase is transposed to five different scale degrees.

FIGURE 84. UCCELLINI: SONATA OTTAVA (OPUS 5, 1649).

In striking contrast to the virtuoso fireworks in the first eleven sonatas of *Libro V*, in Sonata No. 12 the sustained motion of the violin is interrupted only once. This short passage in eighth notes is almost like another organ part, but with the animation and intensity of expression that characterizes the violin, it provides a fascinating contrast to the similar, but unexpressive, sound of the organ. This sonata appears to be a unique case, since Uccellini's later violin sonatas (of the *Ozio regio* of 1660) are again highly virtuosic. Was it perhaps played with improvised ornamentations, as were the *adagio* movements of Corelli's Sonatas of Opus 5?

The last piece of Uccellini's *Libro V, Trombetta [Tromba* in the tavola] *sordina per sonare con Violino solo,* is a curiosity. Its bass is nothing but a *d,* a fourth below the lowest violin pitch, which is repeated more than 200 times, while the violin revels in endless para-phrases of the D-major triad. The bass was probably played on a *tromba marina* (also called *trombetta marina* or *trombetta sordina*).[15]

Uccellini's Opus 6, *Salmi concertati,* contains vocal music. His Opus 7, published in 1660, carries the title *Ozio regio. Compositioni armoniche sopra il Violino & diversi altri strumenti. Opera settima A uno, due, tre, quattro, cinque, e sei.* . . . It is dedicated to Cardinal Mazzarini, who under the name Mazarin was secretary of state at the French court of Louis XIV and to whom Uccellini offered his compositions as an entertainment for his leisure hours (*Ozio regio* = royal leisure). The contents are as follows:[16]

4 Sonatas à 1:	Nos. 1–4	Violino solo
9 Sonatas à 2:	Nos. 5–10	Violino (2)
	No. 11	Violino, Tiorba
	No. 12	Violino, Violone
	No. 13	Violino, Trombone
4 Sonatas à 3:	Nos. 14–16	Violino (2), Basso
	No. 17	Violino (2), Tiorba
4 Sonata or Canzone à 4;	Nos. 18–21	[unspecified]
6 Sinfonia à 5:	Nos. 22–27	[unspecified]
2 Toccata à 6 (for two choirs)	Nos. 28, 29	Violino (4), Basso (2)
8 Corrente à 4:	Nos. 30–37	[unspecified]

8 Corrente à 5:	Nos. 38–45	[unspecified]
6 Corrente à 2:	Nos. 46–51	Violino (2) [. . . da sonarsi tutte due le parti con un violino solo]
1 Toccata à 2:	No. 52	Violino (2) [. . . da sonarsi tutte due le parti con un violino solo]

(The *Tavola* indicates the instruments when particular ones are required: *Sonata undecima à violino è Tiorba; Sonata duedecima à violino, e Violine; Sonata decima terza à violino e Trombone; Sonata decima settima a tre due violini e Tiorba.* [I have not seen Nos. 46–52—ed.]).

The publication consists of five part books: *Canto primo, Canto secondo, Terza parte, Quarta e quinta parte,* and *Basso continuo.* The voice parts of these 52 compositions are sometimes distributed confusingly in the five part books. For example, for the solo sonatas Nos. 1–4 the score is printed in the *Basso continuo,* but the violin part is not in the *Canto primo* but at the beginning of the *Quarta e Quinta parte.* This part book also contains, on facing pages, the alto and tenor of the five-voice Sinfonias, Nos. 22–27, so that in this instance two players could read from the same part book.

The scoring is not always identical within the individual groups. For example, in Group II, Nos. 5–10 are for two violins and b.c., while Nos. 11–13 are scored for violin, bass, and b.c., with diverse bass instruments (No. 11, theorbo; No. 12, violone; No. 13, trombone); and in Group IV Nos. 18–20 are for violin, alto, tenor, bass, and b.c.; and No. 21 is for three violins, bass, and b.c. The two *Toccata a 6.* (Nos. 28 and 29) are written for two choirs, each of which consists of two violins and bass. The scoring is therefore four violins, two basses, and b.c., so that they belong to the small group of compositions for four violins.[17] In Groups IX and X the two upper parts are notated on a two-system score, as if written for two violins ("a due violini"), but they are actually to be played on one violin ("tutte due le parti con un violino solo") in double-stops.

The 21 sonatas at the beginning of *Ozio regio* are the last ones Uccellini wrote. Their structure belongs to an earlier type in which a succession of contrasting sections is interrupted by occasional cadences. The novel principle, introduced about 1640 by Cazzati and Neri, of dividing the sonata into clearly separated movements was either unknown to Uccellini or not accepted by him. An example of his writing follows:

Sonata prima a Violino solo (No. 1)

Section	1a	b	2a	b	c	d	e	f	g	h
Meter	19 D	56 D	38 Tr	16 D	12 Tr	3 D	42 Tr	15 D	6 D	10 D
Tempo	adagio	allegro			allegro		presto	allegro	adagio	adagio ed allegro

In spite of its considerable length of 217 measures, *Sonata prima* has only one cadence, after an initial section consisting of nineteen measures *adagio* and 56 measures *allegro,* both in duple time. The second section is highly varied, with eight subdivisions of contrasting character. The last one is designated *adagio ed allegro,* as is the final section of Sonata No. 3 (see Fig. 85a). To the present-day musician this tempo indication may seem contradictory and senseless, but it should be remembered that *adagio* actually does not mean "slow" but "leisurely," and *allegro* is not really "fast" but "merrily, gaily." In this connection, it may be mentioned that the first section of *Sinfonia prima* (No. 22) carries the indication *allegro e presto*.

The six sinfonias of Group V are similar to Salomone Rossi's binary sinfonias from 1607. Uccellini's are more extended, the first three having 50 measures, the rest 30. Uccellini employs the same form (A A B B) for his *Toccata seconda* (Group VI, No. 29) as well as for all the correnti. *Toccata prima* avoids cadences, while the final Toccata (No. 52) is divided by cadences in a manner similar to that of the sonatas. The correnti are differentiated in the same way as the dances in Cazzati's Opus 15 from 1654: Group VII, in *stil francese*, are in 6/4, while Group VIII, *al Itagliana*, are in 3/2. While the former are marked *per ballare*, the latter (as well as those in Group IX) are designed as idealized dance music not as dance accompaniment.

The contents of *Ozio regio* leave conflicting impressions. Among the negative aspects, the repetition technique of the 1630s and 1640s, which some might say had fortunately slipped into obscurity, are evident here perhaps to excess. The most striking example is a 30-measure section of Sonata No. 16 (for two violins, bass, and b.c.), in which the motif

appears 68 times in what is probably (one hopes!) the climax of the repeat style. In Uccellini's fugal writing, neither the themes nor their treatment rise above the level of his compositions from the 1640s. It appears that Uccellini was not familiar with the innovations of Cazzati and Neri; that is, the disciplined fugue (rather than the freely treated fugato) was not known to him or not accepted by him. There is a tendency toward passage-work consisting only of broken chords, for instance, a 34-measure section at the end of *Sonata nona*.

On the other hand, *Ozio regio* contains a number of noteworthy features. Especially interesting are progressions that, in one way or another, do not fit into the fully developed system of major and minor, mostly because of the use of diatonic degrees at places where this system would require chromatically altered degrees (see Fig. 85). In publications dealing with the keyboard music of the fifteenth, sixteenth, and seventeenth centuries.[18] I have shown that such progressions are quite legitimate and should not be "corrected" by editorial accidentals. Such progressions also occur in seventeenth-century violin music, in compositions by Marini, Farina, and particularly Uccellini. The progression shown in Fig. 85b is known as the English seventh, because it is very frequently used in virginal music, by William Byrd and others.[19] Even earlier compositions, by Machaut and Landini are called to mind by the occurrence, in Sonata No. 16, of a Lydian cadence:

The phrase shown in Fig. 86 also includes a touch of Lydian, that is, the use of an augmented fourth in m.2.[20] This phrase represents the beginning of an extended mod-

FIGURE 85. UCCELLINI: OZIO REGIO (OPUS 7, 1660).

a).b) Sonata terza   c),d) Sinfonia terza

FIGURE 86. UCCELLINI: SONATA QUARTA A VIOLINO SOLO (OPUS 7, 1660).

ulating passage, which—as in the Spanish model—ascends in five transpositions of the fifth:

followed by five returning modulations:

Sonata No. 3 contains a chromatic scale that includes the enharmonic equivalents e♯ and f (see Fig. 87, accidentals as in the original, that is, ♯ instead of ♮, which was not employed at the time).

FIGURE 87. UCCELLINI: SONATA TERZA A VIOLINO SOLO (OPUS 7, 1660).

Ozio regio closes with six correnti and a toccata "a due violini da sonarsi tutte due le parti con un violino solo." These pieces are chiefly interesting from the point of view of violin technique; for the first time in more than 30 years (Marini, 1626; Grandi, 1628; and Farina, 1628), double-stop technique is employed. It is used to a much larger extent than ever before, not only for short passages but also for entire compositions of considerable length. The notation, on two systems designated *Violino primo* and *Violino secondo*, indicates the polyphonic character of the double-stops. It also makes it possible to perform these pieces by two "normal" violinists rather than by a single virtuoso. Fig. 88 shows a passage from the toccata, a composition of almost 250 measures.

FIGURE 88. UCCELLINI: TOCCATA . . . DA SONARSI . . . CON UN VIOLINO SOLO (OPUS 7, 1660).

Uccellini's *Sinfonie boscarecie*, Opus 8 (1665), is preserved only in reprints from 1669 and 1677. With this publication as well as with Opus 9 (1669), Uccellini leaves the intricate field of the sonata and turns to a much less demanding type of seventeenth-century music, the sinfonia (= Symphonia). Part of the title of Opus 8 reads: *A violino solo e Basso. Con l'agiunta di due altri Violini ad libitum, per poter sonare a due, a tre, e a quatro, conforme piacerà.* The full scoring therefore is three violins, bass, and b.c. Compositions with this scoring are not rare in seventeenth-century music, but an entire publication containing pieces for three violins (and bass) exclusively is probably unique. One gets the impression that there were two other good violinists in Modena with whom Uccellini liked to play.

The title, *Sinfonie boscarecie* (Forest Sinfonias), seems to indicate that these pieces were performed in the open air, perhaps in connection with court festivities. Indeed, their form and content are not very demanding. All 37 sinfonias have the same binary structure (‖:A:‖:B:‖) and an average length of about 25 measures (except for the very short No. 32, with only ten measures, and the very long No. 23, with 64). Stylistically they are unpretentious and without individuality. Only No. 34, *La Gran Battaglia*,[21] shows the characteristic and commonplace traits of battle pieces. In at least a dozen of the sinfonias, the melodies conform to the principle of four-measure phrases (*Vierhegibkeit*), a principle that we meet here for the first time in a clear and unmistakable way. Hugo Riemann, who introduced this term and realized its great importance, greatly exaggerated its validity. Its importance is incontestable in dance music, but even here its validity is not comprehensive because correnti rarely have regular (that is, four-measure) phrases. About 1650, the four-measure principle becomes recognizable in other fields, in the operas by Cesti and Cavalli, and also in the sinfonias of Uccellini, who was a leading exponent of this principle. A melody like that in Fig. 89 exemplifies a method of organization that was valid until the end of the nineteenth century, that is, the combination of a four-measure phrase and parallelism of phrases. This melody has a somewhat popular character, which is entirely suitable for a *Sinfonia boscarecia*.

Uccellini's last publication, *Sinfonici Concerti, Brievi, e facili, à uno, à due, à tre, & à quatro strumenti: Ogni cosa con il suo Basso continuo, per Chiesa, e per Camera. Con Brandi, e Correnti alla Francese, e Balletti al Italiana giusta l'uso aprovatissimo della Corte di Parma. Opera nona, e nuova . . .*, appeared in 1667 in Venice. It is dedicated to Ranuccio II of

FIGURE 89. UCCELLINI: SYMPHONIA DECIMA TERZA (OP. 8, C. 1665).

Parma, whom Uccellini was then serving as *Maestro di Capella Strumentale*. The publication contains:

I.	25 Sinfonia	Nos. 1–25
II.	2 Brando alla francese per ballare	Nos. 26, 27
III.	6 Corrente alla francese per ballare	Nos. 28–33
IV.	Introduzione dè Balli al Italiana	No. 34
V.	15 Ballo al Italiana	Nos. 35–49
VI.	2 Canon	Nos. 50, 51

According to the title these sinfonias could be performed in the church as well as in the "chamber," with the continuo being played on the organ in the former case and on the harpsichord in the latter. The dance pieces—brandi, correnti, balletti—are composed "according to the most approved custom of the court of Parma."

The scoring of the sinfonias is as follows: violin and b.c. in Nos. 1 and 2; violin, violone, and b.c. in No. 3; two violins and b.c. in Nos. 4–7; two violins and b.c. in Nos. 8 and 9; two violins, violone, and b.c. in Nos. 10–12; two violins, alto, bass, and b.c. in Nos. 13–16 and 18–25; and four violins and b.c. in No. 17. The dances of Groups II–V are all for two violins, alto, bass, and b.c.; and the two canons of Group VI are for two violins and b.c. The two sonatas for solo violin (Nos. 1 and 2) are not notated in score—as are the earlier solo sonatas—but as a normal thorough bass.

The sinfonias have the usual binary form ‖:A:‖:B:‖ except for the Nos. 1, 2, and 5, which are continuous without repetition. In the title they are said to be *brieve, e facili*, but in truth they are neither particularly short nor very easy to play. They are considerably more extended (mostly having about 40 measures in each section) than the *Sinfonie boscarecie* of Opus 8, from which they differ in several ways: The sinfonias of Opus 9 are frequently subdivided into segments with varying tempo and meter indications, and four-measure phrases play a much less important role here. In Sinfonias Nos. 4, 5, and 6 the two violins stand out with solo passages, those of No. 5 being particularly virtuosic, reminiscent of Castello (Fig. 90).

FIGURE 90. UCCELLINI: SINFONIA QUINTA À DUE VIOLINI (OPUS 9, 1667).

The Opus 9 sinfonias also make frequent use of sequential constructions; the one shown in Fig. 91 is especially interesting because it is based exclusively on the interval of the third.

FIGURE 91. UCCELLINI: SINFONIA VIGESIMA QUARTA A QUATRO (OPUS 9, 1667).

The two brandi and six correnti (Groups II and III) all carry the remark *alla francese per ballare*. They are dance music in the proper sense, as are some correnti of *Ozio regio* (Group VII). The two brandi each consist of four dances, that is, *Brando*, *Gaij*, *Amener*, and *Gavotta*. *Gaij* certainly means *Branle gay*, a dance mentioned in Arbeau's *Orchésographie* (1589) as one of the many kinds of branle. And *Amener* is the *Branle à mener*, an early form of the menuet characterized by phrases of six (rather than four) measures.[22] Uccellini's *Brando primo* is written according to the following scheme (the numbers indicate the number of measures):

Brando	Gaij	Amener	Gavotta
¢‖:12:‖12	3/4‖:8:‖:8:‖	3/4 24	¢‖:4:‖:8:‖

The *Amener*, which is notated without a repeat sign, consists of four phrases of six measures each, the first two of which are identical, so that it has the form A A B C. The second brando consists of four dances and has exactly the same structure as the first. About the same time, three composers living in Modena—G.M. Bononcini, G.B. Vitali, and G. Colombi—wrote brandi that match these pieces in every detail (including the number of measures). Obviously all these brandi represent the same court dance, performed according to the same strictly prescribed ceremonial in both Parma and Modena. The six "French" correnti (Nos. 28–33), *per ballare* and in 6/4 meter, belong to the same type as those of *Ozio regio*. The Italian dances consist of a short *Introduzione dè Balli al Italiana* in binary form (No. 34), and fifteen *Balli al Italiana* (Nos. 35–49), all in triple meter (ten in 3/2, three in 6/4, and two in 3/4). Very likely these are also correnti, not meant for dancing but representing idealized dance music. This contrast was seen in Uccellini's *Ozio regio* but is much more obvious in the works of Bononcini and Vitali.

NOTES

1. Only four compositions from *Ozio regio*, Opus 7 (1670), are listed as *Sonata over Canzone*.

2. In the contents listed in SartoriB, vol. II, p. 106, *Sinfonia sesta* is missing. This is accounted for by the fact that the melody of the canon is in the *Canto secondo* part book, while Sartori clearly studied the *Canto primo* part book.

3. The words *Il Terzo Libro delle* are lacking in the original title but do occur at the bottom of each page of the print. The *Tavola* of the *Basso continuo*, which is always the most complete, has not been preserved.

4. One is reminded of Girolamo dalla Casa's diminutions presented measure by measure in the note values of the vocal original, then in diminution (e.g., *ancor che col partire*, in *Il vero modo . . .* , vol. II, p. 35).

5. Here and in later representations, the movements that in the original have no tempo indications will be called "fast" or "slow" whenever it is clear from the notation that this is the intent.

6. See ApelG, pp. 506 and 533, among others (see Index under "Modulating Passages"). In note 9, p. 85, we referred to the Spanish influence on Buonamente.

7. Modern edition of *Sonatas* Nos. 16 and 17 and a few correnti are in TorchiA, pp. 205ff.

8. Martino Pesenti, who was born blind in Venice about the year 1600, published a book of keyboard music entitled *Correnti, Gagliarde e Balletti, trasportati parte cromatici e parte henarmonici*, in which we find transposition of twenty tonalities, for example, F minor to D minor. See ApelG, p. 475.

9. Both the arias and the correnti are written with regular barlines, while in the sonatas there are few and quite irregular barlines.

10. Modern edition of *Sonata seconda* in RiemannO, vol. IV, p. 135; of *Sonata ottava* in BeckmannVS, No. 2.

11. See HAM, No. 304, taken from J.F. Edelmann, *Six Grand Lessons for the Forte Piano or Harpsichord with an Accompaniment for the Violin*, ca, 1780.

12. See ApelG, p. 528, Fig. 565.

13. "Bis zur 6, Lage ereweitert" (MoserG, p. 74).

14. In Beckmann's modern edition (see note 10) groups of ten to twelve notes are included in a single legato bow, the authenticity of which is questionable. Fig. 84 shows the original grouping.

15. The first edition of MoserG (1922) assumes that it is played with a lowered string. In Nösselt's modern edition this notion is correctly ignored.

16. See note 6, p. 85.

17. In 1668 in Antwerp, Phalèse brought out an edition of *Ozio regio* in two separate books: *Sonate sopra il Violino e diversi altri strumenti . . .* (see SartoriB, vol. I, 1668h) and *Compositioni armonichi sopra il Violino e diversi altri strumenti . . .* (see SartoriB, vol. I, 1668g). The former contains the pieces *a uno, due, tre* and the latter those *a quatro, cinque, e sei*.

18. See ApelA, p. 30, "Harmonik und Melodik," as well as the Foreword to the second edition.

19. See ApelG, p. 777, "Septime." The g-$g\sharp$ dissonance also occurs with Cazzati, as seen in Fig. 93.

20. See ApelA, p. 38, "Die lydische Tonalität."

21. New edition in WasielewskiS, No. XXIX.

22. See the article *Amener* in W. Apel, *Harvard Dictionary of Music* (Cambridge, 1944; 2d ed., 1969). An early example of this type is found in the music of Louis Couperin (ca. 1626–1661), with the title *Menuet de Poitou*.

SOURCES

Sonate, sinfonie, et correnti a 2. a 3. et a 4. per sonare con diversi instromenti . . . libro secondo.
Venice: Alessandro Vincenti, 1639.   RISM U13.
    Poland: Wroclaw, Biblioteka Uniwersytecka (S I and II, b.c.).

Sonate, Arie, et Correnti a 2. e 3. per sonare con diversi instromenti. Venice: Alessandro
Vincenti, 1642.   RISM U14.
    Poland: Wroclaw, Biblioteka Uniwersytecka.
    West Germany: Kassel, Murhard'sche Bibliothek der Stadt Kassel und Landesbibliothek (S I and II, b.c.).

*Sonate, correnti, et arie da farsi con diversi stromenti si da camera, come da chiesa, a uno,
a due, et a tre.* Opus 4. Venice: Alessandro Vincenti, 1645.   RISM U15.
    Italy: Bologna, Civico Museo (Parts I, II, III, b.c.).
    Poland: Wroclaw, Biblioteka Uniwersytecka (Part III, b.c.).
Reprint:
Antwerp: Les héritiers de Pierre Phalèse, 1663.   RISM U16.
    Great Britain: Durham, Cathedral Library (Canto I and II, terza parte, b.c.).
Edition:
Florence: Studio per Edizione Scelte, 1984.

Sonate over Canzoni da farsi a Violino solo, & basso continuo. Opus 5. Venice: Alessandro
Vincenti, 1649.   RISM U17.
    Great Britain: Oxford, Bodleian Library.
    Italy: Florence, Biblioteca Nazionale Centrale.
    Poland: Wroclaw, Biblioteka Uniwersytecka.

*Canto primo dell'ozio regio, compositioni armoniche sopra il violino e diversi altri strumenti
. . . a uno, due, tre, quattro, cinque, e sei.* Opus 7. Venice: Francesco Magni detto Gardano,
1660.   RISM U19.
    France: Paris, Bibliothèque Mazarine (S I).
Reprints:
Antwerp: Les héritiers de Pierre Phalèse, 1668.   RISM U20.
    Great Britain: London, British Library (Violone, b.c.).
Antwerp: Les héritiers de Pierre Phalèse, 1668.   RISM U21.
    Great Britain: Durham, Cathedral Library (first part [Violin I and II]; second part
    [Violin II, Theorbo, Violone, Trombone]; terza parte [Violin solo, Theorbo, Violoncello; b.c.]).

*Sinfonie boscarecie, brandi, corrente, con diversi balli alla francese, e all'itagliana conforme
si costuma ballare nella corte del . . . duca di Modena; ogni cos a violino solo e basso con
l'agiunta di due altri violini ad libitum . . .* Opus 8. Venice: Francesco Magni detto Gardano,
1660.   RISM U22.
    Italy: Pesaro, Biblioteca comunale Oliveriana (Violin I incomplete).
Reprints: *Sinfonie Boscarecie a violino solo e Basso con l'agiunta di due altri Violini ad libitum,
per poter sonare à due, a trè, è a quatro conforme piàcerà. . . .* Opus 8. Antwerp: i Heredi
di Pietro Phalesio, 1669.   RISM U23.
    Belgium: Bibliothèque Royale Albert Iᵉʳ (lacks Violin III).
    Sweden: Norrkoepirn, Stadsbiblioteket (Violin I, II, III, b.c./Violone).
Antwerp: Luca de Potter, 1677.   RISM U24.
    Great Britain: London, British Library (lacks b.c./Violone).
    Netherlands: The Hague, Gemeente Museum (b.c./Violone).

Sinfonici concerti brievi, e facili, a uno, a due, a tre, et a quattro strumenti; ogni cosa, con il suo basso continuo, per chiesa, e per camera, con brandi, e correnti alla francese, e balletti al italiana. . . . Opus 9. Venice: Francesco Magni, 1667. RISM U25.

Italy: Bologna, Archivio dell'Accademia filarmonica (Violin I, II, III, Violone, b.c.); Bologna, Civico Museo.

🍎 *Maurizio Cazzati*

The well-known composer Maurizio Cazzati was born about 1620, probably in Guastalla (between Mantua and Modena). Following short periods in Mantua (1641), Bozzolo (1647), Ferrara (1650), and Bergamo (1653), he was chapelmaster at San Petronio in Bologna from 1657 to 1673. He died in 1677 in Mantua. Cazzati may be regarded as the founder of the Bolognese school, which played a leading role in the second half of the seventeenth century. His Opus 55 was the first publication of solo violin sonatas from Bologna.

Cazzati's first publication of violin music appeared in 1642, with the title *Canzoni a 3. Doi Violini e Violone, col suo basso continuo . . . Opera Seconda*. It contains eight canzonas and two vocal compositions, a *Confitebor* and a *Letatus*. The contents, though small in number, are of great significance, mainly in the development of the structural aspects of the sonata.

Cazzati's canzonas (it is certainly permissible to regard them as sonatas) differ unmistakably from the style of the sonatas of the 1630s and even from those by Uccellini. While these earlier sonatas frequently have no interruptions or are divided into three or four parts by cadences, Cazzati's canzonas consist of a number of sections clearly separated by fermatas over the final chords, double bars, repeat signs, and tempo indications. Here for the first time a present-day scholar may feel justified in speaking of sonatas consisting of several "movements." Four of the eight canzonas have three movements, two have four movements, and two have five. In the following schematic representations, double bars are indicated as they appear in the original.

Canzone prima la Gonzaga

Section	1		2a	b		3	4a	b	5	
Meter	9 D⌢	‖	18 D	8 D⌢	‖	9 D⌢	28 Tr	5 Tr⌢	18 D⌢	‖
Tempo	Slow	‖	Allegro	Largo	‖	Grave	Allegro	Largo	Allegro	‖

Canzone quarta La Greca

Section	1			2	3	4	
Meter	17 D	:	‖ :	22 Tr⌢	7 D⌢	25 D⌢	‖
Tempo	fast		‖	Adagio	Grave	Allegro	

Canzone settima L'Altiera

Section	1		2		3a	b	
Meter	41 D⁀	‖	43 Tr⁀	‖	8 D⁀	14 D⁀	‖
Tempo	fast			‖	Largo	Allegro	

Most of the movements in triple meter have no tempo indications, for instance, those of *Canzone settima*. Whether they are to be played slowly or quickly is difficult to decide.[1] However, it is interesting that in *Canzone prima* the triple-meter section (4a) is designated *Allegro*, although (or because?) it is notated in 3/1 with whole notes (that is, in *tempus perfectum*); while the second movement of *Canzone quarta* is written in 3/2 (*prolatio major*) with the indication *Adagio*. Cazzati tends to write in a homogeneous style, except for occasional *Largo* introductions, as in the third movement of *Canzone prima*. Aside from *Canzone quinta* and *Canzone settima*, all the canzonas are cyclic, in that the last movement recalls the first. In *Canzone seconda* the entire first movement is restated at the end.

Cazzati's fugue technique deserves special attention. The fugal pieces are all in three voice parts—violin I, violin II, and Violone—with a *basso continuo* that is always a *basso seguente*. The themes are lively, in eighth and sixteenth notes. Several of them are "bithematic," meaning that there are two parts to the theme, a and b, in which b is the counterpoint to the answer of a but is also employed as an independent theme later in the music:

```
a _____ b _____
              a _____
```

Cazzati's technique has much older prototypes (for instance, the ricercars of Andrea Gabrieli). In order to describe the structure of the fugal movements it is useful and even necessary to distinguish between *fugato* and *fugue*. A fugato begins with one or even two expositions of the theme, but continues freely with other material; while a fugue consists of a number of expositions separated by episodes. If these terms are applied to the fugal first movements in Cazzati's Opus 2, most of them will belong to the older type, the fugato. Only the first movement of *Canzone settima L'Altiera* can be regarded as a fully developed fugue. It consists of a first rather complete exposition (mm. 1–15); a first episode (mm. 16–23); a second, very short exposition (mm. 24–25); a second episode (mm. 26–28); a third exposition, which is very detailed (mm. 29–41); and a coda (mm. 42–48), in which a motif derived from the theme is heard six times. Although these movements can be described with terms commonly used for the analysis of a Bach fugue, an essential difference exists in the tonal relationships, particularly in the tonal structure of the first exposition. In Bach's fugues the first exposition is governed by the principle of the answer at the fifth, a principle that in the case of the three-voice fugues can be indicated by the formula I–V–I. In Cazzati's fugues the expositions have tonal structures such as I–I–IV, I–IV–I, I–IV–IV, I–I–V, and I–V–V, but none of the type I–V–I.[2]

Canzone quarta La Greca begins with five imitations of the theme *Est-ce Mars* (Fig. 92a), which Sweelinck had used for a series of variations,[3] and then turns to another theme (Fig. 92b). In the closing *Allegro* of this canzona the second theme reappears, but surprisingly the popular song does not. This may seem strange to us, but how popular was this French song in Italy?

FIGURE 92. CAZZATI: CANZONE QUARTA (OPUS 2, 1642).

Several canzonas of Cazzati's Opus 2 include short introductory sections in slow tempo, several with the designation *Largo* or *Grave*. Some of these introductions consist of three or four short "invocations" separated by rests; this impressive structure was also used by some later composers. Fig. 93 shows section 3 of *Canzone prima* (see the schematic representation above).

FIGURE 93. CAZZATI: CANZONE PRIMA (OPUS 2, 1642).

For the close of several canzonas Cazzati uses a pedal point, for example, in Nos. 1, 2, 4, and 5. It is particularly impressive in *Canzone quarta*, where, in the last two measures, the two violins climb higher and higher in fast motion, then suddenly stop, one after the other, as if they had arrived at a precipice. After a short breathing space there is a cadence in quiet motion in which (as occurs often in Uccellini's works) the final major chord is preceded by its minor third (Fig. 94).

FIGURE 94. CAZZATI: CANZONE PRIMA (OPUS 2, 1642).

In 1648, Cazzati published another book with violin music: *Il secondo libro delle Sonate a una, doi, tre, e quattro ... opera ottava*, which possibly was preceded by a now lost *primo libro* between the *Canzone*, Opus 2 of 1642, and the *Motetti*, Opus 5 of 1647. Opus 8 contains fourteen compositions. In the *Tavola* of the *Organo* part book they are arranged in three groups: *A Doi* (Nos. 1–3), *A Tre* (Nos. 4–9), and *A Quattro* (Nos. 10–13). These are followed by *Sonata detta la Vecchia* for six instruments (three violins, viola, trombone, violone, and b.c.). The category *a una* included in the title, is missing in the *Tavola*. This is explained by the fact that Sonatas Nos. 2 and 3 are described as *Violino*

solo, over *Violino e Basso*, so that they could be played by violin and b.c. or violin, bass, and b.c. As a confirmation for *Violino solo* performance, the *Organo* part book contains a score for these two sonatas that combines the violin part and the organ part, exactly as in all the earlier solo sonatas. The group *A Tre* has the trio scoring two violins, bass, and b.c. In the group *A Quattro* a viola is added, so that the scoring is similar to that of the present-day string quartet—two violins, alto, bass, and b.c. Although the title reads *Sonate*, Nos. 1, 8, and 9 are designated *Canzone*; the reason is as difficult to explain here as in Buonamente's *Libro VI*. Nos. 12 and 13 of Cazzati's Opus 8 carry the title *Simphonia*.

As he did in Opus 2, Cazzati again endeavors to divide the sonata (or canzona) into movements. Among the twelve sonatas of Opus 8, five have three movements, five have four, one has five, and one has two. Diagrams of three representative sonatas follow:

Sonata La Calva (No. 2; violin or violin and bass and b.c.)

Movement	1		2		3a	b		4	
Meter	14 D	:	: 41 Tr :		: 3 D	10 D		19 D	
Tempo	Allegro		Vivace		Grave	Allegro		Allegro e presto	

Sonata La Bonga (No. 5; two violins, bass, and b.c.)

Movement	1		2		3a	b		Coda	
Meter	37 D		18 D		14 Tr	37 Tr		5 D	
Tempo	fast		Grave		Largo	Allegro			

Sonata La Giroloma (No. 11; two violins, alto, bass, and b.c.)

Movement	1		2		3a	b	
Meter	30 D		14 D		32 Tr	21 D	
Tempo	fast		Adagio		Allegro	Allegro	

The structural principles of the Opus 8 sonatas differ strikingly from those of Opus 2, in which nearly all the sonatas are cyclic. In Opus 8 only two are of this type: *La Lucilla* (No. 9) and *La Giroloma* (No. 11; see the diagram above), in which section 3b recalls the theme of the first movement. This indicates a tendency to make the movements interdependent, a tendency that, in view of later development, may be regarded as "progress." The second difference concerns the inner coherence of the individual movements. The movements in Opus 2 are very homogeneous, except for an occasional *Largo* introduction or ending, but in Opus 8 quite a few movements consist of two rather extended sections that clearly differ from each other. In the above diagrams see the third movements of *La Bonga* and *La Giroloma*. Sonatas *La Vertua* (No. 1), *La Pezzola* (No. 3), and *La Vecchia* (No. 14) each begin with a slow movement in chordal style, similar to the first movement of the typical *sonata da chiesa* of a later period. Sonatas *La Marenza* (No. 4), *La Bonga* (No. 5), and *La Pepola* (No. 7) close in an unusual but very impressive way: not with an *allegro* but with a homophonic *adagio* of two, five, and twelve measures respectively.

Regarding the movements in fugal style, the statements made about Opus 2 are on the whole valid for Opus 8, particularly for Sonatas Nos. 4–9, which have the same scoring (two violins, bass, and b.c.) as all the works in Opus 2. The majority of these movements are fugatos, but at least two are fully developed fugues: in *La Bonga* (No. 5) and *La Pepola* (No. 7). The initial fugue of *La Bonga* consists of three expositions and two episodes:

Measures:	1–5	6–8	8–15	16–19	20–28	29–36
	Theme, 3 times	Episode	Theme, 4 times	Episode	Theme, 5 times	Coda

The two episodes are developed out of a short motif (and its inversion) that could be regarded as a countertheme. Fig. 95 shows the close of the second exposition and the beginning of the second episode.

FIGURE 95. CAZZATI: SONATA LA BONGA (OPUS 8, 1648).

The tonal relations in the expositions are the same as in Opus 2. In the four-voice fugues, No. 10 follows the scheme I–IV–I–IV and No. 11 the scheme I–IV–IV–IV, both indicating that in the older fugue (also in motets, ricercars, etc.) the answer at the fourth was greatly favored.

Heinrich Riemann, discussing both Opus 2 and Opus 8, says of *Canzone La Lucilla* (No. 9) that its second section (I would say "movement") "is worked out with particular love."[4] He reproduces the entire movement, a *Grave* of ten measures, unfortunately with a modification that agrees with his theory about the upbeat but that actually distorts the character of the music. Fig. 96 shows the beginning of this movement in its original notation, together with Riemann's interpretation, which destroys the weight characteristic of this *Grave*.

Summing up, it can be said that Cazzati employs only two styles of composition: The *Grave* movements are in homophonic style, and the *Allegro* movements are mostly fugatos plus a few real fugues. In the sonatas *a Violino solo* (Nos. 2 and 3), the violin imitates itself, playing the theme on different degrees of the scale. Only once does Cazzati employ a totally different technique: In the triple-meter section of *Sonata La Pepola*, No. 7, the two violins move almost exclusively in parallel thirds.

FIGURE 96. CAZZATI: CANZONE LA LUCILLA (OPUS 8, 1648).

In the Simphonias (Nos. 12 and 13) Cazzati gives a new meaning to this term, that is, of a four-voice composition in chordal style. No. 12 has a slow introduction followed by an extended *Allegro* movement in triple meter that contains several echoes (*Forte*, *Piano*). After a few measures of *Adagio* the triple-meter movement is repeated *Presto*. *Simphonia* No. 13 is considerably shorter. Compared with the sonatas, both pieces are undistinguished.

In his next two publications Cazzati turned to the field of dance music. In Antwerp in 1651, Phalèse brought out the collection *Corenti e balletti di Sign. Mauritio Cazzati*, which very likely is a piracy of an Italian first edition that is lost. Of this Antwerp printing only the *Basso* is preserved,[5] and it is not until an edition of 1659 that a complete copy is preserved: *Correnti balletti gagliarde a 3, e 4. . . . Novamente ristampati. . .* (no opus number).[6] It contains twelve correnti, eleven balletti, one aria, one capriccio, three gagliardas, and one ciacona. All the compositions are *a 3.* (two violins, bass, and b.c.) except the last *Balletto* (No. 23) and *Aria* (No. 24), which are *a 4.* (two violins, viola, violone, and b.c.). The *basso continuo* part book is entitled *Spinetta o Chitarrone*.

The correnti are the customary short pieces in binary form and with sections of irregular length, for instance: ‖:12:‖:15:‖ (No. 4); ‖:8:‖:10:‖ (No. 5); or ‖:13:‖:15:‖ (No. 6). In addition the sections are divided into phrases of irregular length; in this they differ—I think to their advantage—from the dances of a later period, which are subject to the principle of the four-measure phrase. Two interesting details in the correnti should be mentioned here. *Corrente* No. 5 contains another example of the Corelli clash, which had occurred in a balletto by Marini (also note that in the second measure of Fig. 97a violin II does not rise to the tonic but descends to the third). The other interesting detail is the descending sequence in *Corrente* No. 2 (Fig. 97b), which is an early example of a technique typical of the late Baroque period (Corelli and Bach).

FIGURE 97. CAZZATI: a. CORRENTE QUINTA LA BOZOLINA;
b. CORRENTE SECONDA LA GUASTELLESA (1651).

The balletti are even shorter and more irregular than the correnti. The last *Balletto* (No. 23) differs from the other dances of the collection by being written in four voice parts. It is actually a suite (*Sonata da camera*), consisting of *Entrada del Balletto, Balletto*,

Trecia del Balletto, Galiarda del Balletto, and *Corrente del Balletto,* all in A minor except the *Corrente,* which is in A major. All the dances are in binary form (with irregular section lengths) except the *Entrada* and the *Trecia,* each of which is a short continuous piece of eight and nine measures respectively.[7]

Aria (No. 24) consists of a sixteen-bar theme (*Prima parte*) with two variations (*Seconda, Terza parte*). *Capriccio sopra sette notte* [*sic*] (No. 25) is based on the ostinato

The continuo part book directs that it be repeated 82 times. Nos. 26–28 are gagliardas, each followed by its Italian *Voltata.* The second and third gagliardas are in the customary 3/2, but the first, curiously, is notated in **C**. But on closer examination we find a situation similar to that in Marini's *Romanesca* of 1620 (Fig. 30): the piece is notated in 2/2 (**c**), but its real sense is 3/2 as Fig. 98 shows. The purpose of the notation in duple meter is the same as it was with Marini, namely, to indicate a slower tempo; this is confirmed by the fact that *Gagliarda prima* is notated in quarter and eighth notes while the *seconda* and *terza* are in halves and quarters.

FIGURE 98. CAZZATI: GALIARDE PRIMA (1651). a. ORIGINAL NOTATION; b. ACTUAL METER.

One should not confuse the voltata that follows each gagliarda with the volta, a dance that was very popular about 1600, especially in England, where it was often called *Lavolta* or *Levalto.* All three voltatas are ostinato compositions[8] based on the same ground bass but on different scale degrees, in accordance with the key of the respective galliarda: A, G, and E. It always comprises three measures of **c**, which are once more to be interpreted as two 3/2 measures, as shown in the following scheme of the first *Voltata:*

original notation

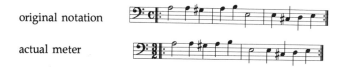

actual meter

From the upper parts it appears that the ostinato of the first and the third *Voltata* is to be played seven times, that of the second, eight times. *Gagliarda seconda* is designated *Del Signor Pietro Nichesola,* while the *Voltata* is said to be *del Autore.*

The last composition of the publication is a *Ciacona* with *Balletto della Ciacona.* The *Ciacona* consists of more than 30 variations of an ostinato comprising two 3/2 measures. Variations 11–13 are particularly interesting. Here the two violins do not perform figuration but play a two-voice upper pedal point, which creates a dissonance against the ostinato in the second measure of each variation (Fig. 99).[9] The *Ciacona* closes with a

FIGURE 99. CAZZATI: CIACONA (1651).

Balletto, a short piece in duple meter (4:‖:6).

In 1654 another publication by Cazzati appeared containing mostly dance music: *Correnti e Balletti a cinque alla francese, et all'italiana, con alcune Sonate a 5. 6. 7. 8 . . . opera XV. . . .*). Only one part book of this edition exists (in the British museum),[10] but a new edition, published in 1667 by Giacomo Monti in Bologna, is completely preserved. It consists of six part books: *Violino I, Violino II, Alto Viola, Tenore Viola, Basso Violone da brazzo (Violone* and *Basso Trombone* in the parts), and *Basso continuo.* It contains 24 correnti, twelve balletti, and four sonatas. The correnti and balletti are all *a 5.* (two violins, alto, tenor, violone, and b.c.), while the sonatas are respectively *a 5.* (two violins, alto, tenor, *Violone overo Trombone,* and b.c.), *a 6.* (two violins, alto, tenor, two basses, and b.c.), *a 7.* (three violins, two altos, tenor, two basses [violone and trombone], and b.c.), and *a 8.* (two violins, two altos, two tenors, two violones, and b.c.).

The correnti are short pieces in binary form with a total length of 20–25 measures. They are alternatingly designated *francese* and *italiana.* Thus they give us an idea of what was meant by these two types around the middle of the seventeenth century in northern Italy. Later they were differentiated as *Courante* (in the Bach suites) and *Corrente.* The only recognizable difference in these pieces is that the *francese* are in 3/4 with three quarter notes to a measure, while the *italiana* are in 3/2 with three half notes to a measure. This probably means that the latter are to be played more slowly than the former, although the reverse was customary in keyboard music: French courantes for harpsichord, for instance, those by Chambonnières, are always in moderate tempo and have as a time signature 3/2 or 6/4; while the Italian correnti, for instance, those by Frescobaldi, are fast and have the signature 3/4.

The balletti of 1654 are slightly more extended than those of 1651, but still consist of two short sections of irregular length, for instance, *Balletto primo* (‖:5:‖:7:‖), or *Balletto sesto* (‖:7:‖:7:‖). An exception is *Balletto terzo,* which consists of two sections each of eight measures. It is to be played *Alla Breve overo come stà, ma presto.* The *come stà* refers to the signature C (which is used for all the other balletti); in other words, *alla semibreve,* ¢ (which requires a tempo twice as slow as *alla breve*). Therefore this balletto is to be played much faster (*ma presto*) than the others (actually twice as fast). Thus it appears that principles of mensural notation were valid as late as 1650. *Balletto duodecimo* is a continuous piece of eleven measures, called *Sopra L'aria ma si turbi, o resereni.* Very likely this is not a popular song, but an operatic aria.

The four sonatas that close Cazzati's Opus 15 were obviously influenced by the Venetian school, especially the last one, whose eight instruments are divided into *Primo choro* and *Secondo choro.* Each sonata consists of three or four movements as clearly separated by repeat signs, fermatas, or double bars as are Cazzati's earlier sonatas.

The last sonata, *detta La Brembata,* consists of three movements, the last of which is to be repeated:

Sonata detta La Brembata. A 8.

Movement	1	2	3	
Meter	9 D⌢	28 D	‖ : 43 Tr : ‖	Si replica alla
Tempo	adagio	allegro	allegro	Sesquialtera se piace.

The sonata begins with a homophonic *adagio* for all the instruments; it consists of three solemn invocations of three measures each. The second movement begins with a five-measure "fanfare" by the *Primo choro,* which is immediately answered by the *Secondo choro* (see Fig. 100). The further course of this movement is completely dominated by the rhythmically precise motifs of the beginning, especially by the one marked m in Fig. 100. The last movement, which is in 3/4 meter, has a structure similar to that of the second but is less impressive.

FIGURE 100. CAZZATI: SONATA DETTA LA BRAMBATA (OPUS 15, 1654).

Cazzati's Opus 18, *Suonate a due Violini col suo Basso continuo per l'Organo, et un ultro à beneplacito per Tiorba ò Violone . . .,* appeared in 1656 in Venice. Of the first edition only the *Organo* part book is preserved, but there exist several complete reprints, among them one that appeared in 1659 in Bologna. It contains twelve sonatas and one capriccio, all for two violins, bass, and b.c., but the bass (which is identical with the continuo, including the thorough-bass figures) is marked *à beneplacito.*

Nine of the sonatas have four movements; *Sonata terza* has three, *Sonata ottava* five, and *Sonata duodecima* two movements, the second of which consists of two sections without interruption. For the first time every movement has a tempo indication, for instance, in No. 2: *largo, adagio, grave,* and *allegro;* and in No. 4: *largo, grave, allegro,* and *presto.* None of the sonatas have the order slow, fast, slow, fast, which is typical of the late *sonata da chiesa.* Each sonata has only one movement in triple meter; this is another indication of Cazzati's striving for structural norms. There is also increased use of repeat signs; they are missing only in some homophonic *grave* movements. Because the four-movement form predominates and tempo indications are used consistently, the sonatas of Cazzati's Opus 18 represent a large advance over those of his Opus 2 and Opus 8 (not to mention those of other composers) toward the formal structure of the fully developed *sonata da chiesa.*

Let us now turn from matters of form to questions of content and of style. The *allegro* movements of Opus 18 are not only slightly shorter on the average than those of Cazzati's early sonatas but also less strictly written. While in the early sonatas at least three movements are fully developed fugues, none of the *allegros* of the Opus 18 go beyond a fugato. In some of these movements, Cazzati uses for the expositions a procedure employed earlier by Merula: the first voice has a rest while the theme is imitated, so that the imitation is clearly audible and not obscured by a counterpoint. See the beginning of *Sonata duodecima La Strozza* in Fig. 101.

FIGURE 101. CAZZATI: SONATA DUODECIMA LA STROZZA (OPUS 18, 1656).

The slow movements of Opus 18 are no less impressive than those of the earlier sonatas but are often written more freely and more individually. The slow movement of *Sonata quinta La Fiasca* consists of three sections: a nine-measure *Grave* for *Violino primo solo*; a *Grave* of the same length in which *Violino secondo solo* plays the same melody transposed to the lower fifth; and an eight-measure *Adagio* for both violins. This is a contrast movement in which the scoring changes, not the tempo or the meter.

Opus 18 closes with *Capriccio sopra sedici note*. Like *Capriccio sopra sette notte*, from 1651, it is an ostinato composition, but much more complex. The earlier capriccio has a two-measure formula that is repeated 82 times, while the present one consists of four separate movements, the first three of which have their own ostinatos (always of sixteen notes). The last movement is based on a triple-meter variant of the first ostinato. The tempo changes from one movement to the next, as do the number of variations, which, by the way, is considerably more limited than in the 1651 capriccio. The following scheme shows the structure of the Opus 18 capriccio, which is a unique example of an "ostinato sonata":

Capriccio sopra sedici note (Opus 18)

Movement	1	2	3	4
	Ostinato I	Ostinato II	Ostinato III	Ostinato IV
Meter	4 D, 6 repeats	8 D, 2 repeats	8 Tr, 4 repeats	2 D, 5 repeats
Tempo	largo	grave	allegro	vivace

Cazzati's next publication for violin, Opus 22, appeared in 1660 in Bologna, with the title *Trattenimenti per camera, d'Arie, Correnti, e Balletti, a due Violini, e Violone, se piace. Con Passacaglio, Ciaccona, & un capriccio sopra 12 note.* . . . It contains fourteen compositions for two violins, violone or theorbo, and spinet (b.c.). The first eleven pieces form a coherent whole, that is, music for a masked ball that may have taken place in the home of Bartolomeo Zaniboni, to whom the publication is dedicated. This group, to which the title *Trattenimenti* (entertainment) chiefly refers, consists of: No. 1, *Aria*; No. 2, *Ballo delle Dame*; No. 3, *Ballo degli Cavaglieri*; No. 4, *Ballo de Contadini*; No. 5,

Ballo de Tedeschi; No. 6, *Ballo de Satiri*; No. 7, *Ballo de Matacini*; No. 8, *Ballo delle Ombre*; No. 9, *Ballo delle Ninfe*; No. 10, *Brando primo*; and No. 11, *Brando secondo*. *Aria* (No. 1) is followed by *Ballo d'Aria*, and each *Ballo* (Nos. 2–9) is followed by *Sua Corrente*. Thus, the entertainment began with an aria (perhaps a song and dance by a single person). Then came dances by the ladies and by the gentlemen, then various groups in characteristic costumes. Finally all persons present danced the two brandi. *Ballo de Matacini* belongs to the same type as *Matassin oder Todten Tantz* in the tablature of Augustus Nörmiger (1598), which evidently was danced in skeleton costumes. Both Nörmiger's and Cazzati's "dances of death" are in 3/8 meter.

Opus 22 closes with three ostinato compositions: *Passacaglio*, *Ciaccona*, and *Capriccio sopra 12 note*. The *Passacaglio* consists of twenty variations of the descending tetrachord in E major; the *Ciaccona* of 24 variations of the ostinato

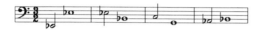

The *Capriccio* consists of twelve variations of a three-measure ostinato containing twelve notes, followed by four variations based on the triple-meter variant of the same ostinato. This capriccio has a much simpler structure than *Capriccio sopra sedici note* in Opus 18.

Cazzati's Opus 30 appeared in 1662: *Correnti, e Balletti per sonare nella Spinetta Leuto, ò Tiorba; Overo Violino, e Violone, col Secondo Violino à Beneplacito*. The publication consists of a score (*Partitura di Correnti . . .*) and a part book for violin II (*Violino secondo di Correnti . . .*). To judge from the title, the pieces are to be played primarily on the spinet, lute, or theorbo, from the score. For performance by a string trio, which is indicated in the title as an alternative, the part books for violin I and violin II would be needed, but only the latter is preserved.

The contents consist of twelve pairs of balletto—corrente (both parts in the same key), two brandi, and one *Aria over balletto*. Some of the balletti are in slow tempo (*largo, adagio*); others are fast (*vivace, presto*); while the correnti are all fast (*presto, allegro*). Phrases of irregular length predominate. Thus, each corrente includes one or more phrases of five measures, for instance, in *Corrente ottava*: ‖:5 4 4 5:‖:5 2 6:‖. *Balletto secondo* is a curiosity that can claim the world's record for brevity: it consists of four (if repeated, eight) measures to be played *presto*, so that the performance takes only a few seconds. One would like to know the reason for this joke.

With his next publication, *Sonate à due, tre, quattro, e cinque. Con alcune per Tromba . . .*, Opus 35, which appeared in 1665 in Bologna, Cazzati returns to the sonata, which he had cultivated in his publications of 1642 and 1648. Opus 35 contains twelve sonatas: two *A due* (two violins and b.c.), four *A 3.* (two violins, bass, and b.c.), three *A 4.* (two violins, alto, bass, and b.c.), and three *A 5.* (trumpet, violin, alto, tenor, bass, and b.c.). In a postscript Cazzati says that the trumpet in the last three can be replaced by a violin. He further advises that *Sonata detta la Caprera*, No. 10, which is in D major, should be played with a stopped trumpet, otherwise the entire sonata has to be transposed down a whole tone, to C major. Exactly the reverse holds for Sonatas Nos. 11 and 12.

While every movement in the sonatas of Opus 18 has a tempo indication, that is not the case in Opus 35, where ten movements (mostly first movements) have no indication of tempo. In Opus 18 four-movement sonatas prevail, while there are only two sonatas of this kind in Opus 35—No. 2, *La Tanara*, and No. 6, *La Marescota*. In the remaining ten sonatas the number of movements varies from two (for instance, No. 5, *La Razza*) to six (for instance, No. 1, *La Gonzaga*). Also, in Opus 18 every sonata has one, and only one, movement in triple meter, while among the sonatas of Opus 35 there are several that have two such movements. All in all, the sonatas of Opus 35 present a less-uniform (one might also say, a less-progressive) picture than those of Opus 18.

The fast movements of the two-voice, three-voice, and four-voice sonatas are all written in fugal style, except for the final movement of *La Marescota* (No. 6), which consists of two homophonic sections: a fourteen-measure *tremolo* in duple meter (affective improvisation?) and a 56-measure *Presto* in 3/4. While in the fast movements of the two-voice sonatas (Nos. 1 and 2) Cazzati limits himself to a fugato, those of the three- and four-voice sonatas are all fully developed fugues (except for No. 6). The final movement of *La Fachenetta* (No. 3), 81 measures of *Presto* in 3/4 meter, is a three-voice double fugue in which additional short motifs are strictly imitated. Particularly important with regard to the development of the fugue are the fast movements of Sonatas Nos. 7–9 because they are all fully developed four-voice fugues, surely the first to be found in violin music. The fugue of *La Sampiera* (No. 8) begins with the "regular" exposition I–V–I–V with tonal answer, as the initial leap of a fifth

becomes a leap of a fourth

The last four-voice sonata, *La Malvasia* (No. 9), has three fast movements (*Allegro, Vivace,* and *Presto presto*), each of which begins with a I–V–I–V exposition. The second and third have tonal answers and are based on the same theme.

The slow movements of Sonatas Nos. 1–9 contain several interesting stylistic details. *La Marescota* (No. 6) has an eight-measure introduction in which the three string instruments (violin I, violin II, and violone) play arpeggio figurations above a D-minor pedal point on the organ. This is probably the earliest example in violin music of an extended passage consisting exclusively of broken chords, a technique used by many later composers, among them Corelli (see Figs. 172 and 173). The second movement of *La Fachenetta* (No. 3) is a *Grave* of 29 measures in which the two violins first alternate, then combine into a sequence that is an early manifestation of a formula that became commonplace 50 years later (see Fig. 102). *Sonata La Sampiera* (No. 8) consists of two movements, the second of which begins with a homophonic *Grave* of fifteen measures and continues with 59 measures of *Largo* in 3/4 meter in which several short motifs— among them a chromatic one—are thoroughly imitated.

Sonatas Nos. 10–12 are written for trumpet, string quartet (*Canto Violino, Alto Viola, Tenore Viola,* and *Violone*), and continuo (for organ and *Tiorba* or *Contra basso*). Here fugal style is replaced by concerto style, with passages for solo trumpet alternating with the string quartet as *tutti*. None of these sonatas has a movement for which a slow tempo

FIGURE 102. CAZZATI: SONATA À 3. LA FACHENETTA (OPUS 35, 1665).

is indicated. It is true that some movements have no tempo indication, but whether there is a slow one among them, remains at least doubtful.

Cazzati's next publication with violin music is *Varii e diversi Capricci per Camera, e per Chiesá . . .*, Opus 50, which appeared in 1669 in Bologna. All 50 compositions are written for two violins, bass, and b.c., with alternative scorings *a 1.*, *a 2.*, and *a 3.* indicated for many pieces. The book contains fourteen capriccios, eleven balli, seven brandi, six gigas, five correnti, four allemandes, two sarabandas, and one gagliarda.

The most important part of the contents are the fourteen capriccios, which in the title are said to be *Varii, e diversi*. Seven are in binary form, and one of these, called *Capriccio detto il Ranuzzi*, is a "bagatelle" with only six measures in each section. Five other capriccios resemble sonatas. Of these, *Capriccio detto il Guastavillani* consists of four movements—*Largo, Allegro, Grave,* and *Allegro*—and is an early example of the *sonata da chiesa*. The last two capriccios are highly individualistic: *Capriccio in Ecco detto il Mareschotti* consists entirely of echoes between violin I and violin II, first several times in half notes, then in longer passages largely made up of broken triads. *Capriccio detto il Gozzadini de diversi Tempi, e Toni* is more than 400 measures long (probably more than 700 if all the repeats are observed). It consists of about twenty sections with different time signatures, among them one marked *Presto* in 3/16, the beginning of which is reproduced in Fig. 103. The *Toni* (keys) also change: at the beginning are D major, E major, A major, and G major; later, F major, B♭ major, and C minor.

FIGURE 103. CAZZATI: CAPRICCIO DETTO IL GOZZADINI (OPUS 50, 1669).

A few remarks are in order about the dance pieces. *Corrente italiana con Varie Partite,* at the beginning of the collection, is not a set of variations but a series of twelve correnti. *Corrente in Tromba detta la Spada* is written in the style of a trumpet fanfare. The gigas always begin with the imitation of a short motif; and in *Giga detta l'Angeletta*, the second section begins with the motif inverted, as do many gigues of Bach (see Fig. 104). The two sarabandas are *presto* and in 3/8 meter, thus differing from the customary character of this dance. Two of the four allemandas are in triple time: *la Ghisilardi* is *presto* in 3/2, and *la Ghisigliera* is *allegro e presto* in 3/4. Finally, we note that *Corrente detta la Palcotta*

FIGURE 104. CAZZATI: GIGA DETTA L'ANGELETTA (OPUS 50, 1669).

(No. 7) contains a measure in which the two violins play six parallel fifths in eighth notes:

This is the most stunning, though by no means the only, indication of an artistic boldness that we regard today with astonishment and admiration, but which was severely criticized by Cazzati's contemporaries, especially by Guilio Cesare Arresti (1617–1692). Cazzati defended his "errors," but because of the controversy, in 1673 he lost his position at San Petronio.

Cazzati's last publication of violin music, Opus 55 of 1670, *Sonate a due Istromenti cioè Violino, è Violone* . . . contains twelve sonatas. The violin part book carries the remark *Violino, ò Cornetto*, a reversion to the old practice of entrusting the upper part to either a string or a wind instrument. The bass is for violone, the b.c. for *Organo, ò Tiorba*. This publication is probably the first to contain exclusively compositions for violin, bass, and b.c., in other words, duets for violin (or cornetto) and violone. The organ (or theorbo) functions mostly as a *basso seguente* and only occasionally as a supporting bass.

The sonatas each consist of three or four movements; the first is to be repeated, and sometimes the second or the third as well. Three sonatas consist only of fast movements: No. 6 (*Allegro, Vivace,* and *Allegro*), No. 9 (*Vivace, Vivace,* and *Allegro*), and No. 11 (*Vivace, Presto,* and *Vivace*).

Most of the movements belong to the category of imitative counterpoint, which is handled with great diversity. At one end of the scale is the final movement of Sonata No. 10, a fully developed two-voice fugue of 45 measures during which the theme appears fifteen times. At the other is the last movement of No. 12, in which the theme in its full form appears twice at the beginning, then completely disappears from the violin part, and is quoted in the violone part a few times in a shortened form. In six movements (for instance, in the first movement, *Largo*, of Sonata No. 3) Cazzati employs for the exposition the same curious procedure used by Merula, Uccellini, and himself in his Opus 18; the *dux* has a rest when the *comes* enters, so that the second instrument is as clearly audible as the first, without being obscured by a counterpoint.

Sonatas Nos. 5, 9, 10, and 11 begin with *Allegro* movements whose themes belong to a well-known type from a later period; that is, they resemble concertos by Vivaldi and Bach that open with "three hammer strokes." In Sonata No. 9, which consists of three fast movements, the three strokes occur in the themes of all three movements; this is a particularly impressive realization of the cyclic principle (see Fig. 105).

FIGURE 105. CAZZATI: SONATA NONA, LA MALCHIAVELLA (OPUS 55, 1670).

Two movements have unusual constructions: The initial movement of *Sonata duode-cima. La zoppia*, a 35-measure *Largo*, consists exclusively of alternating motifs, as follows:

Measure	1	2	3	4	5	6	7	8	9	10	11	12	13	14	15	
Violin	a		a		a		a		b		b		c	a	c	etc.
Violone		b		b		b	a		a			a	c	b	c	

Another peculiar and surprising construction occurs in the second movement of *Sonata decima, La Casarenga*, a *Largo* of 35 measures. The dancelike rhythm that prevails through-out comes neither from Italy nor from France but obviously from Spain, the home of the fandango and similar dances. Fig. 106 shows the beginning of this movement, for which the stirring sounds of the theorbo are more suitable than the rigid chords of the organ; and for the upper part, the cornetto is preferable to the violin.

FIGURE 106. CAZZATI: SONATA DECIMA, LA CASARENGA (OPUS 55, 1670).

Manuscript Rés. Vm⁷ 673 of the Bibliothèque nationale of Paris (often referred to as the MS. Rost) contains eleven compositions by Cazzati (Cassati, Casati). Eight are copied from his Opus 18; the rest (Rost Nos. 36, 65, and 67) have not been identified but most likely are copied from other publications by this master.

With his Opus 55, Cazzati, at the age of 50, leaves violin music. His production in this field is preserved in ten publications (out of a total of 88 publications of music), five of which are given over to the sonata (or canzona). The others contain mostly dance music, an area to which he has contributed much more than is commonly assumed: with more than 100 pieces he is second only to Bononcini, who wrote more than 170 (see table, p. 226). Cazzati's historical importance lies in the fact that in his first pub-lication of violin music, Opus 2 of 1642, he gave the sonata a form that remained valid for almost 250 years. His sonatas each comprise several sections so clearly separated that they can be considered movements. About half of them consist of four movements. Many of his sonatas are captivating, with ingenious ideas and interesting treatment of themes or motifs. He should be praised, not censured, for the serious and wholly nonvirtuosic character of his style.

NOTES

1. But see HouleM for methodology.
2. There is a similar situation in the organ music of the period. See ApelG, p. 378, concerning a 1631 print of Johann Klemm a.d.J.
3. *Jan Pieterszon Sweelinck, Werken voor Orgel en Clavicembel*, edited by M. Seiffert (Amsterdam, 1943), p. 211.
4. RiemannH, pp. 146ff.
5. See SartoriB, vol. II, 1651d.
6. Ibid., 1659b.
7. What is the *Trecia*? In the balletti of J.H. Schmelzer we encounter the *Trezza* (see DTÖ, vol. LVI, p. 9), which is quite different from Cazzati's duple-meter *Trecia*, which resembles a courante or a gagliarda.
8. The name is from the Italian *voltare* (turn) and refers to the turning back of the ostinato.
9. Similarly and somewhat earlier, Frescobaldi did the same in *Partite sopra Passacagli* in his *Secondo libro delle toccate*, of 1627. See ApelG, p. 464, Fig. 494.
10. See SartoriB, vol II, p. 123.

SOURCES

Canzoni a 3. doi violini, e violone col suo basso continuo, e nel fine un Confitebor & un Letatus, a 3. voci. . . . Opus 2. Venice: Bartolomeo Magni, 1642.   RISM C1578.
　　Poland: Wroclaw, Biblioteka Uniwersytecka (V I, Violone).
　　West Germany: Wolfenbüttel, Herzog-August-Bibliothek, Musikabteilung (V I and II, Violone, b.c.)
Reprint:
Bologna: Evangelista Dozza, 1663 (3d printing).   RISM C1579.
　　Great Britain: Oxford, Bodleian Library.
　　Italy: Bologna, Civico Museo (V I, Violone, b.c.).

Il secondo libro delle sonate a una, doi, tre, e quattro istromenti. . . . Opus 8. Venice: Alessandro Vincenti, 1648.   RISM C1587.
　　Great Britain: Oxford, Bodleian Library (V I and II, Violetta, Violone, Organ).
　　Italy: Bologna, Archivio dell'Accademia filarmonica; Bologna, Civico Museo.
　　Poland: Wroclaw, Biblioteka Uniwersytecka.

Correnti e balletti a cinque, alla francese e all'itagliana con alcune Sonate a 5. 6. 7. 8. . . . Opus 15. Venice: Alessandro Vincenti, 1654.   RISM C1596.
　　Great Britain: London, British Library (V II; lacks V I, Alto Viola, Tenor Viola, Bass Violone, b.c.).
Reprint:
Bologna: Giacomo Monti, 1667 (*ristampata da Mario Silvani*).   RISM C1597.
　　Great Britain: Oxford, Bodleian Library.
　　Italy: Bologna, Archivio dell'Accademia filarmonica.

Sonate a due violini col suo basso continuo per l'organo, & un altro a beneplacito per tiorba, o violone. . . . Opus 18. Venice: Francesco Magni, 1656.   RISM C1602.
　　Poland: Wroclaw, Biblioteka Uniwersytecka (Organ; lacks V I and II, Violone).
Reprints:
Antwerp; Les héritiers de Pierre Phalèse, 1657.   RISM C1603.
　　Netherlands: The Hague, Gemeente Museum (V I).

Bologna: Gli eredi di Vittorio Benacci, 1659.   RISM C1604.
Italy: Bologna, Civico Museo (4 parts).

Sonate a due violini con suo basso continuo. Antwerp; Les héritiers de Pierre Phalèse, 1674.   RISM C1605.
　　Great Britain: Durham, Cathedral Library.
　　United States: New York Public Library at Lincoln Center.
　　West Germany: Lüneburg, Ratsbücherei und Stadtarchiv der Stadt Lüneburg, Musikabteilung (V I and II, b.c.).
. . . et un'altro a beneplacito per tiorba o violone. Bologna: Giacomo Monti, 1679.   RISM C1606.
　　Italy: Bologna, Civico Museo (4 parts).

Trattenimenti per camera d'arie, correnti, e balletti, a due violini, e violone, se piace, con passacaglio, ciaccona, & un capriccio sopra 12 note. . . . Opus 22. Bologna: Antonio Pisarri, 1660.   RISM C1613.
　　Italy: Bologna, Archivio dell'Accademia filarmonica; Archivio di San Petronio (V I and II; lacks Violone, Spinetta); Civico Museo.
Edition:
Monumenta Bononiensia, vol. 13. Bologna: Antique Musicae Italicae Studiosi, 1971 (facsimile).

Correnti, e balletti per sonare nella spinetta, leuto, o tiorba; overo violino, e violone, col secondo violino a beneplacito. . . . Opus 30. Bologna: Antonio Pisarri, 1662.   RISM C1624.
　　Italy: Bologna, Civico Museo.
Reprint:
. . . Partitura di correnti e balletti. . . . Bologna; Evangelista Dozza, 1663.   RISM C1625.
　　Italy: Bologna, Civico Museo.
Edition:
Florence: Studio per Edizione Scelte, 1979.

Sonate a due, tre, quattro, e cinque, con alcune per Tromba. . . . Opus 35. Bologna: Mario Silvani, 1665.   RISM C1631.
　　Italy: Bologna, Archivio di San Petronio; Civico Museo (7 parts).
Reprints:
Venice: Francesco Magni detto Gardano, 1668.   RISM C1632.
　　Italy: Bologna, Civico Museo (Tenor-Viola, Violone); Rome, Biblioteca dell' Accademia dei Lincei e Corsiniana.
Antwerp: Lucca de Potter, 1667.   RISM C1633.
　　Belgium: Brussels, Bibliothèque Royale Albert Iᵉʳ (V I and II).

Varii, e diversi capricci per camera, e per chiesa, da sonare con diversi istromenti, a uno, due, e tre. . . . Opus 50. Bologna: s.n., 1669.   RISM C1650.
　　Italy: Bologna, Archivio dell'Accademia filarmonica; Civico Museo (V I and II, Violone/Theorbo, b.c.).

Sonate a due istromenti cioè violino e violone. . . . Opus 55.   Bologna: s.n., 1670.
RISM C1656.
　　Italy: Bologna, Civico Museo (3 parts).

Works without opus number:
Correnti e balletti . . . a 3. e 4. Antwerp: Les héritiers de Pierre Phalèse), 1651.   RISM C1666.

France: Paris, Bibliothèque Geneviève Thibault (B).
Reprint:
Correnti, balletti, gagliarde a 3. e 4. . . . novamente ristampati. Venice: Francesco Magni,
1659.   RISM C1667.
  Italy: Bologna, Archivio dell'Accademia filarmonica (V I and II, Violone, Spinetta/
  Chitarrone).
Edition:
Monumenta Bononiensia, vol. 13. Bologna: Antique Musicae Italicae Studiosi, 1971.

Miscellaneous:
Eleven works for violin, eight of which are concordant with Opus 18, are preserved in
France: Paris, Bibliothèque nationale, MS. Rés. VM⁷ 673 (MS. Rost).

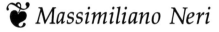

Massimiliano Neri

Massimiliano Neri, who was born about 1615, was first organist at San Marco in
Venice from 1644 to 1664. He then went to Cologne as the Elector's organist and
chapelmaster. He died after 1666. In the prefaces of his publications, which appeared
during his activity in Venice, he calls himself "De gli Accademici Erranti di Brescia
l'Affaticato" (Once an academic of the Erranti of Brescia). In his Opus 2 (1651), he
says that he and his descendants were raised to nobility in 1626 by Emperor Ferdinand
III (to whom the collection is dedicated) because of the merits of his father, Gio.
Giacomo Neri.

Neri's first publication, *Sonate e Canzone a quatro da sonarsi con diversi stromenti in Chiesa,*
et in Camera. Con alcune Correnti . . . opera prima . . . , appeared in 1644. According to
Eitner's *Quellenlexikon* there were two complete copies of five part books, one in Berlin,
the other in Breslau (now Wroclaw). Today, the Berlin copy is lost, and at the University
Library in Wroclaw only three part books are preserved: *Violino II, Alto Viola,* and *Viola*
over Fagotto.[1] Very likely the continuo part from the Berlin copy has been missing since
about 1830, as in both Winterfeld's copy and in Wasielewski's *Instrumentalsätzen* (1874),
a corrente from Neri's Opus 1 is reproduced without the *basso continuo.*
  Opus 1 consists—somewhat in contradiction to the *a quatro* of the title—of four canzonas *a 3* (two violins, alto, and b.c.), two canzonas and two sonatas *a 4* (two violins,
alto, bass, and b.c.), and six correnti about which the title says: "Correnti pure a quatro,
che si ponno sonare a tre, a due ancora, lasciando fuori le parti di mezzo" (which can
be played *a 3* or *a 2*, leaving out the middle part). Each composition carries the indication
of a church mode, for instance, *Canzone prima a 3. Ottavo tuono* and *Corrente prima. Terzo*
tuono.
  Although Neri's Opus 1 is incompletely preserved, the existing part books yield many
details, mainly concerning the structure, which is a very important aspect of the sonatas
of the period. All the compositions are separated into movements—by fermatas, double
bars, or repeat signs—as clearly as those in Cazzati's sonatas. Occasionally the separation
is made even more specific by leaving the remainder of the line blank and starting the

next movement on a new line, like a new paragraph. Most of the sonatas or canzonas (once more, it is impossible to differentiate between them) consist of four or five movements, but No. 2, *Canzone secunda a 3.*, has six and No. 5, *Canzone prima a 4.*, has three. Nearly all of them begin with a lively fugato ending with a repeat sign; obviously this first movement is to be played twice. The only exception is the first movement (a fugato) of *Sonata seconda a 4.* (No. 8), which is to be played *adagio* and consequently lacks the repeat sign. Schematic representations of two compositions follow:

Canzone terza a 3. Settimo tuono (two violins, bass, and b.c.)

Movement	1		2	3		4	5	
Meter	36 D ⌒ :	‖ : 13 Tr ⌒	‖ 24 Tr ⌒	‖ 12 D ⌒	‖ 32 Tr ⌒	‖
Tempo	fast	‖ adasio		‖ fast (?)	‖ adasio	

Canzone prima a 4. Quinto tuono (two violins, alto, bass, and b.c.)

Movement	1		2a	b	c	d	e	3a	b	
Meter	12 D ⌒ :	‖ : 4 D	5 D	5 D	9 D	6 D ⌒	‖ 22 Tr	6 D	‖
Tempo	fast	‖ adasio	presto	adasio	presto	[adasio]	‖ largo	fast	

Although the violin I and *basso continuo* parts are missing, it is apparent that in *Canzone terza* movements 1, 3, and 5 are fugues, while movements 2 and 4 are homophonic. The third movement is based on a chromatic theme. Fig. 107 shows its beginning, with violin I added.

FIGURE 107. NERI: CANZONE TERZA A TRE (OPUS 1, 1644).

In the second movement of *Canzone prima* the former short *adasio* and *presto* sections alternate five times, homophonic, the latter in fugue style. The very stimulating surprise is reminiscent of similar effects in the works of older Venetian masters such as Castello and Fontana. Fig. 108 shows the beginning of this passage (without violin I).

FIGURE 108. NERI: CANZONE PRIMA A QUATRO (OPUS 1, 1644).

Sonata prima a 4. is yet another realization of the concerto principle. Its fourth movement begins with a solo for violin I consisting of a four-measure *Adasio* in half notes and a seven-measure *Largo* in sixteenth and 32d notes; this is repeated by *Violino Secondo solo* at the lower fifth; and the movement ends with a seven-measure *Largo a due* (violins I and II). The *Largo* solo passages consist of the repetition of a one-measure formula.

The second and fifth correnti of Opus 1 are preserved in Winterfeld's transcription, though without the *basso continuo*. All six correnti are in binary form and nearly symmetrical; for instance, *Corrente quinta* has the form ‖ : 11 : ‖ : 12 : ‖ .

In 1651 Neri published his Opus 2, *Sonate da suonersi con varii strumenti. A tre sino a dodici. . . . Consecrata alla Sacra Caesarea Real Maestà di Ferdinando Terzo.* (It is dedicated to the same emperor as is Scarani's *Libro primo* of 1630.) The publication contains fifteen sonatas, of which Nos. 1–3 are *a tre*, Nos. 4 and 5 *a quattro*, No. 6 *a cinque*, Nos. 7 and 8 *a sei*, No. 9 *a sette*, No. 10 *a otto*, No. 11 *a nove*, nos. 12 and 13 *a dieci*, and Nos. 14 and 15 *a dodici*. Eitner wrote that there was a complete copy (seven part books) in Berlin and in Wroclaw, at the same libraries that once owned complete copies of Neri's Opus 1.[2] Today the Berlin copy is lost, and of the Wroclaw copy only three part books exist: *Canto primo, Canto secondo,* and *basso continuo.*

Nonetheless, we are in a better position here than with Opus 1, since the following compositions are preserved: Nos. 1–3 (for two violins, alto, bass, and b.c.) in Wroclaw, though without the *Basso*; No. 5 (for two violins, alto, bass, and b.c.) in Winterfeld's transcription and in WasielewskiS, No. XIX; No. 10 (eight voice parts) in Winterfeld's transcription (fragments in WasielewskiS, No. XX); and No. 14 (twelve voice parts) in Winterfeld's transcription. Both Winterfeld's and Wasielewski's transcriptions lack the *basso continuo*, but it is preserved in Wroclaw.[3] This part contains remarkable ensemble indications for all the compositions; for instance, for *Sonata prima: Canto sec., C. primo, Basso, a tre, Violini soli, Basso solo.* They also show that Sonatas Nos. 7–15, that is, those for six to twelve parts, are divided into two choirs, in the Venetian tradition.

The first composition of Opus 2, *Sonata prima a tre,* resembles *Sonata prima a quatro* of Opus 1. It contains soloistic passages and a short *adasio* section that is played three times, the third time being enlarged by echo repetitions (sections 2, 4, and 6 in the following diagram):

Sonata prima a tre (two violins, bass, and b.c.)

Movement	1		2		3a	b		4	
Meter	27 D ↷		10 Tr ↷		7 D ↷	15 D ↷		10 Tr ↷	
Tempo			adasio		adasio	largo		adasio	
Instrumentation					Violins soli				

	5		6a	b	
	28 D ↷		14 Tr	38 D ↷	
			adasio	allegro	
	Bass solo				

The sonata consists of six movements clearly marked by double-bars and fermatas. The movements are sometimes separated by beginning the new movement on a new system. The third movement, a duet for the two violins, begins with a homophonic introduction in long note values (3a) and continues with a fugato in sixteenth notes. Like the solo passages in *Sonata prima* of Opus 1, the tempo indication is *Largo*. The introduction is an example of incipit repeat, a technique that is recognizable in many other sonatas by Neri. Fig. 109 shows the beginning of the movement *Violini soli*.

FIGURE 109. NERI: SONATA PRIMA A TRE (OPUS 2, 1651).

The repetition of the refrain (4) is followed by movement 5—28 measures of *Basso solo* that are not preserved, since the *Basso* part is missing.

Sonata seconda a tre consists of four movements: a 24-measure fugue, in which the theme appears twelve times, at the end in stretto;[4] a homophonic *adasio* of nine measures in triple meter; a slow movement of twelve measures, in which a chromatic motion

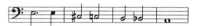

is played three times; and a fast 40-measure movement in 6/4 with a *presto* coda of eleven measures in which the theme of the initial fugue reappears.

Sonata quinta a 4.,[5] in spite of its considerable length (200 measures), consists of only three movements. The first is a coherent fugue, while the other two are subdivided into several sections by multiple changes of tempo and meter. Since this sonata contains three fairly long parts in triple time, the meter is indicated for each of them:

Sonata quinta a 4. (two violins, viola, bass, and b.c.)

Movement	1		2a	b	c	d	e	
Meter	46 D ⌢		20 Tr(3/2)	9 D	17 D	8 D	22 Tr(6/4) ⌢	
Tempo	fast		adasio	allegro	più presto	adasio	allegro	

	3a	b		c	d	
	6 D ⌢	56 Tr(3/4)		4 D	10 D ⌢	
	adasio	allegro, adasio		allegro	presto	

The long triple-meter section, 3b, marked *allegro, adasio*, contains two different progressions, which alternate as follows:

	3b(3/4)					
No. of measures	6	10	8	4	28	
Tempo	allegro	adasio	[allegro]	adasio	[allegro]	

This sonata has an unusual number of tempo changes. The first movement is a fugato rather than a fugue, but it begins with an exposition that in every detail observes the practices of the fully developed fugue (for instance, those of Bach): The theme appears four times alternating tonic/dominant, with tonal modification for the answer. Certainly, such an exposition is rare in the period about 1650. Fig. 110 shows the essential details of this exposition. In the further course of this fugato Neri works with parts of the theme, especially with the countermotif, marked b in Fig. 110. The beginnings of the subdivisions of the second movements are shown in Fig. 111. This movement is not uniform but undergoes frequent changes of construction. The third movement is even more varied: The first section (3a) is a short *adasio* in homophonic style and in duple meter. The second (3b) is 56 measures long, in 3/4 meter, and in fugal style. Two themes are treated alternately, the first *allegro* the second *adasio*, as is shown in the above scheme (in Wasielewski's edition the indication *adasio* in m. 7 and the *allegro* in mm. 17 and 29 are missing). Section 3c consists of a few measures of *allegro* that are a shortened version of the *allegro* in 2b. In the final *presto* (3d), the idea of the *più presto* of 2c recurs. Thus, this sonata is cyclic—as are so many of the period—but in a special manner, since the end does not recall the first movement but the second and third sections of the second movement.

FIGURE 110. NERI: SONATA QUINTA A QUATRO (OPUS 2, 1651).

FIGURE 111. NERI: SONATA QUINTA A QUATRO (OPUS 2, 1651).

Of the multivoice and double-choir sonatas, Nos. 7–15 (six to twelve parts), only two are completely preserved: *Sonata decima a 8.* and *Sonata decima quarta a 12.*, both in Winterfeld's copy without *basso continuo* (which, however, is available at Wroclaw). *Sonata decima* has a *Primo Choro* of three violins and theorbo I, a *Secondo Choro* of three *Flauto* (i.e., recorders) and theorbo II. The first movement consists of four solos[6] without interruption: the three recorders (mm. 1–15), the two theorbos (mm. 14–23), the three violins (mm. 23–37) and finally the three recorders and the two theorbos (mm. 44–72). The second movement is subdivided into several sections: mm. 73–81 for all the instruments in full chordal style, mm. 82–98 for the three recorders, mm. 99–121 for violins I and II and viola, and mm. 122–155 for the two theorbos. The third movement begins with a repetition (mm. 152–159) of mm. 73–81, the section in full chordal style; in the final section, in triple meter (mm. 159–200), the various groups of instruments appear briefly one after the other and finally combine for a most impressive closing effect: three measures *piano* (that is, an echo) by the three recorders, the same instruments that began the work.

Sonata decima quarta a dodici is likewise preserved in Winterfeld's copy. *Choro primo* consists of two cornetti, four trombones, and bassoon; *Choro secondo* of two violins, two violas, theorbo (or viola), and trombone (possibly one from *Choro primo*). The opening nineteen-measure *tutti* is repeated at the end, expanded by four measures. This sonata contains less-expanded "concertini" than does *Sonata decima* but more frequent changes of sonority. Both compositions, particularly the first, are of the concerto grosso type, but much more so than the sinfonias by Francesco Sponga (Usper) of 1619. Both are inestimable jewels of Venetian instrumental music that should be rescued from oblivion. It would require only a letter to Berlin for Winterfeld's score, and to Wroclaw for the *basso continuo*, to bring new life to two splendid compositions from about 1650.

NOTES

1. Modern editions of *Canzone seconda a 4.* in WasielewskiS, No. XVIII; *Sonata prima a 4.* in RiemannB, No. 98. The latter, however, distorted (the ornaments in the opening measure of the short *adagios* on pp. 180–181 are invented; the *Largo* on p. 180 is *Violino primo solo*, that on p. 181, *Violino secondo solo*; the *a due* is omitted from the next section, etc.). The Staatsbibliothek in Berlin (DDR) owns scores of Neri's Opus 1 and Opus 2 copied by von Winterfeld (1784–1852), photocopies of which were provided to me. These contain the two works published in WasielewskiS, Nos. XVIII and XIX, as well as two correnti from Opus 1, *Sonata decima a 8.* and *Sonata decina quarta a 12.* from Opus 2, and the motet *Dignare*.

2. R. Eitner, *Biographisch-bibliographischen Quellen-Lexikon* . . . , 2d ed., Graz, 1959.

3. Clearly, Winterfeld used the Berlin copy, in which (in spite of Eitner's information) the *basso continuo* must have been lacking in 1830. Equally clear is that Wasielewski employed Winterfeld's copy, because he published only pieces contained in that copy. It is interesting that the mensural notation (♦♦ = | ♩ ○ |) was correctly (or at least not incorrectly) interpreted by Winterfeld as | ♩ ○ | while Wasielewski misunderstood it as | ♩ ♩ ○ |.

4. See RiemannH, pp. 152–154. The trills are not in the original.

5. Modern edition in WasielewskiS, vol. 19.

6. Later such solos were labeled *concertini*.

SOURCES

Sonate e canzone a quatro da sonarsi con diversi stromenti in chiesa, & in camera, con alcune correnti pure a quatro, che si ponno [sic] a tre, e a due ancora, lasciando fuori, le parti di mezzo. Opus 1. Venice: Bartolomeo Magni, 1644.   RISM N402.
   Poland: Wroclaw, Biblioteka Uniwersytecka (Violin II, Alto-Viola; lacks Violin I, Viola/Bassoon, b.c.).

Sonate da sonarsi con varii stromenti a tre sino a dodeci. . . . Opus 2. Venice: Stampa del Gardano, appresso Francesco Magni, 1651.   RISM N403.
   Poland: Wroclaw, Biblioteka Uniwersytecka (S I and II, b.c.; lacks A,T,B, part 5).

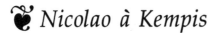 Nicolao à Kempis

Nicolao à Kempis was born about 1600, possibly in Florence, although his professional activity is confined to the Flemish Netherlands from at least 1628. He died in Brussels in 1676.

Within a span of five years the Antwerp printer Phalèse published three books of music by Nicolao à Kempis, who calls himself the organist at St. Gudula in Brussels. The titles of the books are as follows:[1] *Symphoniae unius, duarum [sic] et trium violinorum . . .* (1644); *Symphoniae unius, duorum, trium, IV. et v. instrumentorum, adjunctae quatuor 3. instrumentorum & duarum vocum operis secundi liber primus . . .* (1647); and *Sumphoniae unius, duorum, trium, IV. et V. instrumentorum, adjunctae quatuor 3. instrumentorum & duarum vocum opus tertium et ultimum . . .* (1649).[2]

Because these publications are very close to each other in time, with contents similar in form and style, it will be best to treat them as a single unit.

Book I contains 45 symphonias, Book II 26 symphonias and four motets, Book III 27 symphonias and four motets. The following table indicates the scoring of the symphonias. The extensive use of wind instruments reminds one of Venetian practice:

Instrumentation	Book I	Book II	Book III	Totals
a 1. (violin and b.c.)	Nos. 1–13	Nos. 1–4	Nos. 1–4	21
a 2. (two violins and b.c.)	Nos. 14–30	Nos. 5–12	Nos. 5–12	33
a 2. (violin, bass viola, and b.c.)*	Nos. 31–38	Nos. 13–17	Nos. 13–17	18
a 3. (various instruments)**	Nos. 39–45	Nos. 18–20	Nos. 18–21	14
a 4. (various instruments)***		Nos. 21–24	Nos. 22–25	8
a 5. (two violins, alto viola, tenor viola, bass viola, and b.c.)		Nos. 25, 26	Nos. 26, 27	4

*The scoring cornetto, bassoon, and b.c. is indicated as an alternative.

**The scoring for Book I, Nos. 39–45, Book II, Nos. 19 and 20, and Book III, No. 20, is two violins, bass viola, and b.c. Book II, No. 18, and Book III, No. 19, are scored for cornetto, violin, trombone, and b.c. Book III, No. 18, is for two violins, trombone, and b.c. Book III, No. 21, is for two violins, cornetto, and b.c. or three violins and b.c.

***Book II, Nos. 21, 22, and 24, and Book III, No. 25, are for two violins, tenor viola, bass viola, and b.c. or two violins, trombone, bass viola, and b.c. Book II, No. 23, and Book III, No. 24, are for cornetto, two violins, bass viola, and b.c. Book III, No. 23, is for two violins, tenor viola, bass viola, and b.c. or two violins, trombone, bass viola, and b.c.

What Kempis calls *Symphoniae,* like Mont'Albano's *Sinfoniae* of 1629, are clearly sonatas. It is interesting to note how changeable the term *sinfonia* was in the music of the seventeenth century: compare the sinfonias by Rossi (1607–1622), Sponga (1614, 1619), Marini (1617, 1629, 1655), Buonamente (1626), Uccellini (1639, 1660), and Cazzati (1648), as well as those in operas by Monteverdi (*Orfeo, L'Incoronazione*), Landi (*Il Sant'Alessio*), and many others. Against a background so full of changes it is easier to understand why Bach called his three-part inventions *Sinfoniae*.

The three publications by Kempis contain 98 symphonias or, more properly speaking, sonatas, and prove him to be one of the most productive sonata composers of the seventeenth century. At first, it seems almost impossible to give a proper idea of such a comprehensive output, but, it turns out that Kempis worked according to a scheme for structure as well as for style. Like Merula (and perhaps under his influence), Kempis invented for himself a form to which he basically adheres for all his sonatas and which he only occasionally modifies. Normally it consists of two main sections, the second of which is repeated.

The repetition is not indicated by the sign :‖: commonly used at the time, but by a symbol that looks like an early version of the present-day *dal segno* (𝄋). It is placed at the beginning and end of the section to be repeated. For clarity, the initial notes of the repeated section are printed again at the end of the second section (in other words, at the end of the entire sonata). Thus, without any ambiguity, Kempis's basic form is A B B. In the great majority of cases, A is in duple meter, while B consists of two subsections, the first in triple time, the second in duple. Thus, the normal form used by Kempis can be represented by the scheme D ‖: Tr | D :‖. The last subsection is short in comparison with the others, especially with the first. The following diagram of three representative sonatas shows the number of measures in each section:

Book I, No. 32	|52 D	‖: 27 Tr |	8 D :‖
Book II, No. 15	|60 D	‖: 24 Tr	22 D :‖
Book III, No. 1	|38 D	‖: 34 Tr	10 D :‖

Kempis uses this form strictly in 75 sonatas. In eleven others the repetition is omitted, obviously because the single sections are unusually long. The form | D | Tr | D ‖ is found most frequently in Book III (Nos. 6, 18, 20, 21, 25, 26, and 27). In three sonatas (Book I, Nos. 27 and 36, Book II, No. 7), the repeated sections are replaced by new music, so that the metric structure | D | Tr | D | Tr | D ‖ results. In some cases it is modified in other ways, for instance, | Tr ‖ : D | Tr : ‖ (Book I, No. 17) or | D ‖ : Tr : ‖ (Books III, No. 13). Four sonatas are in triple meter throughout and have no inner cadences, among them *Symphonia supra Ciacona* (Book I, No. 45), while Book III, No. 12, called *Ein lustelijken Mey*, is entirely in duple time. Neither composition is a sonata, but both are variations.

Tempo indications are rather rare and almost completely limited to a *presto* (sometimes *allegro*) for the last section. In Book I this indication appears in only two sonatas, in Book II in eleven, in Book III in fifteen. Thus, at least in this detail a certain progress is recognizable. Usually the *presto* sections are notated in short note values and are preceded by a few measures in long values marked *piano*. (When Kempis employs this word, it is in the sense of *adagio*.) Fig. 112 shows the beginning of the last section of Symphonia No. 15 from Book II.

Kempis used certain style details time and again, especially in the 21 symphonias (or sonatas) for *violino solo* (violin and b.c.). Many of them begin with a theme in long note values (whole notes, half notes) that remind one of the ricercar-like themes in Uccellini's *Libro V* (see p. 109). However, Kempis's treatment of such themes is much

FIGURE 112. KEMPIS: SYMPHONIA TERZIA A 2. (1647).

more casual. Uccellini's sonatas usually begin with four statements of the theme (normally in the order organ, violin, organ, violin), and it sometimes reappears here and there in the organ part. Kempis, on the other hand, never entrusts his theme to the organ, and he uses it only twice in the violin part in a most unusual procedure. The first two or three measures contain the theme in sustained notes; fast passages follow, and after an additional six to ten measures there is a full cadence. The second phrase begins with the theme in transposition to the fourth or the fifth and continues with slightly modified passage-work. The remaining part of the first section is filled with figuration of one kind or another. Thus, in the first section of Kempis's solo sonatas, imitation is limited to two widely separated statements of the theme. To illustrate this strange procedure, Fig. 113 shows the beginning of the Symphonia No. 4 from Book III, in which the theme is answered only once, after twelve measures (the bass is omitted since it is merely an accompaniment). The same procedure is in the sections in triple meter, though not as frequently. The closing sections in duple meter are usually filled with lively figurations.

FIGURE 113. KEMPIS: SYMPHONIA QUARTA. VIOLINO SOLO (1649).

The symphonias for two or more instruments (two violins and b.c.; violin, bass, and b.c.; etc.) usually begin with an imitative figure, but this is all that Kempis concedes to the demands of fugal style. The frequent division into phrases (often of eight measures) ending with a full cadence is contrary to fugal style. All this indicates a northern attitude quite different from that which prevailed in Italy.

   The symphonias for two instruments quite frequently contain soloistic passages of about seven to ten measures, usually at the end of the duple- or the triple-meter section, but occasionally in the middle of these sections. In Book I such passages occur, if at all, in two or three symphonias—a precise statement is not possible here, since the part book for the second instrument (violin II or base) is missing. In Book II, among the thirteen symphonias for two instruments (Nos. 5–17 in the table above), there are five such passages; in Book III, there are nine in the same number of symphonias (also Nos. 5–17), so that one may justly conclude that in the course of his creative activity Kempis paid increasing attention to the idea of a soloist or, to put it differently, to the concerto principle. Most of these solo passages consist of rather commonplace figuration, but the two solos in Symphonia No. 6 of Book III, reproduced in Fig. 114, have some individuality. Dotted rhythm occurs quite frequently in Kempis's compositions.

FIGURE 114. KEMPIS: SYMPHONIA SECUNDA DUORUM VIOLINORUM (1649).

Two of Kempis's symphonias are variations. The last piece of Book I, *Symphonia septima supra Ciacona*, a composition of 84 measures in 3/2 meter, consists of an introduction of nine measures, a middle section of 60 measures—the *Ciacona* itself—and a fifteen-measure postlude. The *Ciacona* is a quasi-ostinato consisting of 30 variations of a basic formula of two measures that is in a slightly modified form each time it appears, for instance:

Occasionally modulations into other keys take place. The other variation work, No. 12 in Book III, *Ein lustelijken Mey*, is the Flemish folk song that John Bull employed about 1620 for variations for the organ or virginal. Kempis's contribution is for two violins and b.c. It consists of a 36-measure "theme" and a *Variatio*, both filled with lively and diverse figurations.

To my mind, the most attractive of Kempis's compositions—one that may well be applauded today—is *Symphonia quarta A 4* from Book II, written for a string quartet (two violins, tenor viola, and bass viola) with b.c., and is inscribed *Sopra Cuccuc vel Sol mi*. The piece owes its charm to the numerous cries of the cuckoo, which are played quite irregularly and unexpectedly, in one or another of the upper parts, most of the time as

but sometimes as

Another attractive element is that all the parts (except the continuo) have frequent rests resulting in a very loose texture. Figurations play a more limited role here than in other compositions by Kempis. Yet another pleasant feature is that the piece closes with a three-measure echo that ends with a final, distant cry of the cuckoo in the first violin.

NOTES

1. *The New Grove*, vol. I, p. 186, mentions a lost book of masses and motets for voices and continuo published in Antwerp in 1650. Possibly there was an additional *operis secundi liber secundus* that has not survived. Two modern editions in RiemannO, vol. IV, p. 142, and RiemannB, No. 99 (both from Book I) are so garbled that they are unusable.

2. *The New Grove*, vol. I, p. 186, dates this publication 1642 (*sic*), calls it Opus 4, and indicates it is for one to six instruments; but see Opus 4 below.

SOURCES

Symphoniae unius, duarum, et trium violinorum.... Antwerp: Les héritiers de Pierre Phalèse, 1644.   RISM K377.

    West Germany: Kassel, Murhard'sche Bibliothek der Stadt Kassel und Landesbibliothek (parts I and 3, b.c.).

Symphoniae unius, duorum, trium, IV. et V. instrumentorum, adjunctae quatuor 3. instrumentorum & duarum vocum ... liber primus. Opus 2. Antwerp: Magdalène Phalèse, 1647.   RISM K378.

    Great Britain: Durham, Cathedral Library (parts 1–5, b.c.); London, British Library.

Symphoniae unius, duorum, trium, IV. et V. instrumentorum, adjunctae quatuor 3. instrumentorum & duarum vocum.... Opus 3. Antwerp: Magdalène Phalèse, 1649.   RISM K379.

    Great Britain: London, British Library (parts 1–5, b.c.).
    Germany: Berlin, Staatsbibliothek (part 4).

Symphoniae unius, duorum, trium, IV. V. et VI. instrumentorum.... Opus 4. Antwerp: Magdalène Phalèse, n.d.   RISM K380.

    Great Britain: London, British Library (part 4).

 *Marco Antonio Ferro*

Marco Antonio Ferro, who died in Vienna in 1662, was lutenist at the court of Emperor Ferdinand III in Vienna. In his Opus 1, dedicated to the emperor, he calls himself Cavalier Aurato *(knight of the golden spur) and* Conte Palatino Cesareo. *Obviously, he was a courtier of high rank.*

The only known work by Ferro is his Opus 1, *Sonate a Due, Tre, e Quattro...*, published in 1649 in Venice. It consists of five part books: *Violino Primo, Violino Secondo, Viola da Braccio, Basso di Viola da Gamba,* and *Basso Continuo.*[1] It contains twelve sonatas scored as follows: Nos. 1 and 2, violin, bass, and b.c.; Nos. 3 and 4, two violins, bass, and b.c.;

Nos. 5 and 6, violin, alto, bass, and b.c.; Nos. 7, 8, and 10–12, two violins, alto, bass, and b.c.; and No. 9, four violas. The instruments to be used for each sonata are indicated in the parts, and (except for Nos. 6 and 9) an alternative group of instruments is specified:

	INSTRUMENTATION	ALTERNATIVE INSTRUMENTATION
No. 1	Violino, Viola da gamba	Violino, Tiorba, Viola da gamba (or Tiorba)
No. 2	Violino, Viola da gamba	Violino, Tiorba
Nos. 3 and 4	Violino, Violetta da braccio, Viola da gamba	2 Violini, Tiorba
No. 5	Violino, Tenore da gamba, Viola da gamba	Cornetto, Trombone, Tiorba
No. 6	Violino, Tenore da gamba, Viola da gamba	
No. 7	2 Violini, Violetta da braccio, Viola da gamba	2 Cornetti, Violetta da braccio, Fagotto
No. 8	2 Violini, Violetta da braccio, Viola da gamba	2 Cornetti, Fagotto
No. 9	4 Viole	
No. 10	4 Viole	2 Violini, Violetta da Braccio, Tiorba
No. 11	2 Violini, Violetta da braccio, Viola da gamba	2 Cornetti, Trombone, Tiorba
No. 12	2 Violini, Violetta da braccio, Viola da gamba	2 Cornetti, Violetta da braccio, Tiorba

Ferro's publication is interesting for its documentation of the violetta, an instrument that is difficult to identify.[2] It had been employed by Castello in his *Libro primo* of 1621 as a substitute for the trombone.

The content of Ferro's sonatas does seem to me sometimes to be disappointing. It is difficult for me to take serious interest in a composer who writes such trivialities as the passage shown in Fig. 115.

FIGURE 115. FERRO: SONATA SECONDA (OPUS 1, 1649).

However, even here there are details that merit our attention. Sonata No. 2 begins with a six-measure solo for violin I, which is answered by the bass instrument at the lower twelfth. Ferro uses the concerto technique here, though to a much lesser extent than Castello did in his sonatas from 1621 and 1627.

The third movement of Sonata No. 1 contains one solo for the bass and one for the violin. They do not consist of lively figurations but of a succession of whole notes that are obviously to be played slowly:

Were these sustained notes played as written, or were they enriched by improvised figurations, as was done in the slow movements of the sonatas in Corelli's Opus 5 from 1700, or possibly the "affetto" passages of Biago Marini and others? Sonatas Nos. 5 and 6 each close with a *Presto* movement that begins like a fugue but ends as a three-voice fanfare: an amusing trick that, no doubt, was much applauded by the Viennese court.

The most noteworthy detail in Ferro's Opus 1 is the third movement of Sonata No. 6, a fourteen-measure *Presto* that is an unexpectedly early example of a running bass; that is, a bass that always moves in short notes of the same value (usually eighth notes), while the upper parts have free rhythmic values, from half notes to sixteenths. Riemann discusses the history of this technique (he calls it *gehender Bass*) and indicates that its earliest examples are to be found in sonatas by G. B. Vitali written between 1660 and 1670.[3] But, Ferro's example is about fifteen years earlier than Vitali's, suggesting that the origin of the running bass goes back at least to the 1640s.

NOTES

1. In the only copy in the University Library at Wroclaw, the continuo is missing; however, Ferro's sonatas are complete in EinsteinC, vol. XIV.

2. The instrument is described by Lanfranco in *Scintille di musica*, (Brescia, 1533), as a fretless little violin (violette), and by Zacconi, in *Prattica di musica*, 1592, as viol (*violetta piccola* = treble viol), while the term is employed by Praetorius, in *Syntagma musicum*, part II, 1619, for both viol and violin. In the mid-seventeenth century the term might easily indicate viola or viola da gamba, for as late as 1732, Johann Walther, in *Musikalisches Lexikon*, writes that it might be either *da braccia* or *da gamba*, and is employed for middle parts, (= French "taille de violon"?).

3. H. Riemann, *Handbuch der Musikgeschichte*, vol. II, part 2, pp. 165ff.

SOURCES

Sonate a due, tre, & quatro. . . . Opus 1. Venice: Stampa del Gardano, 1649.   RISM F543.

Poland: Wroclaw, Biblioteka Uniwersytecka (V I, V II incomplete, Viola da braccio, Viola da gamba; lacks b.c.).

Andrea Falconiero

Andrea Falconiero (Falconieri) was born in Naples in 1585 or 1586. From 1610 to 1647 he was active primarily as a lutenist in various cities of northern Italy—Parma, Florence, Modena, Genoa—as well as in Spain and France. He returned to Naples in 1639 as lutenist, and in 1647 followed Trabaci as royal chapelmaster, a post he occupied until his death in 1656.

In 1610 and 1619 Falconiero published books with vocal music, but it was not until 1650, six years before his death, that a collection of instrumental pieces appeared: *Il primo libro di Canzone, Sinfonie, Fantasie, Capricci, Brandi, Correnti, Gagliarde, Alemane, Volte per Violini e Viole, over altro stromento a uno, due, e tre con il Basso continuo.*[1] This *primo libro* is not the work of a beginner but a late collection of compositions, some of which may have been written decades earlier. Here for the first time a native of southern Italy comes into our view as a composer of instrumental music.

The publication contains 58 compositions (the *Tavola* is not quite accurate), arranged according to the number of parts: 32 *a tre*, fourteen *a due*, (two violins or violin and bass and b.c.), and twelve *a una*. Within each group, there are canzonas, sinfonias (the first of these is marked *Sinfonia seconda!*), fantasias, dances, and pieces with inscriptions such as *L'Eroica, L'Infante Arcibizarra,* and *La Xaveria Buelta.* It is interesting to note that Falconiero, conforming with the political situation in Naples, uses many Spanish words, such as *tiple* (top or treble voice), *buelta* (volta), *dicha* (called), *echa* (named); for example, *Canciona dicha la Preciosa echa para Don Enrico Butler.*

The most important fact about the contents is that the terms *Canzone, Sinfonia, Fantasia,* and *Capriccio* are used without any recognizable differences in meaning. All are representative of a particular type that consists of two, three, or four sections, each of which is to be repeated, according to the scheme ‖:A:‖:B:‖ or ‖:A:‖:B:‖:C:‖ or ‖:A:‖:B:‖:C:‖:D:‖. The three-sectional form is the most frequent, occurring in ten pieces, with each of the others occurring in six. The various sections are similar to one another, and are usually filled with lively sixteen-note motifs or passage-work. The last section is frequently in triple meter, but it closes with a few measures in duple time. The following schematic representations of three pieces indicate the number of measures in each section:

Canciona dicha la Ennamorada (two violins, bass, and b.c.)[2]
‖: 20D :‖: 10D :‖: 10D ‖: 20Tr 3D :‖

Sinfonia seconda (two violins, bass, and b.c.)
‖: 10D :‖: 17D :‖: 27 Tr 4D :‖

La Parlera (violin, bass, and b.c.)
‖: 11D :‖: 10D :‖: 9D :‖

Tempo indications, which were then quite common in northern Italy, are almost completely absent. Only for the close of the *Folia* is *muy despacio* (very slow) prescribed, and for *Il Rosso Brando, Si sona presto.*

Compositions of this kind are totally unrelated to the north Italian sonata, if only because they lack an essential element of this form, that is, change of tempo—either notated or prescribed. If at all, they might be compared with the sinfonias by Rossi and Buonamente, though these were always in binary form. Falconiero's compositions also differ by a very conspicuous trait, that is, the almost regular use of a feminine cadence, as shown in Fig. 116.

FIGURE 116. FALCONIERO: LA PERLERA (1650).

About five compositions, among them *La Gioiosa Fantasia* and *Il Capriccio bisbetico* (capricious crank), are continuous, without interruption or division into sections. These are perhaps Falconiero's most attractive pieces because they both lack repetitions and the somewhat banal "Falconiero cadence," but they contain a succession of attractive motifs.

Falconiero's *Libro primo* contains several other compositions that should be briefly mentioned. The *Passacalle* consists of 32 variations on the theme

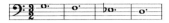

and there is a *Folia* of sixteen variations on the well-known theme (also in 3/2). *Bataglia de Barabaso yerno* [son-in-law] *de Satanas* is a hellish piece of battle music that is reprinted (with some errors) in Torchi's new edition.[3] Also interesting is another battle taking place in hell, inscribed *Riñen* [quarreling] *y pelean* [fight] *entre Berzebillo* [Beelzebub] *con Satanillo, y Canuf, y Canul*, which is followed by a *Bayle* [dance] *de los dichos Diabolos*. It is amusing to note that in the very first collection of violin music from the south we find hell and the devil, perceptions that have always played an important role in the minds of the southern Italians. Falconiero's publication also contains a number of dance pieces: brandi, correnti, gagliardas, allemandes, and voltas.

The article *Falconieri* in MGG lists the publication of a *Sonate a 3* in Venice, in 1650, but I know nothing about it. Manuscript E.M. 83 in the Music Collection of the Österreichische Nationalbibliothek, Vienna, contains a *Sonata 7ª. Del Sig. Andª*, which R. Haas[4] ascribes to Andrea Falconiero. This ascription is highly questionable, since the sonata has traits that clearly point to northern Italy. Very likely, the sonata was written by Andrea Grossi, who lived in Mantua about 1680.

NOTES

1. To be sure, he had published guitar tablatures with his *Musichi . . . libro sexto* of 1619, and he may have published a *sonata a 3* in 1650, now lost but mentioned in *The New Grove* Vol. VI, p. 369.

2. New edition in TorchiA, p. 143.
3. Ibid., No. 53.
4. R. Haas, *Die Estensischen Musikalien* (Regensburg, 1928).

SOURCES

Il primo libro di canzone, sinfonie, fantasie, capricci, brandi, correnti, gagliarde, alemane, volte per violini e viole, overo altro stromento a uno, due, e tre con il basso continuo. Naples: Pietro Paolini & Giuseppe Ricci, 1650.   RISM F85.
   Italy: Bologna, Civico Museo (4 parts).
Edition:
Florence: Studio per Editione Scelte, 1980 (facsimile).

❦ *Giovanni Antonio Leoni*

All that is known about Leoni is that he was active in Rome for a long time. It is assumed that he was born shortly before 1600 and that he died shortly after 1652.

Aside from a motet, the only work by Leoni that is preserved is a publication entitled *Sonate di Violino a voce sola . . . Libro primo Opera terza,* which was published in Rome in 1652 in the form of a score with a violin part. Aside from the customary dedication, it contains a preface to the reader (*A chi legge*) in which Leoni says that he had previously composed many sonatas and symphonias. Various virtuosos were now claiming these works as their property, while others were more modestly content with imitating his style ("Altri poi con maggior modestia contendandosi d'imitar solo lo stile"). Is it possible to identify the musicians who imitated Leoni's style? We shall return to this question after we have examined his compositions.

   Leoni's publication consists of a score and a part book for the violin. It contains 31 sonatas arranged according to church modes: Nos. 1–4, *primo tuono;* Nos. 5–10, *secondo tuono;* etc. Strangely, two of the most common modes, *quinto* and *settimo,* are not represented. There is no *Sonata XVIII,* and two compositions are labeled *Sonata XXX.*

   The form of Leoni's sonatas is governed by two basic principles: They are one-movement works with no interruptions; and most of them consist of three parts according to the scheme D, Tr, D, without repeats. Some phrases cadence with whole notes, but these instances are so infrequent that they seem to be random accidents of the composition and can be ignored in this context, especially since the whole note is often divided into two half notes, thus weakening the cadential character. This occurs in Sonata No. 21, whose first part closes with

There are four exceptions to the three-part arrangement of meters: Nos. 8 and 30 are in five parts (D, Tr, D, Tr, D), No. 7 is in four parts (D, Tr, D, Tr), and No. 19 has only one

part (D). In comparison with the sonatas of such composers as Cazzati, these principles of form are very archaic. The same can be said for the nearly complete absence of tempo indications: in all 31 sonatas there is only one indication of tempo, *allegro* for the last part of the Sonata No. 22.

The violin parts consist to a large extent of figures that are not really virtuosic, since they never go beyond sixteenth notes. Nor do they contain anything noteworthy from the point of view of violin technique, such as high positions or wide leaps. Of considerable interest, on the other hand, is Leoni's use of imitation. In solo sonatas one would expect the theme to be played in alternation by the two participating instruments, violin and organ, as Uccellini did in his solo sonatas of Opus 5 from 1649. Leoni, however, employs another method, which might be called self-imitation. The violin begins with a theme one or two measures long, which by means of various figures is extended into a phrase of eight measures that closes with a half note and a half rest. The second phrase begins with the theme transposed to the fifth or the fourth and continues with other figurations. In nineteen sonatas, Leoni limits himself to these two quotations of the theme, while in the others it appears once more, usually somewhat modified. A typical example is Sonata No. 15 (Fig. 117), in which the theme is "imitated" after twelve measures.

FIGURE 117. LEONI: SONATA XV (OPUS 3, 1652).

The above explanations refer to the first part of the sonatas. In the second and third parts there is much less regularity with respect to self-imitation. Quite frequently, these parts have no imitation at all, and sometimes there are three or even four references to the theme, as in the following table:

Sonata No. 13	40 D	27 Tr	15 D
Theme in mm.	1, 8	1, 8	
Sonata No. 14	53 D	31 Tr	19 D
Theme in mm.	1, 18	1, 5, 18	1, 12
Sonata No. 15	25 D	26 Tr	29 D
Theme in mm.	1, 13	1, 8	
Sonata No. 20	34 D	26 Tr	21 D
Theme in mm.	1, 5, 20		

In the first part of Sonata No. 14 the theme is not imitated until m. 18; and in Sonata No. 13 the theme of the second part is a triple-meter variant of the initial theme, but such manifestations of the cyclic principle are rare.

The organ usually functions as an accompaniment, but in a few cases it plays the theme, always as the initial statement. The theme is imitated after a few measures by the violin (for instance, in the second parts of Sonatas Nos. 1 and 22). The organ part has strikingly few thorough-bass figures, contrary to the case in solo sonatas for violin.

In conclusion I should like to return to the question raised in the first paragraph of this section: Who were the musicians who imitated Leoni's style? Certainly Nicolao a Kempis was one. If one recalls what was said about Kempis's sonatas (see page 000), and if in particular Fig. 117 is compared with Fig. 113, it will be seen that Kempis's self-imitation is identical with Leoni's. The fact that Kempis's symphonias appeared a few years before Leoni's sonatas is not a valid objection, since Leoni says that the compositions had been written at an earlier time.

SOURCES

Sonate di violino a voce sola ... libro primo. Opera terza. Rome: Vitale Mascardi, 1652.   RISM L987.
    Italy: Naples, Biblioteca del Conservatorio di Musica S. Pietro a Maiella (score).
    Poland: Wroclaw, Biblioteka Uniwersytecka (score, lacking title; V).

 *Francesco Cavalli*

Francesco Cavalli was born in 1602 at Crema, in Lombardy. His proper name was Caletto, but he named himself after the governor of Crema, Federico Cavalli, a Venetian patrician, who sent him to Venice in 1616. In 1617 Cavalli became singer of the chapel of San Marco (conducted by Monteverdi). In 1639 he became second organist, in 1665 first organist, and in 1668 chapelmaster of San Marco. Aside from a short stay in Paris (1660–1662), where, upon the invitation of Cardinal Mazarin, he wrote an opera for the wedding of Louis XIV, he spent his entire life in Venice, where he died in 1676.

Cavalli and Monteverdi are associated with Venetian opera, but Cavalli also made a noteworthy contribution to the history of violin music, especially in his *Musiche Sacre* ... of 1656. At the end of this large collection of sacred vocal music (masses, hymns, magnificats, etc.) are six sonatas, one each *a 3., a 4., a 6., a 8., a 10.,* and *a 12.* The publication consists of twelve part books in which, without any obvious reason, the sonatas are called canzonas. The scoring of Sonata No. 1 is for two violins, bass, and b.c.; No. 2 is for two violins, alto, bass, and b.c.; and Nos. 3–6 are scored for double choirs.

In spite of their considerable length, about 200 measures, Sonatas Nos. 1–4 have no inner cadences. They are subdivided only by changes of meter, according to the scheme D Tr D Tr, and short codas (four to six measures) in duple meter. Sonatas Nos. 5 and 6 are shorter and have the scheme D Tr D. Tempo indications are completely lacking.

The first sonata, *a 3.,* begins with a 68-measure fugato in **C**. It is based on a five-measure theme that starts with a descending fourth

and continues in eighth notes. After an exposition in which the theme is played three times on the same degree of the scale, it is played only once more in m. 20 by violin I in transposition to the fifth

Various eighth-note motifs in sequential treatment follow. The second section, 34 measures in 3/2 and obviously a *Largo*, is also a fugato, which begins with an impressive theme:

The third section, eighteen measures in **C**, is yet another fugato, but in fast motion (eighth and sixteenth notes). The last section has the form of a *basso ostinato*, that is, a descending tetrachord

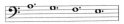

which is repeated twelve times. Above this foundation the two violins play a very peculiar counterpoint: not in continuous motion but in fragments that present an interesting contrast to the sustained notes of the organ bass. The part marked *Violoncino* generally follows the organ bass, but during the seventh to the tenth repeat of the ostinato it goes its own way, adopting the fragmentary style of the violins. Fig. 118 shows the beginning of this passage.

FIGURE 118. CAVALLI: SONATA A 3. (1656).

Cavalli's second sonata, *a 4*, begins with a 67-measure fugato. Its theme starts with an ascending fifth

and is presented in an entirely "regular" four-voice exposition, that is, with tonal answers on the dominant. The second section—similar to that of Sonata No. 1—is a 64-measure *Largo* in 3/2 meter. The third section—also like that of the first sonata—is a short fugato in even meter. The last section, however, presents a quite unexpected picture; it is merely an exact repetition of the first triple-meter section. The same summary procedure is used for the next two sonatas, No. 3, *a 6.* and no. 4, *a 8.* Perhaps there exists a model for this repetition of an entire section in Cavalli's sacred vocal music.

Cavalli's violin compositions are strikingly conservative for their time. This is particularly evident when they are compared with those of Massimiliano Neri, who had the position of first organist at San Marco while Cavalli was second organist and whom Cavalli succeeded when Neri went to Cologne in 1664. Although Cavalli surely knew Neri's publications of 1644 and 1651, he made no use of their important innovations. He was mainly interested in opera and in sacred vocal music.

SOURCES

Musiche sacre concernenti messa, e salmi concertati con istromenti, imni, antifone & sonate, a due, 3. 4. 5. 6. 8. 10. e 12. voci. Venice: Alessandro Vincenti, 1656.   RISM C1565.
   Italy: Bologna, Archivio dell'Accademia filarmonica; Civico Museo.
   Poland: Wroclaw, Biblioteka Uniwersytecka (S II, Violin II, Violincino).
   West Germany: Regensburg, Bischöfliche Zentralbibliothek (12 parts; I: S,A,T,B; II: S,A,T,B; Violin I and II, Violoncino, b.c.).

Giovanni Legrenzi

> *Giovanni Legrenzi was born in 1626 in Clusone, near Bergamo. In 1645 he became organist at Santa Maria Màggiore of Bergamo, and—along with Cazzati—was a member of the Accademia degli Eccitati of that city. In 1656 he moved to Ferrara, and in 1665 to Venice, where in 1672 he became director of the Conservatorio degli Mendicanti, in 1681 vice-maestro and in 1685 primo maestro of the chapel of San Marco. He died in 1690 in Venice. Aside from numerous vocal compositions, including both operas and oratorios, he wrote five books with violin music, which were published between 1655 and 1691, the last posthumously.*

Legrenzi's first publication of violin music, *Sonate a due, e tre, Libro primo, opera seconda,* printed in 1655, contains eighteen sonatas: Nos. 1–6 for two violins and b.c.; Nos. 7–9 for violin, violone or bassoon, and b.c.; and Nos. 10–18 for two violins, violone, and b.c. For Nos. 7–9, the bass instrument is *Violone ò Faghotto,* for Nos. 10–18, only *Violone.*

The structure of Legrenzi's sonatas, primarily characterized by two inner repeat signs, was no doubt taken over from Merula. As in Merula's canzonas, a short coda usually follows the second repeat sign, so that the form A : ‖ : B : ‖ : Coda results. In Sonatas Nos. 1 and 18 the coda is missing, while in Nos. 5, 13, 14, and 17 there is a final section whose length is similar to that of the preceding ones. As in Cazzati's sonatas, the various sections of Legrenzi's sonatas may well be called movements, although they are not always as unequivocally separated as those of the Bolognese master, nor is the separation always indicated identically in the different part books. Many fast movements begin with a slow introduction or close with a slow postlude. A typical example is *Sonata La Spilimbergha* (No. 2; two violins and b.c.), which has the following scheme:

Movement	1		2a	b		Coda	
Meter	55 Tr	:‖	: 7 D↷	27 D	:‖	: 9 D	‖
Tempo	adaggio	‖	adaggio	presto	‖		

Sonata *La Mont'Albana*, No. 11 (is it dedicated to Bartolomeo Mont'Albano, who was about 30 years older than Legrenzi?), with 128 measures, is not only the most extended sonata of Opus 2, but also the only one that consists of four movements:

Sonata La Mont'Albana, No. 11

Movement	1		2a	b	c		3		4a	b	
Meter	48 Tr↷	:‖	: 12 D	5 D	10 D↷	:‖	: 23 Tr↷ :‖		: 3 D↷	27 D↷	‖
Tempo		‖	allegro	adaggio	presto	‖	adaggio	‖	adaggio	fast	

In both Nos. 2 and 11 the movements in triple meter are long in comparison with the others. This is not an accident, but an example of a practice that was quite usual at the time.

The sonatas *a due* (Nos. 1–9) each begin with an imitative movement based on a lengthy theme, which is treated rather casually as a fugato. For instance, the first movement of *Sonata La Foscari* (No. 8; violin, bass, and b.c.) is 31 measures long. Its theme is six measures long and appears only four times: in mm. 1 and 6, and in an abbreviated form in mm. 22 and 25. The middle part (mm. 11–21) is characterized by the alternation of two motifs, each only one measure long.

In the sonatas *a tre* (Nos. 10–18), Legrenzi uses for the first movements more concise themes two to three measures long. They also are mostly treated as fugatos, with a full exposition at the beginning, a middle part filled with various motifs, and a condensed recapitulation of the theme toward the end. The principles of the fully developed fugue are realized most clearly in the initial movement of *Sonata La Mont'Albana* (No. 11), which is the most important composition of Opus 2. We should like to describe it in some detail, referring the reader to the diagram above.

The sonata begins with a 48-measure fugue; surprisingly, it is not in simple meter but in 6/8. Its very attractive theme bestows on the entire movement a character that might be called *allegretto grazioso*. The theme is treated in three full expositions and appears frequently in abbreviated form, especially in the violin part. The second movement consists of three short sections in contrasting tempos: *Allegro, Adaggio,* and *Presto.* The third movement, an *Adaggio* of 23 measures in 3/2 meter, has a homophonic introduction and continues with figurations in eighth notes. The fourth movement also begins in chordal style. Its concluding section is a double fugato whose second theme is the same as the theme of the first movement in a different meter. It is written in eighth-note triplets in a fast 4/4, thus transformed from an *allegretto grazioso* into an *allegro vivace*. Fig. 119 shows the beginnings of the initial fugue and of the final fugato (items 1 and 4b of the diagram).

FIGURE 119. LEGRENZI: SONATA LA MONT'ALBANA (OPUS 2, 1655).

Legrenzi's second collection of violin music, Opus 4, appeared in 1656: *Sonate dà Chiesa, dà Camera, Correnti, Balletti, Alemane, E. Sarabande à tre doi Violini, e Violone, . . . Libro Secondo.* The contents are as follows:

6 Sonata	Nos. 1–6
6 Sonata da camera	Nos. 7–12
6 Corrente	Nos. 13–18
6 Balletto	Nos. 19–24
3 Sarabanda + Alemana	Nos. 25–27

The six first compositions, designated *Sonate [dà Chiesa]*,[1] are, consequently, sonatas in the proper sense of the word, similar to those of *Libro primo*. All of them consist of three movements, except *Sonata La Tassa*, No. 4, which has only two. *Sonata La Brembata*, No. 1, consists of four movements: ‖ A : ‖ : B : ‖ : C : ‖ : D : ‖. Sections B and C are the first and second parts of a dancelike movement in binary form. In almost every sonata, one movement is a typically Venetian contrast movement. Particularly interesting, in both form and content, is *Sonata La Pezzoli* (No. 6), which has the following structure:

Movement	1		2a		b	
Meter	37 Tr⌢	‖:	: 2 D	9 D	2 D	9 D
Tempo	largo		adagio	allegro	adagio	allegro
Instrumentation			Violin I solo		Violin II solo	

c		d			3	
2 D	9 D	13 D	3 D⌢	:‖:	15 D	37 Tr⌢
adagio	allegro	allegro	adagio		presto	largo
Violone solo		a 3.				

The first movement is a *Largo* in 3/2 meter, 37 measures long, in a uniform, essentially homophonic style. There follows a 64-measure contrast movement, in which, unlike most cases, the meter remains constant while the tempo and the scoring change frequently. It begins with three structurally similar solos for violin I, violin II, and violone (two measures *adagio* and nine measures *allegro*), but each employs different musical material. It closes with a section *a 3. (tutti)*, which consists of thirteen measures *allegro*, three measures *adagio*, and fifteen measures *presto*. The third movement, another *Largo*, is an exact repetition of the first one. The repeat sign after the first movement—unless it is a misprint—indicates that the second movement (not the first) is to be played twice. Thus, this sonata is like a triptych whose large and elaborate tableau is flanked by two identical side panels.

The *Sonate da camera* in Legrenzi's Opus 4 (Nos. 7–12) are not chamber sonatas in the usual sense of the word (compositions having the form of a suite, but with individual pieces in binary form, some in duple meter, others in triple). Instead they belong to a category called *sinfonia* in earlier publications (from Rossi's *Libro primo* of 1607 to Uccellini's *Libro secondo* of 1639). Two of Legrenzi's "chamber sonatas" are especially noteworthy: *La Biffi* (No. 8), because its 6/8 motion, is an *"allegretto grazioso"* similar to the first movement of *Sonata La Mont'Albana* from *Libro primo* (see Fig. 119); and *La Forni* (No. 11), an *Adagio* in 3/2 meter in C minor, has impressive dissonances reminiscent of the *durezze e ligature* style of seventeenth-century organ music.

The sonatas are followed by six correnti, six balletti, and three pairs of a sarabanda and an allemande (for instance, *Sarabanda prima* and *Allemanda prima La Pozzi*), a strange combination that is probably unique in the history of the suite.

Legrenzi's *Libro secondo* exhibits two rhythmic peculiarities. The first is a predilection—as in *Libro primo*—for iambic rhythms in triple meter, for instance ♩♪♪♩ or ♪♩♫♫ . The other is the occasional use of quadruplets in 3/2 meter, for example:

Such rhythms are found in three compositions in *Libro secondo*: in *Sonata La Fini* (No. 5), *Sonata da Camera La Strozzi* (No. 10), and *Corrente terza* (No. 15; in 3/4, hence twice as fast). In the music of the late fourteenth century such rhythmic constructions were child's play; in the subsequent period, especially in the sixteenth century, they rarely exist; and in the seventeenth century they are truly a novelty.

In 1663 Legrenzi published his third book of violin music: *Sonate a due, tre, cinque, e sei stromenti. . . . Libro terzo, opera ottava*. It contains sixteen sonatas in five part books: *Violino Primo* in treble clef; *Violino Secondo* in treble and soprano clef (also contains Alto Viola in alto clef and Tenore Viola in tenor clef); *Violino Quarto* contains some parts for Viola da Brazzo in bass clef and Tenore Viola in tenor clef; *Viola da Brazzo* in bass clef (also includes Violone, Basso Viola, and "Fagotto ò Violone," all in bass clef); and *Organo*, with figures in bass, tenor, alto, and treble clefs. The contents are:

Sonatas à 2:	Nos. 1–3	2 Violini
	No. 4	due Violini, e Viola
	No. 5	3 Violini, e Viola da Brazzo, ò Fagotto
	No. 6	due Violini, e Violone
Sonatas à 3:	Nos. 7–10	due Violini, e Violone

Sonatas à 5:	Nos. 11, 12	quattro Violini, e violone
	Nos. 13, 14	due Violini, Alto (Tenore Viola), e Basso
Sonatas à 6:	No. 15	Canti, e Fagotto
	No. 16	[no instrumentation]

(In the part books, Nos. 15 and 16 have parts marked Viola da Brazzo and Tenore Viola, both in bass clef, while the *Viola da Brazzo* part book indicates Fagotto ò Violone for No. 15 and Violone for No. 16.)

For the bass part the following instruments are specified: *Viola da brazzo* (Nos. 4–8, 11, 12, and 15), *Violone* (Nos. 9, 13, 14, and 16), and *Basso Viola* (No. 10), occasionally with *Fagotto* (bassoon) as an alternative (Nos. 5 and 13).

Fourteen of these sonatas have the same form that Legrenzi used in his earlier sonatas: three movements, the second of which is to be repeated: A‖: B:‖ C (in Nos. 3 and 5, C is reduced to a short coda). While the first and last movements are written in a uniform style (except for an occasional *Adagio* introduction to the third movement), the middle movements are subdivided into several sections with a different meter or tempo, in the manner of a contrast movement. A good example is *Sonata La Bonacossa* (No. 7):[2]

Movement	1	‖	2a	b	c	d	‖	3
Meter	31 D	:‖: 6 D	13 Tr(3/4)	13 D	15 Tr(3/2)	:‖: 19 D
Tempo	fast	‖ adagio	allegro	presto	adagio	‖ allegro

The two six-voice sonatas have slightly enlarged forms. *La Basadonna* (No. 14) consists of three movements plus a coda; while *Sonata La Buscha* (No. 13) has four complete movements, of which the second and third are contrast movements.)

Among the numerous interesting aspects of Legrenzi's Opus 8, is the organization of the initial movements. They are all relatively short, comprising 30–50 measures, and written in fugal style with themes that are individually designed and often include typically violinistic leaps of an octave. The themes of the four sonatas in trio scoring (two violins, bass, and b.c.) are reproduced in Fig. 120. They are not only significant on their own account but also in comparison with the thematic idiom of later masters such as Vitali, Bononcini, Corelli, and even Vivaldi. Legrenzi uses various methods for the treatment of these four themes.

FIGURE 120. LEGRENZI: SONATE NOS. 5–8 (OPUS 8, 1663). a. LA ROSETTA; b. LA BEVILAQUA; c. LA BONACOSSA; d. LA BOIARDA.

In *La Rossetta* he begins with a full exposition and continues with free variants or abbreviations of the theme, with no countermotifs, so that the pastoral character of the theme is preserved. In *La Bevilaqua*, on the other hand, the first movement is a fully developed fugue with three expositions, two episodes, and coda. In *La Bonacossa*, Legrenzi writes only two expositions: the first has three full statements of the theme; while in the second the complete theme is played only at the beginning (in violin I) and at the end (in the bass), and in between it is reduced several times to its second, particularly interesting, half (marked 2. in Fig. 120). Finally, in *La Boiarda* there are also only two expositions, both limited to a single statement of the theme in violin I. Here the rather extended episode is based on a highly individual, short, and energetic motif, which appears at the end of the theme (marked M in Fig. 120).

The five- and six-voice sonatas (Nos. 9–14) have fewer salient features than do the trio sonatas but contain many details of interest and importance. *La Cremona* (No. 10) is noteworthy, first of all, for its name, which pays homage to the famous city of violin building. It is written for four violins, bass, viola, and organ continuo. It has the following structure:

Movement	1		2a	b	c	d		3a	b	
Meter	55 Tr(3/2)	:‖:	6 D	5 D	4 D	20 Tr	:‖:	6 D	18 D	‖
Tempo	slow	‖	adagio	presto	adagio	fast	‖	adagio	presto	‖

The first movement (very likely it is to be played slowly, as are the initial movements of No. 2, *La Pia*, and No. 16, *La Crispa*) is a five-voice double fugue based on two simple but impressive themes:

and

They form the point of departure for a movement that is admirable for both its contrapuntal mastery and its expressiveness. The second movement, a contrast movement, consists of a homophonic *Adagio* (2a), a short *Presto* in imitative style (2b), another homophonic *Adagio* (2c), and fast final section (2d) in which two imitated themes alternate. The final movement (3) begins with a homophonic *Adagio* and closes with a *Presto* fugato.

Sonata La Mosta (No. 3; two violins and b.c.) closes with a *Presto* movement containing many rhythmically interesting passages, such as the one in Fig. 121. They exhibit two kinds of rhythmic conflict: eighth notes against eighth-note triplets and the simultaneous use of eighth-note triplets and a dotted rhythm.[3]

FIGURE 121. LEGRENZI: SONATA LA MOSTA (OPUS 8, 1663).

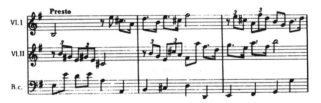

In 1673, Legrenzi's fourth publication of violin music appeared: *La Cetra ... Libro Quarto Di Sonate A due Tre e Quattro Stromenti, Opera Decima.*[4] Like his Opus 2 (1655) and Opus 8 (1663), Opus 10 contains only sonatas. Their scoring is as follows, with the alto voice played by *Violino alto* and the bass by *Viola da brazzo*:

Sonatas à 2:	Nos. 1–3	due Violini
	Nos. 4–6	Violino e Viola da Brazzo (No. 4 is marked
		ò Fagotto in the b.c. part book)
Sonatas à 3:	Nos. 7–12	due Violini e Viola da Brazzo
Sonatas à 4:	No. 13	quatro Violini
	Nos. 14–16	due Violini, Alto e Viola da Brazzo
	Nos. 17, 18	quattro Viole da Gamba ò come piace

The last two sonatas are notated with two different clefs, so that they can be played in two keys a third apart (No. 17 in G minor or E minor; No. 18 in E minor or C minor). Obviously, the lower position is for the scoring *a quatro viole da gamba*, the higher one for the scoring *come piace*, perhaps for two violins, alto, bass, and b.c.

In Opus 10 the tendency toward a four-movement form is evident (while in Legrenzi's earlier sonatas the three-movement form, introduced by Merula, prevails). However, details of the structure remain uncertain, since the separating barlines are frequently missing, and in many cases the meaning of the repeat sign (:‖:) is not clear. Without entering into a discussion of all the problems, we will show the schemes of two sonatas whose structure can be unequivocally determined:

Sonata terza, Due Violini e Viola (No. 9)

Movement	1a	b	c	d	e	
Meter	10 Tr(6/8)	3 D	3 Tr(6/8)	3 D	13 Tr(6/8)	‖ :‖:
Tempo	allegro	presto	[allegro]	[presto]	[allegro]	

	2a	b		3		4a	b	c	
:‖ :‖:	8 D	2 Tr(3/2)	‖	21 D	:‖ :‖:	14 D	8 D	11 D⌒	‖
	Presto	adagio		presto		adagio	allegro	presto	

Sonata terza. A quatro (No. 15)

Movement	1		2a	b	c		3		4a	b	
Meter	27 D⌒	‖ :‖:	3 D⌒ 6 D		23 Tr(3/2)⌒	‖	18 D	:‖ :‖:	47 Tr(3/4)	5 D⌒	‖
Tempo	fast		adagio allegro	adagio			presto		presto	adagio	

In the sonatas of Opus 10, as in the earlier ones, many movements are written in a lively and interesting change of tempo, meter, and content. In both sonatas represented above (and in Nos. 5, 6, 8, 10, and 12) the repeat signs before movement 2 and after movement 3 mean that these two movements are to be played twice as a unit.

The greater freedom and the greater variety in the structure of the sonatas of *La Cetra*—the last ones Legrenzi wrote—apply even more to their content. Strict imitation of themes is replaced by free working with motifs, certainly not everywhere, but all the more conspicuously where it does occur. Right at the beginning of the first sonata Legrenzi uses this technique; the first movement opens, not with a theme and its imitation, but with three different motifs, as shown in Fig. 122.

FIGURE 122. LEGRENZI: SONATA PRIMA A DUE VIOLINI (OPUS 10, 1673).

The main section of the movement (mm. 1–23) consists entirely of the varying succession of these three motifs, as indicated in the following scheme:[5]

Measure	1	3	4	5	7	8	9	9	11	13	15	16	18	20	21	23
Violin I	a		c		b		c		b		c		b		a	
Violin II		b		a		c		b		c		a		c		b

The short closing section (mm. 24–32) is fashioned by numerous restatements of yet another motif. A very similar technique is used for the initial movement of *Sonata prima a 4 Violini* (No. 13). It is constructed entirely of four recurring motifs, as is shown in the following representation of the first half:

Measure	1	2	3	4	5	6	7	8	9	10	11	12	13	14	15	16	17
Violin I	a				b		c				b			a			
Violin II		a				b		c					a				d
Violin III			a				d		b		a			b		c	
Violin IV				a				d		a		a			b		c

The subsequent movements of this very interesting and most significant sonata are similarly written in motivic style. Many other movements in Legrenzi's Opus 10 are developed out of motifs, a technique that is so important that I should like to illustrate it by yet another example. Fig. 123 shows the beginning of the first movement of *Sonata sesta a 3.* (No. 12).

This motivic technique, handled with such mastery by Legrenzi, has a certain looseness, in striking contrast to the strictness of the principle of imitation. It bestows on Legrenzi's *La Cetra* a unique position in the music of the seventeenth century. Is it too far-fetched to relate this looseness and ease to the atmosphere of Venice, which is so different from that of Bologna and Modena?

Legrenzi plays a decisive role in the development of a principle that has universal validity until the end of the nineteenth century, that is, change of key in the inner

FIGURE 123. LEGRENZI: SONATA SESTA A 3. (OPUS 10, 1673).

movements of a sonata or symphony, etc. In his Opus 2 of 1655, all the movements of *Sonata La Donata* are in C major, except for a five-measure *Adagio* in E major. In his later publications, every sonata has changes of tonality, frequently even within a movement or a section. The following scheme shows the tonality changes in *Sonata terza. A quatro* (No. 15), whose structure is indicated above (capital letters stand for major keys, small letters for minor keys):

fast	adagio	allegro	adagio	presto	presto	adagio
d–A	F–C	d–C	C–A	F–A	d–D	g–D

In 1691, one year after Legrenzi's death, his nephew and pupil, Giovanni Vareschinni, published an Opus 16 with the title *Balletti Correnti a cinque Strumenti, con il suo basso continuo per il Cembalo.* It contains nine groups of balletto—corrente in the scoring two violins, alto, tenor, bass, and b.c. Compared with Legrenzi's important work in the field of the sonata, this collection of dances is rather insignificant. Correnti Nos. 3, 6, and 9 are not written in the binary form commonly used for dances: *Corrente terza* is continuous, without inner repetition; and *Corrente sesta* has the form of a French rondeau: A B A C A, with four measures for each of the five sections. *Corrente nona* has an entirely different and very unusual structure. It is based on a *basso ostinato* of eight measures that is repeated thirteen times, resulting in a total length of 104 measures. One would like to know whether it is by intention or by chance that these three exceptional correnti appear at equal distances, at the ends of the first, second, and third parts of the collection.

NOTES

1. The indication in both the *tavola* and the music is simply "Sonata," while the title pages indicate "da chiesa."
2. It is remarkable that, with two exceptions (Nos. 2 and 14) the opening movements of the sonatas contain no tempo indications, while the remaining movements or sections do contain them, although frequently not in all voices.
3. As far as I know, it is here that we encounter for the first time a problem that also arises in several compositions by Bach, for instance, in the *Courante* of his first *Partita* for harpsichord. Should the dotted rhythm be played exactly against the triplets (as in Beethoven's "Moonlight" Sonata), or should it be adjusted, in other words, played as

I have no doubt that the latter performance is correct, not only in Legrenzi's *Sonata* (where, by the way, the very fast tempo defeats any attempt of a contrasting perform- ance), but also in Bach's *Courante* and even very frequently in Schubert's compositions, for instance, in variation III (*Un poco più lent*) of his *Andantino varié*, Opus 84, No. 1.

4. A reprint was published in 1682; see the frontispiece.

5. The same technique had been employed by Cazzati in his *Sonata duodecima*, Opus 55 (1670).

SOURCES

Sonate a due, e tre . . . libro primo. Opus 2. Venice: Stampa del Gardano, appresso Francesco Magni, 1655.   RISM L1610.
> Poland: Wroclaw, Bibliotheka Uniwersytecka (Violin I and II, Violone, b.c.).
Edition:
Stephan Bonta, ed. Cambridge: Harvard University Press, 1984.

Sonate da chiesa, e da camera, correnti, balletti, alemane, e sarabande a tre, doi violini, e violone. . . . Opus 4. Venice: Francesco Magni, 1656.   RISM L1612.
> Great Britain: Oxford, Bodleian Library (Violin I and II, Violone, b.c.)
Reprint:
Suonate da chiesa, e da camera, correnti . . . con il basso continuo. . . . Opus 4. N.p.: Giuseppe Sala, 1682. RISM L1613.
> Austria: Vienna (Violin parts in manuscript).
> Great Britain: Durham, Cathedral Library (complete).
Edition:
Albert Seay, ed. London: Oxford University Press, 1979.

Sonate a due, tre, cinque e sei istromenti. . . . libro 3. Opus 8. Venice: Francesco Magni, 1663.   RISM L1619.
> Italy: Bologna, Archivio dell'Accademia filarmonica (Violin I, II, III, IV, Viola, Organ); Civico Museo.
> Poland: Wroclaw, Biblioteka Uniwersytecka.
Reprints:
Venice: Francesco Magni, 1664.   RISM L1620.
> France: Paris, Bibliothèque de Saint-Geneviève (6 parts).
Bologna: Giacomo Monti, 1671.   RISM L1621.
> Italy: Bologna, Accademia di San Petronio (6 parts); Archivio dell'Accademia filar- monica (Organ); Civico Museo (Violin I); Ferrara, Biblioteca comunale Ariostea.
> United States: Berkeley, University of California, Music Library (Violin II, III, IV, Viola).
Venice: Giuseppe Sala, 1677.   RISM L1622.
> Belgium: Brussels, Conservatoire Royal de Musique, Bibliothèque (Violin I and II, Violone/Viola, Organ).
> Great Britain: Durham, Cathedral Library.

La Cetra . . . libro quarto di sonate a due, tre, e quattro stromenti. Opus 10 (=11) Venice: Francesco Magni detto Gardano, 1673.   RISM L1625.
> Italy: Bologna, Archivio dell'Accademia filarmonica (Violin I and II, part 3, Viola, b.c.).
Edition:
Monumenta Lombardia, vol. 2. Milan: Antiquae Musicae Italicae Studiosi, 1970 (facsimile).

Reprint:
Venice: Francesco Magni detto Gardano, 1682.   RISM L1626.
    Italy: Bologna, Civico Museo.
    West Germany: Münster, Santini-Bibliothek.

Balletti, e correnti a cinque stromenti, con il basso continuo per il cembalo . . . libro quinto postumo. Opus 16. Venice: Giuseppe Sala, 1691.   RISM L1632.
    Great Britain: Oxford, Bodleian Library (6 parts).

🎗 *Antonio Bertali*

> *Antonio Bertali (Bartali, Barthali, Berthali) was born in 1605 in Verona. In 1624 he entered the service of the imperial court in Vienna as an instrumentalist. In 1649 he became chapelmaster, in which position he encouraged the regular performance of Italian opera in Vienna. He died in 1669. His output consists of about 600 compositions, most of which are now lost.[1]*

Among the extant compositions by Bertali are some for violin, but the accounts given in various dictionaries (MGG, Einstein, Riemann, Grove, etc.; he is not included in RISM) differ widely and are most unreliable.[2] I have used the following material for my studies:

> *Prothimia suavissima sive Duodena Prima sonatarum selectissimarum quae nunc prima Editione in Germania prodierunt cum tribus, quatuor Instrumentis redactae, et Basso ad Organum. Autore, J.S.A.B. . . . 1672.*
> *Prothimia suavissima sive Duodena Secunda . . .* [as above]. *Autore J.S.A.B. . . . 1672.*
> Manuscript sonatas in Kassel, Landesbibliothek, and Uppsala, University Library.
> Manuscript sonatas in Paris, Bibl. Nat. Rés. Vm⁷ 673: *Recueil de 150 Sonates* [also known as Collection Rost].[3]

The main sources are the first two items, the posthumous publications. They are not mentioned in the article *Barthali* in MGG, but are discussed in *The New Grove*. Sébastien de Brossard (1655–1730) determined that the indication *J.S.A.B.* means Antonio Bertali, basing this identification on the Stadel Catalogue for 1672.[4] It is confirmed by the fact that in the Uppsala manuscripts, Sonata No. 2 of *Duodena prima* and Sonata No. 4 of *Duodena secunda* are expressly ascribed to Ant. Barthali. We shall begin with a study of the two printed collections and later turn to the manuscripts.

The two *Prothimia* publications each contain a *Duodena* (a dozen) sonatas. They are all written for three instruments: violin I, violin II, and viola da gamba (plus b.c.), except Book II, Nos. 2 and 12, for which a fourth part, *Fagotto ò Viola* is added (it is printed in the part book for *Viola da Gamba*).

In his catalogue, Brossard said he was certain that there were other composers in the *Prothimia* besides Bertali. This opinion is understandable if one compares the first two sonatas of Book I. No. 1 is a piece of 46 measures in a duple meter with no interruption.

It is subdivided only by the use of three themes, each written in fugato style. No. 2 is about three times as long (147 measures) and is separated by cadences into five sections, the fourth of which includes soloistic passages. Book I, Nos. 5, 7, and 9, and Book II, No. 4, are as short and simple as book I, No. 1, while the others are similar to Book I, No. 2, some of them even more extended and more complex. Without doubt, there are two different types of sonata in the *Prothimia* collection, supporting Brossard's assumption that there are "autres auteurs." However, it is possible that the shorter sonatas are also by Bertali.

The structure of the sonatas, as indicated—or at least suggested—by cadences and occasionally also by fermatas, is very variable. Nos. 1, 7, and 9 of Book I are in duple meter and have no interruptions. About six sonatas consist of two movements, among them are No. 5 of Book I and No. 4 of Book II, which respectively carry the remarks "Replica da Capo" and "Repetier von Anfag bis zum Trippel." Thus, in both works the first movement is to be repeated after the second, resulting in the form A B A, the same as in Legrenzi's *Sonata La Pezzoli*, written in 1665 (Opus 4, No. 6). Is this mere coincidence or is there a connection of some kind? About ten of Bertali's sonatas consist of three (different) movements, for instance, Book I, Nos. 8 and 12, and Book II, Nos. 1 and 5. Even more extended structures are found in Book I, No. 10, and Book II, No. 2, both with four movements; in Book I, No. 3, with five; and in Book I, No. 2, with six. Book II, No. 3, is a set of variations.

The content of Bertali's sonatas is no less variable than the structure. The prevailing principle is the constant change of ideas, some of which are interesting and captivating, others rather trivial and even commonplace. His methods of imitation are likewise highly variable. Bertali knows the principle of the double fugue, of stretto, and of inversion; but he also employs the simplifying procedures of "pause exposition" and of merely accompanying the theme by its parallel third instead of writing a genuine counterpoint.

A number of Bertali's sonatas include extended contrast movements, which are all the more interesting because they contain soloistic passages. Book I, No. 3, has a solo for violin I; Book II, No. 11, a solo for viola da gamba; Book I, No. 11, a solo for violin I and one for violin II; and Book I, No. 2, and Book II, Nos. 1, 7, and 10, each have three solo passages: for violin I, violin II, and viola da gamba. The soloistic passages in Book I, Nos. 2 and 11, and Book II, No. 1, are similar to those of Neri, since they are identical except for transposition. In Nos. 7 and 10 of Book II they are wholly individual, the latter also highly virtuosic, as is true of Castello's sonatas. Each of the three solo passages in Book II, No. 7, begins with the same three-measure introduction (I), then continues with different one-measure motifs (m_1, m_2, m_3), which in the subsequent *tutti* section are combined with each other, first m_1 with m_2, then all three. The following diagram shows the design of this section:

	Violin I solo		Violin II solo		Gamba solos		tutti
Measures	1–3	4–8	9–11	12–18	19–21	22–27	28–52
	I	m_1	I	m_2	I	m_3	Violin I $m_1 \ldots m_2 \, m_1 \ldots$
							Violin II $m_2 \ldots m_1 \, m_3 \ldots$
							Gamba $m_3 \, m_2 \ldots$

Book II, No. 3, represents a special case, an interesting set of variations. The attractive theme is twelve measures long, with a unique structure consisting of a two-and-a-half measure motif that is stated four times on various degrees of the scale and is followed by a two-measure refrain. There are nine variations, for which the bass is identical (in the *basso continuo* part book it is notated only once, with the remark "repeat 8 times and close"). In most of the variations the melody too appears without change in one voice part or another (in variations 3 and 8 in the viola da gamba). In fact, the entire viola da gamba part is quite different from the repeated *basso continuo*, which means that the whole composition is written in four different parts, in contrast to the prevailing scoring of the period for three—the trio sonata. In other sonatas by Bertali four-voice passages occur with some frequency, probably because the viola da gamba is a tenor rather than a bass voice, and the scoring is two violins, tenor, and b.c., not two violins, bass, and b.c.

Sonata No. 11 in Book II is the longest (194 measures) and the most noteworthy of the entire *Promithia* publication. Its structure is shown in the following scheme:

Section	1	2	3a	b	4	5	6a	b
Meter	35 D⌢	10 D	15 D	23 D ⌢	10 D	48 Tr	49 D	4 D
Tempo	fast	slow	allegro		slow		presto	slow
Instrumentation			Gamba solo tutti					

Section 1 is a fugue in which a precise theme is treated in three complete expositions. Section 2, a homophonic *grave* modulates from E♭ major to A minor. Toward the end, the sustained chords are unexpectedly replaced by passage-work in sixteenth notes. This entire section is shown in Fig. 124.

FIGURE 124. BERTALI: PROTHIMIA . . . DUODENA SECUNDA, SONATA 11 (1672).

Section 3a is a fifteen-measure solo for viola da gamba. It consists mostly of the repetition of a short formula, which is taken over by the other instruments in section 3b. Section 4 consists of the alternation of two phrases that remind one of early models (see Fig. 125a). In section 5 a rather commonplace idea is treated somewhat too extensively. But section 6a, *Presto*, begins with a phrase that is unique in the entire history of music: a three-voice trill in which the major tonic triad alternates with the diminished triad on the leading tone (Fig. 125b). The initial theme of the sonata reappears in the further course of this very lively section, and the composition closes with a quiet four-measure coda (6b).

FIGURE 125. BERTALI: PROTHIMIA . . . DUODENA SECUNDA, SONATA 11 (1672).

The University Library of Uppsala owns manuscript copies of six sonatas by Bertali (some of them in two and three copies); two of these are also in the *Prothimia* publication (Book I, No. 2, and Book II, No. 4). Another Uppsala manuscript contains six five-voice compositions that are called sonatas.[5] But because of their shortness (about 40 measures), their binary form, and the absence of tempo indications and changes of meter, they might better be classified as sinfonias. At the Landesbibliothek at Kassel there is a *Sonata a 8.* that I have not been able to study. The Rost Collection[6] includes four sonatas ascribed to Bertali: *Tausend Gülden* (No. 37 of the collection), *La Merula* (No. 74), *La Arisia* (No. 75), and *La Pighetta* (No. 76), all scored for two violins and b.c. or violin, bass, and b.c. *Tausend Gülden* is also found in Uppsala, but as *Sonata a 6.*; *La Merula* is not by Bertali, but is a canzona from Tarquinio Merula's Opus 12, published in 1637 (see Fig. 45b). Whether the other two sonatas in the Rost Collection are correctly ascribed to Bertali or are transmitted in their complete form remains an open question.

Bertali was active and famous mainly as a composer of operas and oratorios, in a field that might be called theater music. His violin sonatas often have a mixture of phrase types, some of which are rather commonplace, others fascinating, and still others bizarre. The most impressive of his sonatas, it seems to me, are *Sonata decima* and *Sonata undecima* of *Prothimia II.*

NOTES

1. But see *Grove*, vol. II, pp. 632ff. for clarification.
2. Much of the misinformation regarding Bertali is corrected in I. Bartels, "Die Instrumentalstücke in Oper und Oratorium der früh-venezianischen Zeit," diss., University of Vienna, 1970; and in S.S. Olsen, "Antonio Bertali's "La strage degl'innocenti': An Edition with Commentary," diss., University of Missouri at Columbia, 1972.
3. *Thesaurus musicus a 3* (Dillingen, 1971) is lost.

4. In his *Catalogue des livres de musique . . . dans le Cabinet du Sr. Sébastian Brossard*, pp. 322–323, Brossard remarked, "J. S. A. Bartali comme je l'ai apris et vu dans les Catalogues du sieur Städel . . . pour l'annèe 1672. Je crois bien que led. sieur Bartali est l'auteur de la pluspart de ces Sonates, mais je suis persuadé qu'il y en a aussi d'autres . . ." (J. S. A. Bartali, as I have seen in the Städel catalogues . . . for the year 1672. I believe Bartali is the author of most of the sonatas, but I am persuaded that there are also other [authors].) *Prothimia* is a very clumsily engraved work, with numerous mistakes. That it comes from a German-language area is demonstrated by such rubrics as "Repetier vom Anfang bis zum Trippel."

5. In the Kassel manuscript, in No. 32, *Sonata a 3*, the viola da gamba is an alternate to the trombone (*Trombone overo Viola da gamba*), while in the Uppsala manuscript the reverse is the case.

6. Cf. the article *Rost* in MGG.

SOURCES

Prothimia suavissima sive duodena prima sonatarum selectissimarum . . . cum tribus, quatuor instrumentis redactae. . . . s.l.: s.n., 1672.   RISM BB 2113 I, 1.
    France: Paris, Bibliothèque nationale.
Reprint:
. . . duodena secunda sonatarum. . . . s.l.: s.n., 1672.   RISM BB 2113 I, 2.
    France: Paris, Bibliothèque nationale.

 *Giovanni Antonio Pandolfi*

Only a few reference books list this composer, who is occasionally mentioned under the name of Mealli. It is true that in his first two publications, from 1660, he calls himself Antonio Pandolfi Mealli, but in his publication of 1669 (which has remained almost completely unnoticed), he unequivocally calls himself Giovanni Antonio Pandolfi. Therefore, Pandolfi must be regarded as his real name. All that we know about him comes from the titles of his publications: In 1660 he was active as musico of *Archduke Ferdinand Carl, probably in Innsbruck. In 1669 he was* musico Instrumenta di Violino *of the city of Messina.*

Pandolfi published the following collections of violin sonatas: *Sonate à Violino solo, per Chiesa e Camera . . . Opera Terza,* Innsbruck, 1660; *Sonate à Violino solo, per Chiesa e Camera . . . Opera Quarta,* Innsbruck, 1660; and *Sonate, cioè Ballatti, Sarabande, . . .* (without opus), Rome, 1669.

The first two publications were published in the same year and are also close in content. Each contains six sonatas, all of which belong to the same type. Very likely, Pandolfi chose this unusual kind of publication for political considerations: Opus 3 is dedicated to the ruling Archduchess (*Archiduchessa renante*) Anna; Opus 4 to Archduke Sigismondo Francesco.[1] From the musical point of view it will be best to treat the twelve sonatas as a unit.

All the sonatas are written for violin solo and b.c. and are printed in score form, just like the solo sonatas of Cima, Castello, Fantana, Narini, Uccellini, and Leoni. Regarding the question whether and to what extent the organist or the harpsichordist participated in the melodic activity of the violin part, the reader is referred to remarks made in connection with Uccellini's *Sonate over Canzoni* of 1649 (p. 108). Pandolfi's sonatas are subdivided into movements separated by full cadences and frequently also by fermatas. The number of the movements varies widely. Sonata No. 3 of Book I has only two movements, each of which is a contrast movement in which the tempo changes three times. Several sonatas have three movements (for instance, Book II, No. 5), others have four (for instance, Book I, No. 1). At the other extreme there are a number of sonatas with seven movements, among them, Book I, No. 5. Comprising 325 measures, it is one of the longest in seventeenth-century violin literature. Five sonatas close with slow movements or sections; and one (Book I, No. 4), consists exclusively of slow movements.

The structures of two sonatas deviate from this overall description. Book II, No. 3, *La Monella Romanesca*, is a set of eight variations on a 24-measure theme. The theme is recognizable only in the bass, where it recurs in sustained notes, unchanged in the five first variations.

Above this bass (which is possibly the *Monella* melody) the violin plays lively figurations whose character changes from one variation to the next. In the fourth variation, the first half is dominated by 32d-note trills, the second half by eighth-note triplets.

The other sonata having a structure all its own is Book II, No. 6, the last of the entire collection. It has a rhapsodic and highly virtuosic introduction. The extended main part, in a quiet 3/4, is wholly nonvirtuosic and emphasizes the *cantabile* style of the violin.

FIGURE 126. PANDOLFI: SONATA SESTA LA VINCIOLINA (OPUS 4, 1660).

The beginning of this part is an imitation of the so-called motto aria, which became established about 1650 in the cantatas and operas of Cesti, Legrenzi, and others. Fig. 126 shows the beginning and the end of the introduction and the beginning of the aria.

The "normal" sonatas, to a large extent, are dominated by rather routine, sometimes highly virtuosic, figurations. In contrast to those of Uccellini, sequential phrases hardly ever occur. Imitation, either between violin and organ, or within the violin part (as in Leoni's sonatas), plays a subordinate role. The following is a list of noteworthy details:

1. In several sonatas, Pandolfi composes an entire movement or a lengthy section as a passacaglia based on one or another ostinato: the descending tetrachord (Book I, No. 4)

the descending scale (Book I, No. 3)

or the succession of two chromatic tetrachords (Book I, No. 2)

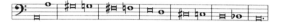

This ostinato perhaps indicates a (misinterpreted) knowledge of ancient Greek music theory.

2. There are several passages based on the principle of modulating passages, which plays a prominent role in Uccellini's sonatas. Pandolfi, however, uses this principle more freely, with the closing measures of the modulated repetitions sometimes differing from each other.

3. In many sonatas the closing part of a movement, especially of the final one, is composed as an organ pedal point, which is used by the violin as a welcome opportunity for virtuosic fireworks.

4. Very frequently Pandolfi writes extended trills, which often end with a rapid reiteration of the leading tone. Caccini calls this *trillo*, and Pandolfi indicates it by the abbreviation *tr.*, as in Fig. 127. Similar, though much less virtuosic, trills had already been used by Mont'Albano in his publication of 1629.

FIGURE 127. PANDOLFI: SONATA SECONDA LA VIVIANA (OPUS 4, 1660).

5. Several sonatas contain short, pregnant chromatic progressions, such as

The diminished third is occasionally employed, for instance:

(in Book II, No. 2) or

(in Book II, No. 5).

6. In some sonatas a dot is printed above each note, as in Fig. 128. What do these dots mean? A special kind of bowing (détaché)? Or do they serve to prevent application of the French practice of *notes inégales*? In other words, do they mean that the notes are to be of equal length?

FIGURE 128. PANDOLFI: SONATA QUINTA LA CLEMENTE (OPUS 3, 1660).

For Pandolfi—as for many other violin composers of the seventeenth century—it is valid to say that his *Allegro* movements or sections are not very significant, while the slow parts are very attractive, sometimes very beautiful. A particularly impressive movement occurs in Book I, No. 5, *Sonata La Clemente*. With seven movements and a total of 325 measures, it is the longest piece of the two publications from 1660). The *Adagissimo*, 10 measures in E minor, takes on the expression of lament and sorrow. This movement can be interpreted as another motto aria: one can imagine it sung to a text expressing grief over the death of a hero. Fig. 129 shows the beginning.

FIGURE 129. PANDOLFI: SONATA QUINTA LA CLEMENTE (OPUS 3, 1660).

After Pandolfi had moved from Innsbruck to Messina, he published his third collection of violin music: *Sonate cioè Balletti, Sarabande, Correnti, Passacagli, Capricietti, & una Trombetta a uno e dui Violini con la terza parta della Viola a beneplacito* .., which was printed in 1669 in Rome. It contains eighteen pieces, six *a tre* (two violins, bass, and b.c.), eight *a due Violini* (two violins and b.c.), and four *a Violino solo* (violin and b.c.). The *viola* (viola da gamba?) in the first group is optional (*Viola a beneplacito*, as the title says). Indeed, it is identical with the organ bass, as is indicated in the part book by the inscription *Organo e Basso di Viola insieme*.

Twelve of the compositions are dances: one sarabanda (No. 7), one balletto (No. 15), two suites *Capricietto—La sua Corrente* (Nos. 2 and 6), two suites *Capricietto—La sua*

Corrente—La sua Sarabanda (Nos. 3 and 5), and five suites *Balletto—La sua Sarabanda* (Nos. 8–12). Sonata No. 14 is also a sort of suite, consisting of *Passacaglio, Arietta,* and *Brando.* The *Passacaglio* is a four-measure ostinato (essentially the descending tetrachord *C Bb Ab G*) played eighteen times. An extended composition named *La Sparta Forta* (No. 13) consists of *Trombetta, Arietta, Battaglia, Corrente,* and *Sarabanda.* Its first movement reminds one of the *Trombetta* in Uccellini's *Libro Quinto* from 1640, with which it shares not only its name but also its style, an endless series of broken D-major chords. Three capricietti (Nos. 1, 16, and 17) are actually sonatas; for instance, No. 1 has three movements—*Largo, Adagissimo,* and *Vivace. Capricietto,* No. 18, the last composition of the collection, consists of four variations based on the same bass and has the structure ‖: 14 :‖: 14 :‖.

NOTE

1. Opus 1 and Opus 2 are unknown.

SOURCES

Sonate a violino solo, per chiesa e camera. . . . Opus 3. Innsbruck: Michael Wagner, 1660.   RISM P832.
    Italy: Bologna, Civico Museo.
Edition:
Ernst Kubitschek, ed. Innsbruck, Edition Helbing, 1986 (Musik am Hofe zu Innsbruck, No. 4089).

Sonate a violino solo, per chiesa e camera. . . . Opus 4. Innsbruck: Michael Wagner, 1660.   RISM P883.
    Italy: Bologna, Civico Museo.

Sonate cioe balletti, sarabande, correnti, passacagli, capriccetti, e una trombetta a uno e dui violini con la terza parte della viola a beneplacito. Rome: Amadeo Belmonte, 1669.   RISM P834.
    Great Britain: London, British Library (Violin I and II, Basso di Viola).
    Italy: Lucca, Biblioteca del seminario arcivescovile presso la Curia.

🍃 Giulio Cesare Arresti

Giulio Cesare Arresti was born in Bologna in 1617, according to some sources, in 1625 according to others. In 1668 he became chapelmaster at San Salvatore. From 1649 to 1661 and again from 1671 to 1699 he was organist at San Petronio. He was one of the founders of the Accademia Filarmonica in 1666, and was elected its president several times. He died after 1704. In 1659 Arresti wrote an abusive tract about Maurizio Cazzati's contrapuntal skills, to which Cazzati replied in 1663 (Cazzati resigned as maestro di capella of San Petronio in 1671).

In 1663 Arresti published his Opus 2, *Messe a tre voci* . . . , which contains mainly vocal compositions for three masses (*De Resurrectione, De Spiritu Sancto,* and *De Communi omnium festorum*). At the end of the first mass a *Sonata a 2.Violini* is added. It consists of three movements, an *Allegro* in fugue style, an *Adagio,* and an extended movement in 3/2 meter called *Aria,* whose three sections are combined in an interesting manner. The first is a solo for violin I, the second a similar solo for violin II, and the third a duet in which motifs from the first section alternate with those from the second.

In 1665, Arresti's Opus 4 appeared: *Sonate a 2. & a Tre. Con la parte del Violoncello a beneplacito* This is the earliest documentation of the violoncello or at least of its present name.[1] The publication contains twelve sonatas, eleven in the scoring two violins, bass, and b.c., and one, No. 8, for violin, bass, and b.c. The sonatas are ascribed to the twelve church modes: *Sonata Prima, Primo Tono* to *Sonata XII, XII. Tono.* Thus, they provide material for the difficult problem of the meaning of the church modes in polyphonic music.

The sonatas consist of three or four movements, of which the final movements are especially noteworthy. As in the sonatas of Opus 2, nearly all are in 3/2 and are named *Aria.* However, they have a different structure. They begin with a solo section for violin I (with b.c.), followed by an equally long section for all the instruments, in which the melody of the first section is played by violin II, not as a solo, but accompanied by violin I, violoncello, and *basso continuo.* This procedure can be schematically represented as follows (the b.c. is omitted):

Violin I	A	B
Violin II		A
Violoncello		C

Five final movements are composed according to this scheme: in Sonatas Nos. 4 and 5 (with fourteen measures in each section), No. 7 (with eight measures), No. 9 (30 measures), and No. 11 (ten measures). Essentially the same, but somewhat more complicated structure is found in the final movement of Sonata No. 1, which consists of four sections as follows: 1. fourteen measures for violin I solo and b.c.; 2. fourteen measures for violin I, violin II, and b.c. with the melody exchanged between the two violins as described above; 3. seven measures for all instruments; and 4. these seven measures repeated with the two violins exchanged. The idea of performing a melody by one violin and then the other violin is derived from vocal music, an assumption confirmed by the designation *Aria*.

As mentioned above, the scoring of *Sonata ottava—A 2., Violino e Violoncello a vicenda—* differs from that of the rest of Opus 4. The designation *a vicenda* (in exchange) probably refers to the fact that the movements of this sonata largely consist of complementary motifs that migrate from the violin to the violoncello. Finally, it should be noted that Arresti often makes use of the so-called Corelli clash, almost as frequently as G.M. Bononcini does.

Arresti is not a great composer, but he deserves better than being remembered for his intrigues against Cazzati or his pedantic criticism of Corelli. The last movements of his sonatas have singular and quite interesting forms. There are also several particularly lively and playful movements among Sonatas Nos. 4, 5 (see Fig. 130), and 11.

FIGURE 130. ARRESTI: SONATA QUINTA (OPUS 4, 1665).

NOTE

1. The name "violoncino" occurs in the 1641 collection of sonatas by G. B. Fontana. The earliest solo repertory seems to be the *Ricercari per violoncello solo* (1684) of Domenico Gabrieli, in manuscript at San Petronio in Bologna.

SOURCES

Messe a tre voci, con sinfonie, e ripieni à placito, accompagnate da motetti, e concerti .... Opus 2. Venice: Francesco Magni, 1663.   RISM A2484.
    Italy: Bologna, Civico Museo (S I and II, B, Violin I and II, Organ); Orvieto, Biblioteca dell' Opera del Duomo (B).
    Poland: Wroclaw, Biblioteka Uniwersytecka.

Sonate a 2, & a tre, con la parte del violoncello a beneplacito. Opus 4. Venice: Francesco Magni detto Gardano, 1665.   RISM A2486.
    Great Britain: Oxford, Bodleian Library.
    Poland: Wroclaw, Biblioteka Uniwersytecka (Violin II, Violoncello; lacks Violin I, b.c.).

🎵 Pietro Andrea Ziani

Pietro Andrea Ziani was born sometime before December 21, 1616, in Venice. In 1640 he became organist at the church of San Salvatore in that city. From 1657 to 1659 he was active as Cazzati's successor as chapelmaster at Santa Maria Maggiore in Bergamo, and 1663 in Vienna as vice-chapelmaster for the emperor's mother, Eleonora. In 1669, he became first organist at San Marco in Venice (succeeding Cavalli), and in 1677 he became a teacher at San Onofrio in Naples, where he died in 1684. He wrote numerous operas, oratorios, masses, cantatas, and arias.

During the years 1666 and 1667 Ziani was at the Saxon court in Dresden, where he performed his operas and some chamber music. Here he wrote his Opus 7: *Sonate a 3., 4., 5., 6. voci,* which was published in Freiberg near Dresden (*Freiberga. Appresso Giorgio Beutlero*), with a dedication (in German) to Elector Johann Georg II. The publication has no date, but it probably appeared during or shortly after Ziani's stay in Dresden, that is, in 1667 or 1668. This publication contains twenty sonatas: Nos. 1–6 *a 3.,* Nos. 7–14 *a 4.,* Nos. 15–18 *a 5.,* and Nos. 19 and 20 *a 6.* In 1678 a reprint was published in Venice with the title *Sonate a tre quattro cinque, et sei stromenti.* The publisher, Giuseppe (Gioppe) Sala—not Ziani—dedicated it in Italian to a Venetian nobleman. This reprint contains only fourteen sonatas, lacking Nos. 3, 6–9, and 14 of the original publication.[1] Since the original was available to me for only a brief survey, the following study is based on the shortened reprint of 1678 and uses its numbering of the sonatas.[2]

Sonatas Nos. 2, 11, and 12 each consist of four movements; No. 10 has five movements; and Nos. 1, 3–9, 13, and 14 each have three. In the last group, the movements of Nos. 1, 3, 4, 7, 8, and 14 are labeled *Prima Parte, Seconda Parte,* and *Terza Parte.* Does this mean that these movements should be separated by longer rests? Except for No. 8, the movements of these *Parte* sonatas are in the order fast, slow, fast. This tempo order is of fundamental importance for the later development of the sonata (by Haydn and Mozart) and the concerto (from Corelli to Beethoven).

In Ziani's three- and four-voice sonatas the fast movements are nearly all fugues. They are skillfully written but are based on uninspired themes. The slow movements of the sonatas, written in homophonic style, are more attractive.

More important and interesting than the three- and four-voice sonatas are those *a 5.* and *a 6.* It is not mere chance that Giuseppe Sala, publisher as well as editor of the 1678 reprint, took over all these sonatas from the original publication, but considerably reduced the number *a 3.* and *a 4.* The first of the five-voice sonatas (No. 9) begins with a fugue whose theme has a totally different character from what was customary at the time. It comes from the world of the organ ricercar, which had been cultivated in Venice almost 100 years before by Andrea Gabrieli. The theme spreads over seven measures in long note values:

It is introduced in a correspondingly long exposition: the last voice, the *Basso,* does not enter until m. 19. The second movement of this sonata is a homophonic *Adagio,* and the third is a fugue whose theme is a 6/4 variant of the theme of the first movement. The second and third of the five-voice sonatas (Nos. 10 and 11) also begin with ricercar movements based on themes of similar character, though they are somewhat less extended:

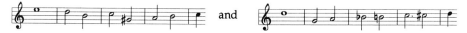

The last of the five-voice sonatas (No. 12) begins with a very impressive *Adagio* in homophonic style. The second movement is composed as a double ricercar, that is, as a fugue based on two themes, both in long note values:

The initial movements of Sonatas Nos. 13 and 14, for six instruments, are not ricercars but fugues whose themes consist of fast eighth notes. Especially in No. 13 the eighth-note motion is so prevalent that the composition takes on the character of a *perpetuum mobile*. Its third movement, however, is like a ricercar in 3/1, with a theme consisting of whole and half notes.

About ten sonatas by Ziani are found in manuscripts (in Oxford and in Vienna), and I have not been able to study them. It is not known whether they are copies of his published sonatas or are additional compositions. Thus, Ziani's very important work in the field of violin music cannot be presented here as fully as it should be.

NOTES

1. SartoriB, p. 564, lists the Freiberg original under 1691(?). I do not know the reason for this excessively late dating.

2. The part books of the 1678 edition are marked *Violino Primo, Secondo, Alto* (in alto clef), *Tenor Viola* (in tenor clef), *Basso* (for No. 9, *Basso Viola*), and *Organo* (employing treble, soprano, alto, tenor, baritone, and bass clefs).

SOURCES

Sonate a 3, 4, 5, 6 voci. . . . Opus 7. Freiberg: Georg Beuther, ca. 1678.   RISM Z176.
Czechoslovakia: Kromeriz, Umelecko-historické muzeum (Violin I and II, Viola, B, Organ).
France: Paris, Bibliothèque nationale.
Reprint:
Sonate a tre, quattro, cinque, et sei stromenti. . . . Venice: Giuseppe Sala, 1678.   RISM 2177.
Great Britain: London, British Library (Violin I and II, Alto Viola, Tenor Viola, B, Organ); Oxford, Bodleian Library.

🎧 Giovanni Maria Bononcini

Giovanni Maria Bononcini was born in 1642 in Montecorrone (near Modena) and died in 1678 in Modena. In 1671 he became violinist and in 1673 maestro di capella at the cathedral of Modena. He was a member of the Accademia Filarmonica of Bologna, probably since 1671. Together with Uccellini, Vitali, and Colombi he belongs to the violin school of Modena, which had close relationships to the Este court. During his short life he published nine books with violin music, from Opus 1 in 1666 to Opus 12 in 1678. Together they contain 29 sonatas, over 180 shorter pieces (dances, arias, and ariettas), and fifteen canons.[1]

Bononcini's first publication appeared in 1666, with the title *Primi Frutti del giardino musicale a due Violini*. The first part contains twelve sonatas with the scoring two violins and b.c.; the second comprises a brando, four arias, and four correnti *A due Violini, e Violone ò vero Spinetta per Camera*.

The sonatas consist of two or three movements clearly separated by fermatas, double bars, or repeat signs. Only *Sonata sesta* (the longest, with 135 measures) has more movements, that is, five. It is also the only one that begins with a slow movement, a homophonic *Adagio* of 25 measures. Most of the sonatas have a structure with two inner repeat signs: _____:‖:_____:‖:_____‖ (probably to be interpreted as A ‖ : B : ‖ C ‖), which had been introduced by Merula and used by Legrenzi in Opus 4 (1656) and Opus 8 (1663). In the closing section, C, Bononcini uses methods similar to Legrenzi's: Sometimes the final section is only a short coda or it is entirely missing, so that the sonata consists of only two movements; sometimes it becomes an independent third movement. The second movements (which are to be repeated) nearly always consist of two sections differing in tempo or meter, as, for instance, in *Sonata terza*:

Movement	1	‖	2a	b	‖	3	‖
Meter	18 D ⌢ :	‖:	21 Tr	22 D⌢ :	‖:	17 D⌢	‖
Tempo	allegro	‖	largo	fast	‖	fast	‖

In Sonatas Nos. 9 and 12 the repeat signs have a different meaning: they divide the first movement into two equal parts, each to be repeated, so that it has the binary form that is obligatory for all the dance pieces and most of the sinfonias of the seventeenth century. Corelli also uses this binary form, for instance, in the first movement of Sonata Opus 3, No. 6. Many of Bononcini's sonatas (e.g., Nos. 2, 4, 5, 10, 11, and 12) are cyclic, since the last movement or the coda is derived from the initial movement.

Except for *Sonata sesta*, Bononcini's sonatas begin with an *Allegro* in fugal style, which in most cases is only a fugato. In Nos. 2, 5, 6, and 7 it is a real two-voice fugue with three expositions, naturally always supported by the harmonies of the continuo. Sonatas Nos. 4, 10, 11, and 12 have unusually extended themes of four to five measures, which are answered unchanged at the unison in such a way that in the opposing voice there is no counterpoint, only rests. Ultimately, this technique, which we have named *pause exposition*, goes back to Merula. It is even closer to Cazzati (see Fig. 101) and Uccellini (Opus 7, Nos. 9 and 10), who used this method for similarly extended themes also answered at the unison.

The movements or sections composed in slow tempo, duple meter, and homophonic style frequently begin with an incipit repeat, as, for instance, in the first movement of *Sonata sesta* (Fig. 131).

FIGURE 131. G.M. BONONCINI: SONATA SESTA (OPUS 1, 1666).

Bononcini's sonatas frequently contain extended passages in disjunct motion: ascending or descending thirds, fourths, or octaves. Two passages of this kind are reproduced in Fig. 132.

FIGURE 132. G.M. BONONCINI: a. SONATA PRIMA; b. SONATA UNDECIMA (OPUS 1, 1666).

Here and there Bononcini writes melodic phrases that suggest a new feeling of charm and grace. They contrast with the seriousness of earlier compositions and seem to be a presentiment of the pleasant melodies of the high Baroque, even of rococo. The dancelike melody of the triple-meter movement of *Sonata quinta* (Fig. 133b) is all the more interesting since it is derived from the theme of the first movement (Fig. 133a), which is strictly formal rather than gracious.

FIGURE 133. G.M. BONONCINI: SONATA QUINTA (OPUS 1, 1666).

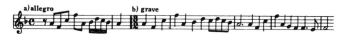

The second part of *Primi Frutti*, the collection of dances, begins with a brando in E minor with the following structure:

Prima Parte	Seconda Parte	Terza Parte	Gavotta	Corrente
¢ ‖ : 12 : ‖ : 12 : ‖	3/4 16	3/4 24	¢ ‖ : 4 : ‖ : 8 : ‖	‖ : 5 : ‖ : 5 : ‖

The *Seconda Parte* and *Terza Parte* of this brando do not have the customary binary form but are continuous. Actually, the *Seconda Parte* consists of two eight-measure phrases that are identical except for their endings: the first closes on the dominant, the second on the tonic, yielding the form A A. The *Terza Parte* consists of four phrases of six measures each, the first two identical, so that the form A A B C results. Thus, the entire brando reproduces in every detail—including the number of measures—the same dance suite as the *Brando* in Uccellini's Opus 9 from 1667 (see p. 116). Bononcini's *Seconda Parte* is therefore a *Branle gay*, his *Terza Parte* a *Branle à mener*. The brando is followed by four arias and four correnti.

Bononcini's Opus 2 of 1667 is entitled *Sonata da camera e da ballo a 1. 2. 3. e 4* . . . It contains 37 dance pieces, which are indicated consecutively in the *Tavola*, but in the book itself they are separated into five groups with different scoring, as follows (A = Allemande; B = Balletto; Br = Brando; C = Corrente; G = Giga; S = Sarabanda):

    I. Allemana, Sarabande, Corente, e Gighe a Violino solo. Da Camera Nos. 1–8: A–S–G–G–C–G–G–G

   II. Allemana, Corente, e Balletti a due Violini. Da Camera Nos. 9–14: A–C–B–C–B–C

  III. Corente a 3. Due Violini e Violone. Da Camera Nos. 15–26: 12 C

  IV. Brando e Corente in stil francese a 3. Da Ballo Nos. 27–29: Br–C–C

   V. Brando e Corente in stil francese a 4. Da Ballo Nos. 30–37: Br–6 C–Aria Discordia Concors, Sua Corente.

It is particularly important that, here within the field of dance music (more properly, "dance-derived music"), a distinction is made between *da camera* and *da ballo*. To the former belong groups I, II, and III, with "weak" scoring for one or two violins; to the latter, groups IV and V, with fuller scoring for three or four instruments. This means that the entire realm of Italian instrumental music should be subdivided not into two fields, *da chiesa* and *da camera*, but into three: *da chiesa*, *da camera*, and *da ballo*; or to put it differently: church music, chamber music, and dance music (more precisely "music for dancing"). Of these fields, chamber music was the most comprehensive. In a way, it corresponded to what is now presented in a concert hall, an important difference being that performance usually took place in a private home, not in public. Various types of instrumental music were played: canzonas, sonatas, sinfonias, toccatas, and arias as well as dance pieces, which, however, were not used for actual dancing (nor were the suites of Bach). Regarding real dance music, such as Bononcini's *da ballo* pieces, the question arises whether something similar can be found in earlier literature. As far as I know, Uccellini was the first to mention this field specifically. His *Ozio regio*, Opus 7 of 1600, contains, among other pieces, eight *Corrente a 4. in stil francese per ballare* (group VII of the contents on p. 110). His Opus 9, which appeared in 1667 (the same year as Bononcini's Opus 2) also contains music for dancing: two *Brando alla francese per ballare* and six *Corrente alla francese per ballare* (groups II and III of the listing on p. 115). For both

Uccellini and Bononcini (as well as for Vitali and Colombi) dance music is always *alla francese*: dancing is patterned after the French. We mention a few additional examples of early dance music: *Balet comique de la Royne* (1592), Marini's "court ballets" in his *Concerto terzo* (1649), and Cazzati's "masked Ball" in his *Trattenimenti* (1660). Of course, this is but a small part of what was written for dancing, because that was music for the moment and is lost forever.

In Bononcini's music, can one perceive a difference between his dances *da ballo* and those *da camera*? In the correnti, the only type found in both categories, the pieces *da camera* are longer and their musical ideas are treated more thoroughly. The decisive difference however, is that of style. While the *da ballo* pieces—correnti as well as brandi— are written in a plain homophonic style, which corresponds to the needs of dance music, the *da camera* pieces contain quite a few attractive details; changing ideas, complementary motifs, short imitations, appoggiaturas, and occasional daring novelties. For example, *Giga*, No. 6, contains an eight-measure passage in which the violin repeatedly returns to *d*, and thereby forms an inner pedal point against which the bass has dissonant notes such as *c*, *e*, and e♭ (Fig. 134).

FIGURE 134. G.M. BONONCINI: GIGA (OPUS 2, 1667).

The brandi at the beginnings of groups IV and V duplicate in every detail, even in the number of measures, the structure of the earlier brando in *Primi Frutti* (see p. 179).

Bononcini's predilection for disjunct motion is even more evident in Opus 2 than in his first publication. Successive thirds, either descending (as in Fig. 132a) or ascending, are found so frequently as to become an unmistakable characteristic of his style. Also typical is his preference for the dissonant cadence generally called the Corelli clash, which we encountered first in a composition by Marini (see p. 56) and later in Cazzati's *Corrente quinta* (see Fig. 97a). While Marini and Cazzati each used it only once, Bononcini wrote it at least as frequently as did Corelli, but fifteen years earlier. Thus it should properly be called the Bononcini clash.

Bononcini makes use of *scordatura* in four pieces, for the first time since Marini's Opus 8 from 1626.[2] For *Giga*, No. 6, the violin has to be tuned

for *Gigas* Nos. 7 and 8,

and for the last piece in the collection, *Aria*, No. 37 (scored for two violins, alto, bass, and b.c.), the two violins are tuned to

and the viola to

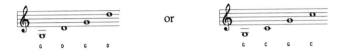

In the original print the *scordatura* (French lute players called it *accord*) is named *Discordua concors* and is indicated by four notes to which letters are added, for instance:

Bononcini's Opus 3 appeared in 1669; *Varii Fiori del Giardino Musicale overo Sonate da Camera a 2. 3. e 4. col suo Basso continuo, & aggiunta d'alcuni Canoni studiosi & osservati.* Its contents, with the original numbering, are:

Nos. 1–7	7 Giga (1–4 a 2., 5–7 a 4.)
Nos. 8–15	5 Allemanda, 3 Corrente (in the order A–C–A–C–A–A–C–A) a 4.
Nos. 16, 17	2 Sonata da Camera (16 a 4., 17 a 3.)
No. 18	Brando in stil francese a 4.
No. 19	Corrente in stil francese a 4.
Nos. 20–30	11 Canon

The scoring is very unusual. Ten of the 30 compositions are to be performed without *basso continuo*, that is, without an accompanying instrument (organ, spinet, or theorbo): Nos. 1–4, 21, and 25 are not represented in the *basso continuo* part book, while Nos. 7, 16, 18, and 19 carry the remark *Tacet*. Thus, for the first time since Buonamente's string trios from 1626 and 1629, we encounter compositions without *basso continuo*: Gigas Nos. 1–4 are duets for violin and viola; *Brando*, No. 18, and *Corrente*, No. 19, are scored for four string instruments (violin, alto, tenor, and bass); and *Giga*, No. 7, and *Sonata*, No. 16, are string quartets in the present-day sense of the word (two violins, alto, and bass). Note that Colombi, who was active in Modena at the same time as Bononcini, published a whole book of compositions scored for string quartet in 1668, one year earlier than Bononcini's Opus 3 appeared.

In the titles of Opus 2 and Opus 3, Bononcini uses the designation *Sonata da camera*. In both publications this term principally refers to single dances—gagliardas, allemandes, correnti—not to groups of dances, as it does in Corelli's *Sonata da camera*. A different situation exists in the case of Opus 3, Nos. 16 and 17, both of which are specifically—that is, in the text and in the *Tavola*—termed *Sonata da camera* but actually belong to the category *sonata da chiesa*. No. 16 consists of *Grave-Allegro-Adagio a tremolo-Grave-Al-*

legro–Affetuoso–Adagio; No. 17 of *Grave–Allegro*. They differ, however, from the sonatas of the period, since—like many sonatas of an earlier time—they proceed without interruption. The *Affetuoso–Adagio* ending of No. 16 is of greater artistic value than anything else in Bononcini's Opus 3. Its deep sonorities, its downward chromatic movement, its daring progressions and combinations of chords—all produce an expression of lamentation that is rare in seventeenth-century violin music. Fig. 135 shows this section; note the dissonance *gb* against *g* at the beginning of m. 5.

FIGURE 135. G.M. BONONCINI: SONATA DA CAMERA A 4 (OPUS 3, NO. 16, 1669).

Brando, No. 18, and *Corrente*, No. 19, have exactly the same structure as those in *Primi Frutti* and in Opus 2.

The eleven canons that close Opus 3 (Nos. 20–30), are not discussed here because they belong more to the field of school counterpoint than to violin music. Right at the beginning of this collection, devoted predominantly to dance music, Bononcini has prominently placed two canons: *Canon 2592 Voci dopo un mezzo sospiro dall'una all'altra devise in 648 Chori . . .*, and on the page with the Preface ("Al benigno lettore") an *Obliogo a 4. Caecus non judicat de Colore*.[3] The canon was especially cultivated in Modena, first by Uccellini, then by Bononcini, and finally by Gio. Battista Vitali, whose *Artificii musicali* of 1689 is a central document of school counterpoint.

In 1671 Bononcini's Opus 4 appeared: *Arie, Corrente, Sarabande, Gighe & Allmande a Violino, e Violone, over Spinetta, con alcune intavolate per diverse accordature*, a collection of 27 pieces. Occasionally successive dances written in the same key can be combined into three-movement suites, for instance, *Aria, Corrente,* and *Sarabanda* in C major (Nos. 7–9) and in F major (Nos. 10–12); *Giga, Sarabanda,* and *Corrente* in D major (Nos. 13–

15) and in E minor (Nos. 16–18; the last *Corrente* in E major); or *Allemanda, Sarabanda,* and *Corrente* in B♭ major (Nos. 21–23).

Nos. 1–6 are all in G major but in a less-meaningful order—*Aria, Corrente, Aria, Corrente, Sarabanda, Corrente*—which can hardly be interpreted as a suite. However, they are all marked *in stil francese,* a designation that Bononcini had already used for a brando in his Opus 3 from 1669. It means the same as the term *da ballare* in his Opus 2 from 1667, that is, dance music in the proper sense of the word. The six dances *in stil francese* are short, with an average length of about fifteen measures, for instance, ‖: 6 :‖: 7 :‖ (*Corrente,* No. 4).

Interesting traits occur mainly in the other pieces, which obviously belong to the *da camera* category. In Correnti Nos. 15, 20, and 23 the tempo changes several times—a liberty that neither Corelli nor Bach would have thought permissible. Two of these correnti are schematically reproduced here:

Corrente, detta La Buffalina (No. 15)

Measures	1–2	3–22		23–30	31–38	39–41	
Tempo	Adagio	Presto	‖:	Adagio	Presto	Adagio	:‖

Corrente, detta La Pegolotta (No. 20)

Measures	1–6	7–14		15–20	21–33	
Tempo	Adagio	Presto	‖:	Largo	Allegro	:‖

In both correnti Bononcini introduces another eccentric feature by suddenly interrupting the sustained sounds of an *Adagio* section with a passage in 32d notes, producing an effect of surprise that reminds one of the early Baroque music of Castello or Fontana. Thus in *Corrente, detta La Pegolotta* the initial calm is disturbed twice, first by a fast passage, then by the change from *Adagio* to *Presto* (see Fig. 136).

FIGURE 136. G.M. BONONCINI: CORRENTE, DETTA LA PEGOLOTTA (OPUS 4, 1671).

For the last four dances (Nos. 24–27) the violin part is printed on two systems, as was done in the last pieces of Uccellini's *Ozio regio* (Opus 7), a work certainly known to Bononcini. However, he surpasses his predecessor in the last three pieces by combining double-stop playing with *scordatura,* a technique he had employed in his Opus 2 from 1667, and which he now calls *accordatura.* The *scordatura* of *Corrente La Castelvetra* (No. 25) is particularly interesting. The violin is tuned

which is nearly the C major tuning,

employed by Biber for No. XII of his "Mystery" sonatas printed about 1674, three years later than Bononcini's and possibly under his influence.[4]

In the same year, 1671, Bononcini's Opus 5 also appeared: *Sinfonia, Allemande, Correnti, e Sarabande a 5. e 6. col suo Basso Continuo.* The contents of this publication are as follows:

No. 1	Sinfonia per introduzione a 5	D minor
Nos. 2–4	Allemanda–Corrente–Sarabanda à 5	D minor
Nos. 5–7	Allemanda–Corrente–Sarabanda à 5	Bb major
Nos. 8–10	Allemanda–Corrente–Sarabanda à 5	G minor
Nos. 11–13	Allemanda–Corrente–Sarabanda à 5	Eb major
Nos. 14, 15	Corrente–Sarabanda à 5	Eb major
Nos. 16, 17	Corrente–Sarabanda à 5	F minor
Nos. 18–20	Allemanda–Corrente–Sarabanda à 5	C minor
Nos. 21–23	Allemanda–Corrente–Sarabanda à 6	Bb major
Nos. 24–26	Allemanda–Corrente–Sarabanda à 6	F major

Here for the first time in Italy we see the succession of dances that Froberger introduced for the German suite in his autograph of 1649.[5] There can be no doubt that Bononcini adopted it from Froberger, who was internationally famous.

As always, the dances are in binary form, the allemandes and correnti with sections of irregular and differing numbers of measures (for instance, the first allemande is ‖: 12 :‖: 11 :‖, the first corrente ‖: 21 :‖: 22 :‖), while the sarabandas have a regular structure with eight and occasionally twelve measures in each section. The allemandes are composed as five- or six-voice fugatos, based on different (sometimes remotely similar) themes or motifs for each section. Only in Allemandes Nos. 11 and 21 does Bononcini write the second section in chordal style interspersed with polyphonic elements. Similar statements are valid for the correnti, although here the polyphonic-chordal style is used more frequently, for instance, for both sections of Nos. 4, 14, 16, 19, and 25. No. 25 presents the same effect of surprise as do some correnti of Opus 4: in the first section the tempo changes from *Adagio* to *Presto* to *Adagio*, in the second from *Allegro* to *Adagio*. The sarabandas are all composed in a strictly chordal style; No. 17, is interesting because of its dynamic designations: in the first section *forte, piano, forte, piano* (each in place for two measures of 3/4); in the second section *forte, piano, più piano e più piano. Sarabanda* No. 26 is marked *Presto* and contains accents and hemiolas (see Fig. 137).

Opus 5 closes with a composition that like several in Opus 3, belong to the field of school counterpoint, which is expressly mentioned in the title: *Et aggiunta d'una Sinfonia a quattro, che si può suonare ancora al contrario rivoltando le parti, e cambiando il Soprano in Basso, l'Alto in Tenore, il Tenore in Alto, et in Soprano il Basso* (a four-voice sinfonia that can also be played in retrograde motion with exchange of voice parts and clefs).

Bononcini's Opus 6, *Sonate da chiesa a due Violini . . . ,* of 1672, contains twelve sonatas in the scoring two violins and b.c., with no bass instrument. Since only one copy is preserved,[6] it is quite possible that the *basso* part book is lost.

FIGURE 137. G.M. BONONCINI: SARABANDA A 6. (OPUS 5, 1671).

The structure of these sonatas is quite different from those of *Primi frutti*, published six years earlier. While most of the early sonatas have the form with two inner repeat signs that was introduced by Merula, the sonatas of Opus 6 consist of three or four movements, clearly separated by fermatas and double bars, but without repeat signs. Thus, they have the new form introduced by Cazzati, which had become obligatory for future development. As may be expected in sonatas written about 1670, the movements are provided with tempo indications; unexpectedly, however, these indications are missing for the triple-meter movements of the first five sonatas. Very likely they are to be played fast, since the triple-meter movements of Sonatas Nos. 6–12 are all marked *Largo* or *Adagio*. Fast movements often begin or close with a few measures in slow tempo. The fast triple-meter movement of Sonata No. 5, written in 12/8, closes with four measures *Adagio* in duple meter, not in the usual time signature C but in 8/12. Of course, this is not intended to mean "eight twelfths" but is a late example of a method frequently used in mensural notation to cancel a sign of proportion.[7]

Like the sonatas of *Primi frutti*, most sonatas of Opus 6 begin with an *Allegro* in freely treated fugal style, that is, with a fugato. Only two begin with a slow movement: *Sonata terza*, with an homophonic *Adagio* of twelve measures; and *Sonata quinta*, with a 29-measure *Largo e affettuoso*, in which an impressive theme—characterized by chromatic suspensions—is treated in imitation (see Fig. 138a). More than half the sonatas are cyclical, the theme of the first movement recurring in a later one. In *Sonata quinta*, which consists of four movements (*Largo e affettuoso*, quick, *Adagio*, and *Allegro*), the first, second, and fourth are unmistakably related by the motif

(see Fig. 138a). Usually the initial theme is modified in a subtler manner, as in Frescobaldi's "variation canzonas" in *Secondo libro di Toccate* (1627). The *Allegro* and *Largo* of Bononcini's *Sonata duodecima* exemplify this kind of cyclic treatment (Fig. 138b).

FIGURE 138. G.M. BONONCINI: a. SONATA QUINTA; b. SONATA DUODECIMA (OPUS 6, 1672).

Several of the fugue movements, for instance, the *Allegro* of *Sonata quinta* (see Fig. 138a) are based on repeated-note themes, a type greatly favored in both the violin and the organ music of the seventeenth century. It can be traced back to the chansons and canzonas of the early sixteenth century, which frequently begin with three iterations of the initial note. The fugal themes are frequently answered tonally, especially in the initial movements (of Nos. 1, 2, 3, 5, 7, 9, and 10). In *Sonata quinta* each of the three themes is answered tonally, the descending fifth

being modified into an ascending fourth

Most of the sonatas of Opus 6 do not close with a sustained chord but with an abrupt stop. In some sonatas of the 1630s and 1640s the final chord is avoided, being replaced by a gradually fading echo. Bononcini, however, used exactly the opposite effect, that is, an abrupt and almost forcible stopping of the music, something more expected in Beethoven than in the seventeenth century. Fig. 139 shows the closing measures of Sonatas Nos. 8 and 10. Nos. 1, 3, 4, 5, and 12 close similarly.

FIGURE 139. G.M. BONONCINI: a. SONATA OTTAVA; b. SONATA DECIMA (OPUS 6, 1672).

Bononcini's next publication, Opus 7, 1672, contains dance music, as is indicated by the title: *Ariette, Corrente, Gighe, Allemande, e Sarabande.* . . . It consists of 24 pieces *a 4.* (two violins, alto viola, violone or spinetta), which can also be played by violin and b.c. or violin, bass, and b.c. Compared with Opus 4 and Opus 5, this collection is disappointing. The fact that neither double-stops nor *scordatura* are used is not to be regretted; more unfortunate is the absence of the artistic daring that is found in many earlier correnti. Most striking, however, is the fact that the principle of a standardized suite, which is fully realized in Opus 5, is missing in Opus 7. True, here and there, two or three successive pieces are in the same key, but these groups consist of entirely different dances, for instance, *Giga, Sarabanda,* and *Corrente* (Nos. 8–10), in B minor; or *Corrente, Allemanda,* and *Corrente* (Nos. 19–21), in D minor. Obviously, Bononcini's Opus 7 is a random selection of remnants, perhaps the initiative of the publisher, Giacomo Monti of Bologna.

Bononcini's Opus 9 is much more important. It appeared in 1675, with the title *Trattenimenti musicali a trè & a quattro Stromenti.* . . . Its contents can be summarized as follows:

    I. Sonate da Chiesa a trè
           Sonata Prima–Quinta   Nos. 1–5
   II. Sonate da Camera a trè
           Allemanda + Corrente Prima–Quarta   Nos. 6–9

III. Sonate da Camera a quatro in Stil Francese

Brando + Gavotta	No. 10
Corrente Prima	No. 11
Balletto	No. 12
Gagliarda	No. 13
Corrente Seconda	No. 14

The first two sonatas *a chiesa* each consist of four movements (No. 1: *Adagio, Allegro* [3/2], *Adagio,* and *Allegro;* No. 2: *Allegro, Allegro* [6/8], *Adagio,* and *Allegro*); the others have three movements. *Sonata quarta* proceeds throughout in slow tempo except for its final movement (note the unusually extended *Largo* section in triple time):

1a	1b	‖ 2	‖ 3	‖
18 D	60 Tr (3/4)⌐	‖ 9 D⌐	‖ 22 D⌐	‖
Adagio	Largo	‖ Adagio	‖ Allegro	‖

Furthermore, all of its parts are related to one another by the cyclic principle: in m. 10 of the first *Adagio* there is a triadic motif that recurs in all the following sections or movements (Fig. 140).[8]

FIGURE 140. G.M. BONONCINI: SONATA QUARTA (OPUS 9, 1675).

The sonatas of Opus 9 differ from those of Opus 1 and Opus 6, first of all, in their scoring. They are not written *a* 2 (two violins and b.c.) but *a* 3 (two violins, bass, and b.c.). The fuller scoring particularly affects the fugues, which are now performed by three imitating instruments. In Opus 1 there are a number of fugues with three expositions (fewer in Opus 6, where very extended themes are often used), while in Opus 9 Bononcini consistently limits himself to two expositions. This results from the fact that all the fugues are nearly the same length: in a fugue of about 25 measures there is room for either three two-voice expositions or two expositions in three voice parts. Even the very extended *Largo* of *Sonata quinta* has only two expositions, since episodes—even within an exposition—occupy considerable space. At any rate, it would be misleading to analyze the fugues of Bononcini or of other Italians using terms associated with the fugues of Bach. A striking example of an unorthodox use of imitation is the beginning of the particularly charming *Sonata seconda* of Opus 9 (see Fig. 141). Should it be regarded as a double fugue?

Part II, Nos. 6–9 of Opus 9, consists of eight *sonate da camera*, which form four pairs of *Allemanda* and *Corrente*, each pair in the same key. Each dance, of course, is binary with approximately the same number of measures in each section, for instance, twelve and eleven in *Allemanda quarta*. In the allemandes as well as in the correnti almost every section begins with a short imitation, and frequently the imitation of the second section

FIGURE 141. G.M. BONONCINI: SONATA SECONDA (OPUS 9, 1675).

is based on the reversed motif of the first. Thus, allemandes and correnti are treated like the gigues in the Bach suites. *Corrente prima* is dominated by dotted and syncopated rhythms that are in sharp contrast to the "running" character of the corrente and completely change its nature.

Part III, No. 10–14 of Opus 9, shows an interesting change of scoring: *Violino secondo* is replaced by *Canto Viola* and *Basso continuo* by *Alto Viola* without thorough-bass figures. Thus we have the unusual scoring violin, two altos, and bass—a string quartet with two violas. The pieces in this part are dance music in the proper sense of the word (*da ballo*), as is indicated by the designation *in stil francese* as well as by their simple, homophonic style. In addition, No. 10, *Brando—Gavotta*, has the same structure as the brandi written for the Este court by Uccellini, Vitali, Colombi, and Bononcini himself.

Bononcini's last publication of violin music, Opus 12, *Arie, e Correnti a trè, due Violini, e Violone . . .*, like all his works since Opus 3, was printed by Giacomo Monti in Bologna.[9] It contains 24 pieces, of which Nos. 1–18 form nine groups of *Aria—Corrente*. Then follow a single *Aria* in E minor (No. 29), a group *Aria—Corrente—Sarabanda* in Bb major (Nos. 20–22), and an *Aria—Corrente* in C minor (Nos. 23 and 24). The three-piece group, which Bononcini had used at times in Opus 4 and to a large extent in Opus 5, was later abandoned by him. In Opus 7 and Opus 9 it is not represented at all, and in Opus 12 by only one example.

Opus 12 consists of three part books—*Violino primo, Violino secondo,* and *Violone* (without *basso continuo*)—and therefore the scoring is that of a string trio. The bass instrument is referred to in the title of the publication as *Violone,* but in the part book it is called *Violoncello,* a name that occurs for the first time in Arresti's Opus 4 from 1665. In his Opus 3 from 1669 Bononcini had written string quartets in the present-day meaning of the term (that is, without *basso continuo*); thus his importance for the development of modern chamber music becomes apparent. Among the dance pieces, the allemandes are distinguished by their variety of ideas and structure. They seem more modern than those in the earlier collections, especially since they do not begin with imitation, in contrast to those of Opus 5, in which each of the two sections is a fugato. A turn to a new style is suggested, but Bononcini was not able to develop it. He died, at the age of 36, in the same year in which his Opus 12 appeared.

NOTES

1. I am grateful to Professor W. Klenz, who permitted me to use his transcriptions of the entire corpus of Bononcini's violin music, and who has written the most exhaustive

study of this master (KlenzB). In the article *Bononcini* in MGG the statement that Bononcini was "Kpm. an San Giovanni in Monte und San Petronio in Bologna" is in error. See KlenzB, p. 14.

2. Uccellini is often mentioned in connection with the history of *scordatura* because of *Trombetta sordina* in his *Libro V* (1649). A. Moser theorized that the bass was to be played on a lowered violin string, but this seems highly unlikely. See n. 15, p. 117.

3. The solution to the canon is as follows: the tones

each with the value of a maxima, will be sung by 2,592 voices in the interval of a *mezzo sospirio* (sixteenth note), which yields a D-minor chord that is broken a thousand times. The numbers are not arbitrary but are derived from the relationship between perfect and imperfect mensurations: $2,592 = 3^4 \times 2^5$; $648 = 3^4 \times 2^3$, or $1/4$ of the first number. In the continuo part book the scheme for No. 22 is reduced to a canon for eight voices, and thus taken from the realm of *musica speculativa* to the realm of *musica practica*.

4. The C-major tuning was later employed for the English guitar, for which the famous violinist F. Geminiani wrote a method, *The Art of Playing the Guitar or Cettra . . .* (London, 1760).

5. See ApelG, p. 541.

6. In the library of the Accademia Filarmonica in Bologna. Facsimile edition in *Biblioteca musica Bononensis*, vol. IV, No. 146. Seven sonatas are transcribed in KlenzB, Supplement, pp. 142–202.

7. See Ape1N, p. 175 (Gafurius). As late as 1707, Murschauser employed this method; cf. Apel, p. 211.

8. In KlenzB, pp. 133–134, all 29 sonatas are presented in a diagram, but the indication of the cyclic principle (through the use of *) is not complete.

9. As late as the eighteenth century (1700?, 1705, 1720) there were further editions published in England; compare KlenzB, pp. 59 ff.

SOURCES

Primi frutti del giardino musicale a due violini e basso continuo. Opus 1. Venice: Francesco Magni detto Gardano, 1666.   RISM B3625.
    Italy: Bologna, Archivio dell'Accademia filarmonica (Violin I and II, b.c.); Civico Museo.

Delle sonate da camera e da ballo a 1. 2. 3. e 4. . . . Opus 2. Venice: Francesco Magni detto Gardano, 1667.   RISM B3626.
    Italy: Bologna, Archivio dell'Accademia filarmonica (Violin I and II, Spinetta/Violone); Ferrara, Biblioteca comunale Ariostea.
Edition:
Monumenta musica mutinesia, vol. 10. Bologna: Antique Musicae Italicae Studiosi, 1971 (facsimile).

Varii fiori del giardino musicale, overo sonate da camera, a 2. 3. e 4. col suo basso continuo, & aggiunta d'alcuni canoni studiosi, & osservati. . . . Opus 3. Bologna: Giacomo Monti, 1669.   RISM B3627.
    Great Britain: London, British Library (Violin II, Viola, Violone).
    Italy: Bologna, Civico Museo (Violin I and II, Violone, b.c.).
Edition:
Biblioteca Musica Bononiensis, section IV, No. 74. Bologna: A. Fiorni, 1983 (?), (facsimile).

Arie, correnti, sarabande, gighe, & allemande a violino e violone, over spinetta, con alcune intavolate per diverse accordature. . . . Opus 4. Bologna: Giacomo Monti, 1671.   RISM B3628.
> Great Britain: London, British Library (Violin, Violone).
> Italy: Bologna, Civico Museo.
Reprint:
Bologna: Monti, 1674.   RISM B3629.
> Italy: Bologna, Civico Museo.

Sinfonia, allemande, correnti, e sarabande a 5. e 6. col suo basso continuo; et aggiunta d'una sinfonia a quattro, che si può suonare ancora al contrario rivoltando le parti. . . . Opus 5.   Bologna: Giacomo Monti, 1671.   RISM B3630.
> Great Britain: London, British Library (Violin I and II, Alto Viola, Tenor Viola).
> Italy: Bologna, Civico Museo (6 parts).

Sonate da chiesa a due violini. Opus 6. Venice: Francesco Magni detto Gardano, 1672.   RISM B3631.
> Italy: Bologna, Archivio dell'Accademia filarmonica (Violin I and II, b.c.); Civico Museo (b.c.).
Reprint:
Suonate a due violini con il basso continuo per l'organo. . . . Opus 6. Bologna: Giacomo Monti, 1677.   RISM B3632.
> Italy: Bologna, Civico Museo.
> West Germany: Münster, Santini-Bibliothek (Violin I and II, Organ).
Edition:
Biblioteca Musica Bononiensis, section VI, No. 46. Bologna, A. Fiornl, 1970 (facsimile).

Ariette, correnti, gighe, allemande, e sarabande; le quali ponno suonarsi a violino solo; a due, violino e violone; a tre, due violini e violone; & a quattro, due violini, viola e violone. Opus 7. Bologna: Giacomo Monti, 1673.   RISM B3634.
> Italy: Bologna, Civico Museo (Violin I, Spinetto/Violone).
Reprints:
Bologna: Giacomo Monti, 1677.   RISM B3635.
> Italy: Bologna, Civico Museo (Violin I and II, Viola).
Venice: Stampa del Gardano, 1677.   RISM B3636.
> Italy: Bologna, Civico Museo (Violin I and II, Viola, Violone).

Trattenimenti musicali a tre, & a quattro stromenti. Opus 9. Bologna: Giacomo Monti, 1675.   RISM B3637.
> Italy: Bologna, Civico Museo (Violin II, b.c.); Modena, Biblioteca Estense (4 parts).

Arie, e correnti a tre, due violini, e violone. . . . Opus 12. Bologna: Giacomo Monti, 1678.   RISM B3641.
> Great Britain: Oxford, Bodleian Library (Violin I and II, Violone).
> Italy: Bologna, Civico Museo (Violoncello); Modena, Biblioteca Estense.

 Giovanni Battista Vitali

Giovanni Battista Vitali was born in 1632 in Bologna, where he studied with Cazzati (whom he calls "mio maestro" in his Opus 1). In 1658 he became a member of the famous chapel of San Petronio; in 1666 he was accepted into the Accademia filar-monica; and in 1673 he became chapelmaster of San Rosario in Bologna. In the following year he went to the Este court in Modena as Sotto maestro di capella, and probably in 1684 he was promoted to maestro. He died in 1692 in Modena. His work for violin is preserved in twelve publications, from Opus 1 of 1666 to Opus 14 of 1692.[1] He must have been well liked, especially as a young composer during his stay in Bologna, because his first five publications were printed within four years, from 1666 to 1669, and were also reprinted several times.

Vitali's first publication carries the title *Correnti e Balletti da Camera a due Violini, col suo Basso continuo per Spinetta, ò Violone.* . . . It contains twelve balletti and twelve correnti, all for two violins and b.c. The correnti make frequent use of dotted rhythms, often alternating between |♩♪♩| and |♩♩♪|, giving these dances a special liveliness. At the close of *Corrente seconda* there is a Neapolitan sixth—a harmonic device whose name refers to the Neapolitan school of the eighteenth century but which was actually used about 1650 by Carissimi (see Fig. 142).

FIGURE 142. G.B. VITALI: CORRENTE SECONDA (OPUS 1, 1666).

Vitali's Opus 2 appeared in the next year, 1667, also in Bologna: *Sonate a due violini col suo basso continuo per l'organo.* It contains twelve sonatas, three of which have three movements, eight have four movements, and one has five. Among the four-movement sonatas, Nos. 4 and 8 have movements entitled *Grave, Allegro, Largo,* and *Vivace* (*Allegro* in No. 8), with a *Grave* introduction for the final movement. The order of movements is typical of the late *sonata da chiesa*; it is also represented by a single example in Cazzati's Opus 50 of 1669.

For the structure of the first fast movements Vitali used various methods. Most of them are two-voice fugues, short enough to be called fughettas, in which the two violins present the theme either in two expositions (with longer episodes) or in three (with shorter episodes), each time with the harmonic support of the organ. In Nos. 2 and 11, the first *Allegros* are composed as three-voice fugues in which the organ fully participates in the presentation of the theme. Consequently, the organ part begins not with chords but as *basso seguente*. Each of these three-voice fugues has three expositions, the last one in stretto. The *allegro* of Sonata No. 8 is completely different; it is entirely homophonic and in four-measure phrases, almost like a balletto.

The running bass, which occurs in a 1649 publication by Marco Antonio Ferro, plays a very important role in Vitali's compositions. In his Opus 2 Vitali employs this technique several times for various sections of a movement, for instance, in the *Vivace* of Sonata No. 6 and in the second *Grave* of No. 10. We shall return to this technique in connection with his later sonatas, in which it is more fully realized.

Even while these sonatas were being printed, preparations for Vitali's next publication were going on. An announcement for Opus 3 appears at the end of Opus 2: "Si stampano al presente Balletti, e Galiarde per ballare, Balletti, Correnti per Camera, e Sinphonie per Teatro, a quatro Istromenti del medemo Autore." Opus 3, which also appeared in 1667 and at the same press (Giacomo Monti, Bologna), is entitled *Balletti, Correnti alla francese, Gagliarde, e Brando per ballare. Balletti, Correnti, e Sinfonie da Camera a quattro Stromenti....* Its contents are:

> I. 6 Balletto per ballare—Sua Corrente alla francese
> 4 Gagliarda
> 1 Canario
> 1 Brando—Sua Corrente
> II. 4 Balletto per Camera
> 3 Corrente
> 1 Sarabanda
> 2 Sinfonia

As in Bononcini's Opus 2, a distinction is made between dance music *per ballare* (group I) and dance music *per Camera* (group II), that is, between actual and idealized dance music. As in Bononcini's books—though not as clearly—the dances *per Camera* differ from those *per ballare* by their more elaborate style. While the latter are essentially homophonic, the former include occasional passages with short imitations or with complementary motifs. Furthermore, a tendency toward four-measure structure, toward sections of eight, twelve, or sixteen measures, is recognizable in the *per ballare* group, while in the *da camera* group only the sarabandas have four-measure phrases, two in each section. The brando at the end of group I reproduces in every detail, including the number of measures, the structure of the four written by Bononcini.

In the announcement in Opus 2, the two sinfonias at the end of Opus 3 are named *per Teatro*. In fact, one may well imagine that these short binary pieces were used in connection with theatre performances, possibly with open-air plays. Many of the earlier sinfonias may have served the same purpose, particularly Uccellini's *Sinfonie boscarecie*.

At the end of Opus 3 Vitali again gave advance notice of his next publication: "Si stampano al presente Balletti, Correnti, Allemande, Gigue, e Sarabande, a Violino, e Violone, con alcuni avertimenti necessarii, per praticarli." Opus 4 appeared in 1668 with the title *Balletti, Correnti, Gighe, Allemande, e Sarabande a Violino, e Violone ò Spinetta con il secondo Violino a beneplacito....* It contains five balletti, eight gigas, five correnti, three sarabandas, two allemandes, and one zoppa. Some dances can be combined to form suites, for instance *Corrente seconda–Giga–Sarabanda* (all in D major) or *Corrente terza–Giga–Sarabanda* (all in E minor). Unfortunately, the *avertimenti [sic]* offered in the advance notice are missing.

Only one of the five correnti has the tempo indication *Allegro*, which is traditional for this dance type, while three others are inscribed *Grave*. In one of these the tempo changes in each of the two sections: Three measures of *Largo* are followed by eight measures of *Allegro*. Fig. 143 shows the beginning of violin I.

FIGURE 143. G.B. VITALI: CORRENTE QUARTA (OPUS 4, 1668).

Vitali's Opus 5, which appeared in 1669, resembles his Opus 2 in that it contains sonatas; *Sonate a due, trè, quattro, e cinque stromenti.* . . . Of its twelve compositions, eleven are called *Sonata*, and No. 11 is labeled *Capriccio*. Nos. 1–5 have the scoring two violins and b.c. Nos. 6–9, two violins, bass, and b.c.; Nos. 10 and 11, two violins, alto, bass, and b.c.; and No. 12, two violins, alto, tenor, bass, and b.c.

The structure of these compositions is fairly uniform; Nos. 9 and 12 have three movements but the rest consist of four. The four-movement sonata played such an important role almost until the end of the nineteenth century that information concerning its origin is most interesting. The creator of the four-movement sonata was Cazzati, the master who was also the first to conceive of the sonata as consisting of separate movements. Of the 42 sonatas (or canzonas) he published between 1643 (Opus 2) and 1670 (Opus 55, his last collection of violin music), 23 consist of four movements. Also of interest is the origin of the *sonata da chiesa*, a sonata of four movements with the tempo order slow, fast, slow, fast. Here too there is an unexpectedly early example by Cazzati, with the following structure:

Cazzati: Sonata la Vecchia (Opus 8, 1648)

Movement	1		2		3a	b		4a	b	
Meter	10 D↷	:‖:	18 D↷	:‖:	7 D	28 Tr ↷	‖	12 D	14 D ↷	‖
Tempo	slow	‖	Allegro	‖	Largo			Grave	allegro e Presto	‖

A single example like this does not prove very much, since the possibilities of combining two tempos are so limited that the succession slow, fast, slow, fast is almost bound to occur. A somewhat different situation exists in Vitali's sonatas. *Sonata quinta* and *sonata ottava* in Opus 2 (1667) and *La Pallavicini* in Opus 5 (1669) have the standard form of the *sonata da chiesa*. However, it is not until we come to Corelli's Opus 1 (1681) that this form occurs frequently enough to be considered the norm; among the twelve sonatas of this collection there are five of the type slow, fast, slow, fast.

An interesting detail in Vitali's sonatas is the length of the themes of his fugal movements. In his Opus 2 some themes differ from those of earlier composers in that they comprise four measures; in other words, the four-measure principle is transferred from the dance to the fugue. In Opus 5 this tendency is even more noticeable. However, the regular form of the theme does not lead to a regular structure of the exposition, since nearly always the answer starts before the theme ends, after three or three and a half measures. Fig. 144 shows two examples in point.

FIGURE 144. G.B. VITALI: a. SONATA LA CAMPORI; b. SONATA LA GRATIANI (OPUS 5, 1669).

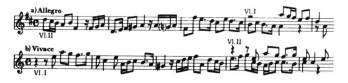

Vitali's Opus 5 includes a particularly impressive example of a running bass in *Sonata La Pallavicina*, No. 4. It consists of *Grave* (nine measures), *Allegro* (30 measures), *Largo* (29 measures in 3/4), *Grave* (eight measures), and *Allegro* (seventeen measures). The first *Allegro* is based throughout on an uninterrupted running bass that creates inner unity by means of a recurrent motif, in the present case using the scale degrees 5-5-3-1

In a very unusual realization of the cyclic principle, the second *Allegro* is based on a continuous running bass in which the same motif recurs.

Capriccio detto il Molza (No. 11), written entirely in F minor, is a particularly impressive composition. In its slow movements soft lament is expressed as beautifully as is wild impetuosity in the fast ones.

In 1682, after Vitali had moved from Bologna to Modena, he published his Opus 7, with the title *Varie Partite del Passamezzo, Ciacona, Capriccii, Passagalli, a tre, due Violini, e Violone, o Spinetta*. It contains:

Partite del Passamezzo	No. 1
Partite d'altra Sorte del Passamezzo	No. 2
Ciacona	No. 3
Capriccio Primo, Secondo	Nos. 4, 5
Passagallo Primo, Secondo, Terzo	Nos. 6–8

All eight compositions are variations; their themes are not melodies but bass formulas. No. 1 consists of six variations of the *passamezzo nuovo* in B minor, No. 2 of three variations on the *passamezzo antico* in D minor. As in all passamezzos, each note of the bass is four measures long (originally one *brevis*, which equals four *semibreves*), within which it is paraphrased by rich figurations down to sixteenth notes. The passamezzo had a full century of continuous life (from about 1520 to 1620), to which masters like Andrea Gabrielli, Byrd, Bull, Sweelinck, and finally Scheidt (in his *Tabulatura Nova* of 1624) made contributions. Forty years later it was revived by the organ composer Bernardo Strozzi (who was active in Messina) in his *Selva di varie compositions* (1664), and another twenty years later by Vitali.

The two capriccios are ostinatos in the proper sense of the word, since they are based on formulas that recur unchanged in each variation. Here Vitali follows his teacher Cazzati, especially in his *Capriccio Primo sopra 12 Note*, whose ostinato is similar to that of Cazzati's *Capriccio sopra 12 note*, from 1660.

The ciacona and the three passagalli are variations based on the descending tetrachord. Especially noteworthy is *Passagallo terzo*, which carries the remark "Li Violini sonano in battuta eguale, ed il basso in battuta ineguale, e poi si cambiano."[2] In the first section the bass consists of ten tetrachord paraphrases, each of four measures in 3/4 meter, while the two violins play in 4/4; in the second section the bass has thirteen tetrachord paraphrases, each of four measures in 4/4, while the violins perform a counterpoint in 3/4. This "polymetric" technique was frequently used from about 1380 to 1550,[3] but Vitali's *Passagallo* is probably as rare an example in the seventeenth century as the ballet music in Mozart's *Don Giovanni* was in the eighteenth. Fig. 145 shows the beginnings of both sections of this composition, which is not only technically interesting but also musically valuable.

FIGURE 145. G.B. VITALI: CAPRICCIO TERZO (OPUS 7, 1682).

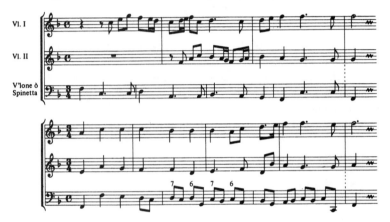

Vitali's Opus 8, from 1683, is entitled *Balletti Correnti e Capricci per Camera a Due Violini e Violone*. The part book for the bass is designated *Violone ò Spinetta* and is fully provided with thorough-bass figures. It contains one group *Balletto—Corrente—Giga*, eight groups *Balletto—Corrente*, and two *Capricci*. In each group the dances are joined by a common tonality as well as thematically (see Fig. 146).

FIGURE 146. G.B. VITALI: BALLETTO PRIMO—CORRENTE—GIGA (OPUS 8, 1683).

The two capriccios are short pieces in binary form, like the dances, but they are written in imitative style. Because of its changing motifs, *Capriccio secondo* is the most attractive piece of the collection, which, on the whole, is not very noteworthy.

Vitali's next publication, Opus 9 from 1684, is much more important: *Sonate da Chiesa a due violini ...*, twelve sonatas for two violins and b.c. Like the sonatas of Opus 2 (1667) and Opus 5 (1669), those of Opus 9 indicate significant development. Among his earlier sonatas there are so many with four movements that H. Riemann called Vitali the creator of the church sonata with its four independent movements.⁴ Strictly speaking, Opus 9 includes only one of this kind, No. 2; No. 7 is possibly another, with the third movement merging into the fourth. In both sonatas the tempos change according to the scheme slow, fast, slow, fast. Most of the sonatas in Opus 9 have five movements. No. 5, for example, consists of *Grave, Largo, Grave, Allegro,* and *Prestissimo,* three slow movements followed by a fast one and a very fast one. The first *Grave* is homophonic, and the *Largo* is a fugato with a very expressive theme of five measures. The second *Grave* is a most interesting ostinato, beginning with two statements of the formula

followed by two statements of its inversion:

two more statements of the original formula, transposed to the lower fifth

and finally two statements of the inverted formula in the same transposition.

Several movements are contrast movements, of the Venetian type, for instance, the final movement of Sonata No. 9, which consists of four sections: *Largo, Allegro, Adagio,* and *Presto,* with the *Presto* based on a running bass.

In the imitative movements the imitation is limited to the two violins, while the bass plays only an accompaniment. The themes are sometimes rather extended (*andamento*) and are occasionally treated according to the method of pause exposition, which was introduced by Merula. Fig. 147 shows the beginning of the second movement of Sonata No. 4, which is another example of a running bass (as are the first movement [*Grave*] of No. 3, the first movement [*Largo*] of No. 4, and the fifth movement [*Presto*] of No. 9).

FIGURE 147. G.B. VITALI: SONATA QUARTA (OPUS 9, 1684).

A very subtle application of the cyclic principle occurs in *Sonata settima*. In mm. 7–
9 of the first *Allegro* there appears, as if by chance, a motif consisting of two descending
fifths:

It is quoted again in the subsequent *Grave* as well as in the final *Allegro*. In *Sonata
duodecima* the first movement (*Vivace*) carries the remark *Soggetto Contrario Riverso*, which
means that the various themes and motifs are answered in inversion. This procedure
results in a very stimulating dialogue by the two violins.

Vitali's church sonatas Opus 9 contain much that is important and impressive. Here
and there, however— for instance, in the final movement of the first sonata—there is a
pleasing yet shallow melody that foreshadows a change in musical mentality.

In 1684, the same year in which Vitali's Opus 9 was published, there appeared both
a lost Opus 10 as well as his Opus 11, *Varie Sonate alla Francese & all'Italiana a sei
Stromenti*. . . . It contains 30 pieces for six instruments, three violins, alto, tenor, and bass
(the bass being *Spinetta ò Violone*). According to a prefatory remark, they can also be
performed by two instruments (*con il primo Violino solo, e Violone*), that is, as string duets.
In most cases, three successive pieces can be combined to form a group in the same
tonality, for instance, Nos. 1–3: *Capriccio–Giga–Gavotta* in Bb major; Nos. 16–18: *Introduzione–Baletto per Camera–Borea* in C major; and Nos. 19–21: *Balletto per Camera–
Giga–Gavotta* in A major. In the title of this publication a differentiation is made between
sonatas *alla Francese* and *all'Italiana*, but it is difficult to say what this means. In the
individual titles as well as in the *Tavola* there are only two pieces *alla Francese*, a balletto
and a corrente. The designation *all'Italiana* appears nowhere, but five balletti are said to
be *per Camera*, a designation that possibly means the same as *all'Italiana*. Some of the
tonal groups (suites) begin with an introductory movement (*Capriccio, Introduzione*) written in a somewhat more elaborate style with short imitations, while the dances are pre-
vailingly homophonic. All the pieces are in binary form, except the last composition of
the entire collection, *Sinfonia per Camera*, with twelve measures *Grave*, 27 measures *Adagio*, and sixteen measures *presto*, which amounts to a short three-movement sonata.
Together with some other compositions by Vitali, it has been reprinted in Torchi's *L'Arte
musicale in Italia*, vol. VII (1867).

Vitali's Opus 12 appeared one year later, in 1685: *Balli in stile Francese a cinque
Stromenti*. . . . It contains 35 dances in the scoring two violins, alto, tenor, and bass (where
the bass is given as *Violone ò Spinetta*). Nine groups, each in the same key, can be formed.
The first seven begin with a *Balletto*, which in most cases is followed by three other
dances, for instance, *Balletto–Giga–Minuet–Borea* in D major (Nos. 1–4) or *Balletto–
Giga–Gavotta–Minuet* in G major (Nos. 5–8). The fifth group includes six dances, the
seventh only three. The collection concludes with a group composed of *Brando–Corrente–
Gagliarda figurata–Gavotta–Minuet* in Bb major and a single *Brando* in F major. The two
brandi each consist, as is customary with this dance, of four sections, which are called
Brando, Gaij (= branle gay), *Amener*, and *Gavotta*, and which have the same structure
as those by Uccellini and Bononcini. The two dances with the title *Gaij* have a noteworthy
rhythm—an alternation of two "dance steps" that are differentiated by the position of

the dotted quarter note (Fig. 148). All the dances are strictly homophonic as is required by the *stile francese*.

FIGURE 148. G.B. VITALI: GAIJ (OPUS 12, 1685).

In 1689, three years before his death, Vitali's Opus 13 appeared: *Artifizii musicali ne quali si contengono Canoni in diverse maniere. Contrapunti doppii, Inventioni curiose, Capritii, e Sonate.* . . . This work turns from the cheerful world of the dance to the serious and strict art of school counterpoint. Not without reason has *Artifizii musicali* been regarded as a precursor of Bach's *Die Kunst der Fuge*. The main contents of Vitali's publication are 51 canons, which lie outside our field of interest. They are followed by two balletti, four capriccios, one passagallo, and two sonatas. The balletti belong to the species called *Inventioni curiose* in the title. In the first one each of the three instruments plays in a different meter: violin I in *tempo ordinario* (**C**), violin II in *dodecupla* (12/8), violone in *tripla* (3/4)—going one step further than the polymetric structure of *Capriccio terzo* of 1682 (see Fig. 145). The second, which is described as "In questo Balletto a due si considera, che il Violino sona per b. molle, e il Violone per diesis." In modern terms, the violin plays in Gb major, the violone in F♯ major, in a unique enharmonic experiment. Fig. 149 shows the beginning (note the A♯ in the key signature of the violone part).

FIGURE 149. G.B. VITALI: BALLETTO (OPUS 13, 1689).

The first of the four capriccios is a short rhythmic study (6: ‖ :6), for the first violin plays ♪ ♪♪ ♪♪ throughout while the violone plays ♪♪ ♪ ♪♪ ♪ in a rapid exchange of notes and rests for which a composition by Stradella may have been the model (see Fig. 161). The three other capriccios are somewhat more extended duets in binary form in which numerous motifs are presented in short imitation. *Passagallo, che principia per B. molle, e finisca per Diesis* is a very extended composition (it is also reprinted in Torchi's *L'Arte musicale*) consisting of 71 variations of a quasi-ostinato of four measures. During these variations the tonality gradually modulates from Eb major to E major, according to the following scheme:

Var.	1–9	10–20	21–28	29–39	40–47	48–55	56–63	64–71	
Key	Eb	Bb	F	C	G	D	A	E	(all major)

The two sonatas at the end of the publication are for violin solo and b.c., the only ones of this type that Vitali wrote. Both consist of five movements, the first of *Largo*,

Allegro, and three movements without tempo indications; the second of *Grave, Prestissimo, Grave, Allegro,* and *Largo* (both have been reprinted by Torchi). For the initial movement of the first sonata Vitali employs self-imitation, a method that had been introduced by Leoni. The fast fourth movement consists entirely of virtuosic broken chords, which had replaced the virtuosic scale formations of an earlier period. Vitali used the same style for the *Prestissimo* of the second sonata (Fig. 150).

FIGURE 150. G.B. VITALI: SECONDA SONATA A VIOLINO SOLO (OPUS 13, 1689).

In 1692, the year in which Vitali died, his son, Tomaso Antonio, published an Opus 140: *Sonata da Camera a tre, due Violini, e Violone* . . . He says that the pieces had been composed "per far concerto a gl'applausi de' Popoli nelle gloriose nozze" (for a popular celebration occasioned by the marriage) of Duchess Margherita Farnese d'Este at Modena. Vitali wrote 41 dances for it. Four or five successive dances are in the same key, so that the entire collection consists of eleven suites. Seven suites begin with a balletto, for instance, the first in B♭ major (*Balletto—Giga—Borea*, and *Minuet*) and the tenth in G minor (*Balletto—Gavotta—Zoppa*, and *Corrente*). Each dance consists of two sections, each of which has four or eight measures, as is fitting for a popular entertainment.

NOTES

1. In the article *Vitali* in MGG, manuscripts in Bologna and Modena are mentioned. The Bologna manuscript is a copy of Vitali's Opus 9 copied in the twentieth century, and the Modena manuscripts are copies of Opus 7.

2. "The violins are in equal time, and the bass in unequal time, then they exchange."

3. An early example is an anonymous *Fortune* (around 1370) containing 5/8 against 6/8, a late one being Pierre de la Rue's *Missa l'homme armé* with 3/8 against 2/4 and 3/4. (See ApelN, pp. 458–459).

4. RiemannH, p. 164. Actually, this is an accomplishment of Vitali's teacher, Cazzati.

SOURCES

Correnti e balletti da camera a due violini col suo basso continuo per spinetta o violone. . . .
Opus 1. Bologna: Marino Silvani, 1666.   RISM V2141.
   France: Paris, Bibliothèque nationale (b.c.).
   Italy: Bologna, Civico Museo (Violin I and II, b.c.); Modena, Biblioteca Estense.
Reprints:
Venice: Francesco Magni, 1670 (*novamente ristampata*).   RISM V2142.
   Italy: Bologna, Civico Museo (3 parts).
Venice: Gardano, 1677 (*con il basso continuo*).   RISM V2143.
   Italy: Bologna, Civico Museo (3 parts).
Bologna: Giacomo Monti, 1680.   RISM V2144.
   Great Britain: Oxford, Bodleian Library (3 voices).
   Italy: Bologna, Civico Museo; Modena, Biblioteca Estense.

Forty four sonatas or ayres in three parts for two violins and a bass. . . . London: John Young, 1702.   RISM V2145.
> France: Paris, Bibliothèque nationale (Violin I).

Sonate a due violini col suo basso continuo per l'organo. . . . Opus 2. Bologna: Giacomo Monti, 1667.   RISM V2146.
> Great Britain: London, Royal College of Music (Incomplete parts); Oxford, Bodleian Library (Violin I and II, b.c.).
> Italy: Bologna, Archivio di San Petronio; Civico Museo.

Reprints:
Venice: Francesco Magni, 1668.   RISM V2147.
> Italy: Bologna, Civico Museo (3 parts).

Bologna: Giacomo Monti, 1671.   RISM V2148.
> France: Paris, Bibliothèque nationale (3 parts).
> Italy: Bologna, Civico Museo.

Suonate a due violini. . . . Venice: Giuseppe Sala, 1682.   RISM V2149.
> Italy: Modena, Biblioteca Estense (3 parts).

Venice: Gardano, 1685.   RISM V2150.
> Great Britain: Oxford, Bodleian Library (3 parts).
> Italy: Bologna, Civico Museo.

Balletti, correnti alla francese, gagliarde e brando per ballare, balletti, correnti e sinfonie da camera a quattro stromenti. . . . Opus 3.   RISM V2151.
> France: Paris, Bibliothèque nationale (Violone).
> Italy: Bologna, Civico Museo (4 parts).

Reprints:
Bologna: Giacomo Monti, 1674.   RISM V2152.
> Great Britain: London, British Library (Violone).
> Italy: Bologna, Civico Museo (4 parts).

Venice: Giuseppe Sala, 1679.   RISM V2153.
> Italy: Asti, Archivio capitolare (Violin II).

Bologna: Giacomo Monti, 1680.   RISM V2154.
> Italy: Modena, Biblioteca Estense (4 voices).

Balletti, correnti, gighe, allemande, e sarabande a violino, e violone, o spinetta con il secondo violino a beneplacito. . . . Opus 4. Bologna: Giacomo Monti, 1668.   RISM V2155.
> Italy: Bologna, Archivio dell'Accademia filarmonica (Violin I and II); Civico Museo; Biblioteca universitaria (Violin I); Modena, Biblioteca Estense.

Reprints:
Bologna: Giacomo Monti, 1671 (*di nuovo ristampata con nuova aggiunta*).   RISM V2156.
> Italy: Bologna, Civico Museo (Violin I, Violone); Modena, Biblioteca Estense (Violin I and II).

Bologna: Giacomo Monti, 1673.   RISM V2157.
> Great Britain: London, British Library (Violin I).
> Italy: Bologna, Civico Museo (3 parts).

Venice: Gardano, 1677.   RISM V2158.
> Great Britain: Durham, Cathedral Library (3 parts).
> Italy: Bologna, Civico Museo (lacks Violone).

Bologna: Giacomo Monti, 1678.   RISM V2159.
> Italy: Bologna, Civico Museo (Violin I, Violone).

Sonate a due, tre, quattro e cinque stromenti. . . . Opus 5. Bologna: Giacomo Monti, 1669.   RISM V2160.

France: Paris, Bibliothèque nationale (Violone, Organ).
Great Britain: Durham, Cathedral Library (Violin I and II, Viola, Violone, Organ).
Italy: Bologna, Archivio dell'Accademia filarmonica (lacks organ); Civico Museo.
Reprint:
Bologna: Giacomo Monti, 1677.   RISM V2161.
France: Paris, Bibliothèque nationale (Organ).
Great Britain: London, British Library (incomplete parts); Oxford, Bodleian Library.
Italy: Bologna, Civico Museo; Modena, Biblioteca Estense (lacks Viola).
Switzerland: Zürich, Zentralbibliothek, Kantons-, Stadt-und Universitätsbibliothek (5 parts).

Varie partite del passemezzo, ciaconna, capriccii e passagali a tre, due violine e violone o spinetta. . . . Opus 7. Modena: Giovanni Gasparo Ferri, 1682.   RISM V2163.
Italy: Modena, Biblioteca Estense (Violin I and II, Violone).
Netherlands: The Hague, Gemeente Museum.

Balletti, correnti e capricci per camera a due violini, e violone. . . . Opus 8. Modena: Giovanni Gasparo Ferri, 1683.   RISM V2164.
Italy: Modena, Biblioteca Estense (Violin I and II, Violone).
Reprints:
Venice: Stampa del Gardano, 1683.   RISM V2165.
Italy: Bologna, Civico Museo.
West Germany: Münster, Santini-Bibliothek (3 parts).
Venice: Gardano, 1685.   RISM V2166.
Great Britain: Oxford, Bodleian Library (3 parts).
Italy: Modena, Biblioteca Estense; Venice, Biblioteca nazionale Marciana (Violin I).

Sonate da chiesa a due violini. . . . Opus 9. Amsterdam: Ioanno Philippo Heus, 1684. RISM V2167.
Great Britain: London, British Library (Violin I incomplete, Violin II, b.c.).
Reprint:
Venice: Gardano, 1684.   RISM V2168.
Great Britain: Durham, Cathedral Library (3 parts).

Varie sonate alla francese, & all'italiana a sei stromenti. . . . Opus 11. Modena: Giovanni Gasparo Ferri, 1684.   RISM V2170.
Great Britain: Durham, Cathedral Library (Violin I, II, III, Alto Viola, Tenor Viola, Violone); London, British Library (incomplete); Oxford, Bodleian Library.
Italy: Bologna, Civico Museo; Modena, Biblioteca Estense.

Balli in stile francese a cinque stromenti. . . . Opus 12. Modena: Antonio Vitaliani, 1685.   RISM V2171.
Great Britain: London, British Library (Alto Viola).
Italy: Bologna, Civico Museo (Violin I and II, Alto Viola, Tenor Viola, Violone); Venice, Biblioteca della Fondazione Querini-Stampalia (lacks Violin I and Alto Viola).
Reprint:
Venice: Giuseppe Sala, 1690.   RISM V2172.
Italy: Venice, Biblioteca della Fondazione Querini-Stampalia (Violin II, Tenor Viola, Violone).

Artificii musicali ne quali si contengono canoni in diverse maniere, contrapunti dopii, inventioni curiose, capritii, e sonate. . . . Opus 13. Modena: eredi Cassiani, 1689.   RISM V2173.
Italy: Bologna, Civico Museo; Milan, Biblioteca del Conservatorio "Giuseppe Verdi";

Modena, Biblioteca Estense.
United States: Washington (D.C.), Library of Congress, Music Division.
Edition:
Louise Reed and Gertrude P. Smith, eds., Northampton (Mass.): Smith College, 1959.

Sonate da camera a tre, due violini, e violone. . . . Opus 14. Modena, Christoforo Canobi, 1692.   RISM V2174.
Italy: Bologna, Civico Museo (Violin I and II, Violone); Modena, Biblioteca Estense.

Livre cinquième du recueil des dances, ballets, allemandes, brandes, courantes, sarabandes, etc., des diverses autheurs de ce temps, à deux parties. Antwerp: Les héritiers de Pierre Phalèse, 1668.   RISM V2175.
Belgium: Bibliothèque Royale Albert Iᵉʳ (S, B, Violin).

🦗 *Gioseppe Colombi*

Gioseppe Colombi was born in 1635 in Modena. At the age of twenty-five he was appointed capo degli strumentisti del Serenissimo Duca di Modena. *In 1674 he became assistant chapelmaster at the court and in 1678 first chapelmaster at the cathedral, positions he held until his death in 1694. His entire life seems to have been spent in Modena, where Bononcini and Vitali (from 1674) also were active.*

Gioseppe Colombi's first publication appeared in 1668: *Sinfonie da camera, Brandi e Corrente alla francese, con Corrente & Arie da Camera, e Suonate per suonare a due, a trè, & a quatro.* . . . It consists of 23 compositions:

I.	8 Sinfonia da Camera	Nos. 1–8
II.	2 Brando alla francese	Nos. 9, 14
III.	5 Corrente alla francese	Nos. 10–12, 15, 16
IV.	6 Corrente da Camera + Aria	Nos. 13, 17–21
V.	2 Suonata	Nos. 22, 23

The publication consists of four part books—*Violino Primo, Violino Secondo, Viola,* and *Basso*—showing that the pieces of Opus 1 are performed by four string instruments only. The bass is without thorough–bass figures, and there is no indication of support by a keyboard instrument (such as *col suo Basso Continuo*) in the title or (such words as *Violone ò Spinetta*) in the part book. Thus, Colombi is the second composer of the "thorough-bass period"—the first was Buonamente, with his string trios of 1626 and 1629—who renounced the use of a keyboard instrument. He was, however, the first who wrote in string quartet scoring—two violins, alto, and bass.[1] All the pieces of the collection are written *a quatro,* so that the scorings *a due* and *a trè* indicated in the title are to be understood in the sense of *a beneplacito.*

Groups I, IV, and, of course, V belong to the category *da camera.* Groups II and III carry the remark *alla francese,* which has the same meaning as Bononcini's *da ballo* and

Vitali's *per ballare*, that is, music for actual dancing. The two brandi reproduce in every detail—including the number of measures—the same structure as Bononcini's *Brando* (without *Corrente*; see p. 179). Eleven compositions for this court dance have been preserved: two by Uccellini (Opus 9, 1667), four by Bononcini (one in Opus 1, 1666; two in Opus 2, 1667; one in Opus 3, 1669), three by Vitali (one in Opus 3, 1667; two in Opus 8, 1685), and two by Colombi (Opus 1, 1668). Nine of these were written between 1666 and 1669; two appeared twenty years later. Uccellini's brandi were written for the Farnese court at Parma, all the others for the Este court at Modena.

Among the correnti in Colombi's Opus 1, the difference between those *alla francese* and those *da camera* is the same as in Bononcini's and Vitali's: the former are strictly homophonic and limited to the typical rhythm of the dance; the latter are more freely and more individually written, occasionally with complementary motifs. Each *Corrente da camera* is followed by an *Aria*, all of which are *Presto* in 3/4 meter and hence are quite different from the customary character of this type. The two sonatas at the end of the collection show by their brevity and stylistic simplicity that they are first experiments. Colombi uses the dissonant Corelli clash, that is, the cadence

as frequently as did his fellow-citizen Bononcini, while the Bolognese Vitali hardly ever uses it.

Colombi's Opus 2 appeared five years later, in 1673: *La Lira armonica, Sinfonie à due Violini, col suo Basso continuo.* . . . The term *Sinfonie* here designates compositions whose individual titles as well as those in the *Tavola* should correctly be *Sonata prima–Sonata duodecima*. The scoring is two violins and b.c.

Nine of these sonatas consist of three movements separated by double bars; Nos. 1 and 2 have only two movements; and only No. 10 has four, as was customary at the time. These works are strikingly brief: even No. 10, with four movements, has only 75 measures, compared with the 120 to 150 measures of most sonatas of the period. And a considerable number of movements have no tempo indication.

The initial movements (in No. 11 it is the second, after a homophonic *Grave*) are short fugues. Those in Nos. 2, 3, 5, 9, 10, and 12 are in two parts, with the *basso continuo* serving as support. The opening movements of the other sonatas are in three parts, with the continuo participating in the imitation of the theme. The themes are mostly of the *andamento* type and are answered at the unison, as in *Sonata quinta* (Fig. 151). Some are shorter, in the manner of the *soggetto*, and are answered at the fourth (Nos. 2, 6, and 8) or the fifth (No. 11). The exposition is usually followed by an episode in sequence style. The second exposition is based on a shortened or slightly varied form of the theme, and the brief coda often consists of a few measures of *Adagio* in chordal style. In the three-movement sonatas the initial fugue is usually followed by a slow movement in homophonic style. In most sonatas the third movement is also homophonic and nearly always in triple meter.

Colombi's Opus 3 appeared in 1674, with the title *Balletti, Correnti, Gighe, Sarabande a due Violini, e Violone, ò Spinetta*. It contains 24 dances in no recognizable principle of order: nine balletti, six correnti, five gigas, three sarabandas, and one aria. Opus 1, which

FIGURE 151. COLOMBI: SONATA QUINTA (OPUS 2, 1673).

also contains dance music, was written for string quartet, while Opus 3 is for string trio. However, Colombi shows a more conservative attitude here by admitting the spinet as an alternative for the string bass. In Opus 1 a distinction is made between dances *da camera* and dances *alla francese* (that is, *da ballo*), but all the dances of Opus 3 are *da camera*, as appears from various stylistic details (occasional use of imitation, complementary motifs, etc.). The six correnti are to be played in slow tempo (*Adagio, Largo*), which would be impossible for a corrente *da ballo*.

Colombi's next publication, Opus 4, appeared in 1676, with the title *Sonate a due Violini con un Bassetto Viola se piace* . . . It contains twelve sonatas, the first ten for two violins, bass, and b.c. The last two *a Due Violini*, that is, without the *Bassetto Viola*, hence for two violins and b.c. Nearly all the statements made for Colombi's Opus 2 are valid for his Opus 4, including the preference for the three-movement form (eight of the twelve sonatas have three movements; No. 8 has two; and Nos. 3, 4, and 12 have four), the shortness of the movements, and the scarcity of tempo indications. The music is of rather limited value and sometimes borders on the trivial, particularly *Sonata undecima*, which may be best regarded as a musical joke. The first and the third movements of *Sonata duodecima* are identical. Both are homophonic *Adagios* (the latter has no tempo indication) that differ only in their meter: the former is in **C**, the latter in 3/2. At the end of *Sonata sesta* the three string instruments stop playing one after the other—an idea that reminds one of Haydn's "Farewell" Symphony (see Fig. 152).

FIGURE 152. COLOMBI: SONATA SESTA (OPUS 4, 1676).

It is odd that in the title of the publication the remark *se piace* is associated with *Bassetto Viola*. This instrument plays an important role in many pieces. Thus in Fig. 152 the effect would be greatly diminished if in the penultimate measure the eighth-note motif were to disappear and only the three quarter notes of the organ were heard.

Colombi's last publication of violin music, Opus 5, appeared in 1689, with the title *Sonate da camera a tre stromenti, due Violini, e Violone, ò Cimbalo.* The scoring is the same as in Opus 3, that is, a string trio in which the string bass can be replaced by a keyboard instrument. The publication contains eleven sonatas and one giga. The sonatas are four-movement suites, each of which consists of a short *Adagio* and three dances of various kinds. Sonatas Nos. 1, 4, and 11 each consist of *Adagio, Balletto, Giga,* and *Corrente,* the same form that Giovanni (Battista) Bononcini (1670–1750) used for his *Trattenimenti* of Opus 1 (1685). Chronologically Colombi appears to be a successor of Bononcini, but in reality it was the other way around: Bononcini was then fifteen years old, Colombi 50. Other sonatas in Colombi's publication consist of *Adagio, Balletto, Corrente,* and *Gavotta* (No. 2), *Adagio, Corrente, Giga,* and *Sarabanda* (No. 9), and *Adagio, Allemanda, Corrente,* and *Sarabanda* (No. 10).

While we have characterized the music in Opus 4 as "trivial," three years later, in Opus 5, Colombi appears as a composer of high rank and individuality. The introductory *Adagios* are fascinating, not so much for the flow of melody but for the interesting progressions, which lead from a lively motivic play over fragmentary configurations to a veritable hocket (Fig. 153).

FIGURE 153. COLOMBI: SONATA UNDECIMA (OPUS 5, 1689).

The dance movements are interesting in various respects. For instance, in Sonatas Nos. 3, 5, 9, and 10 the corrente—originally a fast dance—is marked *Adagio,* and in Sonata No. 10, the *Gavotta*—usually a dance in moderate tempo—is marked *Presto.* The fragmentary style (which was very much in vogue during the 1670s and 1680s, and which probably originated with Stradella) appears occasionally in the dances: for instance, in the *Balletto* of Sonata No. 2, in which the two violins alternate eighth notes and eighth rests, as in Fig. 153, but in fast tempo; and in the *Gavotta* of No. 5 and the *Aria* of No. 7, in which the fragment ♪♩ is played repeatedly in *Presto.*

In the *Balletto* of No. 3, mm. 2–3 contain successive leaps of a fifth

similar to those in Arresti's Opus 4 (1665). There are also short passages with parallel fifths or octaves, for instance, in the *Adagio Corrente* of Sonata No. 3, where violin I plays

while violin II plays

Finally, in his last opus Colombi frequently uses the Corelli clash.

NOTE

1. One might argue that the single surviving exemplar, in the Biblioteca Estense in Modena, is incomplete, the continuo book being lost. This seems unlikely because Colombi's two later prints of dances (Opus 3 and Opus 5) are also written for a string ensemble with no mention of continuo, while the two prints with sonatas (Opus 2 and Opus 4) require a continuo instrument.

SOURCES

Delle sinfonie da camera, brandi e corrente alla francese con corrente, et arie da camera e suonate per suonare a due, a tre et a quattro. ... Opus 1. Bologna: [Giacomo Monti], 1668.   RISM C3435.
   Italy: Modena, Biblioteca Estense.

La Lira Armonica. Sinfonie a due violini, col suo basso continuo. ... Opus 2. Bologna: Giacomo Monti, 1673.   RISM C3436.
   Italy: Bologna, Civico Museo; Modena, Biblioteca Estense.

Balletti, correnti, gighe, sarabande, a due violini, e viole o spinetta. ... Opus 3. Bologna: Giacomo Monti, 1674.   RISM C3437.
   Italy: Modena, Biblioteca Estense.

Sonate a due violini, con un bassetto, viola se piace. ... Opus 4. Bologna: Giacomo Monti, 1676.   RISM C3438.
   Great Britain: Oxford, Bodleian Library (4 parts).
   Italy: Modena, Biblioteca Estense.

Sonate da camera a tre strumenti, due violini, e violone, o cimbalo. ... Opus 5. Bologna: Pietro Maria Monti, 1689.   RISM C3439.
   Great Britain: Oxford, Bodleian Library.
   Italy: Bologna, Civico Museo; Modena,Biblioteca Estense.
   West Germany: Münster, Santini-Bibliothek (Violin I incomplete).

🎵 Pietro Degli Antonii

Pietro Degli Antonii was born in Bologna in 1648 and spent his whole life there. In 1666 he became a charter member of the Accademia Filarmonica; he was elected its president in 1676 and several times in later years. He was chapelmaster of three Bolognese churches: from 1680 at Santa Maria Maggiore, 1686 at San Stefano, and 1697 at San Giovanni in Monte. He died in 1720. Pietro, his brother Giovanni Battista, and Giovanni Battista Vitali represent the second generation of the Bolognese school, which was founded by Cazzati.

Degli Antonii's Opus 1 appeared in 1670, the same year as Cazzati's Opus 55. *Arie, Gighe, Balletti, Correnti, Allemande, e Sarabande. A Violini, e Violone, ò Spinetta con il Secondo Violino a beneplacito* contains 25 pieces. Nos. 1–19 are for two violins and Nos. 20–25 are for one violin (*violino solo*), all with the accompaniment of *Violone ò Spinetta*. Frequently two successive pieces form a pair in the same key, for instance, *Aria prima—Sua Arietta* (Nos. 1 and 2 in D major), *Alemanda prima—Corrente seconda* (Nos. 12 and 13 in Bb major), *Balletto terzo—Corrente terza* (Nos. 16 and 17 in Eb major), and *Giga sesta—Sua Arietta* (Nos. 24 and 25 in A major). The ariettas differ from the arias, not—as might be expected—by being shorter, but by being in triple meter (3/8 or 12/8), while the arias are all in even meter. The pieces are all in binary form with interesting harmonic structures. The first section remains in the tonic key (in only one case does it close in the dominant), while the second section modulates to the dominant or to the parallel key, as in *Alemanda prima*, written in Bb major (Fig. 154). Such modulations can be found in the works of other contemporary composers, but not as clearly and consistently as in Degli Antonii's Opus 1.

FIGURE 154. PIETRO DEGLI ANTONII: ALEMANDA PRIMA (OPUS 1, 1670).

Several times Degli Antonii has the violins play in parallel fifths (in *Giga prima* and *Balletto secondo*) or octaves (in *Balletto terzo*). Whether this was criticized by Arresti, as were the numerous "errors" in the works of Cazzati, is not known. At any rate, Degli Antonii's career—in contrast to Cazzati's—made steady progress.

In the following year, 1671, Pietro Degli Antonii published a second collection of dances, with the title *Balletti, Correnti & Arie diversi à Violino, e Violone per Camera, & anco per Suonare nella Spinetta, & altri Instromenti. . . . Opera terza.* The publication consists only of a score in small oblong format; from it and the remark *& anco per Suonare nella Spinetta* one may conclude that Opus 3 was also intended to be performed as keyboard music. The eighteen dance pieces are grouped in pairs, for instance, *Balletto primo* and *Sua Corrente, Balletto Quarto* and *Sua Giga,* and at the end, the rather unusual pair of *GIGA* and *Sua Sarabanda.* Often, at cadences as well as within a phrase, a trill is indicated by *t.* As far as I know, this is the first occurrence of this notation in violin literature. Pandolfi used *tr.* in his two publications from 1670, not as an abbreviation for a trill but in combination with a written-out *trillo* (see Fig. 127). Stylistically, the pieces of this collection are simpler than those of Opus 1.

Degli Antonii's next publication of violin music, Opus 4, appeared in 1676: *Sonate a Violino solo con il basso Continuo per l'Organo.* As was traditional for solo sonatas, the publication consists of a score and a part book for the violin. These twelve sonatas are subdivided into sections or movements that differ in tempo, meter, or style, but only rarely are they separated by double bars. For instance, *Sonata terza* consists of *Allegro, Aria Grave, Grave,* and *Allegro* but has only one double bar, before the second *Allegro.* Possibly this means that the first three movements should be played without interruption. At any rate, Degli Antonii's sonatas differ strikingly from those of his predecessor Cazzati in their lack of structural clarity. In Sonatas Nos. 1, 2, 9, and 12 Degli Antonii uses for one of the movements the designation *Posato* (steady, deliberate), a very telling word for a quiet tempo that has never been included in books of musical terms. He shows a striking preference for slow tempi: *Largo, Lento, Grave,* and *Posato* appear much more frequently than *Allegro, Vivace,* or *Presto.*

For the fast movements of his sonatas, Degli Antonii used various methods of composition. The *Allegro* of No. 1 is a two-voice fugue, the final *Allegro* of No. 3 a loosely worked-out fugato, while the method of self-imitation introduced by Leoni prevails in the *Vivace* at the beginning of No. 5. Other fast movements are duets in which the violin and the organ participate on an equal basis, by moving in parallel thirds or sixths, or alternate in complementary motifs, for instance, in the 12/8 *Allegro* of No. 4. Finally, there are several fast movements written as virtuoso violin solos, for instance, the *Presto* of No. 7 and the final *Vivace* of No. 11.

Degli Antonii's fast movements—especially those written in imitative style or in the manner of duets—are not particularly remarkable. His slow movements, on the other hand, are among the most beautiful compositions in the violin literature of the late seventeenth century. Here he appears to be in the domain of the vocal music of the time, with regard to both form and style. The *Aria grave* of *Sonata terza* is another example of the motto aria, which originated in the fields of opera and cantata, and which Pandolfi had used in his sonatas from 1670 (see Fig. 129). In the *Aria grave* of *Sonata seconda* and in the final movement of the *Sonata quarta,* Degli Antonii uses the principle of announcing the motto. In the third movement, *Grave,* of *Sonata terza* another device of theatrical music is imitated, that is, the recitative, whose words are answered by the echo. Fig. 155 shows the beginning of this movement.

FIGURE 155. PIETRO DEGLI ANTONII: SONATA TERZA (OPUS 4, 1676).

In the *Largo* at the beginning of *Sonata undecima*, which is in 3/2, the note group

occurs three times. This highly chromatic phrase includes a diminished fifth and a diminished third. And several times in *Sonata settima* (for instance, at the close of the first *Adagio*), a phrase occurs that represents the very opposite, the forced turning away from chromaticism, that is, a cadential formula in which the leading tone is suppressed and only the tonic is repeated, for example,

instead of

Both phrases are mannerisms borrowed from contemporary vocal music.

Ten years after Opus 4, in 1686, Degli Antonii's Opus 5 appeared with the same title: *Suonate a Violino solo col Basso Continuo per l'Organo*. It is also in the form of a score, but without a part book for the violin. The publication contains eight sonatas of the same type as those of Opus 4. One difference—one may or may not call it progress—is that the sonatas are more clearly divided into movements. In addition to various terms of fast and, especially, slow tempos, there are indications for nuances of performance, for instance, *Con spirito* (No. 8), *Affettuoso* (No. 3), and *un poco piano* (No. 1).

Stylistically, the sonatas of Opus 5 differ from those of Opus 4 by their greater emphasis on imitation, particularly in the fast movements, all of which are written in imitative style. However, as is to be expected in solo sonatas, the principle of imitation is rather loosely applied, insofar as the themes appear only at the beginning (in a fugato), only in the violin (self-imitation), or separated by long episodes.

Opus 5 shows the same preference for slow movements as in Opus 4. They are not only more numerous (a total of 48 against 26, in the two collections) but also sometimes more extended. Here, in *Largo* and *Grave*, in *Affettuoso* and *Posato*, Degli Antonii shows himself to be a great master. His impressive violin melodies are like arias "sung" above the sustained sounds of the organ. A particularly beautiful example is the *Grave* of *Sonata terza* (Fig. 156), which also contains an exceptional application of the incipit repeat: The initial four-measure phrase is restated not (as in most cases) in the dominant, but in the parallel key, thus involving a change from minor to major.

FIGURE 156. PIETRO DEGLI ANTONII: SONATA TERZA (OPUS 5, 1686).

Equally impressive is the beginning of the *Adagio* of *Sonata prima*. The initial phrase is played twice at a high pitch; then, transposed to the dominant, it is played two octaves lower, in the dark region of the violin. The *Adagio affettuoso* of Sonata No. 3 and the *Aria grave* of No. 8 belong to the motto aria type, as do several movements in Opus 4.

In 1680 there appeared a collection entitled *Scielta delle Suonate a due Violini, con il Basso Continuo per l'Organo, raccolte da diversi Eccellenti Autori*, edited by Marino Silvani. It contains as No. 5 a trio sonata by Pietro Degli Antonii, the only sonata of this type that has been preserved among his compositions. It consists of five movements, all of which have indications of slow tempo: *Largo, Lento, Grave, Lento,* and *Grave*. Although the second movement gives the impression of an *Allegro*, this accumulation of slow movements is unique in the history of the sonata.

SOURCES

Arie, Gighe, Balletti, Correnti, Allemande, e Sarabande, a violino, e violone, ò spinetta, con il secondo violino a beneplacito. . . . Opus 1. Bologna: Giacomo Monti, 1670.   RISM D1346.
   Italy: Bologna, Archivio dell'Accademia filarmonica; Civico Museo.

Balletti, Correnti, & Arie diverse à violino, e violone per camera, & anco per suonare nella spinetta, & altri istromenti. . . . Opus 3. Bologna: Giacomo Monti, 1671.   RISM D1348.
   Italy: Bologna, Civico Museo.
   West Germany: Munich, Bayerische Staatsbibliothek, Musiksammlung.

Sonate a violino solo con il basso continuo per l'organo. . . . Opus 4. Bologna: Giacomo Monti, 1676.   RISM D1349.
   Great Britain: Oxford, Bodleian Library.
   Italy: Bologna, Civico Museo.

Suonate a violino solo col basso continuo per l'organo. . . . Opus 5. Bologna: Giacomo Monti, 1686.   RISM D1350.
   Great Britain: Oxford, Bodleian Library.
   Italy: Bologna, Civico Museo; Modena, Biblioteca Estense.

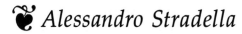 Alessandro Stradella

Alessandro Stradella was born in 1644 in Rome, where he stayed until 1677. During this time he wrote numerous operas, oratorios, and cantatas, many of them for the Colonna and Pamfili families as well as for the Teatro Tordinona, which was closed in 1676. Stradella's last five years were filled with travel and adventures—in Venice, Turin, Genoa, and possibly other places. He was murdered in Genoa in 1682 because of a love affair.[1]

About twenty cantatas, six oratorios, twenty motets, eight operas, nine serenades, and about 60 other vocal compositions can be attributed to Alessandro Stradella with certainty. Twenty-six works for violin are known, nearly all of them preserved in manuscript. I have used the following sources:

1. Modena, Biblioteca Estense, Mus. F 1129 (ModF): Twelve compositions.

2. Modena, Biblioteca Estense, Mus. G 210 (ModG): Six compositions.

3. Turin, Biblioteca Nazionale, Foà 11 (Foà): Nineteen compositions, seven of them not in Modena.

4. *Scielta delle Suonate a due Violini, con il Basso Continuo per l'Organo, raccolte, da diversi Eccellenti Autori* . . . 1680. This collection, edited by Mario Silvani, contains as *Sonata sesta del Sig. Alessandro Stradella* composition No. 8 from ModF.

5. *Sonate a tre di Vari Autori* . . . (1700?). No. III in this collection is a *Sonata del Stradella*, which is not found in the manuscripts.

The three manuscripts are scores written after 1700. Unfortunately, they contain many errors, few thorough-bass figures, and hardly any tempo indications. The sonata mentioned in the last source above, has six indications of tempo, while in the manuscripts there are only nine tempos indicated for 25 sonatas with more than 100 movements. This deficiency makes it difficult to comprehend and interpret these works as originally conceived. Twelve compositions are scored for violin and b.c.; nine for two violins and b.c.; two for two violins, bass, and b.c.; and three are multivoiced, for six, seven, and ten instruments respectively. In the manuscripts nearly all the compositions are called *Sinfonia*, but they are actually sonatas (as are the *Sinfonie* in Colombi's Opus 2), except for a single composition in the manuscript Foà (f. 38), which is a set of variations.

The great majority of the sonatas consist of four movements, a norm that had been adopted by many other composers during the 1660s and 1670s. Six of Stradella's sonatas deviate from it: one with three movements (ModF, No. 1 = Foà, f. 84 = XXIIV[2]) two with five (Foà, f. 99 = XV; and ModG, No. 4 = XXII), two with six (ModG, No. 2 = XXII; and ModF, No. 4 = Foà, f. 17v = VI), and one with seven (Foà, f. 26 = XI). There is a striking preponderance of movements in binary form, most of them in triple meter and therefore taking on the character of a dance (a corrente or a giga). Legrenzi was probably the first to write a movement in binary form, that is, the second movement of his *Sonata La Brembata* (Opus 4, No. 1, of 1656). Nearly all of Stradella's sonatas close with such a movement, and in some of them the second movement is also written in binary form. The following schematic representation shows the structure of Sonata ModF No. 7 (= Foà, f. 9 = IX).

Movement	1	‖ 2	‖ 3	‖ 4	‖
Meter	26 D	34 Tr(3/4)	30 D	59 Tr(6/8)	
		12 : ‖ : 22		11 : ‖ : 48	

Especially impressive is the binary movement at the end of Sonata ModG, No. 3 (= II). Its D-major tonality, 12/8 meter, dotted rhythm, and lyrical melody (mostly in four-measure phrases) give it the character of a siciliano or a pastorale. Fig. 157 shows the beginnings of the first and second sections.

FIGURE 157. STRADELLA: SINFONIA (ModG NO. 3).

Quite frequently Stradella fashions the beginning of a movement with an incipit repeat, as at the start of Sonata No. 7 from ModF (= Foà, f. 9 = IX), shown in Fig. 158. Since the incipit repeat is nearly always used for slow movements, one might be inclined to interpret this opening, which sounds like a fanfare, as a *Largo* or a *Grave* followed by an *Allegro* in m. 8. Or should it be interpreted as an energetic *Allegro* from the beginning?

FIGURE 158. STRADELLA: SINFONIA (ModF NO. 7).

The latter is the opinion of Gino Roncaglia, whose very detailed study of Stradella's instrumental compositions says of this sonata, "Il 1° tempo e deciso ed energetico."[3] This work shows how difficult it is to understand and perform Stradella's instrumental compositions properly when tempo indications are lacking.

Stradella's movements in fugal style are based on well-designed, concise themes that comprise at the most two measures, sometimes only one. Although the themes are quoted quite frequently within the course of a movement, no particular attention is paid to the consistent alternation of expositions and episodes, as prescribed by the rules. In harmony Stradella turns out to be one of the most progressive masters of his time, be it in the frequent use of passing modulations, chromatic alterations, or occasional harmonic changes. Especially remarkable is the close of the sixth movement of the very long sonata Foà, f. 26 (= XI). With its strange turns and windings it reminds one of Berlioz (Fig. 159).

FIGURE 159. STRADELLA: SINFONIA (FOÀ, F. 26).

In several cadences the descent to the tonic is chromatically subdivided by the insertion of the minor third between the major third and the second, for instance,

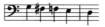

One of the most noteworthy movements is the last one of Sonata ModF, No. 12 (= XVII) for two violins and b.c. Like many movements in Stradella's sonatas it is in binary form, with a total length of sixteen measures and a repeat sign in the middle of m. 5. Its special quality is the extensive dismembering of the voice parts, which are cut up by rests into shorter and shorter fragments; one is reminded of the medieval hocket. In conformance with this abrupt style of writing, the movement and, consequently, the sonata itself, concludes not with a sustained chord but with a detached eighth note, moreover without the usual double bar but in its place a scroll and the word "finis." Fig. 160 shows the beginning and end of the second section. One may not necessarily agree with Roncaglia, who interprets this movement as an expression of anxiety (*senso di ansia*), but he is certainly right in saying that it would be hard to find an example or model of this form with such originality.[4]

FIGURE 160. STRADELLA: SINFONIA (ModF, NO. 12).

FIGURE 161. STRADELLA: SINFONIA (FOÀ, F.65).

Stradella uses the same abrupt style, though with an entirely different meaning in the last movement of Sonata Foà, f. 65 (= XVI). The almost uninterrupted use of the rhythm ♩♪♪ in alternation between the two violins and the bass gives it a majestic character (Fig. 161). It is reminiscent of the "bows" in Narini's *Retirata* from 1655 (see Fig. 37), which might be regarded as Stradella's model.

Sinfonia Foà 11, f. 38ff. (= XII), is a set of 25 variations. They are based on an unchanging bass of thirteen whole notes that form three groups of four notes plus a closing note:

The variations to be played by the violin are not very noteworthy, except for Nos. 15, 16, and 24, which are to be performed with double-stops.

Stradella is particularly famous for his three multivoice compositions, which belong to the category of the concerto grosso, as is indicated in their titles:

1. ModF, No. 1: *Sonfinia per violini e Bassi a due Concertini distinti*; Foà, f. 84: *Sonata a 4 Due Violini, e due Cornetti divisi in due Chori*. This composition (= XXIV) is for six instruments divided into two choirs each of two violins and bass (according to Foà, two violins and bass and two cornetti and bass). It has three movements. Of special interest is the opposition of the violins and cornetti in the Foà version.

2. ModF, No. 2: *Sinfonia a Violini e Bassi a Concertino e Concerto grosso distinti*; Foà, f. 69: *Sonata di Viole, cioe Concerto grosso di Viole e Concertino di 2 Violini e Leuto*. This composition (= XXV) is written for seven instruments divided into a three-voice *concertino* (two violins and bass) and a four-voice *concerto grosso* (violin, alto, tenor, and bass). It has four movements.

3. Foà, f. 111; *Sonata a otto viole con una tromba, le viole divisi in due chori*. This composition (= XXVI) has ten parts, with a four-voice *Primo Choro* (two violins, tenor, and bass) and a six-voice *Secondo Choro* (trumpet plus two violins, alto, tenor, and bass). There are four movements, of which the second and fourth are called *Aria* and are binary. The trumpet plays the highest part of the second choir in the clarino range, *a* to *c♯"*.

As early as 1619, Francesco Sponga (Usper) had written a *Sinfonia* that can be regarded as a concerto grosso, and the same is true of some sonatas by Massimiliano Neri, from 1651. Thus, Stradella is the third in a series of composers that continues with Torelli, Corelli, and Vivaldi and ends with Bach. In the treatment of the opposing groups, Sponga and Neri employ essentially the same method as the later masters, insofar as the "solo" passages are occasional insertions in a composition that is primarily *a Tutti*. But Stradella's concertos consist basically of alternations of the two groups that are only occasionally (especially at the beginning) joined with the *Tutti*. Fig. 162 shows a passage from the first movement of Concerto No. 2.

FIGURE 162. STRADELLA: CONCERTO, NO. 2.

Note that Stradella does not use the term *Concerto grosso*, as became customary later, for the entire composition, but for the larger of the two groups, while the smaller one is called *Concertino*. Quite logically, in *Concerto* No. 1, both groups are called *concertino*, since they are equally scored. Stradella's vocal compositions also contain several instrumental movements of the category *Concerto grosso*.[5]

Although Stradella's violin compositions contain a few weak passages or movements, they offer much boldness, elan, and brilliant invention. They are the work of a very sensitive and restless artist, whose creative work depended on the inspiration of the moment—an impression that is also given by his life, which was so full of changes and adventures.

NOTES

1. See E. F. McCrickard, "Allessandro Stradella's Instrumental Music," diss., University of North Carolina, 1971.
2. The Roman numerals refer to the new edition, ibid., vol. 2.
3. RoncagliaS, vol. III, p. 9.
4. Ibid., pp. 5–6.
5. Stradella's vocal compositions are discussed in RoncagliaS, vols. I and II.

SOURCES

Scielta delle suonate a due violini, con il basso continuo per l'organo raccolte da diuersi, eccelenti autori. Bologna: Giacomo Monti, 1680.   SartoriB 1680[a].
  Italy: Bologna, Civico Museo; Biblioteca del Conservatorio (Violin I).

Suonate a tre di vari autori. . . . s.l.: s.n., 1700(?).   SartoriB 1700[l].
  Italy: Bologna, Civico Museo; Biblioteca del Conservatorio (Violin I).
Edition:
Eleanor McCrickard, ed. Cologne: Arno Volk Verlag, Hans Gerig, 1980 (collected instrumental music).

Manuscripts:
Modena, Biblioteca Estense Mus. F 1129.
Modena, Biblioteca Estense Mus. G 210.
Turin, Biblioteca Nazionale Foà 11.

🎵 Giovanni Buonaventura Viviani

Giovanni Buonaventura Viviani was born in Florence in 1638. From 1656 until 1672 he was a violinist and from 1672 to 1676 director of court music in Innsbruck. In 1677–78 he was in Venice and Rome, and in 1692 he became chapelmaster of the cathedral of Pistoia. Between 1677 and 1682 he wrote a number of operas, which were performed in Venice and Naples.

In 1673 Giovanni Viviani's Opus 1 appeared: *Sonate a trè, due Violini, e Viola . . .* , a collection of twelve sonatas for two violins, bass, and b.c. They have widely varying structures. The simplest one is No. 4, with three movements each of a uniform character. The most complex is *La Vendramina*, No. 2, in which six movements can be distinguished, several of which are contrast movements. This sonata includes a short soloistic section for each of the three instruments, as is shown in the following diagram:

Movement	1	2a	b	c	3a	b	c
Meter	26 D	3 D	5 D	4 D	11 D	11 D	4 D
Tempo		Adagio	Presto	Adagio	Presto	Adagio	Presto
Instrumentation		Violino II solo				Violino I solo	

Movement	4a	b	5	6a	b
Meter	9 D	Tr	8 D	11 D	4 D
Tempo			Adagio	Allegro	Adagio
Instrumentation	Viola solo	a 3.			

Sonata La Bergonza, No. 7, also has two soloistic sections, one for violin I and one for violin II.

Sonata La Dieda, No. 9, begins with a 30-measure movement entitled *Toccata*. Indeed, it has the structure of an organ toccata since the two violins (the viola part book reads *Toccata a due Violini tacet*) play lively figurations above sustained notes on the organ (C, F_1, G_1, C).

In Viviani's fast movements we sometimes encounter short, rhythmically precise motifs that are not played imitatively (as might be expected) but simultaneously in all instruments, yielding an effect of sharp strokes. Particularly noteworthy in this respect is the first movement of Sonata No. 11, the beginning of which is shown in Fig. 163. What is the significance of its title, *La Barbara*? Surely Viviani did not have Saint Barbara in mind but the same affect that Bartók expressed much more realistically in his *Allegro barbaro*, where *barbaro* means "barbarous" or "brutal"—a meaning, however, unknown in the seventeenth century. This is an indication of the pitfalls connected with the interpretation of the numerous character titles in seventeenth century Italian repertory.

In 1678 Viviani published his Opus 4, another collection of violin music of interest from the bibliographical point of view. It appeared in the same year in two editions: one in Venice with the title *Capricci armonici da chiesa e da camera a Violino solo . . .* , the other in Rome with the title *Sinfonie, Arie, Capricci, Allemande, Corrente, Gighe, Introduttioni, Sarabande, etc. . . . .* In the Venetian edition (as in his Opus 1) Viviani calls himself *Maestro*

FIGURE 163. VIVIANI: SONATA UNDECIMA. LA BARBARA (OPUS 1, 1673).

di Capella di Sua Maestà Cesarea in Innspruck, but not in the Roman edition, which he dedicated to a citizen (*Il Signor Asdrubale Cardelli*). It is possible that in 1678 he left (lost?) the position at the imperial court and went to Rome. The contents of Opus 4 are as follows:

Symphonia prima, seconda	Nos. 1, 2
Toccata prima, seconda	Nos. 3, 4
Sonata prima, seconda	Nos. 5, 6
Aria prima—sesta	Nos. 7–12
Introduttione prima–quarta	Nos. 13–16
Capriccio primo–terzo	Nos. 17–19
Sinfonia cantabile	No. 20
Sonata prima, seconda per Trombetta sola	Nos. 21, 22

Nos. 1–20 are for *Violino solo* (violin and b.c.), Nos. 21 and 22 for *Trombetta sola* and b.c.

The *Introduttioni* (Nos. 13–16) and *Capriccio secondo* (No. 18) are suites. The rest of the compositions fall into the category of the sonata and consist of three or four movements, except for *Sinfonia cantabile* (No. 20), which has seven movements, some of them very extended (for instance, a 68-measure *Allegro* in 3/4). The style is basically that of a duet with occasional bits of imitation. However, nearly every one of these compositions contains a movement or a section in which the organ is limited to a few sustained notes, so that the violin stands out as a solo instrument. In Nos. 3 and 4 these soloistic movements are at the beginning and are quite extended, hence the designation *Toccata*. The second movement of *Sonata prima* is an *Adagio Aria* followed by five variations. As far as I know, this is the first example of a procedure used by the Viennese classicists, who frequently wrote the *Adagio* movements of their sonatas, symphonies, or string quartets as a theme with variations. Viviani's variations are written on an original nine-measure theme, rather than on a traditional or popular song, as was customary in the seventeenth century. The variations are not called *parte*, but—also for the first time—*Variatio I, Variatio II*, and so on. The work does not consist exclusively of variations, but begins with the theme, followed by the variations, a procedure in which Viviani may be following an Austrian or a German model.

Viviani's *Introduttioni* are actually suites in which the introduction is followed by several dances, for instance, *Introduttione seconda, Allemanda, Corrente, Sarabanda + Variatione*. In *Introduttione quarta (Introduttione, Corrente, Balletto)*, the two first movements are in Bb major, the third in C major. Also in the suite inscribed *Capriccio secondo*

(*Capriccio, Giga, Allemanda, Corrente, Balletto, and Sarabanda*) the first two movements are in G minor, the rest in C minor.

Viviani's six arias are noteworthy for their structure. From the earliest examples of this type in Buonamente's *Libro quinto*, of 1629, to those in Bononcini's Opus 12 (which appeared in the same year as Viviani's Opus 4), the aria is a fairly short composition in binary form (‖: A :‖: B :‖) with a total length of ten to 25 measures, and always in even meter. Viviani enlarges and changes this frame considerably, especially in *Aria prima*, which consists of three independent parts that, as in a sonata, may well be regarded as movements. *Aria seconda—quinta* each consist of two movements, and *Aria sesta* is the only one with just one movement, but with 35 measures in 3/2 it is considerably more extended than the norm. Nearly all the movements have a repeat structure, but by no means the simple one indicated above. They are more complex, as can be seen in the following schematic representation of *Aria prima*:

Movement		1		‖	2		‖	3		
Tempo	c	A	:‖: B A		3/2	Adagio A B A C		3/4	Presto A :‖: B :‖: ‖	
No. of measures		4	12 4			9 8 9 12			10 9	

The first movement closes with a repeat of the first part, in the so-called *Reprisenbar* found in the songs of the German Minnesinger and occasionally in Latin hymns. It is the basic structure of the classical sonata form—repeated exposition, development, and recapitulation.

Sinfonia cantabile (No. 20) is well named, for three of its movements are written in the style of a recitative, and the other movements have a vocal rather than a violinistic character.

Viviani very frequently provides cadences with the sign *t.* for a trill, the same way as Pietro Degli Antonii did for the dances of his Opus 3, from 1671. Other Italian violin composers of his time may have taken the addition of a trill for granted and regarded this notation as unnecessary; some champions of performance practice, especially of improvised ornamentation, maintain this theory.

Viviani's Opus 4 is one of the most important works of the seventeenth-century literature for violin solo. The movements or sections written in imitation of vocal recitative are particularly beautiful. Once more, one is reminded of Pietro Degli Antonii's solo sonatas of Opus 4, from 1676. No doubt, there existed a relationship between the two masters, but what?

SOURCES

Suonate a tre, due violini, e viola. . . . Opus 1. Venice: Francesco Magni, 1673.   RISM V2254.
   Italy: Bologna, Archivio dell'Accademia filarmonica (Violin I and II, Viola, Organ). Reprint:
Venice: Giuseppe Sala, 1679.   RISM V2255.
   Great Britain: Oxford, Bodleian Library (4 parts).

Sinfonie, arie, capricci, alemande, correnti, gighe, introduttione, sarabande, &c. per violino solo. . . . Opus 4. Rome: Giuseppe Vannacci, 1678.   RISM V2256.
   Great Britain: Oxford, Bodleian Library (V principale, Organ).
Reprint:
Capricci armonici da chiesa, e da camera a violino solo cioe sinfonie, toccate, sonate, introduttioni, alemande, corente, gagliarde, sarabande, gighe, balletti, e capricci, et sonate per tromba sola. . . . Venice: Giuseppe Sala, 1678.   RISM V2257.
   Italy: Bologna, Civico Museo.

Veglie armoniche a 1. 2. e 3 voci con violini e senza. Opus 7 Florence: s.n. [Stamperia di S.A.S. alla Condotta, 1690].   RISM V2260.
   Italy: Florence, Biblioteca Nazionale Centrale (B, Violin I).

 # Giovanni Battista Mazzaferrata

Giovanni Battista Mazzaferrata (fl. 1670) was an organist and composer and a pupil of Tarquinio Merula. He was maestro di capella of the cathedral of Vercelli in 1661, and by 1668 he held the same position at the Accademia della Morte in Ferrara. Mazzaferrata composed madrigals, songs, cantatas, psalm settings, oratorios, and one book of sonatas, his Opus 5.

The sonatas of Mazzaferrata's Opus 5 are four-movement works in contrasting meters and tempo (the last, however, consists of four movements all marked *allegro*). They are light, flowing works of harmonically oriented counterpoint foreshadowing the Classical style, according to William Newman.[1]

NOTE

   1. William S. Newman, *The Sonata in the Classic Era*, 3d ed. (New York: Norton, 1983).

SOURCES

Il primo libro delle sonate a due violini con un bassetto viola se piace. Opera Quinta. Bologna, Giacomo Monti, 1674.   RISM M1514.
   Austria: Vienna, Österreichische Nationalbibliothek.
   Italy: Bologna, Accademia Filarmonica (b.c. only).
Reprints:
1678.   RISM M1515.
   Belgium: Brussels, Bibliothèque Royale de Belgique.
   Great Britain: Durham, Cathedral Library; London, British Library.
   Italy: Asti, Biblioteca del seminario.
1688.   RISM M1516.
   Italy: Bologna, Accademia Filharmonica.

🎵 Giovanni Battista Bassani

Giovanni Battista Bassani was born about 1657 in Padua. In 1677 he became organist of the Accademia della morte in Ferrara, and in 1680 chapelmaster to Duke Alexander II della Mirandola. After a short stay in Bologna (1682–83), he returned in 1685 to Ferrara, where he was first active as chapelmaster of the Accademia and in 1689 also as organist and chapelmaster of the cathedral. In 1712 he became chapelmaster of the Basilica Maria in Bergamo, where he died in 1716. In addition to numerous operas, oratorios, and other vocal compositions, he wrote two collections of violin music.

Bassani's Opus 1; *Balletti, Correnti, Gighe, e Sarabande à Violino, e Violone, overo Spinetta, con il Secondo Violino à beneplacito*, contains twelve suites, each consisting of *Balletto, Corrente, Gigha,* and *Sarabanda.* Nearly every dance has an indication of tempo, including some rather modern ones, such as *Largo ma spiritoso* (*Balletto primo, secondo*) and *Non tanto presto* (*Gigha quinta*), but also the seemingly self-contradictory *Vivace, ma Largo* (*Corrente seconda*). All the sarabandas are marked *Presto*, one even *Prestissimo.* Normally the sarabanda is regarded as slow and serious, but in its exotic homeland, Mexico, it was a wild and lascivious dance, and it retained this character for a long time in its European development. About the middle of the seventeenth century the change to a dance of the opposite type became fairly conclusive, but Bassani fanatically emphasizes its original character. The structure of his sarabandas is quite different from what was then customary. The sarabandas by Bononcini, Vitali, and Degli Antonii always consist of two sections of eight measures each, those by Bassani have sections of irregular length, for instance: ‖ : 4 : ‖ : 7 : ‖, ‖ : 11 : ‖ : 20 : ‖, or ‖ : 7 : ‖ : 9 : ‖. Fig. 164 shows the first section of *Sarabanda ottava.*

FIGURE 164. BASSANI: SARABANDA OTTAVA (OPUS 1, 1677).

Corrente sesta and *nona* have the tempo indication *Largo,* which is as unusual as the *Presto* of the sarabandas. Moreover, the bass of the *Corrente nona* is an ostinato in 3/2:

which is stated four times in the first section and three times in the second section, transposed to the lower fourth. In *Gigha prima* the problem of rhythmic performance arises, similar to that in a *Presto* movement in Legrenzi's Opus 8, from 1663 (see. Fig. 121). Both pieces are written in even meter (**C**), but contain numerous eighth-note triplets, leading one to question whether rhythms like ♪♪ are to be adjusted, that is, performed as ᴣ♪ . For Legrenzi's composition the adjusted performance is preferred, but for Bassani's *Gigha* contrast is probably intended, since a motif with sixteenth notes plays an important role. Fig. 165 shows the beginning of this piece.

FIGURE 165. BASSANI: GIGHA PRIMA (OPUS 1, 1677).

Of course, the triplet rhythm is possible here, too, as indicated in small notes, but it seems to me that with the adjustment the piece would lose its charm. In order to bring out the contrast, the tempo should be kept moderate rather than fast. Bassani writes *Allegro*, not *Presto*, as does Legrenzi. Bassani—like Bononcini and Colombi—frequently uses the Corelli clash, but usually a less-dissonant variety, in which the leading tone sounds ahead of the anticipated tonic

In his Opus 1, which he wrote as a young man of twenty, Bassani proves himself to be a musician of high rank. His suites are distinguished by many interesting phrases and brilliant ideas. Particularly beautiful is the melody of *Gigha settimi*, which is characterized by a very charming, alluring motif (Fig. 166).

FIGURE 166. BASSANI: GIGHA SETTIMA (OPUS 1, 1677).

Bassani's second publication of violin music is his Opus 5, which appeared in 1683, with the title *Sinfonie a due, e tre Instromenti, con il Basso Continuo per l'Organo* in Bologna.[1] The publication contains twelve sonatas in the scoring two violins, bass, and b.c. Nos. 1–6 are marked *Violoncello a beneplacito* (*se piace* in an Amsterdam reprint), Nos. 7–12 *Violoncello obligato*. This is somewhat strange, since in the six first sonatas the violoncello has many important and even indispensable passages, for instance, in the *Allegro* of No. 6, the answer to the theme in m. 2.

The form of Bassani's sonatas differs from what was customary at the time, since only three of them consist of four movements, all with the tempo sequence slow, fast, slow, fast. Eight sonatas have five movements; and one, No. 1, has seven movements, with movements 4 and 6 (both *Adagio*) related thematically, and movements 5 and 7 (both *Prestissimo*) identical except for transposition.

The initial movements in fast tempo show a great variety of procedure. In Sonata No. 11 one measure of *Largo* precedes the 60-measure *Presto* in 6/4. This movement resembles a vivacious scherzo, in free style and with ever-changing ideas and motifs. It is a charming piece, comparable to the fourth movements of Sonata No. 6 (*Prestissimo* in 3/4) and Sonata No. 10 (*Prestissimo* in 3/2). In other sonatas the initial *Allegros* are written in fugal style, ranging from the very simple to the very complex. The simplest is the *Allegro* of Sonata No. 12, in which a short sixteenth-note motif is treated so freely that the 25-measure piece can hardly be regarded as a fugato, but rather as an attractive free study in imitative counterpoint. Midway in the range one might place the first *Allegro* of Sonata No. 7, in which a prominent theme is treated in the three-voice fugue with three expositions. More complex are the initial *Allegros* of Sonatas Nos. 3, 4, and 8, which are fully developed double fugues. The climax is the *Allegro* of No. 10, a triple fugue, which is a novelty in the field of Italian violin music.

In *Sonata ottava* (which begins with a five-measure *Grave*) the fast movement (*Presto*) is a 42-measure double fugue whose main theme reminds one of the E♭ minor fugue of the *Well-Tempered Clavier I.* It starts with a descending fifth, an interval that Bassani uses so often in the bass of this movement that the repeated motion V–I takes on the higher meaning of a thematic motif. Fig. 167 shows the thematic situation at the beginning of the first and second expositions.

FIGURE 167. BASSANI: SONATA OTTAVA (OPUS 5, 1683).

Even more noteworthy is the first fast movement (also *Presto*) of *Sonata decima.* Its three themes are played in the first twelve measures by the two violins, while the violoncello and the organ perform a running bass. In the second section (mm. 15–24), the three themes are performed in the bass, separated by rests during which the two violins play in stretto. The third section (mm. 25–39) is analogous to the first, the fourth (mm. 40–47) similar to the second, and in the fifth (mm. 47–58) theme B is played twice by violin I. Fig. 168 shows the themes of this masterwork, together with a schematic representation of the first two sections.

FIGURE 168. BASSANI: SONATA DECIMA (OPUS 5, 1683). R = RUNNING BASS.

Like Bononcini, Stradella, Albergati, and other violin composers of the time—though not Corelli—Bassani shows a tendency to use fragmentary phrases and abrupt endings in his fast movements.

The slow movement, *Adagio*, of Sonata No. 12 is based on a basso ostinato

played twelve times; four times on *d*, four times on *a*, and again four times on *d*. *Sonata decima* contains two particularly beautiful slow movements of a serious, even tragic character. The first movement is an *Adagio* in C minor, and the third is a *Largo* in F minor whose second half begins with a short imitation of the motif

which Bach uses as a symbol of the cross, of suffering.

The first work in the collection *Scielta delle Suonate*, edited by Marino Silvani, which appeared in 1680, is a sonata by Bassani (*Allegro, Presto, Adagio,* and *Vivace*). It is less important than the sonatas of Opus 5, and was obviously written at an earlier time (before 1680).

NOTE

1. It is reproduced in the article *Bassani* in MGG.

SOURCES

Balletti, correnti, gighe, e sarabande a violino e violone, overo spinetta, con il seconde violino a beneplacito. . . . . Opus 1. Bologna: Giacomo Monti, 1677.   RISM B1161.
    France: Paris, Bibliothèque nationale (Violin I).
    Italy: Bologna, Civico Museo.
Reprints:
Bologna: Marino Silvani (Giacomo Monti), 1684.   RISM B1162.
    Great Britain: London, British Library.

Suonate da camera, cioè balletti. . . . Venice: Giuseppe Sala, 1686.   RISM B1163.
United States: New York (N.Y.), New York Public Library at Lincoln Center.

Sinfonie a due, e tre instromenti, con il basso continuo per l'organo. . . . Opus 5. Bologna:
Giacomo Monti, 1683.   RISM B1171.
Great Britain: Oxford, Bodleian Library.
Italy: Bologna, Civico Museo.
Reprints:
Bologna, Marino Silvani (Giacomo Monti), 1688.   RISM B1172.
Italy: Bologna, Civico Museo.
West Germany: Regensburg, Bischöfliche Zentralbibliothek (Violoncello).
Suonate a due, tre instrumenti col basso continuo per l'organo. . . . Antwerp: Hendrik
Aertssens, 1691.   RISM B1173.
France: Paris, Collection André Meyer.
Great Britain: London, British Library; Oxford, Christ Church Library (incomplete).
United States: Cambridge (Mass.), Harvard University, Music Libraries.
XII Sonate da chiesa a tre, due violini, basso e basso continuo. . . . Amsterdam: Estienne
Roger, No. 93, n.d.   RISM B1174.
Great Britain: Cambridge, Pembroke College Library; University Library; London,
British Library.
Netherlands: The Hague, Gemeente Museum.
Sweden: Stockholm, Kungliga Muikaliska Akademiens Bibliotek.
United States: Washington (D.C.), Library of Congress, Music Division.

🎵 *Andrea Grossi*

> *Little is known about Andrea Grossi except the information in his four publications
> of violin music, the only ones that are preserved. He was a descendant of Viadana
> (Lodovico Grossi) and seems to have been a violinist active at the ducal court of
> Mantua at least from 1678 to 1685.*

Andrea Grossi's Opus 1, from 1678: *Balletti, Correnti, Sarabande, e Gighe a tre, due Violini,
e Violone, overo Spinetta,* contains eight suites, four of which consist of *Balletto, Corrente,
Sarabanda,* and *Gigha.* If in the four-movement suites the balletto is replaced by an allemande—an exchange that is certainly admissible—the resulting suite may be called
classical, that is, closing with a giga instead of a sarabanda.[1] Whether the little-known
Andrea Grossi (he is not represented in MGG) was the creator of this form is doubtful.
At any rate he plays an important role in the documented history of the suite, or *sonata
da camera.*

Without exception, all Grossi's dance movements are strictly symmetrical, with the
same number of measures in each of the two sections, for instance:

	Balletto	Corrente	Sarabanda	Gigha
Primo	7 : ‖ : 7	12 : ‖ : 12	8 : ‖ : 8	9 : ‖ : 9
Settimo	12 : ‖ : 12	20 : ‖ : 20	9 : ‖ : 9	11 : ‖ : 11

Here all the dances are subjected to a principle of regularity that was otherwise valid only for the sarabanda. Grossi's predilection for strict regularity is even more apparent in his Opus 2, which appeared in 1679, not only with the same title but also with the same contents as his Opus 1: four two-movement suites (*Balletto* and *Gigha*) and four with four movements (*Balletto, Corrente, Sarabanda,* and *Gigha*). Every one of the 24 dances is, of course, strictly regular in its structure.

Musically, Grossi's suites are rather unimportant, containing nothing that would call for special attention. However, they are noteworthy from the point of harmony. A very elementary, but also very important, question arises in connection with the numberless dances written during the Baroque period: On which degree does the first section end? In the dance pieces of Bach's suites and partitas it is, almost without exception, the dominant. The situation in early violin music is presented in the following table. All pieces in binary form (dances, but also arias, sinfonias, etc.) published between 1642 and 1679 are listed according to the close of the first section: the dominant (D), the tonic (T), or another scale degree (O).

Composer	Date of Publication	D	T	O
Uccellini	1642, 45, 60, 67, 69	11	51	17
Cazzati	1651, 54, 60, 62, 67, 69	22	80	7
Bononcini, G.M.	1666, 69, 71, 71, 73, 75, 78	74	82	19
Vitali, G.B.	1666, 67, 68	40	34	1
Colombi	1668, 74	24	29	—
Degli Antonii, P.	1670, 71	5	37	—
Bassani	1677	19	28	1
Degli Antonii, G.B.	1677, after 1677	13	51	—
Grossi	1678, 79	33	9	6

It appears that in the publications of Uccellini, Cazzati, Bononcini, and P. and G. B. Degli Antonii, the closing of the first section of a majority of these pieces is on the tonic. A turn in favor of the dominant is indicated in Vitali's publications, but in Grossi's it first becomes decisive. In the cases listed under O, Uccellini's and Cazzati's binary pieces sometimes have a cadence on the subdominant, those of the other composers almost exclusively on the parallel key.

Grossi's Opus 3 appeared in 1682. This publication, *Sonate a due, a trè, quattro, e cinque istromenti* . . . contains twelve sonatas, Nos. 1–3 for two violins and b.c.; Nos. 4–6 for two violins, bass, and b.c.; Nos. 7–9 for two violins, alto, bass, and b.c.; and Nos. 10–12 for trumpet, two violins, alto, bass, and b.c. Five sonatas consist of four movements, five others of five, one has three, and one has six movements. Sonata No. 3 has the tempo sequence slow, fast, slow, fast.

The sonatas for string instruments (Nos. 1–9) contain a total of 40 movements. About half of them are strictly written fugues in two, three, or four voices, with a continuo that frequently takes on the older form of a *basso seguente*. Each fugue has three or four expositions of the theme, in which Grossi's love of regularity manifests itself no less clearly, though in a different way, than in the dance movements of his Opus 1 and Opus

2. Each exposition proceeds from high to low, so that the theme is played first by violin I, then by violin II, then by the viola, and so on, in contrast to the normal practice of changing the order of the instruments in the various expositions.

Very frequently several movements of a sonata are related to each other thematically. This principle was then rather old-fashioned, but it is another expression of Grossi's sense of order and regularity. An example in point is *Sonata quarta*, in which the *Largo* (toccata-like, with the pedal point *D*), *Allegro*, *Presto*, and *Prestissimo* all begin with

in various rhythms.

Sonatas Nos. 10–12 for trumpet, string quartet, and continuo—along with the last three sonatas in Cazzati's Opus 35 from 1665 (see p. 129)—are early examples of the art of playing the trumpet. The fugue style, which plays such an essential role in the sonatas for string instruments, is replaced here by the alternation of the trumpet accompanied by the organ and the strictly homophonic string quartet, two contrasting sonorities that combine into a *tutti* at the end of each movement.

Grossi's Opus 4, from 1685: *Sonate a trè, due Violini, e Violine, con il Basso Continuo per l'Organo* . . ., contains twelve sonatas in the trio scoring two violins, bass, and b.c. Compared with his Opus 3, the number of four-movement sonatas has increased (to eight), as has the number of those with the tempo sequence slow, fast, slow, fast. The length of the compositions has also increased—the violin I part book of Opus 3 has 47 pages, that of Opus 4, 62. Grossi's sense of order and regularity manifests itself even more frequently in the practice of imitating the theme from high to low. While the fugues of Opus 3 have a maximum of four expositions, those of Opus 4 have at least five, and some have as many as six, all in the same succession of voice parts. Another regularity occurs in the entrance of the theme: In violin II and in the bass it is always preceded by a rest, but never in violin I. The example shown in Fig. 169, the fifth exposition of the second movement of Sonata No. 8, is one of hundreds of the same type.

Also in Opus 4, Grossi frequently makes use of the cyclic principle. For instance, in *Sonata ottava* the motif

of the second movement reappears in the fourth and fifth movements, and in *Sonata settima* the motif

is treated in a similar way.[2]

FIGURE 169. GROSSI: SONATA OTTAVA (OPUS 4, 1685).

NOTES

1. In keyboard music the sequence Allemande, Corrente, Sarabanda, Giga occurs for the first time in a print after 1690 containing suites by Froberger, with the comment "mis en meilleur ordre." See ApelG, pp. 541–542.

2. An Opus 5 (*Suonate da camera*, Bologna, 1696) was mentioned by Fétis and by Eitner, but appears to be lost. *Sonata quarta*, for two violins and b.c., is in *Scielta delle suonate*, Bologna, 1680 (Sartori 1680ᶜ).

SOURCES

Balletti, correnti, sarabande, e gighe, a tre, due violini, e violone, overo spinetta. Opus 1. Bologna: Giacomo Monti, 1678.   RISM G4724.
    Great Britain: Oxford, Bodleian Library.

Balletti, correnti, sarabande, e gighe a tre, due violini, e violone, overo spinetta. Opus 2. Bologna: Giacomo Monti, 1679.   RISM G4725.
    Great Britain: Oxford, Bodleian Library.
    Italy: Bologna, Civico Museo.

Sonate a due, tre, quattro, e cinque istromenti. . . . Opus 3. Bologna: Giacomo Monti, 1682.   RISM G4726.
    Italy: Bologna, Civico Museo (6 parts).

Sonate a tre, due violini, e violone, con il basso continuo per l'organo. . . . Opus 4. Bologna: Giacomo Monti, 1685.   RISM G4727.
    Italy: Bologna, Civico Museo.
    West Germany: Münster, Santini-Bibliothek (4 parts).

Giovanni Battista Degli Antonii

Giovanni Battista, the younger brother of Pietro Degli Antonii, was born about 1660 in Bologna. He was elected a member of the Accademia Filarmonica in 1684, and sometime later he became organist of San Giacomo Maggiore in Bologna. Of his later life nothing is known except that in 1690 he was still active as organist of the same church.

In 1677 a collection of violin music by Giovanni Battista Degli Antonii appeared in score with the title *Balletti, Correnti, Gighe, e Sarabande da Camera a Violino, e Clavicembalo ò Violoncello . . . Opera Terza.* It contains twelve suites, each consisting of a ballo with one, two, or (in two cases) three other dances, for instance, *Ballo secondo* and *Gigha* in D major, *Ballo terzo, Aria, Gigha,* and *Sarabanda* in F major (but which are printed in the wrong order *Aria, Gigha, Sarabanda,* and *Ballo terzo*). The dances are unpretentious, but not without skill and in good taste.

Degli Antonii's Opus 4 appeared (with no indication of date) with the title *Balletti, Correnti Gighe e Sarabande a trè due Violini e Clavicembalo ò Violoncello. . . .* Like Opus 3, this publication contains twelve suites, each consisting of a ballo followed by one, two, or (in two cases) three other dances, for instance, *Ballo secondo* and *Corrente* in C major, and *Ballo terzo, Corrente, Sarabanda,* and *Gigha* in D major. The scoring is two violins and b.c. These pieces are considerably more significant than the earlier ones. The gigas, with which four suites end, are especially attractive. They are all in major keys, lively, and high-spirited, especially the giga of the third suite (*Ballo terzo, Corrente, Sarabanda,* and *Gigha*), which sounds like joyous hunting music. Fig. 170 shows the beginning of the first section. In the penultimate measure (as in some preceding ones) there is an anapest rhythm, which is extremely rare in Italian violin music.

FIGURE 170. GIO. BATTISTA DEGLI ANTONII: GIGHA (OPUS 4, AFTER 1677).

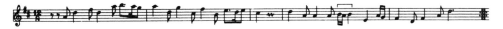

G.B. Degli Antonii's Opus 5 appeared in 1689, with the title *Ricercate a Violino, e Violoncello, ò Clavicembalo.* It consists of ten two-voice ricercars. The ricercar (or ricercata) plays a very important role in organ music, beginning with Marcantonio Cavazzioni's *Recerchari . . .,* of 1523, and ending with the ricercar in Bach's *Musical Offering,* of 1742. In the field of string instruments the situation is quite different. As early as the middle of the sixteenth century, Silvestro Ganassi (*Regola Rubertini,* 1542) and Diego Ortiz (*Traatado de glosas,* 1552) had written ricercars for the viola da gamba, but Degli Antonii was the first to cultivate this type again, nearly 150 years later: in his Opus 1, *Ricercate sopra il Violoncello, ò Clavicembalo,* 1687 (obviously this is a later edition, since his Opus 3 appeared in 1677) and now in Opus 5.

The violin ricercars are duets in the strictest sense of the word, with two equal partners. The compositional technique is the same as that of the bicinia of the late sixteenth century and of Bach's Two-Part Inventions. The lower part (which has no thorough-bass figures) must be played by the cembalist's left hand, except for occasional short passages notated in the tenor clef that can easily be played with the right hand.

Degli Antonii's ricercars are 60 to 80 measures long, with no interruptions, but usually subdivided into three sections in which the meter changes from duple to triple. These sections are related to each other by an identical head motif, which, unexpectedly, recurs only in the lower part. Fig. 171 shows the beginnings of the three sections of *Ricercata quinta*.

FIGURE 171. GIO. BATTISTA DEGLI ANTONII: RICERCATA QUINTA (OPUS 5, 1689).

Degli Antonii's Opus 6: *Balletti a Violino, e Violoncello, ò Clavicembalo*, appeared in 1690 in score. The bass is fully provided with figures and is therefore meant to be played primarily on the cembalo. The publication consists of fifteen dances that form six suites, each of which begins with a ballo. Groups Nos. 1, 2, and 5 each consist of *Ballo, Corrente*, and *Sarabanda* (in No. 2 the last dance is a *Gigha*), the others only of a *Ballo* and *Corrente*. The structure of the two sarabandas is of interest. The numerous sarabandas written since about 1650 retained the character of music for actual dancing, with four or eight measures in each section. Degli Antonii was the first to disregard this limitation and to apply the principle of free continuation that had long been used for other dances: the first sarabanda has the structure 13 : ‖ : 14, the others, 15 : ‖ : 19.

In his Opus 3 and Opus 4 Degli Antonii shows a striking preference for closing the first section of his dances on the tonic (see the table on p. 226). This is also true of his Opus 6: among the fifteen dances there are ten of this type.

SOURCES

Balletti, Correnti, Gighe, e Sarabande da camera a violino, e clavicembalo, o violoncello. . . . Opus 3. Bologna: Marino Silvani, 1677.   RISM D1339.
  Italy: Bologna, Civico Museo.
  West Germany: Wiesentheid, Musiksammlung des Grafen von Schönborn-Wiesentheid.
Reprint:
Bologna, Gioseffo Micheletti, 1688.   RISM D1340.
  Great Britain: Oxford, Bodleian Library.
  Italy: Bologna, Civico Museo.
  West Germany: Munich, Bayerische Staatsbibliothek, Musiksammlung.

Balletti, Correnti, Gighe e Sarabande a tre, due violini e clavicembalo, o violoncello. . . . Opus 4. Bologna: Gioseffo Micheletti, n.d.   RISM D1341.
  Italy: Bologna, Civico Museo.

Ricercate a violino, e violoncello, o clavicembalo. . . . Opus 5. Bologna: Gioseffo Micheletti, 1690.   RISM D1342.
   Great Britain: Oxford, Bodleian Library.
   Italy: Bologna, Civico Museo.

Balletti a violino, e violoncello, o clavicembalo. . . . Opus 6. Bologna: Gioseffo Micheletti, 1690.   RISM D1343.
   Great Britain: Oxford, Bodleian Library.

🎵 *Arcangelo Corelli*

Arcangelo Corelli was born in 1653 in Fusignano (near Faenza). In 1666 he came to Bologna, where he was elected a member of the Accademia Filarmonica, in 1670, when he was barely seventeen years old. In 1675, or possibly earlier, he moved to Rome, where he was elected to the famous Accademia degli Arcadi in 1706 and also received many other honors. He died in 1713. His musical creativity is chiefly preserved in six publications, all of which contain compositions for the violin.[1]

Corelli's Opus 1, printed in 1681, has the title *Sonate a trè, doi Violini, e Violone, ò Arcileuto, col Basso per l'Organo*. It is dedicated to Queen Christina of Sweden, who had accepted Corelli in her celebrated circle of scholars and artists. The publication contains twelve sonatas, which in reprints are correctly named *Sonate da chiesa*. Nine of them consist of four movements, two have three movements, and one has five:

Three Movements

F, S, F	No. 7
FS, F, F	No. 4

Four Movements

S, F, S, F	Nos. 2, 3, 8, 11
S, F, S, FSF	No. 1
S, F, SFFSF, F	No. 5
S, S, S, F	No. 6, 12
FFFS, F, S, FS	No. 9

Five Movements

S, F, F, S, F	No. 10

(F = fast; S = slow. Movements are separated by commas. Letters not separated by commas indicate changes of tempo within a movement.)

Sonatas Nos. 1, 2, 3, 8, and 11, with four movements in the tempo sequence slow, fast, slow, fast, have the form of the final development of the *sonata da chiesa*. As early as 1648 Cazzati had written a sonata of this type, and in Vitali's publications of 1667 and 1669 there are one or two examples, but such isolated cases reflect no more than the inevitable combination possibilities. In Corelli's Opus 1, on the other hand, for the first time this form is a structural principle, so that Corelli must be recognized as the founder of the *sonata da chiesa* in the specific meaning of the term.

The fourth movement of Sonata No. 1, the third of No. 5, and the first and fourth of No. 9 are contrast movements of the Venetian type (as in Neri and Legrenzi). They consist of several sections that differ from each other in meter, tempo, and ideas. In the third movement of No. 5 the tempo changes so often between *Adagio* and *Allegro* that it is difficult to decide whether it is a slow or a fast movement. It seems preferable to interpret it as a slow movement with fast insertions, and the sonata as belonging to the type slow, fast, slow, fast. The contrast movement at the beginning of Sonata No. 9 consists of three *Allegro* sections and a concluding *Adagio*, with the *Allegros* made up entirely of broken-triad formations. In 1649, Uccellini had written a *Trombetta sordina per il Violino* (the last composition of his Opus 5), which consists entirely of arpeggio paraphrases of a D-major triad; and some later composers also wrote extended passages in broken chords. In Corelli's movement, however, the broken-chord phrases are not irrelevant passage-work but significant phrases, which make this movement one of the most interesting and most significant pieces in Opus 1. The principle of contrast is combined here with the principle of repeat, since the third *Allegro* differs from the first only by transposition and contrary motion. Fig. 172 shows the beginnings of the first three sections.

FIGURE 172. CORELLI: SONATA NONA (OPUS 1, 1681).

The final movement of this sonata is built of the same material, that is, a fugato on a theme consisting of five measures in broken-chord formation. The result, however, is not very convincing; arpeggio phrases are suitable for an overture, not for the fugue.

Corelli's Opus 1 contains about ten movements in fugal style. The second movements of Sonatas Nos. 3, 4, and 9 are fully developed fugues with several expositions. The others are fugatos whose theme—sometimes an extended *andamento* (for example, the fourth movement of No. 3, the first of No. 7, and the second of No. 10)—is treated only in an initial exposition, while in the later course of the movement it is reduced to a motif that sometimes also appears inverted (for instance, the fourth movement of No. 9 and the fifth of No. 10). In some movements only the two violins participate in the imitation, for instance, the second movement of No. 12, whose very extended theme Corelli regarded as unsuitable for the bass.

Three slow movements belong to the field of the fugue: the second movement of No. 6 (*Largo*), the third of No. 8 (*Largo*), and the second of No. 12 (*Largo e puntato*). The others are duets in which the two violins frequently begin in homophonic motion, then alternate with short complementary motifs. Five slow movements (the third movement of No. 3 and the first of Nos. 2, 8, 11, and 12) begin with a phrase that, after a rest, is recreated on another scale degree, according to the principle of incipit repeat. In the third movement of Sonata No. 3 the incipit comprises three measures (not four) and is transposed to the upper third (not, as is usual, to the fifth).

Corelli's Opus 2, of 1685, *Sonate da camera a trè, doi Violini, e Violone, ò Cimbalo*, contains eleven sonatas and a *Ciacona*. The sonatas are suites with great variability of form: Nos. 2 and 6 consist of *Allemanda, Corrente*, and *Giga*; Nos. 5 and 8 of *Preludio, Allemanda, Sarabanda*, and *Gavotta*. Eight suites begin with a *Preludio*—a free introduction—as in Vitali's Opus 4, from 1676, where four suites begin with an *Introduttione*. Corelli's introductions are far superior to Vitali's in content and expressiveness, particularly that of No. 7, which is a beautiful example of incipit repeat. In Nos. 3 and 4, Corelli inserts in the third place a free movement in slow tempo (*Grave, Adagio*), an element taken over from the *sonata da chiesa*, which differs from the dances by being written without interruptions rather than in binary form. Suite No. 3 contains two allemandes, one after the *Preludio*, the other after the *Adagio*.

In Opus 1, Corelli had already used the cadence characterized by two successive seconds, which is named after him and which we call the "Corelli clash," but in Opus 2 it appears with striking frequency. As we have seen, it bears Corelli's name unjustly, since it occurs just as frequently in compositions by G. M. Bononcini and Colombi published in the 1660s.

The final composition of Corelli's Opus 2 is a *Ciacona* consisting of 30 variations on the descending tetrachord—the famous theme that Frescobaldi had treated extensively in his *Partite sopra Ciaccona* and *Partite sopra Passacaglii* (both in *Secondo libro di Toccate*, 1626). Corelli begins his *Ciacona* with four variations in *Largo*, then proceeds to an *Allegro* for the main part of the composition. At the beginning of the *Allegro* the descending tetrachord $g–f\sharp–e–d$ is played twice in its pure form as a strict ostinato; thereafter it is paraphrased in manifold ways (as it is in Frescobaldi's composition), so that one may speak of a quasi-ostinato. Above this foundation, the two violins perform lively and varied melodic lines, which—as may be expected in a work by Corelli—always remain within the limits of good taste and musical propriety.

Corelli's Opus 3, which appeared in 1689, has the same title as his Opus 1: *Sonate a tre, doi Violini, e Violone, ò Arcileuto, col basso per l'Organo*. It contains twelve *sonate da chiesa*, whose structures can be represented as follows:

Four Movements

S, F, S, F	Nos. 2, 3, 4, 5, 7, 8, 9, 11
S, F, F, F	No. 1
F, S, F, F	No. 6
F, F, S, F	No. 10

Five Movements

SFSFS, F, F, F, F	No. 12

This tabulation differs in three important ways from the corresponding one for Opus 1: The three-movement form has disappeared; the contrast movement is represented by only one example; and eight sonatas have the tempo sequence slow, fast, slow, fast, which is obligatory for the later *sonata da chiesa*.

The thematic substance in the imitative movements is treated in such a variety of ways that a special study would be required to provide a proper picture. Many of these movements are fugatos in which the complete theme appears only in an initial exposition; thereafter it occurs only in a shortened version. The *Vivace* of Sonata No. 9 comes closest to a three-voice fugue. It consists of a first exposition, a fairly extended episode, and a second exposition. The second movement (*Allegro*) of Sonata No. 2 is a double fugue in the second half of which only the countersubject (an inverted form of the main theme) is used. The third movement (*Largo*) of No. 3 resembles the second movement (*Largo e puntato*) of Opus 1, No. 12, because its very extended theme occurs only in the upper voices, not in the bass. The second movement of No. 2 is a double fugue the themes of which Bach treated more extensively in his *Fuge über ein Thema von Corelli*[2] for organ.

The first movement of Sonata No. 12 resembles the initial movement of Sonata No. 9 in Opus 1. It is a contrast movement in which three short *Adagios* serve as prelude, interlude, and postlude for two extended *Allegros* consisting almost exclusively of broken-triads: the first fourteen measures above the pedal point *A*, the other 40 (!) measures above the dominant *E*. Fig. 173 shows a passage from the latter section. In the subsequent movements of this sonata, broken-chord phrases of various lengths appear again and again, echoing what the first movement offers in such plenitude.

FIGURE 173. CORELLI: SONATA DUODECIMA (OPUS 3, 1689).

Corelli's Opus 3—like his Opus 1—contains half a dozen movements in binary form (such as the third of No. 1 and the fourth of No. 2). This reminds one of Stradella, who frequently includes such binary movements in his sonatas, and whom Corelli certainly had known personally, since both of them lived in Rome from about 1675 to 1677.

Corelli's Opus 4 appeared in 1694: *Sonate à 3. composte per l'Accademia dell'Em.mo e Rev.mo Sig. Cardinale Ottoboni. . . .* It contains twelve suites (*sonate da camera*) consisting of the same elements as those of Opus 2: *Preludio, Allemande, Corrente, Giga, Sarabanda, Gavotta,* and occasionally an *Adagio* or a *Grave*. The variability of grouping is even greater than in Opus 2: every suite has a different form.

Each suite begins with a *Preludio*, seven of which are continuous, while the others either have binary form (Nos. 3, 9, and 12) or are extended contrast movements (Nos. 6 and 10). Among the dance movements there are four gavottas. The one in Suite No. 4 has the regular structure 4 : ‖ : 8, which is customary for this dance, while the others exceed this normal format; for example, the one in No. 3 has the structure 14 : ‖ : 28. Corelli (as well as some other composers of his time) calls attention to this difference by designating the dance in Suite No. 4 *Gavotta*, the others *Tempo di Gavotta*. The tempo and the character of the sarabandas are variable, as so frequently happens in the last decades of the seventeenth century: the *Sarabanda* of Suite No. 3 is slow (*Largo*), while those of Nos. 7 and 8 are fast (*Vivace* and *Allegro*). The *Sarabanda* of No. 3 is the only movement of Opus 4 in which the so-called Corelli clash is used (the dissonant cadence Corelli wrote so frequently in his Opus 2). Finally, in many movements the lower voice part has the form of a running bass, mostly in fast eighth notes (in the fourth movements of Nos. 1 and 7, the second movement of No. 5, and the third of Nos. 8 and 11), once in fast sixteenths (in the second movement of No. 8), and twice in slow eighth notes (in the first movement of No. 2 and the third of No. 4).

The dance movements of Opus 4 are similar to those of Opus 2 in style and content. The free *Adagio* movements show increased expressiveness, especially the *Adagio* of No. 4 and the *Preludios* of Nos. 5 and 8.

Corelli enters a new field with his famous Opus 5, which appeared in 1700. This publication consists of two parts, *Parte Prima Sonate a Violino e Violone o Cimbalo* and *Parte Seconda*, containing *Preludii, Allemande, Correnti, Gighe, Sarabande, Gavotte, e Follia*. It contains twelve compositions for violin solo (and b.c.): Nos. 1–6 are *sonata da chiesa*; Nos. 7–11 are *sonate da camera*; and No. 12 is a set of variations.

Nos. 1–6 are unusual and novel in various respects. First of all, the designation *sonata da chiesa* is not quite suitable for them since the violin is not accompanied by the organ (as in Opus 1 and Opus 3) but by the violone or the cembalo. They are not to be performed in the *chiesa* but in the *camera*, perhaps (as with Opus 4) in the *accademia* of Cardinal Ottoboni. They could be called "church sonatas *per camera*."[3] The form of the sonatas of Corelli's Opus 5 deviates from the normal type of the time: they all consist of five movements, either in the sequence slow, fast, fast, slow, fast (Nos. 1, 2, 4, and 6) or slow, fast, slow, fast, fast (Nos. 3 and 5). Most important, however, is the novelty of their style. They make frequent use of double-stops and full chords. To be sure, double-stops were not new in Italy having been used by Marini (Opus 8, 1626), Uccellini (Opus 7, 1660), G. M. Bononcini (Opus 4, 1671), Stradella (about 1670), and Torelli (Opus 4, about 1690). Corelli, however, used this technique to serve a novel purpose—writing in imitative style. In each sonata the first *Allegro*, and in Nos. 1, 2, and 6 the final one also, begins with an imitative section in which the first and second statements of the theme are played by the violin, the third by the violone or the harpsichord. Fig. 174 shows the beginning of Sonata No. 1.

The further course of these sonatas is very different in each case. In the second movement (*Allegro*) of No. 1 the imitative beginning is followed by a long section of a purely virtuosic character, first a passage with arpeggio chords, then one in sixteenth-note figuration. The fifth movement of No. 1 and the second of Nos. 4, 5, and 6 have similar structures but close with a second, abbreviated exposition of the theme. The second

FIGURE 174. CORELLI: SONATA NO. 1 (OPUS 5, 1700).

movement of No. 3 has exceptionally virtuosic episodes (bariolage, trills in thirds) and closes with an extended cadence over a pedal point. The second and fifth movements of No. 2 are contrapuntal-fugal throughout, except for a short passage in arpeggio chords or arpeggio figurations. The fifth movement of No. 6 is the only one that can be regarded as a fully developed fugue with three expositions and fairly extended episodes that are not highly virtuosic.

Among the nonimitative fast movements there are three final movements (the fifth in Nos. 3, 4, and 5) that are in binary form with the character of a giga. Five movements are of the *perpetuum mobile* type—three in continuous sixteenth-note motion (the fourth movement of No. 3 and the third in Nos. 1 and 6) and two in 3/8 meter with inserted triplets (the third movements of Nos. 2 and 4). It is possible that Corelli adopted this somewhat mediocre type from Antonio Veracini, who had used it several times in his Opus 2, of ca. 1694.

Among the slow movements, the first *Adagio* of Sonata No. 1 stands apart from the others. It is an extended contrast movement (slow fast slow slow fast slow) with a similar structure in each half (slow fast slow). In several slow movements the beginning is shaped according to the principle of incipit repeat, with the incipit varying in length from one and a half measures (fourth movement of No. 2) to as much as twelve measures (third movement of No. 3). Usually the incipit is repeated in the dominant key, but in the third movement of No. 2 it is in the mediant. The third movement (*Adagio*) of No. 1 is particularly expressive, with its extended melody in 3/2 meter.

The slow movements of Opus 5 are famous because of the rich ornamentations that have been added in several reprints, beginning with an edition by P. Mortier of Amsterdam, which carries the following additional remark: "Quatrième Edition, ou l'on a joint les agréments des Adagio de cet' ouvrage, composez par Mr. A. Corelli, comme il les joue." It is a much-discussed question whether and to what extent these ornamentations can be regarded as authentic. Antonio Veracini, in his Opus 2, from about 1694, offers convincing evidence that the basically French practice of improvised (that is, not written-out) ornamentation had been accepted in Italy by writing out a score for most of his slow movements in the cembalo part book (see p. 269). Also, the *Adagio* ending of the first *Allegro* of Corelli's Sonata No. 1, as reproduced in Fig. 175, shows that Corelli was familiar with this kind of ornamentation. Although this is not conclusive, it does support the thesis that the ornamented versions of the *Quatrième Edition* (for instance, the ending of the third movement of Sonata No. 2, shown in Fig. 175b) are somewhat authentic.

In the second part of Corelli's Opus 5, the compositions referred to as *Sonate VI–XI*

FIGURE 175. CORELLI: a. SONATA NO. 1 (OPUS 5, 1700);
b. SONATA NO. 2 (OPUS 5, QUATRIÈME EDITION, N. D.).

are suites (*sonate da camera*) that consist of the same elements are those of Opus 2 and Opus 4. The double-stop playing characteristic of the sonatas of the first part, is limited here to a very few passages, mainly the cadential measures of the second movement, *Corrente*, of No. 7 and the third movement, *Sarabande*, of No. 10. The absence of virtuosic display is easy to justify in a suite. It is interesting that the editor of the *Quatrième Edition* has completely renounced providing ornamented versions for these compositions, which would have been possible and even desirable at least for the short third movements (*Adagio*) of Nos. 9 and 11. The final movement of No. 9, *Tempo di Gavotta*, consists of three sections, the third being an exact repetition of the first:

$$A \; \| : \; B \quad A$$
$$20 \quad 14 \quad 20$$

This is an exceptionally extended example of the so-called *Reprisenbar*, a form that belongs to medieval Germany rather than seventeenth-century Italy, and which we have encountered in a composition by Viviani.

Corelli's Opus 5 closes with a composition called *Follia*, a set of variations on a sixteen-measure theme that can be schematically represented as follows:

This theme, above the common ostinato bass pattern, appears as early as the first half of the sixteenth century (one of many examples is a pavane in the vihuela book *Silva de Sirenas* by Valderravano, 1547). Corelli's extended set of variations is his most famous composition. First of all, it should be noted that it is not a *Folia con 23 Variazioni*, as listed in the Contents of the new edition by Joachim and Chrysander (*Les Oeuvres d'Arcangelo Corelli*, Livre II, London 1890). No composer of the seventeenth century would ever think of using such an "objectional" number as 23. As in all variation sets of this period, the first variation is not numbered, so that the "happy" total of 24 results.

Nearly all the variations are formula variations, a type in which a characteristic formula recurs in each measure, adapted to the respective requirements of the harmony. Variation 15, with a continuous flow of expressive melody, and variation 20, which is written in the style of imitative counterpoint, represent different types. In variations 12, 13, and 14 the meter changes from 3/4 to C, in such a way that each measure corresponds to two 3/4 measures, so that each of these variations comprises eight measures instead of sixteen. Nos. 5–6, 7–8, and 21–22 are paired variations, since they are based on the same formula, which appears first in the upper part, then in the lower one. Corelli does not treat the violone (or the cembalo) as a mere accompanying instrument but as an equal partner. Frequent change of tempo is unusual in variations but here No. 9 is *Adagio*, No. 10 *Vivace*, No. 11. *Allegro*, and No. 12 *Andante*.

Recent research has brought to light a number of compositions that are not found in Corelli's printed collections. They have been published as *Werke ohne Opuszahl* (see note 1), where they are labeled WoO 1–10. WoO 1 is a *Sinfonia* written in 1689 as an introduction for an oratorio by Giovanni Lorenzo Lulier.[4] It is a concerto grosso with a three-voice *concertino* and a four-voice *concerto grosso*, and consists of four movements— *Grave, Allegro, Largo assai,* and *Vivace*. This composition shows that Corelli had cultivated the concerto grosso long before the publication of *Concerti grossi,* Opus 6, in 1712, very likely under the influence of Stradella.

The other *Werke ohne Opuszahl* are less interesting since they do not change the total picture of Corelli's printed compositions. WoO 5–10 are trio sonatas with the tempo sequence slow, fast, slow, fast.

One cannot spend years of studying Corelli's work without dealing with the phenomenon of its almost incredible success, a success without parallel until the beginning of the nineteenth century. Even his Opus 1, which is certainly not a masterpiece, became famous all over the world. Between 1681 and 1700 it was reprinted about ten times, and by the end of the nineteenth century it had almost 100 new editions. How is one to explain this unparalleled success? Only by the fact—so it seems to me—that it was published in Rome, in that greatest and culturally most important city of Italy, where church music (Palestrina, Benevoli), organ music (Frescobaldi, Pasquini),and opera (Landi, Rossi) had long been cultivated, but not violin music. In the metropolis of Rome, Corelli achieved triumphs that laid the foundation for his fame as *the* violin master of the seventeenth century—a fame he does not deserve exclusively but must at least share with such masters as Fontana, Neri, Legrenzi, G. M. Bononcini, Stradella, P. Degli Antonii, and Torelli.

NOTES

1. H.J. Marx, *Corelli, Werke ohne Opuszahl* (1976) contains ten manuscript works and a few doubtful compositions.

2. Breitkopf & Härtel edition, vol. IV, No. 19.

3. Sonatas of this type had been written by G. M. Bononcini (Opus 3, 1699, Nos. 16 and 17), Albergati (Opus 5, 1687), and Ruggieri (Opus 1, 1689).

4. *S. Beatrice d'Este,* libretto by Cardinal Benedetto Pamphili (Modena, 1689). Another oratorio by Lulier with introductory symphonia by Corelli is *L'applause musicale,* with text by F. M. Paglia (Rome, 1693).

SOURCES

The great volume of eighteenth- and nineteenth-century editions of Corelli's music have left us no alternative but to list here only first editions and seventeenth-century editions.

Opus 1

Sonate a tre, doi violini, e violone, o arcileuto, col basso per l'organo. Opus 1. Rome: Giovanni Angelo Mutij, 1681.　　RISM C3658.
> Great Britain: London, British Library (Violin II).
> Italy: Bologna, Civico Museo; Siena, Archivio Musicale dell'opera del Duomo (Violin I and II, Violoncello).

Reprints:

Rome: Mascardi, 1685.　　RISM C3659.
> Austria: Vienna, Österreichische Nationalbibliothek, Musiksammlung (Violin I, Organ).
> Great Britain: Glasgow, Glasgow University Library (Violin I and II).
> Italy: Asti, Archivio capitolare (Organ); Bologna, Civico Museo (Violin I and II, Violone).

Rome: Giovanni Angelo Mutij, 1688 (*nuovamente ristampata*).　　RISM C3660.
> France: Paris, Bibliothèque de l'Arsenal (Organ); Collection Marc Pincherle (Violin I).
> Great Britain: London, British Library (Violin II, Organ); London, Westminster Abbey Library.
> Italy: Rome, Biblioteca dell'Accademia nazionale dei Lincei e Corsiniana (Violin II, Organ); Siena, Biblioteca dell'Accademia Musicale Chigiana (Organ).
> West Germany: Hamburg, Staats- und Universitätsbibliothek, Musikabteilung (Violone).

Sonate a tre, due violini, e violone, o tiorba, col basso per l'organo. . . . nuovamente ristampata. Bologna: Giacomo Monti, 1682.　　RISM C3661.
> Italy: Bologna, Civico Museo (Violin I and II, Organ); Rome, Biblioteca Apostolica Vaticana (Violin II); Biblioteca Musicale governativa del Conservatorio di Santa Cecilia (Violin II).

Reprints:

Bologna: Giacomo Monti, a spese di Marino Silvani, 1684.　　RISM C3662.
> Italy: Bologna, Civico Museo.

Bologna: Giacomo Monti, 1688.　　RISM C3663.
> Great Britain: London, British Library (Violin I).
> Italy: Bologna, Civico Museo; Ferrara, Biblioteca comunale Ariostea; Forli, Biblioteca civica "Aurelio Saffi" (Violin I and II, Violone).

Suonate a tre. . . . Bologna: Marino Silvani, 1697.　　RISM C3664.
> Austria: Vienna, Gesellschaft der Musikfreunde in Wien.
> Italy: Assisi, Biblioteca comunale (Violone); Forli, Biblioteca civica "Aurelio Saffi"; Rome, Biblioteca Musicale governativa del Conservatorio di Santa Cecilia (Violin I and II, Organ).

Suonate a tre . . . nuovamente ristampata. Venice: Giuseppe Sala, 1684.　　RISM C3666.
> Italy: Venice, Biblioteca del Conservatorio "Benedetto Marcello" (Violin II).

Sonate, studiosi e vaghe, a tre. Modena: Antonio Vitaliani, 1685.　　RISM C3668.
> Great Britain: London, British Library (Violin II, Violone, Organ).
> Italy: Bologna, Civico Museo; Forli, Biblioteca civica "Aurelio Saffi" (Violin II).

Suonate a due violini col suo basso continuo per l'organo. Amsterdam: s.n., 1685.　　RISM C3669.
> Great Britain: London, British Library (Violin I; lacks Violin II, Organ).

Suonate a tre, due violini, e violone, col basso per l'organo . . . nuovamente ristampata. Antwerp: Hendrik Aertssens, 1688.　　RISM C3670.

Great Britain: Durham, Cathedral Library.
Suonate a tre ... col basso per l'organo. Amsterdam: Estienne Roger and Marie Susanne de Magneville, [1699].   RISM C3671.
United States: New York Public Library at Lincoln Center.

Opus 2

Sonate da camera a tre, doi violini, e violone, o cimbalo. ... Opus 2. Rome: Giovanni Angelo Mutij, 1685.   RISM C3693.
Great Britain: Glasgow, Glasgow University Library (Violin I and II).
Italy: Bologna, Civico Museo (Violin II, Violone); Rome, Biblioteca dell'Accademia nazionale dei Lincei e Corsiniana (Violin I, II, Violone).
Bologna: Giacomo Monti, 1685.   RISM C3694.
Italy: Bologna, Civico Museo; Ferrara, Biblioteca comunale Ariostea (Violin I and II); Venice, Biblioteca del Conservatorio "Benedetto Marcello" (Violin I).
Sonate da camera ... due violini, e violone, o cimbalo. Modena: Antonio Vitaliani, 1685. RISM C3695.
Italy: Bologna, Civico Museo; Forli, Biblioteca civica "Aurelio Saffi" (Violin I and II); Modena, Biblioteca Estense (Violone).
Suonate da camera. ... Venice: Giuseppe Sala, 1686.   RISM C3696.
Italy: Venice, Biblioteca nazionale Marciana (Violone).
Reprint:
Venice: Giuseppe Sala, 1687.   RISM C3697.
Italy: Venice, Biblioteca nazionale Marciana (Violin I and II).
Sonate da camera ... seconda impressione. Rome: Mascardi, 1686.   RISM C3699.
United States: Chicago, Newberry Library (Violin II).
Sonate da camera ... nuovamente ristampata. Rome: Giovanni Angelo Mutij, 1688. RISM C3700.
Italy: Rome, Biblioteca Musicale governativa del Conservatorio di Santa Cecilia (Violin I and II).
Suonate da camera. ... Antwerp: Hendrik Aertssens, 1689.   RISM C3701.
Great Britain: Durham, Cathedral Library; London, British Library (Violin I).
Sonate da camera ... quarta impressione. Rome: Mascardi, 1691.   RISM C3702.
Italy: Bologna, Civico Museo.
West Germany: Wiesentheid, Musiksammlung des Grafen von Schönborn-Wiesentheid.
Sonate da camera. ... Venice: Giuseppe Sala, 1692.   RISM C3703.
Italy: Forli, Biblioteca civica "Aurelio Saffi" (Violin II).
Sonate da camera a tre. Bologna: Pier-Maria Monti, si vendono da Marino Silvani, 1694. RISM 3704.
Italy: Florence, Biblioteca Nazionale Centrale (Violin II); Forli, Biblioteca civica "Aurelio Saffi" (Violin I and II).
Suonate da camera. ... Venice: Giuseppe Sala, 1697.   RISM C3705.
Austria: Vienna, Österreichische Nationalbibliothek, Musiksammlung (Violoncello handwritten).
Suonate da camera a tre. Amsterdam: Estienne Roger, [1698].   RISM C3707.
Great Britain: Durham, Cathedral Library; London, British Library (Violin I); Manchester, Central Public Library.

Opus 3

Sonate a tre, doi violini, e violone, o arcileuto, col basso per l'organo. ... Rome: Giacomo Komarek (Nicolaus Dorigny), 1689.   RISM C3730.
Czechoslovakia: Olmutz, Státní archív.
France: Paris, Bibliothèque de l'Arsenal.
Great Britain: London, British Library (Violin II, Organ).

Italy: Bologna, Civico Museo; Ferrara, Biblioteca comunale Ariostea (Violone); Forli, Biblioteca civica "Aurelio Saffi"; Modena, Biblioteca Estense; Rome, Biblioteca dell'Accademia nazionale dei Lincei e Corsiniana (Violin II, Organ).

United States: New Haven (Conn.), Yale University, The Library of the School of Music (Organ).

Reprints:

Bologna: Pier-Maria Monti, 1689.   RISM C3731.

Italy: Bologna, Civico Museo; Lucca, Biblioteca del seminario arcivescovile presso la Curia (Violin II, Violone).

Sonate a tre, cioe, duoi violini, e violone. Modena: eredi Soliani, 1689.   RISM C3732.

Italy: Bologna, Civico Museo (Violone); Lucca Biblioteca del seminario arcivescovile presso la Curoa (Violin II, Violone).

West Germany: Hamburg, Staats- und Universitätsbibliothek, Musikabteilung (Violone).

Sonate a tre, doi violini, e violone. Venice: Giuseppe Sala, 1691.   RISM C3733.

Italy: Forli, Biblioteca civica "Aurelio Saffi" (Organ).

Suonate a tre. Antwerp: Hendrik Aertssens, 1691.   RISM C3734.

Great Britain: Manchester, Central Public Library.

Sonate a tre. . . . Venice: Giuseppe Sala, 1694.   RISM C3735.

Austria: Vienna, Österreichische Nationalbibliothek, Musiksammlung (Violone incomplete).

Sonate a tre. . . . Bologna: Pier-Maria Monti, 1695.   RISM C3736.

Italy: Bologna, Civico Museo (Violin II, Organ); (Violin II); Modena, Biblioteca Estense (Violone); Rome, Biblioteca Musicale governativa del Conservatorio di Santa Cecilia (Violin I and II).

Sonate a tre. Rome: Mascardi, 1695.   RISM C3741.

France: Paris, Bibliothèque de l'Arsenal (Organ).

Great Britain: London, British Library.

West Germany: Hamburg, Staats- und Universitätsbibliothek, Musikabteilung (Violone).

Opus 4

Sonate a tre. . . . Opus 4. Rome: Giovanni Giacomo Komarek, 1694.   RISM C3762.

Italy: Bologna, Civico Museo; Forli, Biblioteca civica "Aurelio Saffi" (Violone); Venice, Biblioteca nazionale Marciana.

West Germany: Hamburg, Staats- und Universitätsbibliothek, Musikabteilung (Violin I).

Sonate a 3. . . . Bologna: Pier-Maria Monti, 1694.   RISM C3763.

East Germany: Meiningen, Historisches Staatsarchiv (Violone).

Italy: Bologna, Civico Museo; Forli, Biblioteca civica "Aurelio Saffi."

Reprints:

Bologna: Marino Silvani, 1698.   RISM C3764.

Italy: Ferrara, Biblioteca comunale Ariostea (Violin II).

United States: San Francisco, San Francisco State College Library, Col. Frank V. de Bellis Collection (Violin I).

Sonate da camera a tre . . . seconda impressione. Rome: Giovanni Giacomo Komarek, 1695. RISM C3766.

Great Britain: London, British Library.

Italy: Forli, Biblioteca civica "Aurelio Saffi" (Violin I and II, Violone); Naples, Biblioteca del Conservatorio di Musica S. Pietro a Maiella.

United States: Ann Arbor (Mich.), University of Michigan, Music Library.

Sonate a tre. . . . Venice: Giuseppe Sala, 1695.   RISM C3767.

Italy: Florence, Biblioteca privata Olschki (Violin II); Forli, Biblioteca civica "Aurelio Saffi" (Violone).

United States: Berkeley (Cal.), University of California, Music Library and Bancroft Library.

Sonate, allemande, correnti, sarabande e gighe a tre. Amsterdam: Estienne Roger and I. L. Delorme, (P. Picard), 1696.   RISM C3771.

Great Britain: London, British Library (Violin I); Oxford, Bodleian Library.
West Germany: Wiesentheid, Musiksammlung des Grafen von Schönborn-Wiesentheid.

Accademia ottobonica overo suonate a tre istromenti. . . . Antwerp: Hendrik Aertssens, 1696.   RISM C3772.

Great Britain: Durham, Cathedral Library (Violin II).
Netherlands: Rotterdam, Gemeente Bibliotheek.

Sonate a tre. . . . Rome-Modena: Fortunato Rosati, 1697.   RISM C3773.

Italy: Forli, Biblioteca civica "Aurelio Saffi" (Violin II).

Opus 5

Parte prima sonate a violino e violone o cimbalo. . . . Opus 5. Rome: Gasparo Pietra Santa, [1700].   RISM C3800.

Belgium: Brussels, Conservatoire Royal de Musique, Bibliothèque.
France: Paris, Bibliothèque nationale.
Great Britain: Cambridge, Magdalene College; University Library; London, British Library; Royal College of Music; Liverpool, Public Libraries, Central Library; Oxford, Bodleian Library; University College.
Italy: Ancona, Biblioteca comunale "Benincasa"; Bologna, Civico Museo; Cazzago S. Martino, Biblioteca privata Orizio; Florence, Biblioteca del Conservatorio di Musica "L. Cherubini"; Forli, Biblioteca civica "Aurelio Saffi"; Milan, Biblioteca del Conservatorio "Giuseppe Verdi"; Montecassino, Biblioteca dell'Abbazia; Perugia, Biblioteca del Conservatorio di musica "F. Morlacchi"; Pesaro, Biblioteca del Conservatorio "Gioachino Rossini"; Palermo, Archivio di Stato; Biblioteca del Conservatorio "V. Bellini"; Rome, Biblioteca Casanatense; Biblioteca Musicale governativa del Conservatorio di Santa Cecilia; Siena, Biblioteca dell'Accademia Musicale Chigiana; Venice, Biblioteca e Instituto di Lettere, Musica e Teatro della Fondazione "Giorgio Cini"; Biblioteca nazionale Marciana.
Japan: Tokyo, Bibliotheca Musashino College of Music Library.
Poland: Wroclaw, Biblioteka Uniwersytecka.
Sweden: Stockholm, Kungliga Musikaliska Akademiens Bibliotek.
Switzerland: Ascona, Privatbibliothek Dr. h. c. Anthony van Hoboken.
United States: Chicago, Newberry Library; Rochester (N.Y.), Sibley Music Library, Eastman School of Music, University of Rochester; Washington (D.C.), Library of Congress, Music Division.
West Germany: Hamburg, Staats- und Universitätsbibliothek, Musikabteilung.

Opus 6

Concerti grossi con duoi violini e violoncello di concertino obligato e duoi altri violini, viola e basso di concerto grosso ad arbitrio, che si potranno radoppiare. . . . Opus 6. Amsterdam: Estienne Roger, No. 197, [1714].   RISM C3844.

Austria: Vienna, Österreichische Nationalbibliothek, Musiksammlung.
East Germany: Rostock, Universitätsbibliothek.
Denmark: Copenhagen, Det Kongelige Bibliotek.
France: Carpentras, Bibliothèque Inguimbertine et Musée de Carpentras; Paris, Bibliothèque nationale (Violin I concertino, B).
Great Britain: Cambridge, University Library; Cardiff, Public Libraries, Central Library; London, British Library; Oxford, University College (lacks Violin I concertino).
Italy: Bologna, Civico Museo (lacks Violoncello concertino); Florence, Biblioteca del Conservatorio di Musica "L. Cherubini"; Forli, Biblioteca civica "Aurelio Saffi";

Genoa, Biblioteca delle Liceo Musicale "Paganini"; Naples, Biblioteca del Conservatorio di Musica S. Pietro a Maiella (lacks Violin I and Violoncello concertino); Rome, Biblioteca Musicale governativa del conservatorio di Santa Cecilia (lacks Viola); Venice, Biblioteca del Conservatorio "Benedetto Marcello"; Biblioteca nazionale Marciana.

Netherlands: Utrecht, Instituut voor Muziekwetenschap der Rijksuniversiteit (lacks Violin I and II concertino, Viola).

Poland: Warsaw, Biblioteka Uniwersytecka.

Spain: Madrid, Biblioteca nacional; Zaragoza, Archivo de musica del Cabildo.

Sweden: Lund, Universitetsbiblioteket; Stockholm, Kungliga Musikaliska Akademiens Bibliotek (lacks Violin II and violoncello concertino).

Switzerland: Ascona, Privatbibliothek, Dr. h. c. Anthony van Hoboken; Neuenburg, Bibliothèque publique de la Ville de Neuchâtel.

United States: Chicago, Newberry Library; Cambridge (Mass), Harvard University, Music Libraries; Rochester (N.Y.), Sibley Music Library, Eastman School of Music, University of Rochester; Washington (D.C.), Library of Congress, Music Division.

West Germany: Hamburg, Staats- und Universitätsbibliothek, Musikabteilung; Munich, Bayerische Staatsbibliothek, Musiksammlung; Musikverlag B. Schott's Söhne, Verlagsarchiv (lacks Violin I concerto grosso); Regensburg, Fürst Thurn und Taxis Hofbibliothek.

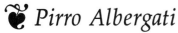 *Pirro Albergati*

Pirro Albergati was born in 1663 in Carati, of a noble family (in the titles of his publications he calls himself Conte d'Albergati). He was a friend of Corelli, and Bononcini dedicated music to him. Apart from accepting the post of chapelmaster in Puiano in 1728, he seems to have led the life of an enlightened amateur. Albergati was most active in Bologna, where he wrote oratorios, cantatas, and operas, and where he died about 1735.

Albergati's Opus 1, *Balletti, Correnti, Sarabande, e Gighe, a Violono, con il Secondo Violino a beneplacito . . .*, appeared in 1682. It contains 24 dances, the first eighteen of which form six three-movement suites. Each suite begins with a balletto, for instance, *Balletto primo, Corrente prima*, and *Sarabanda prima* or *Balletto quarto, Sarabanda terza*, and *Giga terza* (each dance type has its own numbering). The suites are followed by six single dances. The only one that is musically interesting is the penultimate piece, *Corrente sesta*. In contrast to the usual tempo of the corrente, it is a *Grave* in 3/2 meter. It is written in D minor, and modulations into other minor keys (in the second section Eb minor is reached) bestow an exceptionally serious character, which is enhanced by repeated use of the Corelli clash.

In 1683 Albergati published his Opus 2: *Suonate a due Violini col suo Basso continuo per l'Organo, & un altro a beneplacito per Tiorba, ò Violoncello*. It contains twelve sonatas largely in standard form of the *sonata da chiesa*: eight of them consist of four movements with the tempo sequence slow, fast, slow, fast—the same number as, years later, in Corelli's Opus 3.

Albergati's fast movements often show interesting and novel traits that reveal a self-willed—one might almost say, autocratic—temperament. About half of them, especially initial *Allegros*, are fugues in which concise themes are treated in three more or less complete expositions. Frequently the voice parts are interrupted by rests, occasionally simultaneously in all parts, so that a basic principle of fugal style, continuous motion, is violated. The first movement of *Sonata ottava* presents a particularly striking example of this abrupt style (Fig. 176).

FIGURE 176. ALBERGATI: SONATA OTTAVA (OPUS 2, 1683).

The last *Allegro* of Sonata No. 3 is also very peculiar. It begins with a broken-triad phrase in eighth notes for organ and theorbo. After a quarter rest, it is answered by the two violins with an abruptly cut-off scale passage in sixteenth notes. This fascinating alternation is repeated twice. The slow movements also are frequently subdivided by rests into shorter segments.

In 1687 Albergati's Opus 5 appeared: *Pletro* [plectrum] *armonioso Composto di dieci Sonate da Camera a due violini, e Basso con Violoncello obligato*, dedicated to Emperor Leopold I. These compositions, which are called *Sonate da Camera* in the title, are really *Sonate da chiesa*, with the tempo sequence slow, fast, slow, fast. It is clear that we would misunderstand the terms *da camera* and *da chiesa* if we were to interpret them as designations of forms (suite or sonata). Actually, the real difference lies in their literal meanings: *da camera* means in the "chamber," *da chiesa* in the church. The latter are always sonatas; the former are normally suites, but may also be sonatas. This contrast of performance locale is also reflected in the instruments, since *sonate da chiesa* are always accompanied by an organ, *sonate da camera* by a spinet or harpsichord (cembalo). Indeed, the continuo part book of Albergati's publication is inscribed *Cimbalo*.

In Opus 5, Albergati repeatedly uses the term *spicco* (*Allegro e spicco, Largo e spicco*), an abbreviation of *spiccato*, that is, "detached," "accentuated" (Fig. 177). And even more frequently than in Opus 2, he employs a style that had been cultivated by G. M. Bononcini and Stradella: working with single notes or pairs of notes separated by rests (see Figs. 137, 160, and 161).

The abrupt style of these passages was very much in vogue in the violin music of the 1670s and 80s. It also manifests itself in the closings of these movements, which frequently do not end with a sustained chord but abruptly, as in Bononcini's *Sonata ottava* from 1672 (see Fig. 139).

Albergati's *Sonata ottava* has an unusual form. It consists essentially of four movements *Spiritoso* in a regular structure (8 : ‖ : 8, the last 8 : ‖ : 12 : ‖ : 8), between which short

FIGURE 177. ALBERGATI: SONATA PRIMA (OPUS 5, 1687).

Adagios are inserted. These *Spiritoso* movements are very similar to each other. With their 3/4 meter, binary or ternary structure, four-measure phrases, and homophonic style they may well be regarded as correnti. This is the only dancelike element in Albergati's *Sonate da camera.*

SOURCES

Balletti, correnti, sarabande, e gighe, a violino e violone, con il secondo violino a beneplacito. . . . Opus 1. Bologna: Giacomo Monti, 1682.   RISM A601.
    Italy: Bologna, Civico Museo (Violin I and II, Violone).
Reprint:
Bologna: Giacomo Monti, 1685 (*nuovamente ristampata*).   RISM A602.
    Great Britain: London, British Library; Oxford, Bodleian Library.
    Italy: Bologna, Civico Museo.

Suonate a due violini col suo basso continuo per l'organo, & un' altro à beneplacito per tiorba, ò violoncello. . . . Opus 2. Bologna: Giacomo Monti, 1683.   RISM A603.
    Great Britain: Oxford, Bodleian Library.
    Italy: Bologna, Civico Museo.

Pletro armonico composto di dieci sonate da camera à due violini, e basso con violoncello obligato. Opus 5. Bologna: Giacomo Monti, 1687.   RISM A606.
    Great Britain: London, British Library.
    Italy: Bologna, Archivio di San Petronio; Civico Museo; Modena, Biblioteca Estense.
    West Germany: Munich, Bayerische Staatsbibliothek, Musiksammlung (Violin II, handwritten score).

❧ Giuseppe Torelli

Giuseppe Torelli was born in 1658 in Verona. He probably studied in Bologna, where in 1684 he was adopted into the Accademia Filarmonica and in 1686 entered the chapel of San Petronio. From 1698 to 1700 he was active in Augsburg, Vienna, and Ansbach, where by 1698 he had been made maestro di concerto *for the Margrave of Brandenburg. In 1701 he returned to Bologna, where he died in 1709.*

In 1686 Torelli published his Opus 1: *Sonate a trè Stromenti con il Basso Continuo.* . . . It contains ten sonatas scored for two violins, bass, and b.c., and consists of five part books, among them two different ones for *Organo* and *Tiorba ò Violone.* Along with Albergati's

Opus 2, from 1683, it provides early documentation of the practice of reinforcing the organ continuo with a string instrument.

In view of the relatively late date of Torelli's publication, the structure of his sonatas is strikingly variable. The number of movements ranges fro three in No. 1 to six in No. 8. Four sonatas have four movements, Nos. 6, 7, and 10 with the tempo sequence slow, fast, slow, fast.

Torelli's fast movements are strictly written fugues, not fugatos, like nearly all those in Corelli's sonatas. They are based on fairly extended themes, some of which acquire a particularly lively and energetic character by the insertion of a large interval—a fifth, octave, or diminished seventh. Fig. 178 shows two examples of this kind, the second movements of Nos. 5 and 7. The theme in Fig. 178b is similar to that of Bach's Fugue in A minor from *Well-Tempered Clavier II*. Torelli's first expositions are nearly always written according to the rules, on the scale degrees I-V-I and with tonal modification of the answer at the fifth.

FIGURE 178. TORELLI: a. SONATA QUINTA; b. SONATA SETTIMA (OPUS 1, 1686).

Torelli also uses imitative style for some slow movements, particularly impressively in the second movement, (*Largo*) of No. 2. Most of the slow movements, however, are written in the quasi-homophonic style that was obligatory at the time. The second movement (*Adagio*) of No. 1 is strictly homophonic throughout and in the same rhythm ♪♩♩♩♩ , a construction reminiscent of Biagio Marini's *Retirata* from 1655 (see Fig. 37). The bass of the fifth movement of No. 3 is written as a running bass, after a model by Vitali.

Sonata ottava occupies a special place. With its soloistic movements for each of the three instruments it represents another contribution to the repertory of the concerto-sonata.[1] The following diagram shows its structure:

Movement	1	2a	b	3	4
Meter	15 D	24 D	4 D	21 D	30 Tr(3/4)
Tempo	Grave	Allegro	Adagio	Adagio, e affettuoso	Allegro
Instrumentation				Violin I & Violoncello solo	Violin I solo

5a	b	6a	b
27 Tr (3/2)	17 Tr(12/8)	4 Tr(3/2)	44Tr (3/8)
slow	Allegro	Grave	Allegro
Violin II solo		a tre	

In the third movement, both violin I and violoncello are designated *solo*, although the violoncello is actually an accompanying part almost identical with the b.c. The fourth movement is a real solo for violin I, but it consists of nothing but 60 repetitions of a one-measure formula. It has the binary form 13 : ‖ : 17. Except for this disturbing element the sonata is quite attractive.

Torelli's Opus 2, *Concerto da Camera a due Violini e Basso* . . . also appeared in 1686. It also has two part books for the bass: one for violone (without thorough-bass figures) and one for the clavicembalo (figured). A *Tavola* added to the *Violone* part book divides the contents into twelve groups of three dances each, beginning with *Allemanda prima, con Corrente, e Sarabanda; Balletto secondo, con Gigha, e Sarabanda; Allemanda terza, con Gigha, e Gavota,* etc. In each group the three movements are in the same key, as is almost always the case in suites (as opposed to sonatas, in which one of the inner movements is usually in a different key). The succession of keys is unusual and even unique: the first six suites are all in minor keys (C, B, D, E, G, A), the other six in major (G, C, F, D, B♭, A). In each suite, the first dance is an extended movement in duple meter (an allemande or a balletto), the second also extended in triple meter (corrente or giga), the third, a short sarabanda, gavotta, or minuet. The first and second movements of each group are written in a surprisingly elaborate style. Nearly every one starts with an imitation, which is also used for the beginning of the second section and whose theme recurs in other places in the composition. The eighth group begins with a *Capriccio*. The name leads us to expect something unusual, which is borne out by the fact that the two violins do not play continuous melodies but, in the manner of a hocket, alternate in fast motion (*Presto*). Violin I plays the rhythm ♩ ⅞ ♪ ⅞ ♪ ♩ , violin II ⅞ ♪ ⅞ ♪ , while the violone and the harpsichord perform a running bass. Exactly the same rhythmic alternation is used by G. B. Vitali in the first capriccio of his Opus 13, of 1689.

In 1687, Torelli's Opus 3 appeared: *Sinfonie a 2., 3., e 4. Istromenti*. It contains twelve compositions, which in the individual part books are more properly designated *Sonata prima, Sonata seconda,* etc. Nos. 1 and 2 are for violin, bass, and b.c., with *Violoncello non obligato*; Nos. 6–8 for two violins, bass, and b.c., with *Violoncello obligato*; Nos. 9–11 for two violins, alto, bass, and b.c.; and No. 12 for three violins, bass, and b.c. Sonatas Nos. 2, 5, 6, 8, and 10 can be related to the type slow, fast, slow, fast, but only No. 8 represents the pure form, in which every movement stays in the same tempo throughout (except for slow introductions or conclusions to fast movements). In the other sonatas the basic form is modified by one (sometimes two) contrast movements that are subdivided into several sections with different tempi. In all, the sonatas include at least eight contrast movements.

Like the first movement of Sonata No. 9 from Corelli's Opus 1 (see Fig. 172), Torelli's contrast movements often combine the principle of contrast with the principle of repetition, resulting in structures like A B A (first movement of No. 2 and third movement of No. 5), A B A B A (fourth movement of No. 2), A B C B D (first movement of No. 10), and A B A C A (first movement of No. 12). Sonata No. 3 consists of only two movements, each of which is an extended contrast movement, as indicated in the following scheme:

Movement 1 (duple meter)

A	B	A	B
14 Adagio	19 Largo	8 Adagio	12 Largo

Movement 2 (various triple meters)

C	D	E	C	D
16 Largo	6 Allegro	6 Adagio	9 Largo	3 Allegro

As can be seen from the number of measures the sections are abbreviated when repeated. Fig. 179 shows the beginnings of the sections of the first movement. Even these short excerpts show Torelli's skill in chromatic harmony and melody. Note the succession of seventh chords in the *Adagio*. The theme of the *Largo mà spirituoso*, when compared with the theme in Fig. 178, represents an important step toward Bach's "final" realization of this idea.

FIGURE 179. TORELLI: SONATA TERZA (OPUS 3, 1687).

In several sonatas of Torelli's Opus 3 a change of key takes place. It always occurs in the third movement, a *Largo* or an *Adagio*, and is visibly indicated by a change in the key signature:

KEY OF SONATA	KEY OF THIRD MOVEMENT
No. 2: A minor without signature	Largo: E minor with one sharp

No. 5: F major with one flat   Largo: D minor without signature
No. 6: C minor with two flats   Adagio: G minor with one flat
No. 9: G major without signature   Largo: D major with one sharp
No. 11: A major with two sharps   Largo: B minor with three sharps

Here for the first time, this tonal principle, which is so important in the classical sonata, is realized with great clarity.

Torelli's Opus 4 (without date) has the title *Concertino per Camera a Violino e Violoncello*. . . . It consists of two part books and is therefore for two string instruments, without cembalo accompaniment. It contains an extended *Preludio* and eleven suites, each of which consists of an *Introduzione* and two dances, for instance, *Introduzione, Balletto,* and *Corrente* (No. 2) and *Introduzione, Allemanda,* and *Gigha* (No. 7). This publication is important for the development of violin technique, because it uses double-stops for the first time since Uccellini (Opus 7, 1600), G. M. Bononcini (Opus 4, 1671), and Stradella. Two *Introduzione* (Nos. 8 and 11) are in double-stops throughout, and several other pieces include passages with three- or even four-voice chords (Fig. 180a). The *Balletto* of Suite No. 8 contains a long succession of parallel triads. Fig. 180b shows this "illegality," which reminds one of Cazzati.

FIGURE 180. TORELLI: a. CORRENTE; b. BALLETTO (OPUS 4).

Torelli's Opus 5 appeared in 1692, with the title *Sinfonie a tre e concerti a quattro*. . . . It alternates six sinfonias and six concertos: *Sinfonia prima, Concerto primo, Sinfonia seconda, Concerto seconda,* etc.

The sinfonias are in three parts with the scoring two violins, bass, and b.c., with the bass played by *Tiorba ò Violone* and the continuo, which is practically identical with the bass, played by *Organo e Violoncello*. In form, the sinfonias are *sonate da chiesa*. Only No. 6 has the tempo sequence slow, fast, slow, fast. The others have the order fast, fast, slow, fast. This sequence is somewhat modified in Nos. 4 and 5 by the addition of a short *Adagio* at the beginning and end of the first movement. Usually the slow movements are fairly short. Among the 24 movements of the sinfonias, there are only four fully developed *Adagios* or *Largos* with more than ten measures: the third movements of No. 2 (22 measures), No. 5 (thirteen measures), and No. 6 (sixteen measures); and the first movement of No. 6 (25 measures). Thus we see that in this publication Torelli shows a striking predilection for fast movements, and they are the ones that merit our attention.

Among the seventeen fast movements there are ten fully developed fugues ranging from 50 to 90 measures in length. Two of the themes display chromaticism: that of the second movement (*Allegro*) of No. 1

has the same intervallic motion as the C#-minor Fugue of Bach's *Well-Tempered Clavier,* Book I:

And the theme of the second movement (3/2 *Allegro*) of No. 3

contains a diminished fourth and a diminished fifth, intervals to which the diminished third, seventh, and octave are added later. The second movements of Nos. 4 and 6 are double fugues with fast-moving second themes that form an effective contrast to the quiet motion of the first themes. Fig. 181 shows the second movement of No. 4, in which the repercussive motif marked m also appears independently. Certainly this

FIGURE 181. TORELLI: SINFONIA QUARTA (OPUS 5, 1692).

is one of the best fugues written at the time in Italy. Of equal excellence is the fugue at the end of the first sinfonia. Like many final movements, it is in 6/8 meter. Its theme does not have the character of a giga but has a syncopated rhythm, which prevails throughout the fugue and bestows a highly individual stamp of nervous insecurity.

Among the non-fugal movements, the first movement (*Vivace*) of No. 3 is written in homophonic style with phrases of mostly three measures. The second movement of No.

5 catches our attention because a one-measure motif,

recurs in each of its 48 measures, giving the impression of an ostinato or, more properly, of a quasi-ostinato that keeps reappearing in a different voice and on a different scale degree.

The six concertos of Torelli's Opus 5, *a quattro* are scored for two violins, alto, bass, and b.c. Torelli says in an *Avertimento a chi legge*: "Se ti compiace suonare questi Concerti, non ti sia discaro moltiplicare tutti gl'Instromenti, se vuol scoprire la mia intentione" (these concertos are to be played by a small orchestra, with several instruments to each part).

Concertos Nos. 1 and 4 are in four movements—slow, fast, slow, fast; Nos. 3 and 6 are also in four movements—fast, slow, fast, fast. Nos. 2 and 5 have three movements—fast, slow, fast—in the modern form used by Ziani in his Opus 7 (1668) and G. B. Bononcini in his Opus 5 (1687). The slow movements of Torelli's concertos are much shorter than those of his sinfonias: only in Concerto No. 4 are there any that are longer than ten measures (two *Largos*, eleven and thirteen measures respectively). Fugal movements, which play such an important role in the sinfonias, are absent in the concertos. Here sonorous homophony prevails, occasionally interrupted by a short imitation, as, for instance, in the final movement of Concerto No. 3. Another typical trait are rests and cadences, which appear at short distances, for instance in the first movement of No. 5 (Fig. 182). In many movements, particularly final ones, repeat forms are fairly recognizable: A B A (fourth movement of No. 1), A A B A (fourth movement of No. 4), A B A A (first movement of No. 5), A B A C A (fourth movement of No. 6), and A B A C A D (fourth movement of No. 3), as well as other subtler realizations of the ritornello principle.

FIGURE 182. TORELLI: CONCERTO QUINTO (OPUS 5, 1692).

Torelli's Opus 6 appeared in 1698: *Concerti musicali a quattro*. It was printed in Augsburg and dedicated to the Margrave of Brandenburg. It contains twelve concertos in the scoring two violins, alto, bass, and b.c. A preface entitled *Cortese Lettore* advises, "Ti averto che, se in questi concerti troverai scritto solo, dovra esser suonata da uno solo Violino. Il Rimanente poi fà duplicare le parti etiamdio trè ò quattro per stromento, che così scoprirai la mia intentione. . . ." (In these sonatas, if you find the indication "solo" it should be played by a single violin. The other parts can be duplicated even with three or four instruments, in accordance with my intentions.) As in the concertos of Opus 5, Torelli wants each part to be played by several instruments, except for the passages marked *solo*. Concertos Nos. 4, 8, and 10 have four movements in the tempo sequence slow, fast, slow, fast; No. 1 has the sequence fast slow, fast, slow, fast. The remaining eight concertos belong to the three-movement type fast, slow, fast; though in No. 5 the slow part is only a four-measure ending to the first movement.

The concertos of Opus 6 show considerable progress in matters of style over those of Opus 5. While in the earlier concertos the homophonic setting nearly always predominates, the later ones are distinguished by a great variety of procedures. While the homophonic style is used very little, there are movements in which violin I plays the leading role and others that could be called violin duets. In many movements all four instruments are independently active; and finally there are some movements that belong to the category of the solo concerto of the concerto grosso. The Opus 6 concertos contain—in contrast to those of Opus 5—a number of extended slow movements, quite a few of them distinguished by great expressiveness. Especially beautiful is the *Adagio* of Concerto No. 6, which is reproduced in Fig. 183 (the two inner parts, violin II and alto, are omitted).

FIGURE 183. TORELLI: CONCERTO SESTO (OPUS 6, 1698).

Concertos Nos. 6, 10, and 12 include the *solo* passages mentioned in Torelli's preface. The first movement (*Allegro*) of No. 6 contains four sections of eight to twelve measures for violin I solo, alternating with *tutti* based on one of ritornellos. In the final *Allegro* of this concerto, violin I has only two solo sections but it has some extended ritornellos. In

No. 10 only the first movement, a *Largo* in 3/2 meter, contains solo sections—two for violins I and II, and one for violin I alone. Because of their highly affective character they differ markedly from the surrounding *tutti*, which are in purely chordal style. Concerto No. 12 contains solo passages in the first and last movements, both of them *Allegro*. The first movement contains two sections, of eleven and nineteen measures respectively, in which all the instruments play solo, realizing the principle of the concerto grosso. The surrounding ritornellos (in Torelli's preface they are named *Il Rimanente*) are to be played by three or four instruments to a part. Here, for the first time, the concerto grosso appears in the kind of performance demanded by eighteenth-century practice, as, for instance, in Torelli's best-known publication, Opus 8, of 1708, which contains the six *Concerti grossi* for which he became famous.

The collection *Sonate a tre di diversi Autori* from ca. 1700[2] contains five sonatas, among them one (No. 3) by Torelli. It is a short composition in three movements—fast, slow, fast—and not particularly interesting.

Of Torelli's violin compositions that have been preserved in manuscripts,[3] I know only *Sonate für Violine solo, Violoncello obligato u. Cembalo.*[4] This interesting extended sonata begins with a contrast movement that essentially consists of a virtuoso solo for the violin, a similar one for the violoncello, a chromatic *Adagio*, and a *Presto* with an *Adagio* ending. The second movement is an *Adagio* with double-stop passages for the violin; the third is a short, expressive *Adagio*; and the fourth is an *Allegro* in 6/8 that has double-stops for the violin.

One cannot help comparing Torelli and Corelli—not only because of the similarity of their names. They lived at the same time and belonged to the Bolognese school. Both masters wrote *sonate da chiesa, sonate da camera*, and concertos, but with completely different content. Corelli's music has always been admired—justifiably—for its equilibrium; for its moderation in rhythm, melody, and harmony; for its well-formed beauty—characteristics that have designated Corelli a classicist. None of that occurs in Torelli's music. Some of his compositions, especially in Opus 1, are rather poor, and his work is far from balanced. On the contrary it fascinates by its unexpected and often novel ideas: chromatic themes and progressions, abrupt constructions, conflicting rhythms, and eruptions of virtuosity and experiments in the field of the concerto. Torelli's music, though perhaps not more beautiful, is certainly more interesting than that of his famous contemporary. His work could be more appreciated and studied much better if there were a complete new edition of his violin music!

NOTES

1. The term concerto-sonata indicates a composition containing soloistic sections for each of the participating instruments. This interesting repertory includes sonatas of Castello (1621, 1627), Fontana (ca. 1625), Neri (1651), Legrenzi (1655), and Bertali (ca 1660?), as well as Torelli and a few of his contemporaries.
2. See SartoriB, 17001.
3. See the articles *Torelli* in MGG.
4. In WasielewskiS, No. XXXV.

SOURCES

Sonata a tre stromenti con il basso continuo. Opus 1. Bologna: Gioseffo Micheletti, 1686.   RISM T980.
Italy: Bologna, Civico Museo (Violin I and II, Violoncello, Violone, Organ); Rome, Biblioteca Musicale governativa del Conservatorio di Santa Cecilia (lacks Organ).
Netherlands: The Hague, Gemeente Museum (Violone).
United States: Washington (D.C.), Library of Congress, Music Division (Violin I and II, Violoncello).
Reprint:
Antwerp: Hendrik Aertssens, 1695.   RISM T981.
Great Britain: London, British Library (Violin I and II, Violoncello, Organ).

Concerti da camera a due violini e basso. Opus 2. Gioseffo Micheletti, 1686.   RISM T982.
Italy: Bologna, Civico Museo (Violin I and II, Violoncello, b.c.).
Reprint:
Amsterdam: Estienne Roger, n.d.   RISM T983.
Great Britain: London, British Library (Violin II).

Sinfonie à 2. 3. e 4. istromenti. Opus 3. Bologna: Gioseffo Micheletti, 1687.   RISM T984.
Great Britain: London, British Library (Violin I and II, Viola).
Italy: Bologna, Archivio dell'Accademia filarmonica (Violin I and II, Alto Viola, Violoncello, Organ); Civico Museo; Modena, Biblioteca Estense.
Netherlands: The Hague, Gemeente Museum.
West Germany: Münster, Santini-Bibliothek (*Violoncello).
Reprint:
Antwerp: Hendrik Aertssens, 1689.   RISM T985.
France: Strasbourg, Institut de musicologie de l'Université.
Italy: Bologna, Archivio dell'Accademia filarmonica; Rome, Biblioteca nationale centrale "Vittorio Emanuele II°" (Violoncello).

Concertino per camera a violino e violoncello. Opus 4. [Bologna], Marino Silvani, n.d. RISM T968.
France: Paris, Bibliothèque nationale (Violin, Violoncello).
Great Britain: London, British Library.
Italy: Bologna, Civico Museo.
Editions:
Franz Gieling, ed. Winterthur: Amadeus and New York: Editiono Eulenberg, 1977.
S. Bonfarit, ed. Milan: Carisch, 1973.

Sinfonie a tre e concerti a quattro. Opus 5. Bologna: Gioseffo Micheletti, 1692.   RISM T987.
Great Britain: Oxford, Bodleian Library (Violin I and II, Viola, Violoncello, Violone, Organ).
Italy: Bologna, Archivio di San Petronio; Civico Museo.
Reprints:
Amsterdam: Estienne Roger, n.d.   RISM T988.
Great Britain: London, British Library (Organ).
West Germany: Wiesentheid, Musiksammlung des Grafen von Schönborn-Wiesentheid (Violin I and II, Viola, Violoncello, Organ).
Venice: Giuseppe Sala, 1698.   RISM T989.
Italy: Bologna, Civico Museo (6 parts).

Concerti musicali a quattro.. Opus 6. Augsburg: Lorenz Kroniger & Theophil Göbels Erben, Johann Christoff Wagner, 1698.   RISM T990.
  France: Paris, Bibliothèque nationale.
  Italy: Bologna, Civico Museo.
Reprints:
Amsterdam: Estienne Roger, n.d.   RISM T991.
  France: Paris, Bibliothèque nationale (Violin I and II, Organ/Violoncello).
  Great Britain: London, British Library (Violin I and II, Viola, Organ/Violoncello).
Venice: Giuseppe Sala, 1701.   RISM T992.
  Italy: Bologna, Civico Museo.

🎵 *Giovanni (Battista) Bononcini*

Born in 1670 in Modena, Giovanni Battista, the son of Giovanni Maria Bononcini, was a child prodigy. As early as 1688 he was chapelmaster in Bologna at San Giovanni in Monte. Between 1692 and 1693 he was in Rome; from 1698 to 1712 he was active in Vienna and from 1720 until about 1732 in London. Little is known about his later life. He died in 1747 in Vienna.

Giovanni (Battista) Bononcini's Opus 1 appeared in 1685, with the title *Trattenimenti da camera a tre, due Violini, e Violone, con il basso continuo per il Cimbalo*. In a postscript to the *Dilettante Cortese*, Bononcini says he had written this work at the age of thirteen, after having studied music (*esercizio nel suono*) for three years and counterpoint (*studio nel Contrapunto*) for one year. The publication—whose title he borrowed from Opus 7 by his father, who certainly was his teacher—contains twelve *Trattenimenti*, each of which consists of *Adagio, Balletto, Giga* (or *Corrente*), and *Sarabanda*. The introductory *Adagios* are short movements, five to ten measures in length, which reveal a remarkable mastery by the young composer, see, for example, Fig. 184.

FIGURE 184. GIO. (BATTISTA) BONONCINI: TRATTENIMENTO TERZ. (OPUS 1, 1685).

The balletti are all marked *Allegro*, but three correnti (normally fast dances) are marked *Largo* (*Trattenimenti* Nos. 2, 5, and 6); two gigas (also normally fast) are marked *Largo* (Nos. 3 and 12); and the (normally slow) sarabandas are in fast tempi (*Allegro, Presto*, even *Prestissimo*) except for No. 4, *Largo*. This change of a dance tempo into its opposite occurs for the first time in Bassani's Opus 1 (1667), where several correnti and gigas are slow (*Largo*) and all the sarabandas are *Presto* or *Prestissimo*. The giga of group 12 is not notated in the usual fast 12/8 or in even meter with triplets (which would amount to the same thing), but in slow even meter (*Largo*) with dotted eighth notes— a very unusual change of the rhythm of this dance.

Bononcini's Opus 2 appeared in 1685 also, with the title *Concerti da camera a tre, due Violini, e Violone, con il basso continuo per il Cembalo.* Unfortunately, only the violin II part book is preserved.[1] From this it appears that the publication contained twelve *Concerti*, each of them a suite of the same form as in Opus 1, the only difference being that for the third movement the giga is used three times, the corrente four times, and the allemande five times. The balletti are all *Allegro* except for Nos. 4 and 5, which are marked *Largo*; the correnti are all *Largo*; and three sarabandas are slow (*Largo* or *Adagio*) and nine are fast (*Allegro*, *Vivace*, or *Presto*). As far as can be determined from the single part book, the style of the *Concerti* is the same as that of the *Trattenimenti*.

Bononcini's Opus 3, the third publication to appear in 1685, is entitled *Sinfonie a 5. 6. 7. e 8. Instromenti, con alcune a una e due Trombe, servendo ancora per Violini.* It is dedicated to Gio. Paolo Colonna, chapelmaster of San Petronio. Bononcini calls himself Colonna's *discepolo*, probably wanting to show that, although he was not yet fifteen years old, he was in full command of multivoice and even double-choir composition. The scoring of the twelve sinfonias ranges from five voice parts (two violins, alto, tenor, bass, and b.c.) to eight parts in two choirs (two violins, alto, and bass and two violins, tenor, and bass). Nos. 5 and 8 are for one trumpet (*tromba*), Nos. 9 and 10 for two. Unfortunately the publication is not completely preserved; in the unique copy (in Bologna) the main part, violin I, is missing.

Bononcini's *sinfonias*—like those in Bassani's Opus 5—are in every respect *sonate da chiesa*. They consist of four movements—slow, fast, slow, fast—except for the trumpet sonatas, in which this form is enlarged by extended solo movements. For the fourth movement of No. 3, the sixth of No. 8, and the third of No. 9, Bononcini uses the designation *spicato*, which two years later appears in Albergati's Opus 5 in the shortened version *spiccio*.

While Bononcini's Opus 1, Opus 2, and Opus 3 are interesting as early works, his Opus 4, written in 1686, when he was sixteen, shows artistic maturity. *Sinfonie a tre Istromenti, col Basso per l'Organo* is dedicated to Count Pirro Albergati. It contains twelve *sonate da chiesa* scored for two violins, bass, and b.c., with the bass played by a violoncello and the continuo (b.c.) by the organ together with violone or theorbo, for which an extra part book is added. Seven sinfonias have four movements with the tempo sequence slow, fast, slow, fast; No. 11 has the tempos slow, slow, slow, fast; Nos. 4 and 8 have three movements—fast, slow, fast; and Nos. 5 and 12 have enlarged forms with extended solo sections.

The *Allegro* movements are mostly fully developed fugues, with some quite remarkable themes. In the fourth movement (*Vivace*) of No. 9, the theme begins with an impressive downward leap of a fifth; and in the first movement of No. 4, the theme starts with a upward chromatic motion (Fig. 185). Several movements are double fugues, for instance, the second of Nos. 1 and 2 and the third of No. 4. Occasionally a fugal movement has a loosened character, being based on a short motif rather than

FIGURE 185. GIO. (BATTISTA) BONONCINI: a. SINFONIA NONA; b. SINFONIA QUARTA (OPUS 4, 1686).

on an extended theme (for instance, in the second and fourth movements of both No. 6 and No. 7).

Among the slow movements are the contrast movements that open Sinfonias Nos. 1 and 2. Here the *Adagio* is interrupted two or three times by *Allegro* passages. The second movement (*Largo*) of No. 4 has a running bass.

The most noteworthy compositions of Bononcini's Opus 4 are Nos. 5 and 12, in which—as in the trumpet sonatas of Opus 3—the basic form is enlarged by the addition of soloistic sections. Both sinfonias contain for each of the three instruments solo sections of remarkable extension, from 30 to more than 50 measures. *Sinfonia quinta* can be schematically represented as follows:

Movement	1	2	3	4a	b
Meter	41 Tr (3/2)	42 D	29 D	7 Tr (3/2)	24 Tr (6/8)
Tempo	Adagio	Allegro	fast	Largo	Presto
Instrumentation			Violin I solo	Violin II solo	

	5a	b		6a	b	
	4 D	54 Tr (3/8)		5 D	‖ : 21 : ‖ : 28 : ‖ Tr (3/8)	
	Grave	Vivace		Grave	Vivace	
	a tre	Violoncella solo				

This scheme is strikingly similar to that of *Sonata ottava* from Torelli's Opus 1 (see p. 246). Both compositions contain a group of three soloistic movements before the final movement, which is *a tre*. Such an identity of structure of two works written in the same city (Bologna) and published in the same year (1686) cannot be mere coincidence. One gets the impression that they resulted from some sort of competition, from which Torelli, though twelve years older, did not necessarily emerge the winner. As mentioned before, his sonata suffers from the fact that the violin I solo in the fourth movement consists of nothing but the repetition of a one-measure formula. However, in making this comparison, it should be borne in mind that Bononcini's sinfonia is the Opus 4 of a child prodigy, Torelli's sonatas the Opus 1 of a slowly maturing composer. (We shall see that yet another Bolognese participated in this competition, Giorgio Buoni.)

Bononcini's Opus 5, *Sinfonie da chiesa a quattro, cioè due Violini, Alto Viola, e Violoncello obligato*, appeared in 1687. It contains twelve sonatas in the scoring two violins, alto, bass, and b.c., with the continuo to be played on the organ, as it always is in compositions *da chiesa*.

Sinfonias Nos. 1, 4, 6, and 9 have the form slow, fast, slow, fast; and No. 5, has the sequence slow, slow, slow, fast. The other seven consist of three movements—fast, slow, fast—a form that was to be of basic importance for the future development of music: it is valid not only for the concerto from Corelli to Brahms but also for many sonatas of the early classical period. Usually this form is traced back to the Italian operatic overture, especially to Alessandro Scarlatti's *Del Male il Bene* (about 1697). However, it is documented considerably earlier in violin literature: first in Ziani's Opus 7 (about 1668), which contains at least five sonatas with the tempo sequence fast, slow, fast. This form was used by Torelli for Sonata No. 1 of his Opus 3 (1687) and by Bononcini for Sinfonias Nos. 4 and 8 of his Opus 4, but in his Opus 5 for the first time it is the preferred form.

As for matters of content and style, we shall limit ourselves to some remarks about the slow movements. Three of them (the second movements of Nos. 3, 5 and 10) are fugues of 25 to 30 measures in length. In striking contrast are the third movement of No. 4 and the first of No. 9, in which the abrupt style is used in slow tempo: the former has twelve measures in the rhythm ♩ ♪ ♪♪ ♪ ♪ ♩, the latter, inscribed *Grave, e staccato*, has 33 measures of ♩♪♩ ♪♩♩ ♩ . Both contain many seventh chords, often on the strong beat, before the rest. About twelve slow movements are written in homophonic style, with occasional inserts of short imitation. In some of them Bononcini (as did other composers of his time) makes extended and effective use of modulation. Thus, the second movement of *Sinfonia seconda* (which is in Bb major), after a short opening in G minor, begins in the tonic (Bb major); modulates to D minor, A minor, C minor, A minor, and G minor; and ends with a half-cadence on D major. An interesting chromatic modulation is found in the second movement (*Adagio*) of *Sinfonia duodecima*, which is in A major. It begins in F♯ minor, but reaches F major in m. 21, Bb major in m. 25, and G minor in m. 27; then goes on to a half-cadence on C♯ major in m. 35.

In the same year, 1687, Bononcini's Opus 6 appeared: *Sinfonie a due strumenti, Violino, e Violoncello, col Basso Continuo per l'Organo*. It contains twelve *sonata da chiesa*, two of which consist of three movements (No. 8: fast, slow, fast; and No. 12: slow, fast, slow). All the others have four movements in the tempo sequence—slow, fast, slow, fast—which plays the main role here even more decisively than in Corelli's Opus 3, which appeared two years later.

Like his Opus 4 (though not Opus 5), Bononcini's Opus 6 includes some movements in fugal style that are not based on an extended theme but on a short motif such as

(second movement, *Presto*, of No. 2), or

often shortened to

(second movement, *Vivace*, of No. 9). Among movements that are not fugues there are some with individual stamp and structure. The final movement (*Allegro*) of *Sinfonia sesta* is a rondo in 3/8 in which an eight-measure refrain alternates with episodes in which the violin and the violoncello compete in playing arpeggios and trills. In the second movement of *Sinfonia settima*, an *Allegro* in 4/4, the two instruments play a *perpetuum mobile* of 50 measures. The fourth movement of *Sinfonia prima*, an *Allegro* in 3/8, consists of the alternation of two sharply contrasting progressions, a descending sequence in sixteenth notes and an ascending triad in quarter notes. Among the slow movements, there are two (the third movement of No. 2 and the first of No. 12), in which Bononcini imitates vocal recitative, after the model of Pietro Degli Antonii. Both movements close with a change from the minor to the major third. Fig. 186 shows the beginning and end of the first movement of No. 12.

FIGURE 186. GIO. (BATTISTA) BONONCINI: SINFONIA DUODECIMA (OPUS 6, 1687).

Between the ages of fifteen and seventeen, in a remarkable outburst of juvenile creativity, Bononcini wrote six collections of violin music, containing much that is novel and artistically important. Much later (in 1721, 1722, and 1732) he published additional collections of violin music.

NOTE

1. SartoriB, Vol. 2, p. 171, in discussing 1685e, mistakenly lists a complete copy in Paris.

SOURCES

Trattenimenti da camera a tre, due violini, e violone, con il basso continuo per il cembalo.
Opus 1. Bologna, Giacomo Monti, 1685.   RISM B3604.
   Great Britain: London, British Library.
   Italy: Modena, Biblioteca Estense.

Concerti da camera a tre, due violini, e violone, con il basso continuo per il cembalo. . . .
Opus 2. Bologna, Marino Silvani (Giacomo Monti), 1685.   RISM B3605.
   Italy: Bologna, Civico Museo (Violin II).
Reprint:
Bologna: John Walsh, author, n.d.   RISM 3606.
   East Germany: Berlin, Deutsche Staatsbibliothek. Musikabteilung; Leipzig, Musik-
   bibliothek der Stadt Leipzig.
   France: Paris, Bibliothèque nationale.
   Italy: Genoa, Instituto musicale.
   United States: Boston, Boston Public Library—Music Department; Chicago, New-
   berry Library; University of Chicago, Music Library; Los Angeles (Cal.), University
   of California, William Andrews Clark Memorial Library; Washington (D.C.), Library
   of Congress, Music Division.

Sinfonie a 5. 6. 7. e 8. istromenti, con alcune a una e due trombe, servendo ancora per violini.
. . . Opus 3. Bologna: Marino Silvani (Giacomo Monti), 1685.   RISM B3607.
>   Italy: Bologna, Civico Museo (11 parts; lacks Violin I).

Sinfonie a tre istromenti, col basso per l'organo. . . . Opus 4. Bologna: Giacomo Monti, 1686.   RISM B3608.
>   Great Britain: London, British Library (Violin I and II, Violoncello, Violone/Tiorba, Organ).
>   Italy: Bologna, Civico Museo.
>   United States: Berkeley (Cal.), University of California, Music Library (Violone/ Tiorba).
>   West Germany: Münster, Santini-Bibliothek (Violin II).

Sinfonie da chiesa a quattro, cioè due violini, alto viola, e violoncello obligato. . . . Opus 5.
Bologna: Marino Silvani (Giacomo Monti), 1687.   RISM B3609.
>   Italy: Bologna, Civico Museo.
Reprint:
Bologna: Marino Silvani (Giacomo Monti), 1689.   RISM B3610.
>   Italy: Siena, Biblioteca dell' Accademia Musicale Chigiana (Organ).

Sinfonie a due stromenti, violino, e violoncello, col basso continuo per l'organo. . . . Opus 6.
Bologna: Marino Silvani (Giacomo Monti), 1687.   RISM B3611.
>   Italy: Bologna, Civico Museo.

Sonatas, or chamber aires, for a German flute, violin or common flute; with a through bass for the harpsichord, or bass violin. . . . Opus 7. London: John Walsh, No. 494, n.d.   RISM B3612.
>   Great Britain: Leeds, Leeds Public Libraries, Music Department, Central Library.
>   United States: Washington (D.C.), Library of Congress, Music Division.

Duetti da camera. . . . Opus 8. Bologna: Marino Silvani (Pier Maria Monti), 1691.   RISM B3613.
>   Belgium: Brussels, Conservatoire Royal de Musique, Bibliothèque.
>   Italy: Genoa, Instituto musicale; Modena, Biblioteca Estense; Venice, Biblioteca nazionale Marciana.
>   West Germany: Wiesentheid, Musiksammlung des Grafen von Schönborn-Wiesentheid.
Reprint:
Bologna: Marino Silvani, 1701.   RISM B3614.
>   Austria: Vienna, Österreichische Nationalbibliothek, Musiksammlung.
>   France: Paris, Bibliothèque nationale.
>   Italy: Assisi, Biblioteca comunale; Bologna, Civico Museo; Naples, Biblioteca del Conservatorio di Musica S. Pietro a Maiella; Ostiglia, Fondazione Greggiati.
>   West Germany: Wiesentheid, Musiksammlung des Grafen von Schönborn-Wiesentheid.

Works without Opus Number
Divertimenti da camera pel violino, o flauto. London: At the musick shops, 1722.   RISM B3615.
>   Great Britain: London, British Library.
>   United States: Washington (D.C.), Library of Congress, Music Division.
Reprints:
London: At Mrs. Corticelle's house, 1722.   RISM B3616.
>   Great Britain: Cambridge, Rowe Music Library, King's College.

Divertimenti da camera traddotti pel cembalo da quelli composti pel violino, o flauto. London: At the musick shops, 1722.   RISM B3617.
> East Germany: Berlin, Deutsche Staatsbibliothek, Musikabteilung.
> France: Paris, Bibliothèque nationale.
> Great Britain: Cambridge, Fitzwilliam Museum; Cardiff, Public Libraries, Central Library; Glasgow University Library; London, British Library.
> United States: Washington (D.C.), Library of Congress, Music Division.

XII Sonatas for the chamber for two violins and a bass doubled. London: s.n., 1732.   RISM B3618.
> Belgium: Brussels, Conservatoire Royal de Musique, Bibliothèque (Violin I and II, Bass).
> France: Paris, Bibliothèque nationale.
> Great Britain: Cambridge, Rowe Music Library, King's College; Pembroke College Library; Pendlebury Library of Music; University Library; London, Royal Academy of Music; British Library; Leeds, Leeds Public Libraries, Music Department, Central Library.
> Italy: Venice, Biblioteca nazionale Marciana.
> United States: Charlottesville (Va.), University of Virginia, Alderman Library; Los Angeles (Cal.), University of California, William Andrews Clark Memorial Library (lacks Bass); Washington (D.C.), Library of Congress, Music Division.

Preludes, allemandes, sarabandes, courantes, gavottes & gigues ... à 2 flûtes ou violons & une basse. Amsterdam: Pierre Mortier, n.d.   RISM B3619.
> Netherlands: The Hague, Gemeente Museum (Flute II).
> West Germany: Wölfenbuttel, Herzog-August-Bibliothek, Musikabteilung (Flute I and II, Organ).

Ayres in three parts, as almands, corrants, preludes, gavotts, sarabands and jiggs, with a through bass for the harpsichord. London: John Walsh & Joseph Hare, n.d.   RISM B3620.
> Belgium: Brussels, Conservatoire Royal de Musique, Bibliothèque (Violin I and II, Bass).
> Great Britain: Durham, Cathedral Library; London, British Library; Leeds, Leeds Public Libraries, Music Department, Central Library; Oxford, Bodleian Library.

Reprint:
London: John Walsh & Joseph Hare, No. 348, n.d.   RISM B3621.
> Great Britain: London, British Library.

❦ *Carlo Antonio Marini*

> *Carlo Antonio Marini was born in 1671 in Albino (near Bergamo). From 1681 to 1705 he was active at Santa Maria Maggiore of Bergamo, first as a boy soprano, later as a violinist. During this time he published seven books with violin music and one with solo cantatas, some of which are incompletely preserved. In his Opus 1 he calls himself Marino, but later Marini.*

Opus 1, which Marini published in 1687 at the age of sixteen, has the title *Sonate da Camera a trè Strumenti* and is scored for two violins, bass, and b.c. It contains ten suites, each of two movements—a balletto (except for No. 8, which starts with a sinfonia) followed by another dance. For example, No. 1 consists of *Balletto—Sua Arietta*, No. 10 of *Balletto— Sua Borea*. The dances are skillfully written and are often quite lively, but like many dances written at the time, they do not rise beyond the level of pleasantness. Throughout *Balletto* No. 6 Marini uses the rhythm ♪♪♪ simultaneously in both violins. Although it has a rather monotonous effect, it is an interesting contribution to the abrupt style of the time.

In 1692, Marini published his Opus 2: *Balletti, Correnti, Gighe, e Minuetti diversi a trè, due Violini, e Violoncello, ò Spinetta*, of which only one part book, *Violin II*, is preserved. It consisted of twelve suites, each with four movements—*Balletto, Corrente, Gigha*, and *Minuet*. Some balletti are inscribed *Largo*, No. 1 is *Presto*, and the others have no indication of tempo. Not much more can be deduced from the single part book that is preserved.

Marini's Opus 3 appeared in 1697: *Suonate a trè, et a cinque, doi e trè Violini, Viola, et Violoncello obligato, col basso per l'Organo*. It contains twelve sonatas, Nos. 1–8 *a trè* (two violins, bass, and b.c.), Nos. 9–12 *a cinque* (two violins, alto, tenor, bass, and b.c.). These sonatas have an unusually large number of slow movements. Nos. 3, 5, 6, 7, and 10 have the tempo sequence slow, fast, slow, fast; but Nos. 2 and 4 each have three slow movements (slow, slow, slow, fast), and No. 1 has four (slow, slow, slow, slow, fast). The rest begin with fast movements, which are followed by four or five others in various tempi.

The fast movements of the sonatas *a trè* are mostly fugues with three expositions and often with extended themes, of six measures (in the fifth movement of No. 1 and the third of No. 8) or even seven (the fourth movement of No. 2). There are some fugues among the slow movements; for instance, the *Largo* of No. 2, which is distinguished by its pregnant and expressive theme (Fig. 187). For other slow movements Marini—like many before him—uses incipit repeat: they begin with a closed phrase, which is repeated in the dominant key.

FIGURE 187. MARINI: SONATA SECONDA (OPUS 3, 1697).

Marini's four sonatas *a cinque* (Nos. 9–12) include some movements of the concerto type. Thus, the final movement of Sonata No. 11, an *Allegro* in 3/8 begins with a violin solo of ten measures that recurs twice in alternation with *tutti*. The second movement (*Allegro*) of Sonata No. 10 has a similar structure, with solo passages for the violoncello and very lively *tutti*.

Marini's Opus 4 contains solo cantatas. His Opus 5 appeared in 1700, with the title *Suonate alla francese a trè*. Since only the part book for violin I is preserved, not much can be said about its contents. It contained twelve suites of *Overtura, Corrente, Giga,* and *Gavotta* (Nos. 3, 4, 7, and 12) or with similar structures. Later there appeared an Opus 6, *Sonate a trè e quattro* (1701); Opus 7, *Sonate a trè* (1705); and Opus 8, *Sonate a Violino solo*. In view of the valuable contents of Opus 3, Marini's violin music deserves a detailed study.

SOURCES

Sonate da camera a tre strumenti. . . . Opus 1. Bologna: Giacomo Monti, 1687.   RISM M687.
>   Great Britain: London, British Library (Violin I and II, Violone, Spinetta).
>   Italy: Bologna, Civico Museo; Modena, Biblioteca Estense.

Balletti, correnti, gighe, e minuetti diversi a tre, due violini, violoncello, o spinetta. . . . Opus 2. Venice: Giuseppe Sala, 1692.   RISM M688.
>   Great Britain: London, British Library (Violin II; lacks Violin I and Violoncello/Spinetta).

Suonate a tre & a cinque, doi e tre violini, viola & violoncello obligato, col basso per l'organo. . . . Opus 3. Amsterdam: Estienne Roger, No. 248, n.d.   RISM M689.
>   France: Paris, Bibliothèque nationale (Violin I and II, Violoncello, Organ).
>   Switzerland: Zurich, Zentralbibliothek, Kantons-, Stadt-und Universitätsbibliothek, (Violin I and II, Violin III/Alto Viola, Violoncello, Organ).

Suonate alla francese a tre. . . . Opus 5. Amsterdam: Estienne Roger, No. 200, n.d.   RISM M691.
>   Great Britain: London, British Library (Violin I).

Sonate a tre & a quattro, doi violini, viola & violoncello, con il basso per l'organo. . . . Opus 6. Venice: Giuseppe Sala, 1701.   RISM M692.
>   West Germany: Wiesentheid, Musiksammlung des Grafen von Schönborn-Wiesentheid (Violin I and II, Viola, Violoncello, Organ).

Reprint:
Amsterdam: Estienne Roger, No. 106, n.d.   RISM M693.
>   France: Paris, Bibliothèque nationale (Violin I and II, Violoncello, Organ; lacks Viola).

Suonate a tre, due violini, violoncello obligato, con il basso per l'organo. . . . Opus 7.   RISM M694.
>   Austria: Vienna, Österreichische Nationalbibliothek, Musiksammlung (Violin I and II, Violoncello, Organ; Violone part handwritten).

Reprints:
Amsterdam: Estienne Roger, n.d.   RISM M695.
>   Great Britain: York, Minster Library (5 parts).

. . . *nouvelle édition, corrigée de plus 300 fautes.* Amsterdam: Pierre Mortier, n.d.   RISM M696.
>   Great Britain: London, British Library (Violin I and II, Violoncello).
>   West Germany: Jever, Marien-Gymnasium, Bibliothek (Violoncello, Organ).

Sonate a violino solo con il suo basso continuo. . . . Opus 8. Venice: Antonio Bortoli, 1705.   RISM M697.
>   Italy: Venice, Biblioteca del Conservatorio "Benedetto Marcello," fondo Correr, and fondo Torrefranca.

West Germany: Wiesentheid, Musiksammlung des Grafen von Schönborn-Wiesentheid (Score; handwritten b.c.).
Reprint:
Amsterdam: Estienne Roger, n.d.   RISM M698.
   Belgium: Brussels, Conservatoire Royal de Musique, Bibliothèque.
   Great Britain: London, Royal College of Music.
   Netherlands: The Hague, Gemeente Museum.
   West Germany: Karlsruhe, Badische Landesbibliothek, Musikabteilung.

🦎 *Giovanni Maria Ruggieri*

All that is known about Giovanni Maria Ruggieri is that in 1715 he was chapelmaster in Pesaro. In his Opus 1 he calls himself a dilettante, non professionale. *Very likely he came from Venice, where all his operas were performed. His publications of violin music, Opus 1 to Opus 4, appeared there as well.*

Ruggieri's Opus 1, 1689, has the title *Bizarrie armoniche esposite in dieci suonate da camera due, cioè Violino, e Leuto ò Tiorba, col suo basso per il Violone ò Spinetta.* The scoring is violin, bass, and b.c., with the bass to be played by a lute or a theorbo. Unfortunately, the violone part book is missing in the only copy that has been preserved (in the library of Graf Schönborn, Wiesentheid). In a preface, *A chi suona,* Ruggieri designates his compositions as "Scherzi d'una penna dilettante, non professionale." Although they are early works they should be taken seriously because they contain many interesting details, and are by a composer who later created some highly important works.

   The title of the publication calls the ten compositions *suonate da camera,* but in every respect they are *sonate da chiesa* except for their scoring. They were not accompanied by the organ but by a bowed or plucked bass instrument or by the spinet.[1] Five of the sonatas contain extended soloistic movements and belong to the type called concerto-sonata. The following is a schematic representation of *Sonata quinta:*

Movement	1		2a	b		c	d		3a	b	
Meter	20 D		4 D	16 Tr (6/8)		5 D	2 D		29 D	9 TR (12/8)	
Tempo	Adagio		Allegro				Adagio		Largo		
Instrumentation			Violin solo							Theorbo solo	

	4		5	
	27 TR (3/2)		38 Tr (12/8)	
	Adagio		Allegro	
	A due			

Ruggieri outdoes his predecessors not only in the number of his concerto-sonatas but also in the virtuosity of the soloistic movements. The second movement of Sonata No. 5 contains the passage shown in Fig. 188.

FIGURE 188. RUGGIERI: SUONATA QUINTA (OPUS 1, 1689).

Sonata No. 10, also an extended concerto-sonata, is in the key of E major and is notated with the modern key signature of F♯, C♯, G♯, and D♯. In the opening *Largo*, the theorbo plays thirteen repetitions of the three-measure ostinato

The violin part contains many fairly long rests, of two or two and a half measures. Very likely they were filled in by the violone, so that the movement had the structure of a duet between the violin and the violone above the theorbo ostinato. In mm. 11 and 12 of the second movement (*Allegro*), the scale degree *f* is notated with a ♯, which, together with the ♯ of the key signature, results in f **x**.

The article *Ruggieri* of MGG mentions *Scherzi geniali ridotti a regola armonica in dieci suonate da camera a trè*, Opus 2, of 1690. Unfortunately, I have not been able to trace this book. Too bad—one would have liked to know what these "genial jests" contained!

Ruggieri's Opus 3 appeared in 1693, with the title *Suonate da chiesa, a due Violini, e Violone, ò Tiorba, con il suo Basso Continuo per l'Organo.* Seven of its ten sonatas have the tempo sequence slow, fast, slow, fast. In three others (Nos. 4, 8, and 10) it is enlarged by the use of contrast movements, for instance, in No. 10: slow, fast slow fast, slow fast slow, fast.

Aside from four movements in binary form (the fourth in Nos. 3, 7, and 9 and the first in No. 8), all the fast movements are fugues. Their structure, by which I mean the treatment of their themes, is (as is usual in that period) still far removed from a norm such as exists in the fugues of Bach. Thus, the first *Allegro* of Sonata No. 1 has four expositions, the first two based on the full theme (two and a half measures), the last two on the shortened theme (one measure) in stretto. On the other hand, in the second movement (*Allegro*) of No. 5, after a full initial exposition, the four-measure theme appears only once more, in violin I. And the fourth movement (*Allegro*) of No. 5, the "compositional jewel of the ten sonatas,"[2] is a double fugue, with both themes also used in their inverted form.

A number of slow movements consist of the first violin (sometimes the second also) playing an uninterrupted expressive cantilena, often lasting more than 40 measures (as in the first movement of No. 10).

In 1697, Ruggieri published his Opus 4, with the same title as Opus 3. He must have been widely recognized as a famous composer, since he dedicated the work to Emperor Leopold I. Like Opus 3, it contains ten sonatas, seven of them with the tempo sequence slow, fast, slow, fast. However, in Nos. 4, 6, and 10 the first slow movement is reduced to a short introduction of four or six measures, so that the structure approximates the three-movement form fast, slow, fast, which Ruggieri actually uses for Sonatas Nos. 1 and 3. Sonata No. 8 has four movements with the sequence slow, slow fast, slow, fast;

No. 5 has three with fast slow, fast slow, fast. Thus, Opus 4 represents an important step toward three-movement form.

Most of the fast movements are fully developed fugues, many of them with interesting and individual traits. The third movement of No. 1, the first of No. 3, and the second of No. 6 are based on themes with syncopated rhythm. Here a rhythmic insecurity is intended and realized—a very rare occurrence in the entire field of fugal writing. The third movement (*Allegro*) of No. 5 is an extended inversion fugue, whose theme

is answered by

While the sonatas from this period usually close with a dancelike movement in binary form and in uneven meter, the final movements of Nos. 3 and 5 are written in the style of a ricercar from the late sixteenth or early seventeenth century. Both movements are in *alla breve* meter and are based on themes consisting mainly of whole and half notes. The final movement of No. 8 is a fugue of 67 double measures with the following theme:

The final movement of No. 3 is a double fugue whose main theme (Fig. 189) is nearly identical with that of the Eb major fugue at the end of Bach's *Clavierübung II*.

FIGURE 189. RUGGIERI: SONATA TERZA (OPUS 4, 1697).

Surely, Ruggieri knew the organ ricercars of the older Venetian masters, especially those of Andrea Gabrieli. Perhaps he was also familiar with the work of another Venetian who was much closer to him in time, Pietro Andrea Ziani, whose sonatas, written about 1667, contain several movements in the style of a ricercar.

Among the slow movements there are two particularly impressive ones. The second movement (*Largo*) of No. 1 is a double fugue of 49 measures in 3/4 meter with a chromatic countertheme; it is probably the first slow fugue (let alone, double fugue) in the history of violin music. And the second movement (*Largo e affettuoso*) of No. 8 begins and ends with the imitation of a highly expressive theme (in Fig. 190, the descending second in m. 3 is the augmentation of the preceding suspensions), which is followed without interruption by a *Presto* in which various motifs are treated in short imitation. This is undoubtedly one of the most original and most beautiful movements from the last decades of the seventeenth century.

FIGURE 190. RUGGIERI: SONATA OTTAVA (OPUS 4, 1697).

Ruggieri is a musician who deserves even more attention than he has received from the "modern" edition of his Opus 3. From the somewhat amateurish, yet often very interesting, beginnings of his *Bizarrie armoniche*, he matured into a master. Though rooted in tradition, he created much that is novel and artistically important. It would be well worth searching for his *Scherzi geniali* from 1690.

NOTES

1. As in G. M. Bononcini's Opus 3 (1669) and Albergati's Opus 5 (1687).
2. L. Nowak, in his new edition of Ruggieri's Opus 3, in DM, No. 425 (1944); also NowakS.

SOURCES

Bizzarie armoniche esposte in dieci suonate da camera, a due, cioè violino, e leuto o tiorba, col suo basso per il violone, o spinetta. . . . Opus 1. Venice: Giuseppe Sala, 1689.   RISM R3103.
    West Germany: Wiesentheid, Musiksammlung des Grafen von Schönborn-Wiesentheid (Violin, Tiorba; lacks b.c.).

Suonate da chiesa a due violini, e violone o tiorba, con il suo basso continuo per l'organo. . . . Opus 3. Venice: Giuseppe Sala, 1693.   RISM R3104.
    Austria: Vienna, Österreichische Nationalbibliothek, Musiksammlung (Violin I and II, Violone, Organ).
Edition: Leopold Nowak, ed. Vienna: Verlag Doblinger ("Diletto Musicale," Nos. 421–430). 1949–1977. (ten sonatas published individually).

Suonate da chiesa a due violini, e violoncello, col suo basso continuo per l'organo. . . . Opus 4. Venice: Giuseppe Sala, 1967.   RISM R3105.
    Austria: Vienna, Österreichische Nationalbibliothek, Musiksammlung.

🎵 Antonio Veracini

Antonio Veracini was born in 1659 in Florence. His father, Francesco, had established a music school there and was certainly his teacher. As far as is known, Antonio Veracini spent his entire life in Florence, where he died in 1733. He was the uncle and teacher of the famous Francesco Maria Veracini.

Antonio Veracini's Opus 1, *Sonate a trè, due Violini, e Violone, ò Arcileuto, col Basso per l'Organo* appeared in 1692 in Florence. It is dedicated to Archduchess Vittoria di Toscana, at whose court Veracini was then active. The publication contains ten sonatas, Nos. 1, 3, 6, 8, 9, and 10 having the tempo sequence slow, fast, slow, fast. Sonata No. 4 consists of four fast movements, but the first one begins with a three-measure *Adagio* that reappears twice, slightly varied and reduced to two measures. Fast tempo predominates also in No. 5; in No. 7, however, slow tempo prevails. The majority of the fast movements (fifteen of a total of twenty) are skillfully written fugues, among them one double fugue (the third movement of No. 7). While the fugues written in even meter are more or less traditional, those in uneven meter are quite novel and charming, with a light, almost dancelike character. Particularly attractive is the final movement of Sonata No. 10, the beginning of which is reproduced in Fig. 191. The short vertical strokes above the sixteenth notes of the first two measures indicate *staccato*, in contrast to the third measure, which is to be played *legato*. Veracini uses these *staccato* signs in several other movements, for instance, the fourth of the No. 2, the first of No. 4, and the second of No. 10.[1]

FIGURE 191. VERACINI: SONATA DECIMA (OPUS 1, 1692).

Veracini's Opus 2 appeared without a date, most likely in 1694. Its title is *Sonate da camera a Violino solo*. It consists of two part books, *Violino*, and *Cimbalo ò Violone*. Its ten compositions are not suites — as might be expected from the designation *Sonate da camera* — but sonatas in the proper sense of the word. They are not to be performed in the *chiesa* but in the *camera*, and are to be accompanied by the harpsichord (*cimbalo*) rather than the organ. Sonatas Nos. 4 and 7 have three movements—slow, fast, slow; Nos. 3 and 8 have five—slow, fast, slow, fast, fast or slow, slow, fast, slow, fast; and the remaining six have four movements—slow, fast, slow, fast.

Imitations, which are not at all impossible in compositions for violin and harpsichord (or organ)—Pietro Degli Antonii uses them very frequently in his solo sonatas of Opus 5 (1686)—hardly ever occur in Veracini's Opus 2. Only in the second movement (Vivace) of No. 1 are there reminders of the technique of self-imitation, which Leoni had invested in his *Sonate di Violino a voce sola* (1652). Many of Veracini's fast movements, especially the final ones, are in binary form, somewhat like dances with lively and pleasant melodies (for instance, the fourth movements of Nos. 1 and 2, the second of No. 2, the third of No. 7, and the fifth of No. 8). Others are virtuosic in the style of a *perpetuum mobile* (for instance, the second movements of Nos. 3, 5, and 10 and the third of No. 8).

The slow movements of Veracini's Opus 2 are particularly interesting, chiefly because most of them, among them all ten initial movements, are printed in score in the *Cimbalo* part book. Here we again encounter a method that was used in the first half of the seventeenth century—from Cima (1610) to Pandolfi (1660)—for all publications of solo violin music. However, with Veracini only the slow movements—not the entire sonatas—are printed in score. The reason is that the violinist improvised ornamentations, which required a flexible tempo, and the accompanist could follow only with the help of a full score. This interpretation is confirmed by the *a tempo* in m. 9 of the first movement of No. 5 and m. 4 of the first movement of No. 9. This instruction indicates the end of free tempo and, at the same time, the end of improvised ornamentations (Fig. 192). Thus, Veracini gives the first concrete proof of that practice, which is widely known through Corelli's Opus 5 of 1700.

FIGURE 192. VERACINI: SONATA IX (OPUS 2, CA. 1694).

Veracini's Opus 3, his last publication of violin music, appeared in 1696: *Sonate da camera a due, Violino, e Violone, ò Arcileuto, col Basso per il Cimbalo*. It consists of three part books: violino, violone ò arcileuto, cimbalo. The ten compositions, like the *sonate da camera* of his Opus 2, are sonatas, all with the tempo sequence slow, fast, slow, fast.

Stylistically, these sonatas differ from those of Opus 2 mainly in that the first fast movements (that is, the second movements) are all fully developed fugues. For example, in the first *Vivace* of Sonata VI the theme occurs six times in the violin as well as in the bass (violone and harpsichord). Fig. 193 shows the beginning of this movement.

The final *allegros* are all in triple time, with pleasant melodies. The fourth movements of Nos. 1, 4, 5, and 8 have no interruptions, while the other final movements are in binary form.

FIGURE 193. VERACINI: SONATA VI (OPUS 3, 1696).

Only five of the slow movements (the first movements of Nos. 1, 2, 4, 5, and 8) are printed in score; this means that the practice of improvised ornamentations is much more limited here than in Opus 2.[2] Among the *Largo* movements, for which Veracini "cannot be praised enough,"[3] two are particularly impressive examples of Baroque expressiveness: the first movement of Sonata No. 7 (which is also a beautiful example of incipit repeat technique) and the third movement of No. 8, with its very sensitive "unending melody" (27 measures with no rest).

NOTES

1. Pandolfi's Opus 3, of 1660, contains dots that may have indicated *staccato* performance.
2. The same movements are printed in score in the violine part book except for the first movement of No. 5, whose moving bass line is not suitable for free tempo.
3. See MoserG, p. 79, where the sonata is incorrectly listed as "für zwei Violinen."

SOURCES

Sonata a tre, due violini, e violone, o arcileuto col basso per l'organo. . . . Opus 1. Florence: Antonio Navesi alla Condotta, 1692.   RISM V1197.
    Great Britain: Cambridge, Rowe Music Library, King's College (Violin I and II, Violone, Organ); London, British Library (incomplete).
    Italy: Bologna, Civico Museo; Florence, Biblioteca Nazionale Centrale.

Reprint:
Amsterdam: Estienne Roger; Utrecht: Estienne Tabuteau, n.d.   RISM V1198.
  Great Britain: London, British Library (lacks Organ).
  Sweden: Lund, Universitetsbiblioteket (lacks Violin I).

Sonate da camera a violino, e violoncello, o basso. Opus 2. Amsterdam: Estienne Roger,
No. 69 (1694?).   RISM V1199.
  Sweden: Lund, Universitetsbiblioteket (Violin, b.c.).

Sonate da camera a violino solo. . . . Opus 2 [*sic*]. Modena: Fortuniano Rosati, n.d.   RISM
V1200.
  France: Paris, Bibliothèque nationale (Violin, Violin/Cembalo in score).
  Great Britain: Oxford, Bodleian Library.

Sonate da camera a due violino e violone o arcileuto col basso per il cimbalo. . . . Opus 3.
Modena: Fortuniano Rosati, 1696.   RISM V1201.
  Belgium: Brussels, Conservatoire Royal de Musique, Bibliothèque (Violin, Violone,
  Cembalo).
  France: Paris, Bibliothèque nationale (Violin, Violone).
  Great Britain: London, Royal College of Music; Oxford, Bodleian Library.
  Italy: Bologna, Civico Museo.
  United States: New Haven (Conn.), Yale University, The Library of the School of
  Music (Violone).
Reprint:
Amsterdam: Estienne Roger, n.d.   RISM V1202.
  Great Britain: Durham, Cathedral Library (Violin, Violone, Cembalo).
  Sweden: Lund, Universitetsbiblioteket.

Bartolomeo Bernardi

*The year and place of Bartolomeo Bernardi's birth are not known. Most likely he
was born about 1660 in Bologna, where he became a student of Torelli. In his Opus
1 (1692) he calls himself* Academico filarmonico. *He spent his later life in Copenhagen, where in 1703 he was musician of the royal chapel and in 1710 its master.
He died there in 1732.*

Bernardi's Opus 1: *Sonate da camera a trè, due Violini, e Violoncello col Violone ò Cimbalo,*
appeared in 1692 in Bologna. It contains twelve compositions of a very uniform structure.
The first movement is a *Preludio* in slow tempo (*Grave, Largo, Adagio,* or *Andante*). The
second is an *Alemanda Allegro,* except in No. 6, which has an *Alemanda Largo.* The third
movement is slow (*Adagio, Largo,* or *Grave*). The fourth is a *Gavota, Giga,* or *Sarabanda* in
fast tempo (*Presto* or *Allegro*), except in No. 7, which closes with a *Largo, Corrente alla
Francese.* Thus, Bernardi's *sonate da camera* are a mixture of elements of the suite and
the *sonata da chiesa.* Quite obviously, Corelli's *Sonate da camera,* Opus 2, of 1685, served
as a model, especially No. 4, with its alternation of free and dancelike movements (*Presto,
Allemanda, Adagio,* and *Giga*)—the structure that Bernardi uses for all his compositions.

Bernardi's rather frequent use of the Corelli clash (for instance, in the third movements of Nos. 1, 5, and 11; the fourth of No. 3; the first of No. 4; and the first and second of No. 9) also reminds one of Corelli. The designation *spicco* in *Preludes* Nos. 3, 5, and 7 (all *Largo, e spicco*) connect Bernardi with Albergati, as does his predilection for abrupt, energetic progressions. Bernardi's sonatas occasionally lack stylistic unity, for example, the *Alemanda Allegro* of No. 11 (15:‖:10) is written in half, quarter, and eighth notes throughout, except for the first five measures of the second section, which are in sixteenth notes. This unusual trait was noticed early by Johann Adolph Scheibe, who wrote that Bernardi's "works are completely stripped of all taste. They are mindless and without organization."[1]

Bernardi's Opus 2 appeared in 1696, also in Bologna, with the title *Sonate a trè Due Violini, e Violoncello, con il Bassi per l'Organo*. Its ten sonatas, in contrast to those of Opus 1, are real *sonate da chiesa*, accompanied by the organ. Sonatas Nos. 2–6, and 9 have the normal structure slow, fast, slow, fast; while No. 1 has the reversed order fast, slow, fast, slow. Nos. 7 and 8 each consist of six movements, some of them rather short; and No. 10 is completely in fast tempo, interrupted only once by four measures in slow motion.

The fast movements show a remarkable variety of ideas and progressions. There are three-part fugues (second movement of No. 2 and the sixth of No. 8), a double fugue (second movement of No. 6), a fugato (third movement of No. 7), a two-part fugue (second movement of No. 5), and a double fugue with supporting bass (second movement of No. 10). The second and fourth movements of No. 9 and the fourth of No. 10 are written in uninterrupted sixteenth notes (*perpetuum mobile*), such as Veracini had written. Others are in binary form (for instance, the first movement of No. 1 and the fourth of No. 2) or in entirely free form (the fourth movement of No. 3 and the first of No. 8). The second movement of No. 3 is based on thirteen repetitions of a *basso ostinato* consisting of the seven tones of the descending scale

The first *Allegro* of *Sonata settima* is a purely chordal movement, in which violin I plays a succession of unchanging broken-chord figures (Fig. 194).

FIGURE 194. BERNARDI: SONATA SETTIMA (OPUS 2, 1696).

Exactly the same style was used by Johann Jacob Kuhnau in his *Neuer Clavier Übung erster Teil* (*Präludium* of *Partie* No. 5), which had appeared seven years earlier. It would

be rather foolish to speak here of influence. Both pieces, however, are interesting as predecessors of the first *Prelude* of Bach's *Well-Tempered Clavier I.*

Bernardi's slow movements, on the whole, are not very important. The most impressive is the *Adagio* at the beginning of *Sonata nona*. It consists of two sharply contrasting sections: in the first, the two violins perform a continuous dialogue above a running bass; the second consists of short, expressive phrases in homophonic style and in abruptly changing keys.

Opus 3, *Sonate a Violino solo col Basso Continuo* was published in Amsterdam with no date. Bernardi wrote it after 1700, as "Compositore e Sonatore di Violino di S. M. il Re di Danmarkia e Norwegia," when he was in Copenhagen. The highly virtuosic style of these six very extended violin sonatas exceeds that of Corelli's Opus 5 (1700), especially in double-stop playing.

NOTE

1. Johann Adolph Scheibe, . . . *Critischer Musicus, Neue . . . Auflage* (Leipzig, 1745) p. 760, note.

SOURCES

Sonate da camera a tre, due violini e violoncello col violone, o cimbalo. . . . Opus 1. Bologna: Pier-Maria Monti, 1692.   RISM B2039.
    Great Britain: London, British Library.
    Italy: Bologna, Civico Museo; Rome, Biblioteca Musicale governativa del Conservatorio di Santa Cecilia.

Sonate a tre, due violini, e violoncello, con il basso per l'organo. . . . Opus 2. Bologna: Carlo Maria Fagnani, 1696.   RISM B2040.
    Great Britain: Oxford, Bodleian Library.
    Italy: Bologna, Civico Museo.
    Switzerland: Zurich, Zentralbibliothek, Kantons-, Stadt- und Universitätsbibliothek.
Reprint:
Amsterdam: Estienne Roger and Jean Louis Delorme, n.d.   RISM B2041.
    Great Britain: London, British Library.
    West Germany: Wiesentheid, Musiksammlung des Grafen von Schönborn-Wiesentheid.

Sonate a violino solo col basso continuo. . . . Opus 3. Amsterdam: Estienne Roger, n.d. RISM B2042.
    France: Paris, Bibliothèque nationale.
    Netherlands: Utrecht, Instituut voor Muziekwetenschap der Rijksuniversiteit.
    West Germany: Wiesentheid, Musiksammlung des Grafen von Schönborn-Wiesentheid.

🎵 Tomaso Antonio Vitali

Tomaso Antonio Vitali, son of Gio. Battista Vitali, was born in Bologna in 1663. In 1674 he went with his father to Modena. In 1675, at the age of twelve, he became a musician at the Este court. Later he was made chapelmaster there. He died in Modena in 1745.

Tomasi Antonio Vitali's first publication, *Sonate a trè, Due Violini, e Violoncello, col Basso per l'Organo*, appeared in 1693, without opus number. It contains twelve sonatas. Nos. 1–4, 7, and 9–11 have the tempo sequence slow, fast, slow, fast; the others have five or six movements. Except for some movements in binary form, mostly final movements (for instance, the sixth movement of No. 6 and the second and fourth of No. 8), nearly all the fast movements are fugues. Side by side with monothematic fugues (for instance, the second movements of Nos. 1, 10, and 12 and the fourth of No. 7), Vitali writes no fewer than five double fugues (the second movements of Nos. 2, 7, and 11 and the fourth of Nos. 2 and 8), and even two triple fugues (the second movement of No. 4 and the fourth of No. 5). Fig. 195 shows the beginning of the triple fugue from Sonata No. 4.

FIGURE 195. T. A. VITALI: SONATA QUARTA (OPUS 1, 1693).

Among the slow movements there are two marked *Grave* (the first movements of Nos. 4 and 9), that have a running bass, which is normally used for fast movements. In the fourth movement (*Andante*) of No. 6, violin I has an ostinato of five measures, which is repeated six times. Since this movement stands between two marked *Grave*, this *Andante* probably means a (moderately) fast tempo. The third movement (*Largo*) of No. 12 has an unusual structure. Its main instrument is the violoncello, which plays an uninterrupted and very expressive melody, while the two violins are restricted to the performance of short phrases separated by lengthy rests. Several times Vitali uses the indication *stacco*, which, like *spicco*, indicates the "detached" manner of playing so much in favor at the time.

In the same year, 1693, Vitali's Opus 2 appeared: *Sonate a doi Violini, col Basso per l'Organo*. In agreement with the title, the scoring is two violins and b.c., that is, without the customary bowed bass (violoncello). The publication contains twelve sonatas. Nos. 1, 4, 5, 7, 9, and 12 have four movements in the order slow, fast, slow, fast. Sonatas Nos. 2, 6, 8, and 10 have the same tempo sequence in three movements (slow fast, slow, fast or slow, fast slow, fast); and Nos. 3 and 11 have enlarged forms.[1]

In the fast movements the number of fugues is considerably smaller than in Opus 1. Moreover, the imitation is limited to the two violins, with the organ restricted to the role of supporting bass. Some of these fugues (for instance, in the second movements of Nos. 1 and 6) are monothematic; in others (the third movement of No. 3 and the second of No. 7), a countertheme is used. Among the nonfugal movements there is a canon (second movement of No. 11) and a *basso ostinato* (fourth movement of No. 9), as well as a number of movements in binary form (the second of No. 3 and the fourth of No. 5) or in free form (for instance, the fourth of No. 1 and the fifth of No. 3). The slow movements are mostly short introductions or transitions. The first movement of No. 5 carries the designation *Largo, e spiccato*; it is in binary form (8 :‖: 13), which is rather rare in slow movements, and has irregular phrases that compensate to a degree for the flatness of effect caused by the many arpeggios. Fig. 196 shows the beginning of this movement, which is used again, in its entirety, for the final movement, with the tempo changed from *Largo* to *Allegro* and the even meter changed to 12/8 (♩♪♩♪ instead of ♫♫).

FIGURE 196. T. A. VITALI: SONATA QUINTA (OPUS 2, 1693).

Vitali's Opus 3 appeared in 1695, with the title *Sonate da camera a trè, due Violini, e Violone*. With this scoring—that is, without an accompanying keyboard instrument—Vitali adopted a tradition exclusive to Modena. In 1688 Colombi published a collection of compositions for string quartet, and ten years later G. M. Bononcini issued one for string trio. Vitali's publication contains twelve compositions, the first ten of which are three- or (mostly) four-movement suites, for instance, *Rondon, Gavotta*, and *Canario* (No. 5) or *Preludio, Rigodon, Gavotta*, and *Minuet* (No. 4). These suites are followed by a *Sopra l'Aria del Pass'emezzo* (No. 11) and a *Sonata* without dance movements (No. 12). Five movements in the suites (the second in Nos. 2, 7, and 9; the first in No. 5; and the fourth in No. 8) are named *Rondon* and represent the French *rondeau*, consisting of a refrain and two couplets (A A B A C A). The modern dances—Borea, Gavotta, Minuet, Rigadon, Bocane (what does this mean?)—are short pieces of little musical significance, mostly with the structure 4 :‖: 8.

The most important composition in Opus 3 is No. 11, *Sonata sopra l'Aria del Pass'emezzo*, in which Vitali writes three variations of the *passamezzo antico*, employing the same method as did his father and many older masters. However, his variations— *Largo, Allegro*, and *Allegro* in 12/8—are more substantial and more interesting than those by the elder Vitali. The last composition of Opus 3, a sonata consisting of *Overtura, Allegro, Largo*, and *Allegro*, is a unique case since the two *Allegros* not only have the same content (as in the *Largo* and *Allegro* of Sonata No. 5 in Opus 2) but are absolutely identical.[2]

Today, Tomaso Antonio Vitali is almost exclusively known as the composer of a highly virtuosic *Chaconne*, which is probably not his work. At any rate, it is a composition written long after 1700.

NOTES

1. In Sonata No. 11 two movements marked *Andante* follow one another. It seems that the first, marked 3/2, is slow, the second, in **C**, fast. This interesting evidence shows that even then *Andante* was an indication of more than a single tempo.

2. Vitali's last publication, *Concerto di sonate a Violino, Violoncello, e Cembalo*, Opus 4, appeared in 1701. A modern edition appeared in the *Smith College Archives*, vol. XI (Northampton, 1954).

SOURCES

Sonate a doi violini, col basso per l'organo. . . . Opus 2. Modena: Christoforo Canobi, 1693. RISM V2176.
> Belgium: Brussels, Conservatoire Royal de Musique, Bibliothèque (Violin I and II, Organ).
> Italy: Bologna, Civico Museo; Modena, Biblioteca Estense.
> West Germany: Wiesentheid, Musiksammlung des Grafen von Schönborn-Wiesentheid.

Sonate a tre, doi violini, e violoncello, col basso per l'organo. . . . Opus 2 [*sic*]. Modena: Antonio Ricci, 1693.   RISM V2177.
> Great Britain: London, British Library (Incomplete); Oxford, Bodleian Library (Violin I and II, Violoncello, Organ).
> Italy: Bologna, Civico Museo; Modena, Biblioteca Estense (lacks Violoncello).

Sonate da camera a tre, due violini e violone. . . . Opus 3. Modena: Fortuniano Rosati, 1695. RISM V2178.
> Italy: Turin, Biblioteca nazionale universitaria.
> Switzerland: Zurich, Zentralbibliothek, Kantons-, Stadt- und Universitätsbibliothek.

Concerto di sonate a violino, violoncello, e cembalo. . . . Opus 4. Modena: Fortuniano Rosati, 1701.   RISM V2179.
> Italy: Bologna, Civico Museo (Violin, Violoncello, Cembalo).

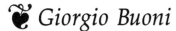 *Giorgio Buoni*

Giorgio Buoni was born in 1647 in Bologna and died there after 1693. He was active as a priest and teacher at San Petronio, especially as the leader of the Concerto dei Putti, that is, of the students, one of whom was G. B. Bononcini. In 1693 Buoni published three collections of violin music, each containing twelve compositions, some of which were written much earlier; in fact, the Preface to Opus 1 says that the pieces therein are "fatti nehl'Anni passati del mio Concerto."[1]

Buoni's Opus 1 is entitled *Divertimenti per camera a due Violini, e Violoncello*. (The bass part book carries the inscription *Cembalo* and is fully provided with thorough-bass figures.) The publication contains twelve suites, all consisting of *Sinfonia, Balletto, Corrente* (or *Giga*), and *Sarabanda*.

The sinfonias are slow (*Grave*). All the other movements are in binary form and fast, especially the sarabandas, nearly all of which have the tempo indication *Presto*. In Balletti Nos. 1, 2, and 10 the two violins begin with a phrase of one and a half measures, followed by a rest of the same length that is bridged only by the thorough-bass. Obviously these rests are an opportunity for the cembalo player to improvise with the right hand an imitation of the preceding violin phrase.

The contents of Buoni's Opus 3, *Allettamenti per camera a due Violini, e Basso*, are very similar to those of Opus 1. Its twelve suites have the same scoring, the same contents, and the same form as those of Opus 1, "fatti negl'Anni passati del mio Concerto" (. . . composed in the years before [I became the leader of] my concerto [dei Putti]).

Buoni's *Divertimenti* (Recreations) and *Allettamenti* (Allurements) carry their names justifiably. They contain attractive music for young musicians and even today—after 300 years—might serve for musical education.

The contents of Buoni's Opus 2 are totally different. *Suonate a due Violini, e Violoncello, col Basso per l'Organo* contains twelve *sonata da chiesa*. Nos. 1, 2, 7, and 10 are of the type slow, fast, slow, fast; and Nos. 3, 6, and 9 are fast, slow, fast. The remaining five have more complex structures. The fast movements are fugues with two or three exceptions, for instance, the fourth movement (*Vivace*) of No. 8, which begins with homophonic 6/8 chords. These fugues are often not treated strictly but contain free variants of the themes or new motifs and use other methods that aim at variety rather than unity. The slow movements are less interesting, often long and monotonous.

Sonatas Nos. 5 and 12 contain extended soloistic sections for each of the three instruments and are therefore concerto-sonatas, like those in Torelli's Opus 1 (1686) and in G. B. Bononcini's Opus 4 (1686). Buoni's compositions are unusually long: No. 5 has 385 measures, No. 12 a total of 429. They have the same structure as those of the other masters. The following diagram of Buoni's Sonata No. 12 may be compared with those of the concerto-sonatas by Torelli (p. 248) and Bononcini (p. 257).

Movement	1	2	3a	b	4a	b
Meter	35 D	90 D	3½ D	46½ D	11 Tr (3/4)	54 Tr (6/8)
Tempo	Adagio	Allegro	Adagio	Presto	Adagio	Allegro
Instrumen-tation			Violin I solo		Violin II solo	

5	6	7	8
8 D	32 Tr (6/8)	7D	142 Tr (3/8)
Allegro	Allegro	Adagio	Vivace
tutti	Violoncello solo	tutti	tutti

Fig. 197 shows the beginning of the solo section for violin I.

FIGURE 197. BUONI: SONATA DUODECIMA (OPUS 2, 1693).

Comparison with the Bononcini work shows strong similarity in the rather complicated structures. In both Bononcini's Opus 4 and Buoni's Opus 2 the concerto-sonatas
appear as Nos. 5 and 12. This may be evidence that Bononcini (perhaps also Torelli?)
was a student of Buoni and a member of his Concerto dei Putti. In addition, the suites
in Bononcini's Opus 1 have exactly the same structure as those in Buoni's Opus 1 and
Opus 3. Although Buoni's publications appeared seven years later than that of his pupil,
their contents go back to a much earlier time.

NOTES

1. Under *Buoni* in MGG (Supplement) we learn that all three prints have similar
contents. This is mistaken; only Opus 1 and Opus 3 are similar.

SOURCES

Divertimenti per camera, a due violini, e violoncello. . . . Opus 1. Bologna: Pier Maria Monti,
1693.   RISM B4948.
    Great Britain: Oxford, Bodleian Library.
    Italy: Bologna, Civico Museo.
    West Germany: Münster, Santini-Bibliothek (Violin I and II, Cembalo).

Suonate a due violini, e violoncello, col basso per l'organo. . . . Opus 2. Bologna: Pier Maria Monti, 1693.   RISM B4949.
  Great Britain: London, Royal College of Music (incomplete); Oxford, Bodleian Library.
  West Germany: Münster, Santini-Bibliothek (Violin I and II, Bassetto, Organ).

Allettamenti per camera a due violini, e basso. . . . Opus 3. Bologna: Pier Maria Monti, 1693. RISM B4950.
  France: Paris, Bibliothèque nationale.
  Great Britain: Oxford, Bodleian Library.
  Italy: Bologna, Civico Museo.
  West Germany: Münster, Santini-Bibliothek (Violin I and II, Cembalo).

Antonio Caldara

Antonio Caldara was born about 1670, probably in Venice, where he sang in the chapel of San Marco. In the title of his Opus 1, of 1693, he calls himself Musico di Violoncello Veneto. *There is only fragmentary information about his life until 1716, when he was called to Vienna by Emperor Charles VI. He was active there as vice-chapelmaster, with J. J. Fux as first chapelmaster. Caldara is famous for the numerous operas and other vocal compositions he wrote for the Viennese court. He died in Vienna in 1736.*

Caldara's Opus 1 appeared in 1693 in Venice, with the title *Suonate a trè, due Violini, con Violoncello, e parte per l'Organo.* It contains twelve *sonate da chiesa,* ten with the tempo sequence slow, fast, slow, fast (in No. 8 the two inner tempi are combined into a single movement: slow, fast slow, fast). Nos. 3 and 11 have three movements: fast, slow, fast.

  In his fast movements Caldara proves himself a master of the fugal style. Most of them are fully developed three-part fugues with five or six expositions and lovely, variable episodes. Exceptions to this rule are the fourth movement of No. 1 and the second of No. 2, in which the imitation is limited to the two violins; and the fourth movements of Nos. 5 and 9, both of which are in binary form, though they begin with an imitation. The second movement of No. 6 represents yet another deviation from the rule; here a ricercar-like theme

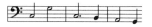

is played uninterrupted, almost like an ostinato, but on different degrees of the scale (*c, g, eb, bb*) and migrating from one voice part to another, while the other instruments play lovely motifs. The second movement of No. 9 is based on the theme

which, along with two themes by Torelli (Figs. 178 and 179), foreshadows the theme of the A-minor fugue of the *Well-Tempered Clavier I*. In the second movement of No. 12, an extended contrast movement, when the violoncello plays a trill of six measures, the *Musico di Violoncello Veneto* is speaking to his audience.

Caldara's slow movements are expressive and affective. There is hardly any in which the diminished-seventh is not present, be it in the melody in downward motion, or in the harmony as a dissonant chord. The most beautiful is the third movement (*Adagio*) of Sonata No. 7. This sonata is written in the "joyful" key of E major, to which the "lamenting" E minor of the *Adagio* is an impressive contrast. Also noteworthy are the first movement (*Grave*) of No. 1, whose melody flows for seventeen measures without interruption by a rest; and the first movement (*Largo*) of No. 8, in which a chromatic theme whose main degrees are

is treated as a migrating ostinato, similar to that in the second movement (*Presto*) of No. 6. Caldara frequently opens his slow movements with a short imitation, though he never employs the very common incipit repeat.

The most attractive of Caldara's sonatas is probably the three-movement No. 11. The first movement, *Vivace*, is based on a precise theme, which is followed, as is frequently the case in Caldara's sonatas, by a figure in dotted sixteenth notes. The second movement, *Adagio*, begins with yet another motif that reminds one of Bach's A-minor *Fugue*. And the third movement, *Allegro*, is a double fugue that uses the theme of the first movement as a countertheme in an interesting realization of the cyclic principle. Figure 198 shows the beginnings of the three movements.

FIGURE 198: SONATA UNDECIMA (OPUS 1, 1693).

Vivace

Adagio

Allegro

Caldara's Opus 2, from 1699: *Suonate da Camera a Due Violini, con il Basso Continuo*, contains eleven sonatas (suites) and a *Chiacona*, obviously modeled after Corelli's Opus 2, of 1685. This statement is also valid for the form of the suites: like Corelli's they are put together in various ways but consist of the same elements: *Preludio, Allemande, Corrente, Sarabanda, Giga*, and *Gavota*, excluding the *Minuet* and such "modernistic" dances as the *Borea* or the *Canario*.

Stylistically, Caldara's suites differ from Corelli's by the more frequent use of initial imitation. In Corelli's Opus 2 only one movement begins with a full imitation (the *Sar-*

abanda of No. 9), while Caldara uses this method very frequently. Particularly noteworthy in this respect is the *Allemande* of No. 7, whose impressive initial motif—which includes a diminished-seventh—reappears repeatedly. Technically as well as artistically this movement stands far above the mediocre level of the *sonata da camera* of the time.

The *Chiacona* consists of 40 variations of a four-measure theme

which is not paraphrased but is strictly maintained. While Corelli transposes his ostinato only twice (variation 11 is in E minor, variations 12 and 13 are in D major), Caldara uses numerous modulations—from B♭ major to F major, G minor, D minor, C minor, and E♭ major, and in between back again to F or B-flat. For the transition from one key to another he nearly always inserts one or two measures. The upper parts are in singing style rather than being virtuosic, in keeping with the *Largo* tempo of the entire composition.

In addition to the two printed publications there are more than 30 solo and trio sonatas in manuscript. Very likely, they all originated during Caldara's stay in Vienna, after 1716.

SOURCES

Suonate a tre, due violini con violoncello, e parte per l'organo. . . . Opus 1. Venice: Giuseppe Sala, 1693.   RISM C57.
    Great Britain: London, Westminster Abbey Library.
Reprints:
Venice: Giuseppe Sala, 1700.   RISM C58.
    Austria: Vienna, Österreichische Nationalbibliothek (Violin II, Organ).
    Italy: Bologna, Civico Museo.
Amsterdam: Estienne Roger, n.d.   RISM C59.
    Great Britain: London, British Library; Oxford, Bodleian Library.
    West Germany: Wiesentheid, Musiksammlung des Grafen von Schönborn-Wiesentheid.

Suonate da camera a due violini con il basso continuo. . . . Opus 2. Venice: Giuseppe Sala, 1699.   RISM C60.
    Italy: Bologna, Civico Museo.
Reprint:
Venice: Giuseppe Sala, 1701.   RISM C61.
    Austria: Österreichische Nationalbibliothek.
    Italy: Turin, Biblioteca nazionale universitaria.

🍇 *Giuseppe Iacchini*

Iacchini (Iachini, Jachini) was born in Bologna in 1663. In 1688 he became a member of the Accademia filarmonica, and in 1689 he joined the chapel of San Petronio as violoncellist. He was active in that position until shortly before his death, in 1727.

Iacchini's Opus 1 was published before 1685 (the year in which his Opus 2 appeared), with the title *Sonate a Violino e Violoncello, et a Violoncello solo, per camera*. The publication consists of two part books and contains eight compositions for two string instruments: Nos. 1–6 for violin and violoncello, Nos. 7 and 8 for violoncello and an undetermined bass instrument.

In spite of the designation *per camera*, these compositions have the basic form of the *sonata da chiesa*, except for several final movements: In No. 2 it is a *Gavota*; and Nos. 4, 6, 7, and 8 have binary *Arias*. Five of the six violin sonatas have the tempo sequence fast, slow, fast; while No. 3 and the two violoncello sonatas each have four movements—slow, fast, slow, fast. Their contents are as modest as their length: the third movement (*Allegro*) of No. 5 is the longest, with 42 measures in 3/4 meter. However, just because of their brevity and simplicity, these sonatas could well have been employed as teaching material and in duet playing.

Iacchini's Opus 2, which appeared in 1695 in Bologna, has the title *Sonate da camera a trè, e quattro Stromenti, col Violoncello obligato*. It contains ten sonatas, Nos. 1–6 *a quattro* (two violins, alto, bass, and b.c.), Nos. 7–10 *a trè* (two violins, bass, and b.c.). Nos. 1, 3, 4, 6, 7, and 10 carry the remark *col Violoncello obligato*, and differ from the others in that the violoncello does not merely reinforce the cembalo but occasionally plays an independent role. Especially in the final movements of Sonatas Nos. 1, 3, 4, and 6, the violoncello, playing fast passages, stands out as a solo instrument.

As in Opus 1, the pieces in Opus 2 are *sonate da chiesa*, but with three suitelike elements: the final movement of No. 1 is an *Aria*, while Nos. 5 and 9 close with a *Corrente*. Sonatas Nos. 2, 5, 9, and 10 have four movements—slow, fast, slow, fast; and Nos. 1, 3, 4, 6, and 8 have the unusual tempo sequence slow, slow, fast; namely, *Largo, ma andante*, *Grave*, and *Presto, e Allegro*.

The four-part sonatas (Nos. 1–6) are stylistically progressive; the fast as well as the slow movements are written in homophonic style, this term being interpreted in the widest sense of the word, that is, non-fugal. The only exception is the third movement (*Allegro*), of No. 6, a fugue in which only the two violins participate, while the viola and violoncello are restricted to occasional allusions to the theme. This style, typical of the fast movements, could be called fragmentary. It reminds one of the abrupt style of Albergati, to whom Iacchini dedicated his Opus 4 (1701). This style is illustrated in the first movement of Sonata No. 3 (Fig. 199). The slow movements of the four-part sonatas are only short introductions or transitions.

The three-part sonatas (Nos. 7–10) also contain a number of fast movements in fragmentary style (for instance, the first movement of No. 8 and the second of No. 9). There are several extended fugues, for instance, the second and fourth movements of

FIGURE 199. IACCHINI: SONATA TERZA (OPUS 2, 1695).

No. 10, each with four expositions, and the third movement of No. 7, with five. The third movement of No. 8 carries the inscription *Presto. A Cappella*, which I fail to understand. Among the slow movements, the first (*Largo, ma andante*) of No. 7, a very expressive movement, is a fugue with three expositions and long episodes.

Iacchini's Opus 3, from 1697, is entitled *Concerti per camera a Violino, e Violoncello solo, e nel fine due Sonate a Violoncello solo col Basso*. It is similar to Opus 1 in that it contains string duets—eight for violin and violoncello, and two for violoncello and bass. The former are designated *Concerti* because the two instruments compete ("concertize") with parts of equal importance; the latter are called *Sonate* because the bass is merely an accompaniment. In the part books, however, all the pieces are named *Sonata*.

Except for the four-movement No. 10, all the sonatas have three movements, but only Nos. 2, 4, and 5 unequivocally with the tempo sequence fast, slow, fast. The last movement of No. 1 and the first of No. 3 are inscribed *Andante*, which is neither fast nor slow; and in Nos. 6, 7, and 8 the first movement is a balletto in binary form with different tempo indications for each section, for instance, *Largo:‖:Presto* (No. 7) and *Andante:‖:Presto* (No. 8). Thus, the traditional practice of writing fast and slow movements is not observed. Nor is it possible to relate these compositions to either of the main categories of seventeenth-century violin music—*sonata da chiesa* or suite. Half the movements have tempo indications only; others, as in suites, carry names of dances (Balletto, Gavotta, Corrente, Minuet); and still others are written in binary form. Thus Iacchini's Opus 3 leads away from the established traditions, contributing to the diffusion of style that began around 1700.

Stylistically, the compositions are similar to those of Opus 1, but in Opus 3 the violoncello plays an even greater role, for instance in Sonata No. 7, the beginning of which is an example of the motto aria (Fig. 200).

FIGURE 200. IACCHINI: SONATA VII (OPUS 3, 1697).

After 1700 Iacchini published two more collections *per camera*: Opus 4, 1701, with compositions for three and four instruments; and Opus 5, 1703, with pieces for three to six instruments. Opus 5 contains important compositions which "are surprising in their inspired ideas and craftsmanship and in no way inferior to Torelli's."[1]

NOTE

1. See the article *Jacchini* in MGG.

SOURCES

Sonate a violino e violoncello, et a violoncello solo per camera. . . . Opus 1. s.l., s.n., n.d. RISM J1.
    Italy: Bologna, Civico Museo (2 parts).

Sonate da camera a tre, e quattro stromenti, col violoncello obligato. . . . Opus 2. Bologna: Pier-Maria Monti, 1695.   RISM J2.
    Great Britain: Oxford, Bodleian Library (Violin I and II, Viola, Violoncello, b.c.).
    Italy: Bologna, Civico Museo.
    West Germany: Wiesentheid, Musiksammlung des Grafen von Schönborn-Wiesentheid (lacking Viola and Violoncello).

Concerti per camera a violino, e violoncello solo col basso. . . . Opus 3. Modena: Fortuniano Rosati, 1697.   RISM J3.
    Italy: Bologna, Civico Museo (2 parts).

 *Tomaso Albinoni*

> *Tomaso Albinoni was born in 1671 in Venice. Aside from a short stay in Florence (1703) and Munich (1722), he seems to have spent most of his life in Venice, where he died in 1751. He was a man of independent means, who in addition to numerous vocal works (operas, arias, and cantatas), composed a large number of instrumental compositions. They exist in nine printed publications that appeared from 1694 until about 1722, and in manuscript.*

In his Opus 1, *Suonate a trè, doi Violini, e Violoncello, col Basso per l'Organo* (1694), Albinoni calls himself *musico di Violino dilettante Veneto*. The publication contains twelve *sonate da chiesa* in the traditional trio scoring and, for the first time, all with the tempo sequence slow, fast, slow, fast. Thus they represent the final stage of the form commonly associated with the term *sonata da chiesa*. It was tentatively used as early as 1667 by G. B. Vitali and 1669 by Cazzati; it came to predominance around 1680 and to exclusiveness in Albinoni's Opus 1. Its position was so fortified by the masters of the eighteenth century that today the terms *sonata da chiesa* and "SFSF" are commonly, but quite wrongly, regarded as identical.

Aside from three final movements in binary form (in Nos. 2, 6, and 10), all the fast movements are strictly worked-out fugues, two of them (the second movements in Nos. 1 and 6) even triple fugues. The themes, particularly those of the initial fugues, are well designed and impressive. Fig. 201 shows the theme of the second movement of No. 5, whose energetic octave leaps remind one of Vivaldi; and that of the second movement of No. 8, which, quite logically, begins with large leaps, continues with diatonic steps, and ends with chromatic motion. Quite understandably, Bach used the same theme for a keyboard fugue.[1] In Sonatas Nos. 3, 7, 9, and 11 (perhaps also in No. 12) Albinoni uses the cyclic principle, deriving the theme of the fourth movement from that of the second.

FIGURE 201. ALBINONI: a. SONATA QUINTA; b. SONATA OTTAVA (OPUS 1, 1694).

Albinoni's slow movements do not quite reach the high level of affective expression as those by Caldara, but they are well designed and of noble character. Particularly noteworthy is the first movement (*Grave*) of No. 6, which has a running bass and, in m. 10, a recitative played by violin I and answered by violin II one step higher (Fig. 202). The first movement (*Grave*) of No. 9 also has a running bass. In the first movement (*Grave*) of No. 12 the two violins perform imitations of changing motifs above a basso ostinato consisting of nine repetitions of a basic formula of two and a half measures. This is one of the most beautiful slow movements in Albinoni's Opus 1.

FIGURE 202. ALBINONI: SONATA SESTA (OPUS 1, 1694).

Albinoni's Opus 2 appeared in 1700, with the title *Sinfonie, e Concerti a cinque, Due Violini, Alto, Tenore, Violoncello, e Basso.* It contains—exactly like Torelli's Opus 5, of 1692—six sonatas and six concertos in alternation: *Sonata prima, Concerto primo, Sonata seconda,* and so on. The scoring is two violins, alto, tenor, bass, and b.c., with the addition of a seventh part book, *Violino de Concerto,* for the concertos.

The sonatas, like those of Opus 1, all have the tempo sequence slow, fast, slow, fast. All the fast movements are fugues in which the five voice parts participate equally in the imitation; in other words, they are five-part fugues. Did Albinoni know the five-part fugues of the earlier Venetian composer Ziani? Very likely he did, since the second edition of Ziani's Opus 7 appeared in Venice in 1678. The second movement (*Allegro*) of No. 3 is a very skillfully written triple fugue. In the second movement (*Allegro*) of No. 2 the theme appears in stretto throughout, a technique that Albinoni had already used in the second movement (*Allegro*) of No. 2 of Opus 1. The slow movements are violin duets with three-part chordal accompaniment, except for a few in full homophonic style, for instance, the first movement (*Grave*) of No. 1. The violins continue in an expressive dialogue, in which pathetic motifs in dotted sixteenth notes (which Caldara was also very fond of) play an important role. The other instruments accompany either with three-part chords in quarter notes or with a three-part running bass in eighth-note motion. Here Albinoni has created a new and noteworthy style. It would be interesting to find out whether it was further developed in the eighteenth century.

The six concertos are entirely different. As is obligatory for a concerto, they have three movements with the tempo sequence fast, slow, fast. In No. 6 it is enlarged to fast, slow fast slow, fast. The scoring is very interesting. The additional part book, *Violino de Concerto*, is not (as one might expect) a "concertizing" soloistic violin part. It mostly duplicates either violin I or violin II; sometimes it becomes independent, but only as an addition to the accompaniment. In the former case, the scoring is for five parts, in the latter for six. But in many places three violins play in unison, so that there are only four different voice parts. Fig. 203 shows several passages from the first *Allegro* of Concerto No. 5. It illustrates the various roles played by the three violins (the lower parts are omitted since they are of no special interest). In mm. 9–12 the three violins play in unison, hence *a quattro* (with the three lower parts); in mm 13–17 they play three different parts, resulting in a scoring *a sei*; and in mm. 18–19 *Violino I* and *Violino de Concerto* are identical, so that the scoring is *a cinque*. The passage in mm. 13–17 is a solo for violin I.

FIGURE 203. ALBINONI: CONCERTO QUINTO (OPUS 2, 1700).

The first movement of No. 5 is a rondo R A R B R C R D, of which Fig. 203 shows the section R B. The first movement of No. 4 has the same form, with extended soloistic sections for both the violin and the violoncello. The third movement (an *Allegro* in 3/4) of No. 6 has a rondo structure also, that is, R R A R R B R R C, with violin I and violin II alternating in the repetition of the ritornello. The *Violino de Concerto* duplicates violin I throughout so that the entire movement has the normal scoring *a cinque*. Most of the slow movements are very short and *a cinque*, except the second movement of No. 4, a nine-measure *Adagio*, which is entirely *a sei*.

How shall we evaluate the musical substance, the artistic quality of the compositions in Albinoni's Opus 1 and Opus 2? The trio sonatas of Opus 1, with their skillfully written fugues, are conservative and, at the same time, very stimulating, as Bach discovered; and their slow movements are impressive, with noble character and continuous melodies. In the sonatas of Opus 2 Albinoni turns out to be a master of the five-part fugue and of the expressive violin duet with three-part accompaniment. The six concertos of Opus 2 have a novel structure, but their content is nothing but a meaningless play of arpeggios, repetitions, and broken chords—in a word, merely harmony, without melody. They are a typical product of musical pioneer work.[2]

After 1700 Albinoni published several other collections of violin music, among them *Sonate per Violino solo, Violone, e Basso continuo* (without opus number, about 1716) and *Concerti a cinque* (Opus 9, ca. 1722).

NOTES

1. Bachgesellschaft (BG), No. 438. The theme of the third movement of No. 2 was also arranged by Bach: BG, No. 437.
2. These works were highly appreciated by Albinoni's contemporaries. Joh. Gottfried Walther arranged Nos. 4 and 5 for organ.

SOURCES

Suonate a tre, doi violini, e violoncello col basso per l'organo. . . . Opus 1. Venice: Giuseppe Sala, 1694.   RISM A698.
    Austria: Vienna, Österreichische Nationalbibliothek.
    Italy: Bologna, Civico Museo (Violin, Organ).
Reprints:
Venice: Giuseppe Sala, 1704.   RISM A699.
    West Germany: Paderborn, Erzbischöfliche Akademische Bibliothek; Wiesentheid, Musiksammlung des Grafen von Schönborn-Wiesentheid.
Amsterdam: Estienne Roger, No. 67, n.d.   RISM A700.
    Great Britain: Cambridge, Rowe Music Library, King's College; London, British Library; Royal College of Music.
    France: Paris, Bibliothèque nationale.
    Sweden: Leufsta Bruk (Private collection De Geer).
Amsterdam: Estienne Roger, s.n.   RISM A701.
    Great Britain: London, Royal College of Music.
    France: Paris, Bibliothèque nationale.
Amsterdam: Estienne Roger and Michel Charles Le Cène, No. 67, n.d.   RISM A702.
    France: Paris, Bibliothèque nationale.
    United States: Washington (D.C.), Library of Congress, Music Division.

Sinfonie e concerti a cinque, due violini, alto, tenore, violoncello, e basso. . . . Opus 2. Venice: Giuseppe Sala, 1700.   RISM A703.
> Austria: Vienna, Österreichische Nationalbibliothek (Violin I and II, Violoncello).
> Italy: Bologna, Civico Museo (Violin I and II).
> United States: Berkeley (Cal.), University of California, Music Library and Bancroft Library.

Reprints:
Venice: Giuseppe Sala, 1707.   RISM A704.
> Italy: Bologna, Civico Museo.
> West Germany: Wiesentheid, Musiksammlung des Grafen von Schönborn-Wiesentheid (de concerto, Alto Viola, Tenor Viola, Violoncello, Organ).

Venice: Estienne Roger, s. No., n.d.   RISM A705.
> East Germany: Dresden, Sächsische Landesbibliothek, Musikabteilung (lacks b.c.).
> Netherlands: The Hague, Gemeente Museum.
> United States: Washington (D.C.), Library of Congress, Music Division.

Amsterdam: Estienne Roger, No. 7, n.d.   RISM A706.
> France: Paris, Bibliothèque nationale.
> Great Britain: Cambridge, Rowe Music Library, King's College; University Library; London, British Library.
> Netherlands: The Hague, Gemeente Museum.
> Sweden: Leufsta Bruk (Private collection De Geer).
> Switzerland: Zurich, Zentralbibliothek, Kantons-, Stadt- und Universitätsbibliothek.
> United States: Berkeley (Cal.), University of California, Music Library and Bancroft Library.
> West Germany: Regensburg, Fürst Thurn und Taxis Hofbibliothek (Violino de concerto, b.c.).

Concertos in seven parts for three violins, tenors and bass violin with a thorough bass for the harpsichord. . . . [London]: John Walsh, P. Randall and Joseph Hare, n.d.   RISM A707.
> Great Britain: Cambridge, Pembroke College Library; London, British Library; Manchester, Central Public Library (Incomplete).
> United States: Urbana (Ill.), University of Illinois, Music Library.
> West Germany: Münich, Bayerische Staatsbibliothek, Musiksammlung.

London: John Walsh and P. Randall, n.d.   RISM A708.
> Sweden: Stockholm, Kungliga Musikaliska Akademiens Bibliotek.

Balletti a tre, due violini, violoncello e cembalo. . . . Opus 3. Venice: Giuseppe Sala, 1701. RISM A709.
> Italy: Bologna, Civico Museo; Rome, Biblioteca dell'Accademia nazionale dei Lincei e Corsiniana.

Reprints:
Venice: Giuseppe Sala, 1704.   RISM A710.
> Austria: Vienna, Österreichische Nationalbibliothek, Musiksammlung (Violone handwritten).
> France: Paris, Bibliothèque nationale.

Venice: Giuseppe Sala, 1706.   RISM A711.
> West Germany: Wiesentheid, Musiksammlung des Grafen von Schönborn-Wiesentheid; Paderborn, Erzbischöfliche Akademische Bibliothek.

Amsterdam: Estienne Roger, No. 260. n.d.   RISM A712.
> France: Paris, Bibliothèque nationale.
> Sweden: Leufsta Bruk (Private collection De Geer).

Amsterdam: Estienne Roger, s. No., n.d.   RISM A713.
> Great Britain: Cambridge, Rowe Music Library, King's College.
> United States: Washington (D.C.), Library of Congress, Music Division.

Amsterdam: Estienne Roger and Michel Charles Le Cène. n.d.   RISM A714.
    Great Britain: Oxford, Bodleian Library.
Amsterdam: Pierre Mortier, n.d.   RISM A715.
    Great Britain: London, British Library; Liverpool, Liverpool University, Music Department (incomplete).
    Sweden: Stockholm, Kungliga Musikaliska Akademiens Bibliotek.

Albinoni's balletti's in 3 parts for two violins and a thorow bass consisting of preludes, alemands, sarabands, corants, gavots and jiggs.... London: John Walsh and Joseph Hare, n.d. RISM A716.
    Great Britain: Cambridge, University Library.
London: John Walsh, n.d.   RISM A717.
    Great Britain: London, British Library; Tenbury, St. Michael's College Library.
    Italy: Venice, Biblioteca nazionale Marciana.
    United States: Charlottesville (Va.), University of Virginia, Alderman Library.

Sonate da chiesa a violino solo e violoncello o basso continuo.... Opus 4. Amsterdam: Estienne Roger, No. 12, n.d.   RISM A718.
    France: Paris, Bibliothèque nationale.
    United States: Washington (D.C.), Library of Congress, Music Division.
Reprints:
Amsterdam: Estienne Roger, n.d.   RISM A719.
    Sweden: Uppsala, Universitetsbiblioteket.
London: John Walsh and Joseph Hare, n.d.   RISM A720.
    East Germany: Leipzig, Musikbibliothek der Stadt Leipzig.
London: John Walsh, P. Randall and Joseph Hare, n.d.   RISM A721.
    Great Britain: London, Royal College of Music.

Concerti a cinque, due tre violini, alto, tenore, violoncello e basso per il cembalo.... Opus 5. Venice: Giuseppe Sala, 1707.   RISM A722.
    Italy: Bologna, Civico Museo (lacks Alto Viola); Venice, Biblioteca del Conservatorio "Benedetto Marcello" (fondo Correr) (lacks Alto Viola).
    West Germany: Wiesentheid, Musiksammlung des Grafen von Schönborn-Wiesentheid.
Venice: Giuseppe Sala, 1710.   RISM A723.
    Italy: Bologna, Civico Museo.
    Switzerland: Zurich, Zentralbibliothek, Kantons-, Stadt- und Universitätsbibliothek.
Amsterdam: Estienne Roger, No. 278, n.d.   RISM A724.
    France: Paris, Bibliothèque nationale.
    Great Britain: London, British Library; Oxford, Bodleian Library.
    United States: Ann Arbor (Mich.), University of Michigan, Music Library.
Amsterdam: Estienne Roger, n.d.   RISM A725.
    France: Paris, Bibliothèque nationale (lacks Viola II, Violoncello, Cembalo; [another edition] Violin I).
    United States: Los Angeles (Cal.), University of California, William Andrews Clark Memorial Library.
... n[ouvelle] edition exactement corigée. Amsterdam: Michel Charles Le Cène, No. 278, n.d.   RISM A726.
    France: Paris, Bibliothèque nationale (lacks Violin de concerto, Violin I and II, b.c.).
    Netherlands: The Hague, Gemeente Museum.
Amsterdam: Michel Charles Le Cène, n.d.   RISM A727.
    Great Britain: Oxford, Bodleian Library.
    United States: Washington (D.C.), Library of Congress, Music Division.

Amsterdam: Pierre Mortier, n.d.   RISM A728.
> Great Britain: Cambridge, Rowe Music Library, King's College; York, Minster Library (incomplete).
> Sweden: Lund, Universitetsbiblioteket; Leufsta Bruk (Private collection De Geer).
> United States: Rochester (N.Y.), Sibley Music Library, Eastman School of Music, University of Rochester.

Trattenimenti armonici per camera; divisi in dodici sonate à violino, violone e cembalo....
Opus 6. Amsterdam: Estienne Roger, No. 3, n.d.   RISM A729.
> East Germany: Rostock, Universitätsbibliothek.
> Sweden: Stockholm, Kungliga Musikaliska Akademiens Bibliotek.

Reprints:
Amsterdam: Estienne Roger, n.d.   RISM A730.
> France: Paris, Bibliothèque nationale.
> Great Britain: Cambridge, University Library.
> Italy: Bologna, Civico Museo.
> United States: Berkeley (Cal.), University of California, Music Library and Bancroft Library.

Trattenimenti armonici per camera.... An entertainment of harmony. Containing twelve solos ... for a violin with a through bass for the harpsichord or bass violin. London: John Walsh and Joseph Hare, n.d.   RISM A731.
> Great Britain: Cambridge, Rowe Music Library, King's College; London, British Library.
> United States: New Haven (Conn.), Yale University, The Library of the School of Music; Coral Gables (Fla.), University of Miami, Music Library.

London: John Walsh, n.d.   RISM A732.
> France: Paris, Collection André Meyer.
> United States: Washington (D.C.), Library of Congress, Music Division.

Concerti a cinque con violini, oboè, violetta, violoncello e basso continuo.... Opus 7. Amsterdam: Estienne Roger, No. 361, n.d.   RISM A733.
> France: Paris, Bibliothèque nationale (libro primo: Violin I; libro secondo: Violin I and II, Viola, Violoncello).
> Sweden: Linköping, Stifts- och Landesbiblioteket Institut (Violin I and II, Oboe I); Lund, Universitetsbiblioteket; Leufsta Bruk (Private collection De Geer).
> Switzerland: Zurich, Zentralbibliothek, Kantons-, Stadt- und Universitätsbibliothek.
> West Germany: Wiesentheid, Musiksammlung des Grafen von Schönborn-Wiesentheid.

Reprints:
Amsterdam: Estienne Roger, n.d.   RISM A734.
> Great Britain: Cambridge, University Library.

Amsterdam: Estienne Roger and Michel Charles Le Cène, No. 361, n.d.   RISM A735.
> East Germany: Berlin, Deutsche Staatsbibliothek, Musikabteilung.
> France: Paris, Bibliothèque nationale.
> United States: Ann Arbor (Mich.), University of Michigan, Music Library; Washington (D.C.), Library of Congress, Music Division.

Baletti, e sonate a trè, à due violini, violoncello, e cembalo, con le sue fughe tiratte à canone....
Opus 8. Amsterdam: Estienne Roger and Le Cène, No. 493, n.d.   RISM A736.
> Austria: Vienna, Gesellschaft der Musikfreunde in Wien.
> East Germany: Berlin, Deutsche Staatsbibliothek, Musikabteilung.
> Great Britain: London, British Library.
> Sweden: Linköping, Stifts- och Landesbiblioteket Institut (lacks Violin II).
> United States: Washington (D.C.), Library of Congress, Music Division.

Reprint:
Amsterdam: Jeanne Roger, No. 493, n.d.   RISM A737.
    East Germany: Dresden, Sächsische Landesbibliothek, Musiksammlung.
    France: Paris, Bibliothèque nationale (Violin I and II).
    Sweden: Stockholm, Kungliga Musikaliska Akademiens Bibliotek (Violin I and II, Violoncello).

Concerti a cinque, con violini, oboe, violetta, violoncello e basso continuo. . . . Opus 9. Amsterdam: Michel Charles Le Cène, No. 494, n.d.   RISM A738.
    France: Paris, Bibliothèque nationale.
    Great Britain: Cambridge, University Library; London, British Library (lacks Violetta).
    Italy: Naples, Biblioteca del Conservatorio de Musica S. Pietro a Maiella (libro primo: Violin I).
    Sweden: Lund, Universitetsbiblioteket; Stockholm, Kungliga Teaterns Biblioteket.
Reprint:
Amsterdam: Jeanne Roger, No. 494, n.d.   RISM A739.
    Italy: Naples, Biblioteca del Conservatorio de Musica S. Pietro a Maiella (Violin I principale).
    West Germany: Münster, Santini-Bibliothek.

Concerti a cinque con violini, violetta, violoncello e basso continuo. Opus 10. Amsterdam: Michel Charles Le Cène, No. 581, n.d.   RISM A740.
    France: Paris, Collection André Meyer (Violin I principale, Violin I di concerto, Violin II, Viola, Violoncello, Organ).
    Netherlands: Utrecht, Instituut voor Muziekwetenschap der Rijksuniversiteit.
    Sweden: Leufsta Bruk (Private collection De Geer).

Works without opus number:

Sonate a violino solo e basso continuo . . . e uno suario ò capriccio di otto battute a l'imitatione del Corelli del Sig. Tibaldi. Amsterdam: Jeanne Roger, No. 439, n.d.   RISM A741.
    Belgium: Brussels, Conservatoire Royal de Musique, Bibliothèque.
    Great Britain: London, British Library.
    United States: Berkeley (Cal.), University of California, Music Library and Bancroft Library; Washington (D.C.), Library of Congress, Music Division.

Sonata in B for violins in 3 parts . . . as also a solo for a violin by Carlo Ambrogio Lonati . . . to be continu'd monthly with the best and choicest sonatas and solos . . . for the year 1704. s.l.: s.n., 1704.   RISM A742.
    Great Britain: London, Minet Library (lacks composition by Lonati).

Albinoni's aires in 3 parts for two violins and a through bass, containing almand's, saraband's, corrant's, gavots, and jiggs, &c., collected out of the choicest of his works with the aprobation of our best masters the whole carefully corrected and fairly engraven. London: John Walsh and Joseph Hare, n.d.   RISM A743.
    Great Britain: Cambridge, Rowe Music Library, King's College; University Library; Durham, Cathedral Library; London, British Library (lacks b.c.).

Appendix

There are quite a number of seventeenth-century Italian composers of violin music who are not represented in this book. The following list of names known to me (there are sure to be many more) helps to place in perspective the 61 composers discussed by Apel. Works by these musicians can be located in RISM (not only in the composer volumes but also in the *Recueils imprimés*), SartoriB, and manuscript inventories in the literature:

Alessandro Botta Adorno
Ignazio Albertino
Paris Francesco Alghisi
G. Alrovandini
Gian Maria Appiano
F. Attilio Ottavio Ariosti
Giuseppe Antonio Avitrano
Antonio Luigi Baldassini
Francesco Ballarotti
G. B. Bassano
Filippo Carlo Beliosi
F. C. Belisi
Giovanni Bianchi
Ipolito Boccaletti
Francesco Antonio Bomporti
Giovanni Battista Borri
Archangelo Borsaro
Domenico Brassolino
Giovanni Batista Brevi
Antonio Brunelli
Nicola Casimi
D. Giuseppi de Castro
Giacomo Cattaneo
Marcantonio Colonna
Carlo Fideli
Andrea Fiorè
D. G. Francalanza
Giovanni Francalanza
P. Franceschini
Giovanni Pietro Franchi
Domenico Gabrielli
Gasparo Gaspardini

Giovanni Ghizzolo
Giovanni Battista Gigli
Alberto Gozzi
Giovanni Lorenzo Gregori
A. Grimandi
A. Guerrieri
B. Laurenti
Bartolomeo Laurenti
Isabella Leonarda
Carlo Ambrogio Lonati
Giovanni Frederico Maestro
Carlo Mannelli
D. Marcheselli
Domenico Marcheselli
Nicolo Mateis
C. Mazolini
Salvatori Mazzella
Giacomo Medico
Pietro Migale
Antonio Molli
Clementi Monari
Pier-Maria Monti
Pompeo Natale
Piro Nichesola
Aurelio Paolinai
Steffano Pasino
Tomano Pegolotti
Giacomo Perdieri [Predieri]
G. A. Perti
Giovanni Battista Piazza
Carlo Piazzo
G. Pistolezza

Gioseffo Placuzzi
Gabrielo Puliti
Giovanni Ravenscroft
Giovanni Antonio Rigatti
Giovanni Rosenmiller
Nicola Casimi Romano
N. N. Romano
Clemente Rozzi
Francesco Rognoni Taegio
Giulio Taglietti

Luigi Taglietti
Francesco Todeschini
Bernardi Tonini
A. M. Turati
Giovanni Giacomo Valther
Elia Vannini
N. N. Veneziano
Pietro Verdina
Benedetto Vinacese
Domenioco Zanata

Bibliography

AfMw	*Archiv für Musikwissenschaft*, Wiesbaden.
AM	*Acta Musicologica*, Leipzig.
ApelA	Willi Apel, *Accidentien und Tonalität in den Denkmälern des 15. und 16. Jahrunderts*, Berlin, 1936; 2d ed., Baden-Baden, 1972 (*Sammlung Musikwissenschaftliche Abhandlungen*, vol. 24).
ApelD	Willi Apel, "Drei plus Drei plus Zwei = Vier plus Vier," *AM*, XXXII (1960).
ApelG	Willi Apel, *Geschichte der Orgel und Klaviermusik bis 1700*, Kassel, 1967; English translation, *The History of Keyboard Music to 1700*, Bloomington, 1972.
ApelH	Willi Apel, *Harvard Dictionary of Music*, Cambridge, 1944; 2d ed., 1969.
ApelN	Willi Apel, *Die Notation der polyphonen Musik, 900–1600*, Leipzig, 1970; original English edition: *The Notation of Polyphonic Music, 900–1600*, Cambridge, 1942.
ApelV	Willi Apel, *Die italienische Violinmusik im 17. Jahrhundert*, Wiesbaden, 1983.
AschmannA	R. Aschmann, *Das deutsche polyphone Violinspiel im 17. Jahrhunderts*, Zürich, 1962.
BeckmannS	G. Beckmann, *Das Violinspiel in Deutschland vor 1700: 12 Sonaten für Violin und Klavier. . .*, Leipzig, 1921.
BeckmannVS	G. Beckmann, *Das Violinspiel in Deutschland vor 1700*, Leipzig, 1918.
BibB	*Bibliotheca Musica Bononiensis*, Ser. IV, No. 150, Bologna, 1969.
BoydenH	D. D. Boyden, *The History of Violin Playing from its Origins to 1761*, London, 1965.
CEKM	*Corpus of Early Keyboard Music* (various editors), 36 vols., 1963–1973.
ChilB	Oskar Chilesotti, *Bibliotheca di rari musicali*, Milan, 1885.
CulM	Michael Culver and Bruce Dickey, "Musik für Zink: eine Quellenkatalog," *Basler Jahrbuch für historische Musikpraxis* V (1982):263–314.
DannB	E. Dann, "Heinrich Biber and the Seventeenth-century Violin," diss., Columbia University, 1968.
DM	*Diletto musicale* (various editors), Vienna.
DunnS	T. D. Dunn, "The Sonatas of Biaggo Marini, Structure and Style," *MR*, XXXVI (1975):161.
EdelmannS	J. F. Edelmann, *Six Grand Lessons for the Forte Piano or Harpsichord with an Accompaniment for the Violin*, [London], ca. 1780.

EinsteinC   *A Collection of Instrumental Music . . . copied by Alfred Einstein,* 20
                   manuscript vols., Smith College Library, Department of Music,
                   Northhampton (photocopies, n.p.; n.d.).

EinsteinG   Alfred Einstein, "Ein Concerto Grosso von 1619," in *Festschrift*
                   Hermann Kretzschmar. . . , Leipzig, 1918.

EitnerQ   Robert Eitner, *Biographisch-Bibliographisches Quellen-Lexikon der*
                   Musiker und Musikgelehrten. . . . 10 vols., Leipzig, 1899–1904.

FreywaldV   Volker Freywald, *Violinsonaten der Generalbass-Epoche in*
                   Bearbeitungen des späten 19. Jahrhunderts (Hamburger Beiträge zur
                   Musikwissenschaft, vol. 10), Hamburg, 1973.

FrotscherG   G. Frotscher, *Geschichte des Orgelspiels und der Orgelkomposition,*
                   Berlin, 1935.

GieglingS   F. Giegling, *Die Solosonata (= Das Musikwerk XV),* Cologne, 1959.

GoldschmidtS   Hugo Goldschmidt, *Studien zur Geschichte der italienischen Oper im*
                   17. Jahrhundert, Leipzig, 1901.

GrebeC   G. Grebe, *P. Cima: Drei Sonaten,* Hamburg, 1969.

Grove   *The New Grove Dictionary of Music and Musicians,* Stanley Sadie,
                   ed., 20 vols., London and New York, 1980.

HAM   A. T. Davison and W. Apel, *Historical Anthology of Music,* 2 vols.,
                   Cambridge, 1946, 1950.

HouleM   George Houle, *Meter in Music 1600–1800,* Bloomington, 1987.

IselinM   D. J. Iselin, *Biagio Marini. . . ,* Hildburghausen, 1930.

Ist   *Istitutioni e monumenti dell' arte musicale italiana,* Milan: Ricordi,
                   1931–1939.

Jacquot   Jean Jacquot, *Le Lieu théâtrale à la renaissance,* Paris, 1963.

KlenzB   W. Klenz, *Giovanni Maria Bononcinoi of Modena,* Durham, 1962.

KolnederB   W. Kolneder, *Das Buch der Violine,* Zürich, 1972.

LedererF   Josef-Horst Lederer, "Ferdinand III," *Grove,* vol. 6, p. 470.

LeonhardtT   Gustav Leonhardt, *Francesco Turini: 6 Sonaten,* Vienna, 1956.

MarxC   H. J. Marx, *Die Überlieferung der Werke Arcangelo Corellis: Catalogue*
                   Raisoné, Cologne, 1980.

McCrickardS   E. McCrickard, "Alessandro Stradella's Instrumental Music," diss.
                   University of North Carolina, 1971.

MGG   F. Blume, ed., *Die Musik in Geschichte und Gegenwart,* 16 vols.,
                   Kassel, 1949–1979.

MiskinB   H. G. Miskin, "The Solo Sonata of the Bologna School," *MQ,* 29
                   (1934):92.

MoserG   A. Moser, *Geschichte des Violinspiels,* 2d ed., H.-J. Noselt, ed.,
                   Tutzing, 1966.

MQ   *The Musical Quarterly,* New York.

MR   *The Music Review,* Cambridge.

MSD   *Musicological Studies and Documents*

NettlB   Paul Nettl, "Giovanni Battista Buonamente," *ZfMw* IX (1927):30–
                   31.

NewmanS   W. S. Newman, *The Sonata in the Baroque Era,* Chapel Hill, 1959.

NowakS   Leopold Nowak, ed. (Giovanni Ruggieri, comp.), *Sonata prima*
                   (secondo, terza, etc.), Diletto Musicale, Vienna, 1949–.

RiemannB   H. Riemann, *Musikgeschichte in Beispielen,* Leipzig, 1912.

RiemannH   H. Riemann, *Handbuch der Musikgeschichte,* 2 vols., Leipzig, 1912.

RiemannO   H. Riemann, *Old Chamber Music,* 4 vols., London, 1900.

RISM   *Répertoire international des sources musicales,* Munich and Duisburg.

RitterG   A. G. Ritter, *Geschichte des Orgelspiels,* Leipzig, 1884.

RMI   *Rivista musicale italiana,* Turin.

RoncagliaS   G. Roncaglia, "Le Composizione strumentale di Alessandro Stradella," *RMI* 44 (1940):91ff, 377ff; and 45 (1941):1ff.

RR   Recent Researches in the Music of the Baroque Era (series), Madison, Wisconsin.

SartoriB   C. Sartori, *Bibliographia della musica strumentale italiana*, 2 vols., Florence, 1952, 1968.

Scelte   *Studio per Edizione Scelte*, Florence.

SchenkT   E. Schenk, *Die italienische Triosonata (= Das Musikwerk*, vol. VII, Cologne, 1954.

ScheringB   A. Schering, *Geschichte der Musik in Beispielen*, Leipzig, 1931.

ScheringG   A. Schering, "Zur Geschichte der Solosonata in der ersten Hälfte des 17. Jahrunderts," in *Riemann-Festschrift*, Leipzig, 1909, pp. 309ff.

Selfridge-Field   Eleanor Selfridge-Field, *Grove*, vol. 16, p. 549.

SutkowskiM   A. Sutkowski, ed., *Opere Complete di Tarquinio Merulo*, Brooklyn, Institute of Medieval Music, 1974.

TorchiA   L. Torchi, *L'Arte musicale in Italia. . .*, vol. 7, Milan, 1908.

TorchiM   L. Torchi, *La Musica istrumentale in Italia nei secoli XVI, XVII e XVIII*, Torino, 1901; reprint from *RMI* IV–VII (1897–1901).

TylerG   James Tyler, *The Early Guitar: A History and Handbook*, Oxford, 1980.

WasielewskiS   J. W. von Wasielewski, *Instrumentalsätze vom Ende des XVI. bis Ende des XVII. Jahrhunderts*, Berlin, 1874, 1883, 1893, 1904, 1910, and 1920.

WasielewskiV   J. W. Wasielewski, *Die Violine und ihre Meister*, Leipzig, 1893.

WinternitzF   E. Winternitz, *Gaudenzio Ferrari, His School and the Early History of the Violin*, Varallo Sesia, 1976.

WolfH   Johannes Wolf, *Handbuch der Notationskunde*, Leipzig, 1909.

ZfMW   *Zeitschrift für Musikwissenschaft*, Leipzig.

Index

WILLI APEL (1893–1988)

Professor Emeritus of Music at Indiana University. His publications include *Gregorian Chant, The History of Keyboard Music to 1700,* and *The Harvard Dictionary of Music.*

 ## THOMAS BINKLEY

Professor of Music and Director of the Early Music Institute at Indiana University. He founded the Studio der frühen Musik in Munich and has been on the faculties of the Schola Cantorum Basiliensis and Stanford University.

EDITOR: NATALIE WRUBEL

BOOK AND JACKET DESIGNER: SHARON L. SKLAR

PRODUCTION COORDINATOR: HARRIET CURRY

TYPEFACE: PALATINO

COMPOSITOR: IMPRESSIONS

PRINTER: MALLOY LITHOGRAPHING